Musical Experience in Our Lives

PRAISE *FOR MUSICAL EXPERIENCE IN OUR LIVES.* . . .

"I opened this book and was immediately engaged. This is a book about alignment, about broadening our perspectives on music education, about identifying the range of music learners in our society and discovering what they can teach us when we take time to watch and listen.

Jody L. Kerchner and Carlos R. Abril have created a compelling collection that should be a part of every musician's library of inspirational books, and one that provides exceptional models for continuing research into the meaning of musical experience. There is no other publication like this in our music education literature.

Kerchner and Abril hope that readers of this book will consider new directions for music education in response. I say: Follow them—they are leading the way with this publication!"—**Donna Brink Fox**, associate dean of academic and student affairs and Eisenhart Professor of Music Education, Eastman School of Music, University of Rochester.

"Jody L. Kerchner and Carlos R. Abril break new ground in this book by bringing together in one publication a series of narratives and case studies that illuminate the nature and meaning of musical engagement in formal and informal settings across the lifespan. Set in rich social and cultural contexts and authored by scholars with diverse interests, each study brings the reader to the heart of musical experience and meaning-making at different developmental stages—infancy and early childhood, childhood, adolescence, and adulthood and older adulthood. The collection serves as a catalyst for expanding the vision and reach of music education and reassessing the impact of music on the human condition."—**Marie McCarthy**, professor and chair of music education, University of Michigan.

"*Musical Experience in Our Lives* features a veritable pantheon of outstanding researchers and thinkers in the field of music education. They bring to this work important perspectives on the transmission, learning, and joy of music-making from the youngest child to people in their later years.

These qualitative studies provide a detailed description of the sociological dimensions of music learning, helping us to understand that what is learned far transcends a particular classroom, teacher, or setting."—**Carol Scott-Kassner**, retired professor of music education, author, and consultant.

Musical Experience in Our Lives

Things We Learn and Meanings We Make

Jody L. Kerchner and Carlos R. Abril

Published in partnership with
MENC: The National Association for Music Education

ROWMAN & LITTLEFIELD EDUCATION
Lanham • New York • Toronto • Plymouth, UK

Published in partnership with
MENC: The National Association for Music Education

Published in the United States of America
by Rowman & Littlefield Education
A Division of Rowman & Littlefield Publishers, Inc.
A wholly owned subsidary of The Rowman & Littlefield Publishing Group, Inc.
4501 Forbes Boulevard, Suite 200, Lanham, Maryland 20706
www.rowmaneducation.com

Estover Road
Plymouth PL6 7PY
United Kingdom

British Library Cataloguing in Publication Information Available

Library of Congress Cataloging-in-Publication Data

Musical experience in our lives : things we learn and meanings we make /
[edited by] Jody L. Kerchner & Carlos R. Abril.
    p. cm.
 "Published in partnership with MENC, the National Association for Music
Education."
 ISBN-13: 978-1-57886-945-9 (cloth : alk. paper)
eISBN-13: 978-1-57886-947-3

 1. Music—Instruction and study. 2. Music, Influence of. 3. Music—Philosophy
and aesthetics. I. Kerchner, Jody L., 1964– II. Abril, Carlos R., 1970–
 MT6.M9628 2009
 780.71—dc22   2008035000

♾™ The paper used in this publication meets the minimum requirements of
American National Standard for Information Sciences—Permanence of
Paper for Printed Library Materials, ANSI/NISO Z39.48-1992.
Manufactured in the United States of America.

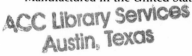

Contents

Acknowledgments

We extend heartfelt thanks to the many contributors, who brought their personal brands of musicianship, pedagogy, and scholarship to this book. Their dedication to the project and patience with the publication process have been exemplary.

We are most grateful for the astute editorial eyes of Frances Ponick (MENC) and the publication team at Rowman & Littlefield—Thomas Koerner, Maera Stratton, and Catherine Forrest Getzie. Thank you for your guidance and careful attention to this project, about which we remain so passionate.

We would like to thank our many colleagues who offered valuable commentary throughout the project. We are especially grateful to Peggy Bennett, Maud Hickey, Katy Strand, and Betty Anne Younker. We also thank the reviewers of the manuscript when the book, in its infant stages, needed focus and finesse.

Finally, we celebrate the lives and musical experiences of those infants, children, adolescents, adults, teachers, student-teachers, and parents who graciously invited us into their musical worlds in order to inform those of us examining, interpreting, writing, and reading about their experiences. By sharing their intimate musical experiences, they underscored the richness of being human and the connection and meaning that music teaching and learning bring to our lives.

J. L. K.
C. R. A.

Introduction

Carlos R. Abril and Jody L. Kerchner

Musical experiences are an important part of our lives, from birth to the cusp of death. In the earliest years of life we perceive and process the music surrounding us in our minds, and produce and respond to music through our bodies and voices. Throughout our lives, we exercise and develop our innate musicality through singing, playing instruments, moving, composing, and listening. Alone and with others, we engage in musical experiences to challenge us, comfort us, and bind us to others. These experiences help us construct meaning and understanding of music, and help us come to understand ourselves, our cultures, and our world.

Many of these experiences are musically educative in that they involve music teaching and learning processes, conscious or unconscious. Other experiences are therapeutic in that they facilitate physical and mental healing. Some musical experiences help to bind two people or large social groups together. The authors of the chapters that comprise this book examine the myriad dimensions of the musical experience within their sociocultural contexts in formal and informal settings. They also seek to emphasize the meaning people construct from these experiences and consider implications for music education.

The purpose of this introduction is to provide a conceptual and theoretical framework for the book. In so doing, we begin by describing the nature of musical experience, its relation to social contexts, and the construction of meaning. We also provide a brief overview of musical experience in relation to the lifespan and explain our reasons for conceptualizing this book as such. We then describe transmission and enculturation, as concepts that situate culture at the heart of music learning. Finally we lay out the plan for the book. We invite you to join us in pondering the overarching questions that guide this book: What is the nature of the musical experience and how does it change throughout the lifespan? How does musical experience impact the construction of personal and social meanings? How do we teach, learn, and transmit culture through the musical experience?

MUSICAL EXPERIENCE

A study of notable musicians and scholars found that most who addressed the nature of musical experience believed "that the ability to experience music is so widespread that it must be considered an inborn capacity for all humans" (Reimer & Wright, 1992, p. 272). That is, people are born with the potential to listen and respond to sound, as well as create and manipulate it. Although the value and significance of the musical experience differs by culture and individual preference, like language it is thought to be a part of all human societies throughout recorded history (Mithen, 2006). The musical experience is a phenomenon of human proportion, throughout our history and throughout our lives. But what are the various dimensions and conceptualizations of the musical experience?

Bennett Reimer (2003) conceptualized musical experience in terms of two broad categories under which people assume various roles: (1) musicianship and (2) listenership. Musicianship roles situate people as creators of the sounds themselves through singing, playing an instrument, improvising, or composing music. The listenership roles, which are once removed from producing music, call "upon a particular way to construct the potential meanings musicians offer into the personal meanings that individuals experience" (Reimer, 2004, p. 35). These include listening to or analyzing music, as well as writing about it or relating it to a people's history or other art forms. The broad categorizations proposed by Reimer provide distinctions among the variety of overlapping, intersecting, and fluid roles that people can play.

Some notions of musical experience have focused on the physical aspects of performance. To authentically experience music, Keil (1995) asserted that people must engage in music through physical involvement. He said, "It's about getting down and into the groove, everyone creating socially from the bottom up" (p. 1). In reacting to aesthetic views of musical experience, Elliott (1995) claimed that humans can have a musical experience during music listening, but that an "experience of the special kind of event-performance we call a musical work requires an understanding of musical performing; it requires that students learn how to perform and improvise completely themselves, as well as to compose, arrange, and conduct" (p. 102). Doing music seems to be at the core of the musical experience.

This might help explain why school music programs in countries like the United States have emphasized music performance (Abril & Gault, 2008).

Examining musical experience from an anthropological perspective, Christopher Small (1998) conceptualized the word "music" as a verb and coined the term "musicking." The term denotes a much wider range of musical experience that includes any form of participation in a musical event or ritual. Small states, "To music is to take part, in any capacity, in a musical performance, whether by performing, by listening, by rehearsing or practicing, by providing material for performance (what is called composing) or by dancing" (1998, p. 9). Musicking can be active or passive, but it always consists of a mutual relationship between the makers of the music and the recipients of those sounds.

Historically, research in music education has examined music behaviors in vacuous conditions, isolating variables from the world in which they reside. While important and useful in their own right, these endeavors usually do not seek to capture musical experience in a broad, holistic manner. In order to understand the complexity of musical experience and its implications for music education, the literature should situate musical experience in its sociocultural contexts. The chapters in this book seek to do that.

Social Dimensions of the Musical Experience

Musical experiences consist of dynamic human interactions within a sociocultural milieu. John Dewey stated, "There is no such thing as sheer self-activity possible—because all activity takes place in a medium, in a situation, and with reference to its conditions" (1902/1956, pp. 30–31). John Blacking (1973) thought that the musical experience itself could teach us about humans and their relationships to one another. Mithen (2006) also recognized the social dimensions of the musical experience, claiming: "Music making is first and foremost a shared activity, not just in the modern Western world, but throughout human culture and history" (p. 205). Although social roles and functions differ by culture and are interdependent with the social context in which they arise, certain cross-cultural threads unite all of musical experience, including music's social nature (Merriam, 1964).

Tia DeNora (2000) asserted that musical experiences, both solitary and communal, help humans construct and reconstruct social order and social realities. Other scholars have suggested that musical experiences are always social, and solitary musical experiences are merely illusionary (Kivy, 1991; Small, 1998). In describing a lone flautist playing music in the night, Small (1998) said, "Although physically alone, he is surrounded as he plays by all the beings that inhabit the world, not only humans, animals and plants but also the land itself . . . and through the sounds he makes he is exploring, affirming and celebrating the ways in which he relates to them" (p. 204).

Consider another example. A teenager alone in his bedroom listens to a new song by a favorite band on a portable music player. This seemingly solitary experience, which is physically and perhaps sonically disconnected from other parts of his environment, is influenced and shaped by its sociocultural context. Consider the following: How did he first become interested in and acquire this recording? How does this music listening experience contribute to the construction of his identity? These questions allude to the social nature of musical experience that straddles past, present, and future.

This book considers musical experience in its broadest and most diverse sense. It includes many events and situations in which humans directly or indirectly engage in or interact with music, heard or imagined. Each chapter seeks to illuminate a specific dimension of the musical experience and the meaning constructed around it, with an eye toward music education.

Meaning in the Musical Experience

A natural consequence of musical experience is the construction of personal and social meaning. As activating agents influenced by their culture, humans determine what is and what is not music based on sounds they produce, hear, or imagine. This determination is based on the relationships among tones, rhythmic patterns, and timbres, as well as concomitant behaviors and ideas. Meaning is not necessarily found in the sounds themselves, but in the ways that people perceive and think about them. Lucy Green (1997) distinguished between two types of meaning: inherent and delineated. Inherent meanings are those that arise from the interrelationships of sounds and silences in the music itself. Delineated meanings are meanings ascribed outside of but in relation to the music. According to Green, both types of meaning are a natural component of the musical experience.

The relationship between producers of music and those who partake in the experience is dynamic. DeNora (2000) proposed that music is not simply the object of people's action, but "music's 'effects' come from the ways in which individuals orient to it, how they interpret it and how they place it within their personal musical maps" (p. 61). Musical meaning is constructed from social, historical, and political contexts; roles valued in a culture; personal associations with music; and people's abilities to perceive organized relationships of musical sounds.

Here is an example of the ways agents of the musical experience might impact one another. Imagine a band performing at a summer music festival for an audience of hundreds. As the band plays, members of the audience perceive those sounds and construct unique meanings based on the characteristics of the music and performance, their emotional or psychological state, prior experiences, and held values and beliefs. In so doing, they respond physically, physiologically, and/or psychologically. Overt responses such as clapping, moving, or shouting might influence the musicians who, in turn, respond through bodily movements or musical alterations. In addition, internal responses to the experience are set in motion, possibly through the strong emotions evoked by the music, the setting, and the group of people, among other things. Emotional experiences in social contexts might even unify groups of people (McNeill, 1995).

The construction of social identity is influenced by musical experiences, and social identity has been found to predict the types of musical experience individuals prefer (MacDonald, Hargreaves, & Meill, 2002). Experience provides people with an opportunity to explore who they are, who they are not, and who they aspire to be. Research has shown that attitudes and preferences toward certain musics are socially constructed (Abril & Flowers, 2007; McCrary, 1993; Morrison, 1998), although privately held views may not coincide with those of a peer group or leader (Alpert, 1982; Finnäs, 1989). Together people participate, practice, and negotiate "meanings that extend, redirect, dismiss, reinterpret, modify, or confirm—in a word, negotiate anew—the history of meanings of which they are a part" (Wenger, 1998, pp. 52–53). DeNora (2000) theorized that music evokes memories of ourselves, and upon further reflection, we associate ourselves—our identity—with place, time, relationships, and feelings. Our reflective thinking recreates our past "selves," which can inform and project onto our future selves.

MUSICAL EXPERIENCE IN OUR LIVES

The vast majority of humans are born with musical potential, but this potential can be realized only through experiences within cultural circles. We traverse outward from the most intimate family groupings (e.g., mother and child) to the more social (e.g., community organizations). Initial experiences with music happen within the family unit (e.g., parents, siblings, caregivers), where they impact one's values, beliefs, and attitudes. One study reported that adults who grew up in families that valued music were more likely to participate in musical experiences as adults (Apfelstadt, 1989). However, adults who had negative experiences with music at home or in the classroom as children might suffer from social or psychological anxiety about music, limiting their musical engagement in childhood through adulthood (Abril, 2007; Sloboda, 2005). It almost goes without saying that each musical experience has a cumulative impact on subsequent musical experiences.

Humans might choose to engage in music throughout their lives. However, the nature and function of these engagements and the roles people play change through the various phases of life. In the early years of life, a baby's environment is awash in musical sounds—people singing, recordings playing, and toys sounding. Yet initial musical experiences in life are often intimate, occurring between primary caregivers and child (Custodero & Johnson-Green, 2003; Ilari, 2005; Trehub, 1996, 1999). Infants experiment with their voices, attempting to imitate sounds and explore their vocal range and capabilities (Fox, 1983, 1990). They respond to musical utterances through bodily movement and communicate with their parents or caregivers through music-like vocalizations (Trevarthen & Aitken, 2001).

Toddlers begin to gain greater control of their responses to and production of music (Moog, 1976; Moorhead & Pond, 1978). They create spontaneous songs that take on freer forms when performed under solitary conditions and repetitive and metric forms in social contexts (Moorhead & Pond, 1978). Young children may even own collections of musical or video recordings that they listen to and watch when they please. In the preschool years, caregivers might enroll children in formal music education programs specifically tailored to their needs and abilities.

Many children's social circles expand as they begin formal schooling (preschool or kindergarten) with peers and adults outside the family. Through other people or other mediated sources (e.g., recordings), children develop a repertoire of learned songs at home, school, playgrounds, and other social spaces (Campbell, 1998). Children's games and play are often accompanied by songs and rhythmic chants (Campbell, 1998; Harwood, 1998). Music in childhood might be used for ritualistic purposes (e.g., birthday celebrations), to teach basic skills or concepts (e.g., alphabet), or for social bonding (e.g., playmates) (Campbell, 1998; Custodero, 2006). Children are likely to dance to music in culturally stylized ways and make increased choices in the music they listen to (Campbell, 1998). Children partake in musical rituals at school, including singing a national anthem or school song, as well as performing in public settings. They also continue engaging in musical rituals within the nuclear and extended family units.

Some children participate in group musical experiences, singing and/or playing in community, religious, or school organizations. Many schools offer children opportunities to study music formally in large-group settings, where they can sing, play instruments, compose, listen to music, and learn to read traditional musical notation. Children with disabilities may be mainstreamed in regular classes or placed in self-contained classes, where musical experiences are adapted to meet students' learning needs. Alternately, music therapists in schools, community centers, and hospitals design musical experiences for people as ways to effect positive changes in their lives that are both musical and extra-musical.

Adolescents might play or sing in school or community music groups or create musical ensembles with their peers or family members. They may teach themselves to play an instrument or write songs to express their emotions. Mass-mediated music (e.g., radio, Internet) has an increasingly powerful influence on the musical decisions and preferences of children and youth (Campbell, 1998; Tarrant, North, & Hargreaves, 2000). Adolescents spend large amounts of time involved in music, particularly through listening (North, Hargreaves, & O'Neill, 2000) and it becomes a prominent facet of the teenage lifestyle (Fitzgerald, Joseph, Hayes, & O'Regan, 1995). Unlike in the early years of life, in adolescence peers exert more influence on teens' musical choices as performers, creators, or listeners than do members of the family unit (Csikzentmihalyi & Larson, 1985; North, Hargreaves, & O'Neill, 2000; Zarbatany, Ghesquiere, & Mohr, 1992). Adolescents' preferences for musical styles and involvement in music performance experiences are related to their personal concepts of self-identity and their perceived notions of what others think of them (North, Hargreaves, & O'Neill, 2000).

In secondary schools (i.e., junior high, middle, and high schools), the numbers of people who enroll in music courses reflect only a small proportion of the entire school population (Reimer, 2004). Of those who study an instrument or voice formally, many abandon music-making because other responsibilities take precedence in adulthood (e.g., higher education, career, family) or because they perceive music to be a vocation reserved for a chosen few (Ernst, 2001). Only a small proportion of the population decides to pursue specialized music study in colleges, universities, and conservatories. Many of these people studying music formally become performers, composers, teachers, critics, therapists, theorists, and administrators. That is not to say that those who study music in formal settings cannot attain careers in music, because many have.

Regardless of career track, most people continue to experience music by listening to recordings, attending concerts, and/or dancing. Some find time to perform in garage bands or other community ensembles. Many adults, whether or not they have studied music formally, create or facilitate musical experiences for others, particularly their own children. Parents use music as a way to communicate and share experiences with their children through songs, games, and movement (Custodero, 2006; Trehub, 1999). They might also enlist family members and friends to perform music during special occasions, celebrations, religious services, or other events and rituals.

Some adults seek challenging and rewarding activities in their lives or have more financial resources for private musical instruction or self-study of an instrument (Ernst, 2001). They may partake in informal large group singing or playing within various social contexts and for various purposes (Bowles, 1991; Coffman, 1997; Darrough, 1992; Ernst, 2001; Titcomb, 2000), move to music during aerobics classes at the gym or in a dance hall

(Cada, 2004), listen to music at home or in the car (Bull, 2003), and use music to soothe or incite emotions (Sloboda, 2005) or to promote healing (Gioia, 2006).

In examining musical experience through the lifespan, this book affords readers an opportunity to step back and view music education from a broader perspective, which includes but is not confined to the school-age years. In recent years, music educators have sought to break free of traditional structures and consider how musical experiences can be made more relevant and accessible to people throughout the lifespan (Myers, 2006). Myers asserted that a "lifespan perspective enlarges and extends the vision of a musically aware society to provide a context for high-quality learning and teaching from nursery school through eldercare" (2006, p. 19). The lifespan perspective of this book is intended to encourage reflective thinking and dialogue in the profession regarding the ways we can increase opportunities for people to experience music throughout their lives.

TRANSMISSION AND ENCULTURATION

Transmission

Transmission refers to the ways in which values, skills, practices, and knowledge are passed from person to person, culture to culture. Activated through human means (e.g., a child singing a song to a friend) and through non-human means (e.g., a song heard on a recording), transmission allows for the sustenance of as well as innovations in culture. According to Jorgensen (2003), transmission, "whether by such means as instruction or osmosis, practice or participation, example or observation, reflection or sensibility, . . . forges new understandings and practices as it also preserves past wisdom and ways of participating in music" (p. 117).

John-Steiner (1997) stated, "In the past two centuries, many aspects of childrearing and the modes of transmission of tradition and knowledge have changed; institutionalization of instruction is one of the most important of these transformations" (pp. 40–41). In other words, schools have become major forces in the transmission of cultural practices and knowledge in many countries around the world.

Nettl (2005) noted three essential forms of music transmission: oral/aural, printed/written, and recorded. While the first two forms have remained the same for centuries, the invention of recorded technologies has shifted the way music is transmitted in many cultures. Filmer (2003) found that current musical transmission is dominated by technologies such as recordings, radio, television, and the Internet. These technologies have greatly expanded the distribution and availability of musical recordings.

Music is no longer solely transmitted through physical contact with other people or in physical repositories such as stores. Music exists on computers, where, through the Internet, millions of music recordings are accessible from home computers around the world, any time of the day or night. Many of these technologies are portable, which allows people to access music virtually anywhere. Personal websites, popular with adolescents and young adults, often include information about their musical tastes. This seems to be a way for teens to reveal sides of their identities in an effort to forge connections with people having similar (or different) musical interests in cyber-communities.

The transmission process is inextricably linked to appropriation—receiving and making meaning of transmitted information. For example, imagine a five-year-old girl watching two other children playing a singing game on a playground. The music and movements she observes are transmitted visually and aurally; the girl sees their hand-clapping pattern and hears the melody and rhythm of the song. She seeks to make sense of the hand patterns, the associated behaviors, and the melody they sing, among other things. She may do so in order to participate with those children or to replicate the game with her own friends at a later time.

Scholars contend that thought is intimately connected to human action and that thinking in action leads to transformation of held cognitive constructs (Dewey, 1902/1956; Schoen, 1983; Wenger, 1998). Transformation of the mind—or learning—can result from a deliberate effort on one's part or serendipitously. It can also happen through the deliberate or unconscious efforts of others (e.g., a teacher or parent). Whether formal or informal, daily experiences provide a curriculum for our lives. Humans not only receive, learn, and act within their cultures, individually and collectively, but they also act as agents in reshaping it. The transmission and appropriation processes create the potential for enculturation, or learning within culture, and forge the way toward innovations.

Enculturation

Enculturation is a term with roots and application in anthropology, where it has been defined as the ongoing process of learning culture throughout life (Merriam, 1964). In a music context, Green (2001) described enculturation as "the acquisition of musical skills and knowledge by immersion in the everyday music and musical practices of one's own social context" (p. 22). Musical experiences, in their various forms and settings, are part of the enculturation process. Thinking about these experiences as being enculturative helps to place culture at the center of all teaching and learning processes.

Types of Enculturation

Enculturation is a lifelong process of learning that results from experience and interactions in physical and social environments. Tishman, Jay, & Perkins (1993) contended that enculturation occurs in "three mutually reinforcing ways: through cultural exemplars, cultural interactions, and direct instruction in cultural knowledge and activities" (p. 150). People are capable of constructing knowledge and understanding of musical experience without direct guidance or instruction from another person and can do so through social interactions, such as playing in a garage band or listening to musical recordings (Green, 2008). Learning that occurs accidentally, without the purposeful guidance of another person, might be called serendipitous learning. In that case, learners might or might not be aware of the things they have learned.

Anthropologist Melville Herskovits (1964) believed that enculturation progressed through two developmental stages. The first occurs in the early stages of life, when a person unconsciously receives cultural information. The second occurs in the later years, when a person is actively involved in receiving, making sense of, reflecting on, and innovating upon that information. The notion that conscious or unconscious learning is dependent on age, however, contradicts contemporary research in music psychology and education, which demonstrates that humans are conscious and reflective from the earliest years of life (Deliege & Sloboda, 1996; Jarvis, Holford, & Griffin, 2003; Younker, 2006).

On occasion people deliberately seek to learn more about a type of music and do so through reading, listening, and attending concerts. Learning that is self-directed and involves little or no guidance from others might be called independent learning. While serendipitous and independent learning are significant facets of enculturation, the careful guidance and mentorship of another, more knowledgeable and experienced person, who serves as a teacher, can result in deeper knowledge, understanding, and skill.

Setting out to help someone learn in a conscious and deliberate manner has been labeled "guided learning" (Campbell, 1998, p. 179). It takes place as part of everyday experiences, when someone more experienced teaches someone less experienced. Guided learning experiences are not part of a planned or sequenced series of learning activities or exercises designed to meet long-term goals, such as those that might be found within a school curriculum.

For example, the director of the senior center steel drum ensemble might ask one of the more advanced drummers in the group to help a less experienced member learn a challenging musical phrase. The more advanced player would probably teach in an intuitive rather than systematic or sustained manner. In this example, instruction would likely be casual and designed in the moment to meet a specific, short-term objective. Experiences such as these often result in reciprocal learning for both the student and the teacher (i.e., the advanced player).

In context, the aforementioned types of learning are closely connected to one another. In examining the ways popular musicians learn, Green (2001, 2006) found that they (1) acquire skills and knowledge on their own or from others, with the encouragement of peers and family members; (2) watch and imitate musicians around them; (3) imitate or refer to music recordings in their own music; and (4) interact with musical styles and forms relevant to them and their sociocultural context. These teaching processes, which resulted in serendipitous and guided learning, are loosely and intuitively planned in the moment, as the need arises.

Learning that occurs through planned and deliberate teaching has been called "structured learning" (Campbell, 1998, p. 179). This type of learning usually, but not exclusively, occurs in the context of schooling or other formalized educational settings. Structured learning is designed and monitored to meet both short- and long-term goals through sequentially designed lessons. It can happen in school, private music lessons, or in learning programs designed by a family member (i.e., home schooling).

Roles in Enculturation

The enculturation process involves people who assume roles as learners and teachers. These roles are not fixed. In some instances, when people teach themselves something new, the roles of teacher and student fuse. Furthermore, the roles of teacher and learner can be reversed within a given setting or situation, depending on who has the greater experience, knowledge, or expertise (Green, 2001). The role of teacher is not exclusively reserved to those officially sanctioned as such. Brand's (2006) exploration of nine teachers working throughout Asia helped to expand the concept of "music teacher" from one officially hired and sanctioned by an agency to work in school classrooms to people who work in any physical or social locale, even on the fringes of society. While the word "teacher" may conjure up the image of a schoolteacher, in this book we use the term more broadly, to describe any person who facilitates learning and is an agent of enculturation, regardless of setting.

Settings and Systems of Enculturation

Enculturation occurs in settings that fall somewhere along a continuum. On one end of the continuum is formal education, which is the direct and purposeful process of teaching and learning in formalized settings. It is thought to provide a space for transmitting culture and for furthering the economy, politics, and culture of a given society (Bruner, 1996). In many societies it is associated with traditional schooling. However, formal education is not limited to pre-K through twelfth grade and college-level schools.

Formal education occurs within the confines of time, place, and curriculum, and is implemented by individuals deemed qualified by a society (Merriam, 1964). Structured learning usually takes place within formal education. It provides a situation in which systematic, sequential, and sustained educational processes unfold. Formal education is a regulated system of enculturation and is required by law for children and adolescents in some societies. While school settings are the predominant form of formal education for children and adolescents in North America, this is not the case in many non-industrialized societies around the world (Strauss, 1984). Other settings for formal education can include homes, private studios, and community or religious organizations.

Swanwick (1988) asserted that education in schools differs from other forms of enculturation in that schools generally have formal systems in place to evaluate, assess, and critique the teaching and learning processes in a formal manner. Schooling is generally a valued commodity in society and often deemed necessary for successful entry into adulthood. Upon successful completion of specific course work and meeting of criteria and standards, learners are awarded a certificate attesting to their achievement (e.g., high school diploma). The knowledge, skills, values, and dispositions that schooling seeks to transmit are generally determined by, agreed upon, and valued by the majority within a specific society—a community of stakeholders, parents, students, school administration and teachers, state and local school boards, and national educational agencies.

Schools that provide music in the curriculum might offer courses in instrumental and vocal performing ensembles or courses in general music, composition, and music theory. In the United States, for example, music study is compulsory in many elementary schools (Abril & Gault, 2006) and more commonly an elective choice in secondary schools (Abril & Gault, 2008).

In contrast to formal education, informal education is not confined by time, place, or curriculum. Lucy Green (2001) defined informal education as "encountering unsought learning experiences through enculturation in the musical environment" (p. 16), by interacting with peers, family, musicians, self-learning strategies, and audiovisual recordings. Informal education can happen in traditional school settings but is not a regulated and monitored component of schooling. Informal education occurs in people's everyday environs. Green states, " [It] takes place in groups, and involves conscious peer-direction and unconscious learning through peer-observation, imitation, and talk. Listening, performance, improvisation, and composition are integrated at the individual and the group level" (2006, p. 16).

Take the following scenario as an example of informal education: A father engages his three-year-old daughter by singing "Itsy Bitsy Spider" in the waiting room of the pediatrician's office to relieve his daughter's anxiety about visiting the doctor. While singing, he moves his hands to correspond with the meaning of the words, in much the same way he learned as a child. In this capacity, he serves as a teacher, guiding his daughter in learning a song and its corresponding movements. On occasion his daughter copies a few of his actions and a couple of words she already knows. Through this musical experience, she begins to learn her musical culture. While functioning primarily as the father's way to entertain and divert his daughter, this informal education experience in which learning is guided is an example of enculturation.

Green (2006) stated that "informal learning practices of the musicians who create these musics [popular music] have not normally been recognised or adopted as teaching and learning *strategies* [original emphasis] within the classrooms" (p. 16). Gardner (1990) stated that there are apparent dissociations between intuitive and symbol knowledge in how students experience (learn) music in school. Students acquire intuitive knowledge informally, while listening, singing, playing, and observing musicians perform. Often there is a misalignment between how students learn naturally and how they are asked to learn in formal educational structures. In considering culture at the heart of all educational processes, from formal to informal, serendipitous to structured, we hope this book helps generate thoughts and ideas for how music education can work toward bringing enculturation in school and in life into greater alignment.

ABOUT THIS BOOK

Our review of research books, textbooks, and trade books made us aware of a lacuna in the music education literature. Historically, most of the music education literature has focused on teaching and learning in formal K–12 settings to school-age people. In other words, it addresses the philosophies, methods, and techniques for teaching music in the classrooms and rehearsal halls of schools. While important, that perspective alone has not provided the profession with ideas on how to move beyond set boundaries. Recent scholarship in music education has led the way in expanding our thinking about music education beyond the school-age years of life (Myers, 2006). In examining the musical experience, meaning, teaching, and learning, we continue along the paths paved by Campbell (1998),

Green (2001), and Brand (2006) but seek to do so through a lifespan perspective.

The chapters that comprise this book seek to provide a wide-angle view of the multifaceted dimension of the musical experience, meaning, and learning, throughout the lifespan. We encourage readers to consider the boundaries surrounding music education (e.g., age, place, time) and how all of us, as music educators, can be more expansive in our reach. In so doing, we may begin rethinking the purpose and aims of music education as it is currently described, discussed, and debated.

We view music learning that occurs during any musical experience as part of enculturation, of both processes and products that congeal without having clear beginning and ending points. Musical experiences that result in the construction of meaning and learning are the spark that can incite deeper understanding of one's self, others, and culture; can inspire subsequent musical engagement and learning experiences throughout life; or can help to reshape a musical culture. The contributors to this book explore shifts in thinking, acting, and feeling related to people's experiences with musical sounds or musical groups in a multiplicity of settings.

The chapters in this book are organized into four major sections that cover the human lifespan in phases. They are (1) infancy and early childhood, (2) childhood, (3) adolescence, and (4) adulthood/older adulthood. Each section illustrates various facets of musical experience reflective of that life phase. We contend that musical experience that occurs during infancy or early childhood is no less sophisticated or meaningful, cognitively or affectively, than that experienced during older adulthood. This is not to say there are no differences in the nature of experience among the age groups. We do not present details of people's musical experience as a model for how people should engage in music, or how or where learning occurs most effectively. Instead, we intend the chapters to provoke you to reflect on your own practices and experiences as a way to consider new directions for music education.

Chapters are written by music educators with experience as teachers, therapists, musicians, and researchers. Their continued work with people of various groups gives them rich insight into the people, settings, actions, thoughts, and phenomena they represent and interpret. The authors employ various qualitative methodologies, including case study, collective case study, narrative inquiry, oral history, and ethnography in presenting their insights into musical experience and learning. To protect the privacy of individuals, pseudonyms for people and places are used unless otherwise noted. Each chapter seeks to make connections with the theoretical and research literature as a way to deepen understanding of the musical experiences being explored. Authors employ terminology from the literature they draw upon; therefore, inconsistencies in terminology among chapters may be encountered. Questions posed throughout the chapters are meant to invite you to think, reflect, and ponder the meaning, aims, and purposes of music education. While the findings of these studies are not meant to be generalized beyond the participants and settings examined, we encourage you to make connections and transfers to your own musical work and play.

REFERENCES

Abril, C. R. (2007). I have a voice but I just can't sing: A narrative investigation of singing and social anxiety. *Music Education Research, 9*, 1–15.

Abril, C. R., & Flowers, P. J. (2007). Attention, preference, and identity in music listening by middle school students of different linguistic backgrounds. *Journal of Research in Music Education, 55*(3), 204–219.

Abril, C. R., & Gault, B. (2006). The state of music in U.S. elementary schools: The principal's perspective. *Journal of Research in Music Education, 54*(1), 6–20.

Abril, C. R., & Gault, B. (2008). The state of music in secondary schools: The principal's perspective. *Journal of Research in Music Education, 56*(1), 68–81.

Alpert, J. (1982). The effect of disc jockey, peer, and music teacher approval of music on music selection and preference. *Journal of Research in Music Education, 30*, 173–186.

Apfelstadt, H. (1989). Do we have to sing? Factors affecting elementary education majors' attitude toward singing. *Update: Applications of Research in Music Education,* Fall–Winter, 24–26.

Blacking, J. (1973). *How musical is man?* Seattle: University of Washington Press.

Bowles, C. (1991). Self-expressed adult music education interests and music experiences. *Journal of Research in Music Education, 39*(3), 191–205.

Brand, M. (2006). *The teaching of music in nine Asian nations: Comparing approaches to music education.* New York: Mellon Press.

Bruner, J. (1996). *The culture of education.* Cambridge, MA: Harvard University Press.

Bull, M. (2003). Soundscapes of the car: A critical study of automobile habitation. In M. Bull & L. Back (Eds.), *The auditory culture reader* (pp. 357–380). Oxford: Berg.

Cada, S. (2004). *Critical programmatic success factors of select arts programs for older adults.* Unpublished master's thesis, Virginia Polytechnic Institute and State University.

Campbell, P. S. (1998). *Songs in their heads.* New York: Oxford University Press.

Coffman, D. (1997). Senior adult bands: Music's new horizon. *Music Educators Journal, 84*(3), 17–22.

Csikszentmihalyi, M., & Larson, R. (1985). *Being adolescent: Conflict and growth in the teenage years.* New York: Basic.

Custodero, L. A. (2006). Singing practices in 10 families with young children. *Journal of Research in Music Education, 54*, 37–56.

Custodero, L. A., & Johnson-Green, E. A. (2003). Passing the cultural torch: Musical experience and musical parenting in infants. *Journal of Research in Music Education, 51*, 102–114.

Darrough, G. (1992). Making choral music with older adults. *Music Educators Journal, 79*(4), 27–29.

Deliege, I., & Sloboda, J. (Eds.). (1996). *Musical beginnings.* Oxford: Oxford University Press.

DeNora, T. (2000). *Music in everyday life.* Cambridge: Cambridge University Press.

Dewey, J. (1902/1956). *The child and the curriculum.* Chicago: University of Chicago Press.

Elliott, D. J. (1995). *Music matters.* New York: Oxford University Press.

Ernst, R. (2001). Music for life. *Music Educators Journal, 88*(1), 47–51.

Filmer, P. (2003). Songtime: Sound culture, rhythm and sociality. In M. Bull & L. Back (Eds.), *The auditory culture reader* (pp. 91–112). Oxford: Berg.

Finnäs, L. (1989). How can musical preferences be modified? A research review. *Bulletin of the Council for Research in Music Education, 102,* 1–59.

Fitzgerald, M., Joseph, A., Hayes, M., & O'Regan, M. (1995). Leisure activities of adolescent schoolchildren. *Journal of Adolescence, 18,* 349–358.

Fox, D. B. (1983). The pitch range and contour of infant vocalizations (Doctoral dissertation, The Ohio State University, 1982). *Dissertation Abstracts International, 43,* 2588A.

Fox, D. B. (1990). An analysis of the pitch characteristics of infant vocalizations. *Psychomusicology, 9*(1), 21–30.

Gardner, H. (1990). *Art education and human development.* Los Angeles: J. Paul Getty Trust.

Gioia, M. (2006). *Healing songs.* Durham, NC: Duke University Press.

Green, L. (1997). *Music, gender, education.* Cambridge: Cambridge University Press.

Green, L. (2001). *How popular musicians learn: A way ahead for music education.* Aldershot, England: Ashgate.

Green, L. (2006). The music curriculum as lived experience: Children's 'natural' music learning processes (chapter 1). In B. Stålhammar (Ed.), *Music and human beings: Music and identity* (pp. 15–25). Örebro, Sweden: Örebro University Press.

Green, L. (2008). *Music, informal learning and the school: A new classroom pedagogy.* Burlington, VT: Ashgate.

Harwood, E. (1998). Music learning in context: A playground tale. *Research Studies in Music Education, 11,* 52–60.

Herskovits, M. (1964). *Man and his works: The science of cultural anthropology.* New York: Knopf.

Ilari, B. (2005). On musical parenting of young children: Musical beliefs and behaviors of mothers and infants. *Early Child Development and Care, 175*(7&8), 647–660.

Jarvis, P., Holford, J., & Griffin, C. (2003). *The theory and practice of learning* (2nd ed.). London: Kogan Page.

John-Steiner, V. (1997). *Notebooks of the mind.* New York: Oxford University Press.

Jorgensen, E. R. (2003). *Transforming music education.* Bloomington: Indiana University Press.

Keil, C. (1995). The theory of participatory discrepancies: A progress report. *Ethnomusicology, 39*(1), 1–19.

Kivy, P. (1991). Music and the liberal education. *Journal of Aesthetic Education, 25*(3), 79–93.

MacDonald, R., Hargreaves, D., & Miell, D. (Eds.). (2002). *Musical identities*. Oxford: Oxford University Press.

McCrary, J. (1993). Effects of listeners' and performers' race on music preferences. *Journal of Research in Music Education, 41*, 200–211.

McNeill, W. H. (1995). *Keeping together in time: Dance and drill in human history.* Cambridge, MA: Harvard University Press.

Merriam, A. P. (1964). *The anthropology of music.* Evanston, IL: Northwestern University Press.

Mithen, S. (2006). *Singing neanderthals.* London: Weidenfeld & Nicolson.

Moog, H. (1976). *The musical experience of the pre-school child* (C. Clarke, Trans.). London: Schott.

Moorhead, G. E., & Pond, D. (1978). *Music of young children: Pillsbury Foundation studies.* Santa Barbara, CA: Pillsbury Foundation for the Advancement of Music Education.

Morrison, S. J. (1998). A comparison of preference responses of white and African-American students to musical versus musical/visual stimuli. *Journal of Research in Music Education, 46*, 208–222.

Myers, D. (2006). Freeing music education from schooling: Toward a lifespan perspective on music learning and teaching. *Journal of Community Music, D*, 1–24. Retrieved December 27, 2007, from www.intljcm.com/archive.html

Nettl, B. (2005). *The study of ethnomusicology: Thirty-one issues and concepts.* Champaign: University of Illinois Press.

North, A. C., Hargreaves, D. J., & O'Neill, S. (2000). The importance of music to adolescents. *British Journal of Educational Psychology, 70*, 255–272.

Reimer, B. (2003). *A philosophy of music education: Advancing the vision* (3rd ed.). Upper Saddle River, NJ: Prentice Hall.

Reimer, B. (2004). Reconceiving the standards and the music program. *Music Educators Journal, 91*(1), 33–37.

Reimer, B., & Wright, J. (Eds.). (1992). *On the nature of musical experience.* Niwot: University of Colorado Press.

Schoen, D. (1983). *The reflective practitioner.* New York: Basic.

Sloboda, J. (2005). *Exploring the musical mind.* Oxford: Oxford University Press.

Small, C. (1998). *Musicking: The meanings of performing and listening.* Hanover, NH: University Press of New England / Wesleyan University Press.

Strauss, C. (1984). Beyond "formal" versus "informal" education: Use of psychological theory in anthropological research. *Ethos, 12*(3), 195–222.

Swanwick, K. (1988). *Music, mind, and education.* London: Routledge Falmer.

Tarrant, M., North, A., & Hargreaves, D. (2000). English and American adolescents' reasons for listening to music. *Psychology of Music, 28*, 168–173.

Tishman, S., Jay, E., & Perkins, D. N. (1993). Teaching thinking dispositions: From transmission to enculturation. *Theory into Practice, 32*, 147–153.

Titcomb, T. (2000). *The social context of informal adult learning: An ethnography of a church choir.* Unpublished doctoral dissertation, Temple University.

Trehub, S. E. (1996). The world of infants: A world of music. *Early Childhood Connections, 2*(4), 27–34.

Trehub, S. E. (1999). Singing as a parenting tool. *Early Childhood Connections, 5*(2), 8–14.

Trevarthen, C., & Aitken, K. J. (2001). Infant intersubjectivity: Research, theory and clinical applications. *Journal of Child Psychology & Psychiatry, 42*(1), 3–48.

Wenger, E. (1998). *Communities of practice: Learning, meaning, and identity.* New York: Cambridge University Press.

Younker, B. A. (2006). Reflective practice through the lens of a fifth grade composition-based music class. In P. Burnard & S. Hennessy (Eds.). *Reflective practices in arts education* (pp. 159–168). Dordrecht, Netherlands: Springer.

Zarbatany, L., Ghesquiere, K., & Mohr, K. (1992). Early adolescents' friendship expectations. *Journal of Early Adolescence, 12*(1), 111–126.

I

INFANCY AND
EARLY CHILDHOOD

1

Songs of Belonging:
Musical Interactions in Early Life

Beatriz Ilari

Music has been present in the education and care of very young children for longer than we know. Anecdotes and recommendations regarding the uses of music with babies and small children are abundant in the research literature and in the writings of Greek philosophers and other scholarly works across diverse cultural and societal contexts throughout the history of mankind (e.g., DeLoache & Gottlieb, 2000; Koskoff, 1989). These reports have made their way across the sea of time and continue to have an impact on musical care-taking behaviors and attitudes towards babies and young children.

Most (if not all) cultures of the world have songs and chants that are created especially for young children (Trehub & Schellenberg, 1995). While in some cultures the mother is the main interpreter (transmitter) of young children's music, in other cultures, the role of musical interpreter belongs to fathers, a special nanny, or an older relative (Ilari & Majlis, 2002). These musical interpreters may sing, hum, and whisper, at times including body gestures, musical instruments, and special percussive effects like tongue clicks and hand claps (Ilari, 2007; Ilari & Majlis, 2002). Lullabies, playsongs, and nursery rhymes are musical styles commonly used to create music experiences for infants around the world. They are usually simple and repetitive, and are often used to serve diverse functions in the caregiver's routine: playing, entertaining, comforting, and sending a tired child to sleep (see Trehub & Schellenberg, 1995). In some cultures, these repertoires may also be shared with different members of the community like relatives, other children, a special shaman, and so on (Ilari, 2007; Ilari & Majlis, 2002). In others, they are used almost exclusively by parents and caregivers when they interact in the musical experience with their little ones.

Not surprisingly, singing has been central to the musical experiences between mothers and infants (see Custodero, Britto & Brooks-Gunn, 2003; Ilari, 2005, 2006a; Trehub, 2002; Trehub & Schellenberg, 1995). The image of a mother singing a song to her restless baby is not only very powerful, but is also an illustration of a practice that diverse societies around the world have encouraged and often considered to be ideal (Green, 1994). Consequently, singing to babies has generally been interpreted as a natural caregiving behavior that, as Green suggested, could be directly linked to "women's 'respectable' roles as domestic music-makers and teachers of children" (p. 66). In many cultures, the expression of emotion through song (and other means) has always been considered to be a feminine feature (see Green, 1994, 1997; Koskoff, 1989). Thus women have been encouraged and expected to sing expressively to their young children.

Interestingly, babies not only distinguish their mothers' voices from other female voices, but they also prefer listening to the former to listening to other voices and sounds (DeCasper & Fifer, 1980). Mothers' vocalizations are important because they provide communication and regulate babies' emotions. As Trevarthen & Aitken (2001) suggested, babies are attracted to the emotional narratives present in the human voice and enjoy participating "in a shared performance that respects a common pulse, phrasing, and expressive development" (p. 12). When engaged in such performances, even a very young child will respond with synchronous and rhythmic vocalizations, body movements, and gestures to "match or complement the musical/poetic feelings expressed by the mother" (p. 12).

Only a handful of studies have examined the ways in which mothers and infants use music in everyday life, and most of them have relied on questionnaires and interviews (Custodero, Britto, & Brooks-Gunn, 2003; Ilari, 2005; Street, 2005), in which individual stories are somewhat diluted in the midst of gathering group data. This collective case study serves to begin filling the gap by providing insight into the musical experiences shared between mothers and infants.

INTRODUCING THE STUDY

This chapter focuses on narratives of one aspect of musical parenting, that is, musical interactions between mothers and young babies. Three narratives were selected from a sample of one hundred semi-structured interviews held with Canadian mothers of six- to nine-month-old infants (Ilari, 2005) who took part in a study of musical memory in early life (Ilari & Polka, 2006). These narratives stood out from the rest for various reasons. The three women who are the main characters of the narratives spoke perfect English. They came from diverse socioeconomic and cultural backgrounds, appeared to be at ease with me (the reseacher), and shared their own stories with pride and in great detail. These women juggled identities as woman, mother, and wife and/or professional. At other times, they challenged established assumptions regarding the roles of music in early childhood development and care. These are the reasons that justified their selection for the present study.

Field notes, semi-structured interviews and infant music-listening diaries were used in the present study to construct the narratives (see Polkinghorne, 1988, 2005). Interview data and field notes were used to a larger extent than diaries in the construction of these narratives. This happened for two reasons. First, I had the chance to meet with the women in their homes and in the university laboratory. By meeting with the women more than once, I had the opportunity to further observe them interact musically with their children and, moreover, to complement interview data that went missing in our first encounter. Second, interview data and field notes were rich in detail and vitality and were frequently deemed more relevant than diary data.

The semi-structured interview constituted the main methodological framework of the study. Considered a window into maternal musical cognition and interactions with infants, the interview included both dichotomous (i.e., yes and no) and open-ended questions regarding maternal socioeconomic, educational, and musical background; musical beliefs regarding music for children; and musical behaviors with the infant, among others (see Ilari, 2005). Due to their openness and willingness to share their lives, the women provided me with a unique opportunity to further investigate *what goes on* in mother-infant musical interactions in the first year of life. This was the core research question of this study. Yet, as expected, the entry into the field brought along some new questions that also required scrutiny. As the women's stories unfolded from their responses to the interview, new questions were raised and readily addressed *in loco*. Questions that emerged within the context of all three interviews included the following: (1) How is music used in the routines of mothers and infants? (2) What musical repertoires are used and how are they selected? (3) In what ways do mothers and infants interact musically? (4) What is the role of musical interactions in the development of attachment in infants? Specific research questions are presented along with the interpretation of each narrative.

MAIN CHARACTERS:
THREE WOMEN AND THEIR SIX CHILDREN

Barbara is a twenty-seven-year-old, English Canadian, stay-at-home mother of four children: Benjamin (age five), Emily (age three), and twins Zachary and William (seven and a half months). She was married soon after she graduated from high school and has never worked outside her home in a Montreal suburb. Her previous musical experiences included playing clarinet in her high school band and singing in the school choir. Amelie is a successful French Canadian businesswoman in her thirties, striving to find balance between motherhood and a career. A single mother by choice, she lives in a modern loft in an affluent Montreal *quartier* with her baby, Sophie (six months). Amelie never studied music formally, although she reports that she likes music. Finally, in a small downtown apartment in Montreal live Aminah, her husband Jamil, and baby Karim (a nine-month-old). In her native Beirut, Lebanon, twenty-nine-year-old Aminah was a first-grade teacher; in Canada she sees herself as a self-employed housewife. Aminah explains that after their immigration to Canada a few years earlier, the family gradually became less religious. Although Aminah portrays herself as Lebanese Canadian, her husband affirms that he is Canadian.

Centered on a mother's perspective, each narrative speaks of a different aspect of musical experience in early mother-infant interactions. A brief interpretation follows each narrative. The converging points of all narratives are discussed at the end of the chapter. These everyday life "vignettes" offer many insights into the compelling nature of music in early mother-infant interactions.

NARRATIVES AND INTERPRETATIONS

Narrative 1: When Singing to a Baby Becomes a Party of Five

I ring the bell of Barbara's suburban home and hear excited voices and hurried footsteps approaching the door. Her son Benjamin, a smiley five-year-old, greets me while holding a yellow plastic giraffe. His mother is right behind him, holding Emily.

As I walk in, Barbara quickly finds a place for me to sit, removing books and toys from the couch. Holding Emily, she sits next to me and explains that the twins are taking a nap. Benjamin sits on the floor at the opposite side of the room, as if examining the situation from a distance. I can tell that Barbara is ready for the interview, so we begin. Each question is answered with a short personal story, an interesting remark, or just a smile. Barbara seems to be pleased that someone has taken interest in her "ordinary life," as she calls it.

When I ask Barbara about her musical activities with the twins, she starts to sing "Itsy Bitsy Spider" in a loud and confident voice. Emily joins in almost immediately. Benjamin, who has now joined us by sitting on the couch, moves in and out of the song, but ends up singing the last verse with the mother-sister duet. When the song ends, they all clap and smile. Barbara explains that singing is a shared family activity, commonly heard in her household.

> We love to sing. This might sound funny to you, but I find that singing is one of the few activities that all my children can do together, at the same time. Of course, there is also sleeping, but that doesn't count [laughs]. . . . When you have four small children, you need to find ways to "keep it together." So we sing a lot. Sometimes we make up songs. Other times, we sing stuff from the TV, the radio, or from CDs.

Barbara also explains that she uses music for different purposes according to the specific contexts. She sings to lull, to entertain, to console, to have fun. According to her, the family frequently sings in the car "so that no one gets cranky or too impatient." She has learned from experience that different repertoires and singing modes are to be used with each individual child:

> Experience is everything, you know. When Benjamin was born, I was very nervous and scared. I was always trying to use music according to advice from friends or from stuff I read on women's magazines or saw on TV shows. I bought many CDs and videos, and was often discouraged when they didn't work as planned. After Emily came along, I had two babies and very little time to read magazines or watch TV. So I started doing music in a natural way with them. I just sang and danced to what I liked (and thought they liked, too), and observed their reactions. For example, Benjamin would sleep very fast if I sang and rocked him to sleep. With Emily, it was completely different; if I sang and rocked her at the same time, she would get excited, make noises and babble, and would not sleep at all. To get her to sleep, I had to hold her steady and walk around a dark room, singing very softly. With Zachary and William it is a completely different story. They both like when I sing, especially Zachary. William doesn't care as much. He really loves to hear the sounds of his musical mobile. If he hears the music playing and he is out of his crib or in another room, he will move his head around, trying to find it.

Next, Barbara starts to sing Benjamin's favorite *Barney* song but is interrupted by a crying baby. She rushes to the nursery, where Zachary is awake. She brings him to the living room, and we continue with our interview. I ask Barbara about the repertoire that she sings/plays for the twins. According to her, the twins like almost everything that their siblings like: lullabies, TV songs, play songs, nursery rhymes, invented songs, radio music. Yet, nothing compares to her voice. She demonstrates this by speaking to Zachary using a very melodious and high-pitched voice. As she does this, Zachary looks at his mother with a big and confident smile.

The interview proceeds. A few minutes later, William's cry is heard on the baby monitor. Barbara asks me to hold Zachary and rushes again to the nursery. Emily follows her. At this point, Zachary reacts to the situation with a frown, and looks at me as if he is about to cry. This is when Benjamin comes to my rescue. He smiles at Zachary and starts to sing his favorite *Barney* song. Like magic, Zachary's frown turns instantly into a smile. Barbara arrives, now with William in one arm and Emily holding her free hand. They all join in and repeat the song. As they end, everyone looks happy— truly a party of five.

Interpretation

Many readers may identify with this narrative. Here we have Barbara, a mother whose actions seem to agree with some common beliefs and stereo- types of early musical interactions (Green, 1997). Even if she does not have any formal music training, her actions appear to coincide with studies and theories regarding early musical development (Trainor, 1996; Trehub, 2001; Trehub & Schellenberg, 1995). With four children, Barbara has learned much about child development, through both experience and intuitive par- enting (Papousek & Papousek, 1987; Papousek, 1996). As an example, she implicitly knows that by using "motherese" she is likely to capture the baby's attention (Fernald, 1989). Her implicit knowledge of music as means of communicating emotions and modulating mood and arousal states helps her choose repertoire to suit different components of the rou- tine (Papousek, 1996; Trehub & Schellenberg, 1995). In her home, music is used to either entertain or calm her children.

Barbara also knows that each of her children is unique with respect to his/her musical responses. She makes use of her empirical knowledge and intuition to ponder some individual differences that she perceives among her children. Barbara is a musical mentor who understands that music can assume diverse roles within the daily family routine (Trehub, 2002; Trehub & Schellenberg, 1995), something that she uses to her own benefit and to suit the needs and likes of each individual child. What makes Barbara a mu- sical mentor and not simply a good mother is her ability to guide her chil- dren's engagement in music. She will rock one child, sing softly to calm an excited baby, and play a favorite sound to delight another. Thus, Barbara's musical parenting behaviors are not mere reflexes. They are by-products of her own experiential reflections, which are based on intuitions, beliefs, thoughts, and problem-solving strategies used in everyday life.

One may wonder about the dynamics of musical interactions within the family. As Barbara interacts musically with one of her four children, how do the other children respond? In this case, it is interesting to see that some of Barbara's intuitive parental and musical caregiving behaviors are readily transmitted to her children. Each family member appears to be learning ways to interact musically with one another, through imitation and im- pregnation (Ilari & Majlis, 2002). They are also helping compose what Trevarthen & Malloch (2002) called "the mini-culture of the family." Evidence of this can be seen when Benjamin sings, probably as his mother does, to calm Zachary. At age five, Benjamin already anticipates a problem (i.e., Zachary's crying) and relies on a specific and familiar strategy (i.e., singing a favorite song) to solve it. This problem-solving strategy is in fact an indirect form of musical parenting.

Barbara's narrative also illustrates music as a form of social group cohesion (Huron, 2001)—in this case, family cohesion. Barbara speaks of music as a way to "keep it together"—having all the family members in synchrony and functioning effectively. In this household, music sharing takes different forms. At times, everyone sings along with Barbara. In other moments, smaller groups of children share music with or without their mother. Through music, a busy mother manages to pay attention to four different children at the same time. Here, music is a powerful means of intra-family communication and bonding.

Narrative 2: Georges Brassens to the Rescue

When I arrive at her loft, Amelie is holding Sophie in her arms. I enter her spacious home and cannot help noticing several pictures of Amelie and Sophie hanging on the walls and in the many silver frames scattered around the living room. Their bond appears to be a strong one. As we both sit on a love seat, Sophie babbles and Amelie responds. They engage in short musical dialogues that sporadically occur throughout the interview.

A few minutes later, Amelie appears to be at ease. She is outspoken and begins to share her personal story. Amelie explains that she was quite successful at a rather early stage of her career; international travel, expensive hotels, and gourmet food were natural parts of her routine. She was, in her own words, "a typical career woman of our times." Yet, as time progressed, she found herself bored and, most of the time, lonely. Additionally, her "biological clock" was ticking, and she became anxious about not being able to bear a child. It was at this turning point that Amelie became pregnant. This is how she depicted herself as an expectant mother:

> I was one of those thrilled and "eager-beaver" future moms, buying all kinds of stuff and preparing her home for the baby's arrival. I spent lots of money on furniture, clothes, CDs, baby gadgets. I wanted Sophie to arrive in the perfect house!

Much to her surprise, Amelie found herself very depressed when Sophie was born. This confident woman was suddenly overcome by fear and anxiety and, as she reported, unable to communicate with little Sophie during her first months of life.

> It was a very difficult moment of my life. Something inside me really wanted
> to communicate with this fragile child, who really needed me. But for some
> strange reason that I cannot explain, I could not come out and do it. I felt re-
> ally depressed.

Luckily, Amelie had friends and family who supported her through the
postpartum depression. Clinically diagnosed with "baby blues," she was in
psychotherapy. In addition to her weekly counseling sessions, she was constantly monitored by her family members. Her mother, for instance, would
come to visit every other day to check on "her two girls." During one of
these visits, Amelie woke up from a nap and overheard her mother singing
"Cornes d'aurochs" (one of her favorite *chansons* by Georges Brassens) to Sophie. The *chanson* was quite familiar to Amelie, because it was background
music during the family's long summer vacation car trips to Moncton, New
Brunswick, where her grandparents lived. Amelie peeked through the half-
open door and was amazed to see how pleased they both were. Sophie and
Grandma looked as if they were "having a blast."

Coincidentally or not, some time later Amelie felt like listening to the
chanson, which she repeatedly played on the CD player. The first few times
she played the CD and watched Sophie from a distance. Then, she started
to come closer to her child. According to her, the first few times Sophie
heard the *chanson*, "she alternated between a 'fixed gaze' and a 'deep look'"
at her mother. Then, one magical day, Amelie was finally able to pick her
up and hold her while Brassens continued to sing. A few days later, mother
and child were moving together to the *chanson*. Then she started to sing
Brassens for Sophie. And it all felt much better.

> This was a magical day. It was as if Sophie and I had just fallen in love with one
> another. For an instance, I felt very happy to be there with my baby, singing a
> song that I really liked, and that reminded me of so many good things.

Amelie ends her story explaining that she is now more confident and
happy about being a mother. When I ask her if she continues to engage in
musical activities with Sophie, she says yes and mentions that the new
Manu Chau CD is their new favorite dancing album. In addition to Brassens,
of course.

Interpretation

Maternal depression is often associated with differences in infant emotion
regulation and attachment (Rosenblum, McDonough, Muzik, Miller &
Sameroff, 2002). This is so because depressed mothers tend to be more withdrawn, and they experience difficulties in interacting with their infants (Field,
Hernandez-Reif, & Diego, 2006). Why was Amelie so depressed when she

wanted "so badly" to have a child? It would probably be tempting for many readers to believe that Amelie's depression was a consequence of her single motherhood. Lone motherhood carries different values across different social locations and circumstances and can be interpreted as either positive or negative. Furthermore, for many people, single motherhood is often associated with a woman's inability to have or maintain a complete family (Moore, 1996) and can become a social stigma (May, 2004). However, it is important to say that Amelie never spoke about lone motherhood as the cause of her postpartum depression or related difficulties. From what I could gather, Amelie was a typical twenty-first-century woman, who was trying to find a balance between her maternal instincts and her professional goals.

Maternal depression is also said to negatively affect maternal attunement (i.e., the ability of a mother to tune in to her baby's needs). According to Trevarthen & Malloch (2002), postpartum depression causes the mother to experience difficulty in providing attuned responses to her baby, as "her speech becomes discordant and unpredictable" (p. 16). In addition, depressed mothers tend to produce quieter and lower-pitched vocalizations that lack a rhythmic regularity, which, in turn, do not encourage the baby to interact musically (Robb, 1999). Maternal attunement is often considered to be a central element in the development of attachment in infants, or the dyadic relationship between mother and infant that results from mutual interactions in the first year of life (Bowlby, 1983). According to Goldberg (1991), the concept of attachment encompasses a combination of social, emotional, cognitive, and behavioral components. Both mother and infant are equally responsible for developing different types of attachment. As Goldberg explains, secure attachment is a reciprocal relationship in which both maternal attunement and infant affect regulation are in synchrony. By contrast, an insecure attachment may develop when the mother is not attuned to, misinterprets, or does not respond to her baby's signals in a timely fashion. The baby, then, regulates his or her affect in ways such as crying, fussing, or withdrawing (Goldberg, 1991; l'Etoile, 2006).

Using her intuition, Amelie found in music a strategy to communicate and develop what seemed to be a secure attachment to Sophie. Both the content of the song, as well as the personal meaning attributed to it, offered prompts for pleasure and closeness, bearing some resemblance to a particular music therapy technique (Bunt, 1998). In other words, Amelie used a mood-altering strategy (Field, 1998), in the form of a preferred song, to interact with her child. The *chanson* provided a comfort zone—a protected environment in which both mother and baby felt safe to communicate with one another. Amelie and Sophie were also dialoguing through a special musical conversation, in which each speaker took turns (see Trevarthen & Aitken, 2001). The presence of music was ubiquitous (i.e., song, dance, proto-conversations).

It was also remarkable to see how Amelie and Sophie made the transition between what could be called therapeutic to pleasing music. The role of music in the routine of this mother-infant dyad changed drastically. Initially Brassens came to rescue Amelie from her depression and to help her communicate with Sophie; after a while the *chanson* facilitated engagement and play between them—it became their song. As with lovers who find meaning in a song that represents their relationship (Ilari, 2006b; Rentfrow & Gosling, 2003), Brassens became a symbol of their love story. Through music, Sophie and Amelie experienced a transformation in their bond, which is now even stronger than before.

Narrative 3: Crossing Borders

As the door of apartment 301 opens, the perfume of rose water fills the air. Aminah explains that she is preparing "a feast for a client." She quickly adds that, besides running all her errands, she also takes care of children other than her own and occasionally cooks Lebanese goodies, which she sells to her friends and acquaintances to "increase the house income and have a little pocket money." As soon as she closes the door, her husband Jamil comes to greet me while he puts baby Karim in a walker that is placed in front of the TV, which had been turned on. Karim looks at me and then ignores my presence, quickly fixating his eyes on the TV screen. Jamil, on the contrary, has all his attention on me and seems to be watching my every step.

We start the interview in his presence, and I sense that Aminah is uncomfortable, more so because Jamil is the one who answers all of my questions. Whenever Aminah attempts to answer, Jamil interrupts her. As the interview proceeds, I start to lose hope of having Aminah's voice being heard. That is when something apparently trivial transforms the entire interview. Britney Spears suddenly appears on TV and sings a fast pop hit. Jamil immediately raises the volume of the TV and shouts: "Hush! Karim's girl is on TV. Look, he is already popular with girls!" We turn to the baby, who is now smiling, moving his body, his arms up as if asking to be held, and staring at his dancing father. Jamil immediately takes Karim in his arms, swinging him around the room. The dancing father-child dyad keeps spinning around, singing and laughing. But things are only warming up. Jamil follows by repeatedly throwing Karim high up in the air. Then, he holds the baby in a single hand, stretches his arm up in the air as high as he can and moves his wrist. Needless to say, Karim laughs hysterically until Aminah yells something in Arabic, to which Jamil mumbles and immediately puts the baby down.

After this "break," we continue the interview. But now Jamil seems to have lost all his interest in it. As soon as I ask the last question, he grabs his keys and tells us that he is leaving. He slams the door and Aminah starts to talk. She asks me to restart the interview; now she answers everything to her liking. She often disagrees with her husband's previous responses. When this happens, she shakes her head, frowns, or sighs. A few times she tells me, "Men don't really know much about children," or "Oh, he is just a man!" She also explains that her husband listens to a lot of radio music with Karim, including Britney Spears, which she dislikes. According to Aminah, her way of playing music or singing to Karim is completely different:

> I like to listen to Lebanese music with Karim. It is my way of feeling closer to my country and my language. When we are [both] in the mood, I like to sing this night song that my mother used to sing when I was little. It is a beautiful song in Arabic; to me it is almost like a silent prayer, something that makes me feel good. We also listen to English children's songs, but I still prefer my Lebanese songs.

Aminah sings a short excerpt of what seems to be a favorite lullaby and continues to talk. We are just about to end the interview when she walks to the stove and pours some soup into a colorful bowl. Karim does not seem to be hungry. This is when Aminah begins to sing what appears to be a funny nursery rhyme in Arabic. At the end of the verse, Karim laughs and Aminah manages to feed him a spoonful of soup. I do not want to interrupt their musical-feeding moment, so I wait and watch them. Once they are done, I leave. The aroma of rose water will always remind me of her.

Interpretation

Even if modern-day men have become gradually more involved in early child care, in most parts of the world the mother is still the primary caregiver for infants (see Abu-Lughod, 1993; Ilari, 2005). How do parental roles change when people immigrate to a new land? How do immigrants parent their children musically in their new country? What cultural dilemmas do they face when selecting repertoires and activities? These are some of the questions that stemmed from Aminah's narrative.

In the present narrative, Aminah portrays herself as the primary caregiver of Karim. In her home, parental roles are clearly defined and mediated by the cultures (and subcultures) of Lebanon and Canada. When people immigrate, they bring along many habits and traditions that are often deeply rooted in their personal identities (Ilari, 2006c). As they experience life in new countries, they often feel as if they have multiple identities—an original one from their place of origin and a new one that is under constant change in the new world. These two identities (or worlds) do coexist, yet they pose some internal conflicts and dilemmas to the individual. Music serves, then, as a bridge to both worlds (Ilari, 2006c). It is interesting to observe that Aminah tries to hold on to her Lebanese culture and identity by singing familiar childhood songs in Arabic to her baby. Her preference for

Lebanese songs suggests that in her musical interactions with Karim, it is her "Lebanese identity" that comes into play. This is understandable, given that exile from one's culture and native community has a direct impact on maternal expression of emotions to her baby (Trevarthen & Malloch, 2002).

What role does gender play in parental interactions with babies? What about infant gender? The narrative of Aminah brings forward some issues of gender differences in parenting of young children. In her home, gender affects parental musical interactions with the baby. On that note, it has been well established that fathers and mothers display different behaviors with young children (Fivush, Brotman, Buckman, & Goodman, 2000; Wille, 1995). For instance, compared to mothers, fathers tend to express positive affect less often and spend a greater proportion of time in physical play with their infants (Forbes, Cohn, Allen, & Lewinsohn, 2004). In addition, mothers and fathers tend to choose different repertoire to sing to their infants (Trehub, Unyk, Kamenetsky, Hill, Trainor, Henderson, and Saraza, 1997). This appears to be true for Aminah and Jamil, who differed in their musical interactions with Karim: While Aminah enjoyed singing stereotypical children's songs and lullabies, Jamil took pleasure in swinging and shaking the baby to pop music. Of course, there is no guarantee that Jamil would show the same music-related behaviors if the child were a girl. Many parental attitudes toward babies are mediated by a combination of both parental roles and infant gender (Graham, 1993; Wille, 1995; Yogman, 2006). They are also culturally bound (Roopnarine, Ahmeduzzanam, Hossain, & Riegraf, 1992). As an example, in some cultures like my own, Brazilian, throwing a baby in the air (as Jamil did) or playing rough games are common gestures that fathers might use to instill bravery in their young sons, but not in their young daughters. As Karim grows up, he is also implicitly learning that far from being a neutral activity, music carries with it many traces of culture, identity, language, and gender (Green, 1994, 1997).

CROSSING THE NARRATIVES: CONVERGING POINTS

Although the three narratives are distinct, some converging aspects of the musical experiences emerge. For instance, singing appeared as an important means for intrapersonal communication and musical transmission. This finding supports previous studies that stress the importance of singing in early musical interactions (Custodero, 2006; Custodero, Britto, & Brooks-Gunn, 2003; Ilari, 2005). Furthermore, in all three narratives, the musical experience played a role in the following:

(1) *Inducing mood and modulating behaviors.* Concurrent with many theories, music was used to induce mood and modulate behaviors of both children

and parents (Crozier, 1998; Shenfield, Trehub, & Nakata, 2003). Intuitively or not, all three mothers learned to use music accordingly to their own and their children's mood and routine, using both empirical knowledge and parental intuitions. At times, musical experiences served to soothe a child or a nostalgic mother. At other times, musical experiences were meant to entertain both mother and baby or used as a strategy to feed a child.

(2) *Learning and growing*. An implicit belief in music as cultural knowledge was common to all narratives. The three women sang songs and listened to music that was directly linked to their own cultures—be it English Canadian, French Canadian, or Lebanese. Barbara sang traditional English children's songs (e.g., "Itsy Bitsy Spider"), Amelie sang Brassens, and Aminah sang a Lebanese lullaby. By singing these songs in their first languages, the three women helped sustain the musical cultures and cultural traditions of their milieu (see Ilari, 2005). In other words, these musical choices did not arise in a vacuum. They were meaningful representations of important features related to the personal, cultural, and social identities of each woman.

(3) *Communicating*. Music was clearly a powerful means of communication of affect between mother and child. In all three narratives, mothers found ways to communicate affect and bond with their children through varied musical forms (e.g., proto-conversations, songs, nursery rhymes, and "motherese"). For Barbara, the communicative aspect of music sharing by mother and infant was also translated into music sharing by siblings. Aminah used a particular repertoire to bond with Karim that distinguished her way of bonding from that of her husband. For Amelie, music provided a powerful communication channel that allowed her to overcome postpartum depression and express her love to Sophie through movement and song. In Amelie's case, music appeared to help them establish a secure attachment (Goldberg, 1991).

The analysis of these three narratives revealed that despite cultural and socioeconomic differences, these three mothers appeared to share some common knowledge regarding musical parenting, as shown in their musical interactions. These mothers relied on their experiences and intuitions to interact musically with their children in a meaningful way. They also used their intuitive parenting to create musical experiences that fostered social, emotional, and musical development in their children.

CONCLUDING THOUGHTS: MUSICAL EXPERIENCE AS A FORM OF BELONGING

The findings of this study provide insight into these three mothers and their children's musical experiences. It was still remarkable to see the synchronicity between the results here and previous studies and theories. Overall, the converging functions of music found in the three narratives suggest that music experience helps facilitate a sense of belonging in the earliest years of life. As Trevarthen & Aitken (2001) suspected, "motherese," proto-conversations, lullabies, adult songs, play songs, nursery rhymes, and other musical forms seem to bring mother and child closer. Through musical interactions, babies and mothers communicate and share affection, modulate mood and behaviors, learn implicit aspects of culture and gender, and build shared repertoires. All of these behaviors and actions are likely to help them strengthen their bonds and gradually create mini-cultures within their families (Trevarthen & Malloch, 2002). From the intrinsic musicality found in proto-conversations to the actual songs that are shared when children are capable of singing parts or a complete song, musical interactions seem to be a tie that binds mother and child, granting them a sense of belonging—to a mother-child dyad, to a family, to a culture. Early musical interactions are important because they may also favor the development of secure attachment in mothers and infants (l'Etoile, 2006).

Bornstein (1995) suggested that the quality of infant attachment may be directly linked to the efforts that parents make to understand their infant's mind. Thus, the narratives of musical parenting presented here carry along with them many implicit beliefs that the three mothers held regarding their infant's cognition. Such beliefs are not only informative of everyday musical experiences, but are also central to our understanding of early social development. Mothers' cognitions regarding their infant's abilities, behaviors, and experiences are important for the establishment of a context in which infants develop their understandings of themselves and of others (Degotardi, Torr, & Cross, 2008). The latter are vital for infants to develop a theory of mind, which is at the core of human social cognition development. Thus, the analysis of maternal narratives of musical parenting may provide deeper insights into the many relationships between music and social bonding (see Crozier, 1998; Huron, 2001).

The implications of the present study for early childhood music educators are many, given that early childhood music education programs attempt to encourage, model, and even mimic maternal musical beliefs and behaviors with infants. First, it is important that early childhood educators understand the central role of mothers in early musical development, as seen in this study and other studies. As some scholars suggest, mothers are musical mentors who appear to be biologically programmed to interact musically with their children (Custodero, 2006; Trehub, 2001, 2002). Nonetheless, educators can extend music learning experiences for parents and children by stimulating parent-child musical interactions through songs, games, and other musical practices. Early childhood music educators can also help parents develop confidence in their singing and better understand the importance of singing in the early years of life.

It is clear that infants need affection, which can be provided through musical interactions with a caregiver. Music educators can help caregivers by providing musical experiences and giving them ideas for ways they can extend these musical practices at home, through proto-conversations, musical games, invented songs, lullabies, or movement. While mothers have been doing this intuitively for centuries and in cultures around the world, early childhood music educators provide something more. In addition to encouraging the natural musicality inherent in parenting, they can expand and enrich the music experience for caregivers and their young ones.

REFERENCES

Abu-Lughod, L. (1993). *Writing women's worlds: Bedouin stories*. Berkeley: University of California Press.

Bornstein, M. H. (1995). Parenting infants. In M. H. Bornstein (Ed.), *Handbook of parenting* (pp. 3–39). Mahwah, NJ: Erlbaum.

Bowlby, J. (1983). *Attachment and loss*. New York: Basic.

Bunt, L. (1998). Clinical and therapeutic uses of music. In D. J. Hargreaves & A. C. North (Eds.), *The social psychology of music* (pp. 249–267). Oxford: Oxford University Press.

Crozier, W. R. (1998). Music and social influence. In D. J. Hargreaves & A. C. North (Eds.), *The social psychology of music* (pp. 84–106). Oxford: Oxford University Press.

Custodero, L. A. (2006). Singing practices in 10 families with young children. *Journal of Research in Music Education, 54*(1), 37–56.

Custodero, L. A., Britto, P. R. & Brooks-Gunn, J. (2003). Musical lives: A collective portrait of American parents and their young children. *Applied Developmental Psychology, 24*(5), 553–572.

DeCasper, A. J., & Fifer, W. (1980). Of human bonding: Newborns prefer their mothers' voices. *Science, 208*(4448), 1174–1176.

Degotardi, S., Torr, J. & Cross, T. (2008). "He's got a mind of his own": The development of a framework for determining mothers' beliefs about their infants' minds. *Early Childhood Research Quarterly, 23*(2), 259–271.

DeLoache, J., & Gottlieb, A. (2000). *A world of babies: Imagined childcare guides for seven societies*. Cambridge: Cambridge University Press.

Fernald, A. (1989). Intonation and communicative intent in mothers' speech to infants: Is the melody the message? *Child Development, 60*(6), 1497–1510.

Field, T. (1998). Early interventions for infants of depressed mothers. *Pediatrics, 102*, 1305–1310.

Field, T., Hernandez-Reif, M., & Diego, M. (2006). Intrusive and withdrawn depressed mothers and their infants. *Developmental Review, 26*(1), 15–30.

Fivush, R., Brotman, M., Buckner, J., & Goodman, S. (2000). Gender differences in parent-child emotion narratives. *Sex Roles, 42*(3&4), 233–253.

Forbes, E. E., Cohn, J. F., Allen, M. B. & Lewinsohn, P. (2004). Infant affect during parent-infant interaction at 3 and 6 months: Differences between mothers and fathers and influence of parent history of depression. *Infancy, 5*(1), 61–84.

Goldberg, S. (1991). Recent developments in attachment theory and research. *Canadian Journal of Psychiatry, 36*(6), 393–400.

Graham, M. V. (1993). Parental sensitivity to infant cues: Similarities and differences between mothers and fathers. *Journal of Pediatric Nursing, 8*(6), 376–384.

Green, L. (1994). Music and gender: Can music raise our awareness? *Women: A Cultural Review, 5*(1), 65–72.

Green, L. (1997). *Music, gender, education.* Cambridge: Cambridge University Press.

Huron, D. (2001). Is music an evolutionary adaptation? *Annals of the New York Academy of Sciences, 930*(1), 43–61.

Ilari, B. (2005). On musical parenting of young children: Musical beliefs and behaviors of mothers and infants. *Early Child Development and Care, 175*(7&8), 647–660.

Ilari, B. (2006a). No matter where you go, babies will always be babies: An informal ethnography on early music learning in Canada and Brazil. *Music Time: Journal of the Early Childhood Music Association of Ontario,* Winter, 1–3.

Ilari, B. (2006b). Música, comportamento social e relações interpessoais [Music, social behavior and interpersonal relationships]. *Psicologia em Estudo, 11*(1), 191–198.

Ilari, B. (2006c). Música e identidade Dekassegui [Music and Dekasegi identity]. In R. Budasz (Ed.), *Anais do SIMPEMUS3* (pp. 35–43). Curitiba: Editora do DeArtes.

Ilari, B. (2007). Music and early childhood in the Tristes Tropiques: The Brazilian experience. *Arts Education Policy Review, 109*(2), 7–18.

Ilari, B., & Majlis, P. (2002). Children's songs around the world: An interview with Francis Corpataux. *Music Education International, 1*(1), 3–14.

Ilari, B., & Polka, L. (2006). Music cognition in early infancy: Infants' preferences and long-term memory for Ravel. *International Journal of Music Education, 24*(1), 7–20.

Koskoff, E. (1989). *Women and music in cross-cultural perspective.* Champaign: University of Illinois.

l'Etoile, S. K. (2006). Infant behavioral responses to infant-directed singing and other maternal interactions. *Infant Behavior and Development, 29*(3), 456–470.

May, V. (2004). Narrative identity and the re-conceptualization of lone motherhood. *Narrative Inquiry, 14*(1), 169–189.

Moore, H. L. (1996). Mothering and social responsibilities in a cross-cultural perspective. In E. B. Silva (Ed.). *Good enough mothering: Feminist perspectives on lone motherhood* (pp. 58–75). London: Routledge.

Papousek, H., & Papousek, M. (1987). Intuitive parenting: A dialectic counterpart to the infant's precocity in integrative capacities. In J. Osofsky (Ed.), *Handbook of infant development* (pp. 669–720). New York: Wiley.

Papousek, M. (1996). Intuitive parenting: A hidden source of musical stimulation in infancy. In I. Deliège & J. Sloboda (Eds.). *Musical beginnings: Origins and development of musical competence* (pp. 147–180). Oxford: Oxford University Press.

Polkinghorne, D. E. (1988). *Narrative knowing and the human sciences.* Albany: SUNY Press.

Polkinghorne, D. E. (2005). Language and meaning: Data collection in qualitative research. *Journal of Counseling Psychology, 52*(2), 137–145.

Rentfrow, P. J., & Gosling, S. D. (2003). The do re mi's of everyday life: The structure and personality correlates of music preferences. *Journal of Personality and Social Psychology, 84*(6), 1236–1256.

Robb, L. (1999). Emotional musicality in mother-infant vocal affect, and an acoustic study of postnatal depression. *Musicae Scientiae, Special Issue*, 123–154.

Roopnarine, J. L., Ahmeduzzaman, M., Hossain, Z., & Riegraf, N. B. (1992). Parent-infant rough play: Its cultural specificity. *Early Education and Development, 3*(4), 298–311.

Rosenblum, K. R., McDonough, S. C., Muzik, M., Miller, A. L., & Sameroff, A. J. (2002). Maternal representations of the infant: Effects on infant response to the still-face. *Child Development, 73*(4), 999–1015.

Shenfield, T., Trehub, S. E., & Nakata, T. (2003). Maternal singing modulates infant arousal. *Psychology of Music, 31*(4), 365–375.

Street, A. (2005). "I'm just a mum": Mothers' perceptions of the role of singing to infants.www.meryc.eu/mediapool/53/535813/data/Street_MERYC_05_paper.pdf

Trainor, L. J. (1996). Infant preferences for infant-directed versus non-infant-directed singing playsongs and lullabies. *Infant Behavior & Development, 21*(1), 77–88.

Trehub, S. E. (2001). Musical predispositions in infancy. In R. Zatorre & I. Peretz (Eds.), *The biological foundations of music* (pp. 1–16). New York: New York Academy of Sciences.

Trehub, S. E. (2002). Mothers are musical mentors. *Journal of Zero to Three, 23*(1), 19–22.

Trehub, S. E., & Schellenberg, E. G. (1995). Music: Its relevance to infants. *Annals of Child Development, 11*(1), 1–24.

Trehub, S. E., Unyk, A. M., Kamenetsky, S. B., Hill, D. S., Trainor, L. J., Henderson, J. L., & Saraza, M. (1997). Mothers' and fathers' singing to infants. *Developmental Psychology, 33*(3), 500–507.

Trevarthen, C., & Aitken, K. J. (2001). Infant intersubjectivity: Research, theory and clinical applications. *Journal of Child Psychology & Psychiatry, 42*(1), 3–48.

Trevarthen, C., & Malloch, S. (2002). Musicality and music before three: Human vitality and invention shared with pride. *Journal of Zero to Three, 23*(1), 10–18.

Wille, D. (1995). The 1990s: Gender differences in parenting roles. *Sex Roles, 33*(11&12), 807–813.

Yogman, M. (2006). Games mothers and fathers play with their infants. *Infant Mental Health Journal, 2*(4), 241–248.

2

From the Teacher's View: Observations of Toddlers' Musical Development

Wendy H. Valerio

The National Association for the Education of Young Children claims that adults who provide developmentally appropriate learning environments for young children incorporate music as an integral ingredient of holistic daily experiences (Bredekamp & Copple, 1997). To do so, these adults must not simply rely on a music specialist to facilitate musical experiences. Rather, they must provide structured and unstructured musical experiences for children, in playful and creative ways. The hope is that children will use music as an integral part of their lives, beyond the preschool years.

Because early childhood music development theories are relatively new, the examination of practices that stem from those theories is even newer. As a result, early childhood music development has been examined mainly through the lens of the music development researcher. The idea that adults may participate as active music-makers who guide young children, including toddlers, through music development, providing music scaffolding experiences, is also relatively new (Adachi, 1994; de Vries, 2005; Gordon, 2003; Reynolds, Long, & Valerio, 2007; Valerio, Reynolds, Taggart, Bolton, & Gordon, 1998). Though researchers have offered theories and descriptions of early childhood music development, none has offered a qualitative description of toddler music development from the toddler teacher's point of view. Such a viewpoint may allow new insights about the musical experience in the life of toddlers.

The purpose of this chapter is to examine the meaning of teachers' observations of toddlers' development within the musical experience. The main research questions were: (1) What do toddler teachers and a music teacher notice about music activities in toddler classrooms? and (2) What common set of understandings do teachers share in regard to toddler music development?

THE STUDY

I used a qualitative design and intensity sampling to gain information from well-informed toddler observers. Those toddler observers were teachers who were experts in toddler classrooms. Moreover, my prior experiences with the participants led me to believe that they would be suitable participants in this study. Researchers can use symbolic interaction with selected groups of keenly perceptive observers to determine how and why social interactions are meaningful to them (Blumer, 1969; Patton, 2002). I used a symbolic interaction approach to examine the data and determine the common set of understandings these teachers share with regard to toddler music development.

Participants for this study were two lead toddler teachers, two toddler teachers, and a music teacher employed by a child development center based in a university. The center serves a diverse group of 180 children between the ages of six weeks and five years. Bonnye (lead teacher) and Linda (teacher) taught Toddler A, a class of ten toddlers between the ages of twelve and twenty-four months. Bonnye was a state certified teacher who had completed two levels of The Program for Infant/Toddler Care (PITC) (WestEd, 1995, 2000). She had twelve years of toddler teaching experience, seven years of after-school kindergarten teaching, and she was pursuing a master's degree in early childhood education. Bonnye served as a teacher for an undergraduate early childhood education practicum at the university associated with the Children's Center. Linda was a teacher with five years of infant/toddler teaching experience, early childhood teaching credentials from a college, and PITC training.

Marilyn (lead teacher) and Salia (teacher) taught Toddler B, a class of twelve toddlers between the ages of twenty-four and thirty-six months. Marilyn held a degree in early childhood education and had completed PITC training. She completed ten years of toddler teaching and seventeen years of teaching among mixed-age groups of young children. Salia began working with young children in high school and college, and completed four years of toddler teaching. Kristen was the music teacher. Kristen had eleven years of experience as a private cello teacher and five years in public and private general music education for infants through children in fourth grade.

The participants and I were familiar with each other. For the past four years, I had supervised early childhood music classes taught by university graduate and undergraduate students to children enrolled at the center. In doing so, I had been in frequent and regular contact with the classroom teachers.

BACKGROUND

Teachers use the Program for Infant/Toddler Care (PITC) approach to toddler caregiving, which emphasizes responsive, relationship-based care (Lally, 1990). To create such an environment, classes are small, and each toddler is assigned to one primary caregiver. Classes remain together, as much as possible, as they progress through the first three years of life in the center. Teachers are expected to respect each family's culture and child-rearing practices.

Teacher responsiveness is the heart of the PITC approach for fostering relationships with toddlers. A teacher who performs optimal responsiveness in her practice includes three elements: contingency, appropriateness, and promptness. By continually watching, asking, and adapting, toddler caregivers enable themselves to provide care that is contingent on toddler behavior, appropriate for each toddler's needs, and prompt, without being hurried or rushed. Mangione (2006) stated, "When we observe responsiveness in action, we see harmonious interactions between adults and babies" (p. 26).

Kristen visited each classroom once a week for the academic year. The musical experiences she provided were based on the tenets of Music Play (Valerio et al., 1998). When offering such music play sessions, Kristen acted as a music guide. She created musical experiences by singing songs and speaking rhythm chants, playfully and repeatedly. As she sang and chanted, she also performed movements, not as choreography, but as physical accompaniment to enhance her breathing and musicianship, and to provide a model of musical coordination for the children.

When providing musical experiences for the toddlers, Kristen continually observed the children in the classroom, but never forced them to participate in teacher-led activities. Instead, she listened and watched for opportunities to use children's sounds and movements as springboards for music interactions and experiences. When she would hear a child utter a sound, she would imitate that sound and create a tonal pattern or rhythm pattern around that sound, incorporating the sound into a song or rhythm chant. When observing a movement performed by a child, she would imitate it and incorporate it into her own movements.

DATA COLLECTION AND TRUSTWORTHINESS

For twelve weeks, Bonnye, Linda, Marilyn, and Salia (the toddler classroom teachers) kept written journals of the toddlers' music activities. They were asked to write down anything they noticed. During the second week of their journaling, I conducted a focus-group interview with the toddler classroom teachers. Kristen, the music teacher, kept a journal of her weekly visits, and during the twelfth week of the study she joined the classroom teachers for another focus-group interview. Kristen also participated in an in-depth individual interview later that week. The interviews were open-ended, yet focused on toddler music activities as observed by the teachers. All interviews were recorded and later transcribed.

To enhance the trustworthiness of this study, I triangulated data by using multiple data sources (Patton, 2002). I also conducted member checks (Creswell, 1998, 2003) and had an expert auditor review the quality of my data analysis (Patton, 2002). I then used the research questions to guide my symbolic interaction analysis of the journal and interview data.

FINDINGS

Study findings are presented with regard to each research question. Following are the themes that emerged.

Q1: What do toddler teachers and a music teacher notice about the music activities in toddler classrooms?

When reviewing the journal and interview data, six categories emerged with regard to what teachers notice about toddler music activities: (1) toddlers and their teachers integrate music throughout each day using conventional songs and improvised songs; (2) toddlers respond with listening, moving, and vocalizing; (3) toddlers respond to purposeful silences; (4) their teachers make music privately and communally; (5) toddlers share music with family members and friends; and (6) music activities are beneficial for toddler language and social development. The following understandings emerged from the analysis.

(1) *Toddlers and their teachers integrate music throughout each day using conventional and improvised songs.* Teachers reported using many conventional songs throughout each day. With regard to conventional songs, Bonnye commented:

> There are about twelve songs we sing on a regular basis every day. These are [songs we sing] five or six times a day. These particular twelve songs are school songs that they love. . . . One of their favorite ones right now is "Swimming" [source unknown], since it's gotten warmer, and it talks about swimming . . . and sometimes it's hot, sometimes it's cold; there's a motion for each little part and they like it because they can't sing it, but they go through the motions.

With regard to improvised songs, the teachers reported that they sing about whatever the children are doing, whenever they are doing it. Linda commented:

> One thing I would like to say is that everything we do involves music. Like during the day, . . . when we are cleaning up, or we are just sitting down doing nothing, we're just singing. Everything we do involves music. They like to dance. We do music on the outside [at the playground]. Whatever we are doing, it always involves music. We change from one routine to another, and we'll sing. When it's time for them to go to the table for their lunch or whatever, we'll sing, "Walking to the table, walking to the table." [Linda improvised this in rhythm.] Sometimes we are sitting on the floor, and we sing, "We're sitting on the floor, we're sitting on the floor," "We're looking in our books." We just make songs out of anything and everything, and they love it.

Marilyn also commented on improvising songs about their daily routines.

> I make up songs when I'm changing their diapers; I'll make up a song. I'll make up a song to get them to come to the potty, because a lot of times they are busy playing with their friends, and they don't want to come to the potty so I will make up a song, like for Ali [to come to the potty].

(2) *Toddlers respond with listening, moving, and vocalizing.* When noticing how toddlers respond to music activities, the teachers reported that all toddlers respond by listening, moving, and vocalizing; however, there are differences between younger toddlers and older toddlers. Of course, in this environment, none of the toddlers was ever forced to participate. When interpreting the music activities of toddlers, in general, the teachers noticed the younger toddlers responding to music by listening and moving, gradually becoming more vocal with age. The older toddlers responded without hesitation by listening, moving, and vocalizing.

All teachers reported that toddlers enjoyed recorded music. Marilyn and Salia played recordings of multicultural music, and their toddlers sang along with the recordings, especially when songs included nonsense syllables such as *la, la, la.* Bonnye and Linda reported that their toddlers loved popular music recorded especially for children.

When asked how toddlers begin to respond to classroom music activities that do not involve recorded music, Bonnye commented:

> They [younger toddlers] . . . use their hands and their arms and their feet while they are saying the music song. So even if it might not sound like they are singing, they are starting to dance with it or do finger motions that go with the song.

Marilyn commented on the older toddlers using movement:

They show us with motion. . . . You can tell by their bodies that that's what they are about to do. . . . You know if they lay on the floor, that's their sleeping song. . . . You kind of know by their body language that that's what they are doing with music.

Kristen, the music teacher, reported that several times when she went to work with the children in the younger group, the class was outside on the playground. As a result, she offered her music activities outdoors. She thinks that this may have been one of the reasons those toddlers were less vocal than they might have been. The younger toddlers did respond by listening when she found creative ways to present her activities. She commented:

Because they were outside, I believe that's why they tended not to be quite as vocal. When I first would arrive and go outside, there would be a few children, because they knew I was there to do music. But they quickly dispersed to do what they do on the playground. I discovered, closer to the end of the semester, that the playhouse was a good tool, because they liked my movement around to the different windows. So I would do different tonal patterns at different windows, [or] different phrases of the song [at each window], or I would appear at the doorway to the house, and they loved that.

When asked how she knew that children in the Toddler A group loved that activity, Kristen stated:

Giggling and smiling and once in a while I would receive a resting tone [vocalization]. Not often, but it didn't really matter as much, because I knew they were absorbing the sounds. I'd like to think they were getting some concept of phrases perhaps as I was moving [and singing around the playhouse].

Children in the Toddler A group vocalized in response to Kristen's music activities, but they showed her what activities they wanted to do through movement. Kristen said,

They [the younger toddlers] did vocalize more with the rhythm patterns and rhythm chants [than with tonal patterns or songs]. Again, it would be a two-macrobeat pattern, usually in duple [meter] such as "Some of them would raise their hands up, which indicates they want to do 'Stretch and Bounce'" [Valerio et al., 1998]. I did not always receive vocalization with that, but a movement response is still a response.

As might be expected, older toddlers began to coordinate their moving and singing and rhythm chanting more accurately than younger toddlers. Kristen recorded the following:

One boy [in the Toddler B group] was singing and performing the motions for our dorian hello song, before I sat on the carpet. When I noticed the motions he was performing, I began singing the dorian hello song, and many of the children joined in singing and/or performing the motions that accompany the song. I performed "Stretch and Bounce" next. Many of the children were performing the motions and a few were chanting along.

(3) *Toddlers respond to purposeful silences.* Kristen used purposeful silences frequently during music classes, and she noted that young toddlers and older toddlers tended to respond differently from each other. She noted that if they vocalized at all, younger toddlers tended only to look at the teacher or were most likely to vocalize during the teacher's purposeful silences or omissions that occurred at the end of songs or rhythm chants. "They [the younger children in the Toddler A group] are not vocalizing as much for those [purposeful silences] at all, but that stare, or the turn of the head, lets me know that they know something is supposed to be there, that something is missing."

Kristen wrote in her journal:

I sang the . . . hello [song] a few times, leaving omissions [purposeful silences] at different times within the song. It was only when I omitted the last pitch [the resting tone] that I received a response. One boy who was wandering around the room sang the resting tone. I repeated this activity twice more, and both times, he sang the resting tone at the end of the song. Miss Linda was there to hear it, and she realized the significance of the resting tone and praised him for his effort.

Kristen talked about children in the Toddler B classroom performing the final note of a song when she omitted it, and they even embellished it. Those older toddlers also began to continue performing during purposeful silences that occurred during the middle of the teacher's song performances. She stated:

But they would [perform the] sound at the end of the song, and that's a big goal for them. And the teachers and I kind of laughed about this one at the end of "The Color Song" [source unknown]. They would sing the last pitch, which is the resting tone, plus the "song" became "sooo—oong." So it was elongated into two syllables.

Kristen then commented:

They [purposeful silences] seem to be more effective in the Toddler B classroom. A purposeful silence or omission is one in which I intentionally leave out part of the song and at this stage, I am really just listening to see if the children fill in the gap. For example, especially in the dorian hello song, I would leave out some of the middle part that contained lots of hand motions to see if I would get a response, and nine times out of ten, Kaylie was right there [singing and doing the motions].

(4) *Toddlers and their teachers make music privately and communally.* As the teachers and toddlers integrated music throughout and within the activities of each day, they performed many music activities that were private, between teachers and one or two toddlers, and many music activities that were for the entire classroom community. Private music activities occurred when teachers sang to children while changing their diapers or when children accompanied themselves by singing during solitary play. One child even woke up from her nap chanting the familiar "Stretch and Bounce" (Valerio et al., 1998) by herself.

Marilyn recalled a private music routine with a child:

> But I do join in with them at the changing table. Me and Devin [sic] have a singing session. He will start with, "Ba-ba," and I'll go, "Ba-ba." Then he'll go, "Ba-ba" again, and I go, "Ba-ba-ba," and he'll go, "Ba-ba-ba-ba." He'll extend it to four, and then I'll do four and then I'll go five, and he'll go five. Then I'll go low, and he'll go deep with his voice. Then I go like a medium tenor voice, and he'll go tenor. Then I'll go high, and he'll go high. And I'll see if he's going to do this again. So I'll do it over again.

From her private music conversations with toddlers, Bonnye noticed a toddler beginning to realize that he could shape the music conversation and get her to imitate him. After observing the private music conversation, several other toddlers in the classroom joined in for a communal music activity. Bonnye said:

> Instead of maybe singing the ba-ba songs [songs sung with neutral syllables] with "ba-ba," the guys decided to change the words on us. They didn't want me to sing yesterday. So, when I started going, "Ba-ba, ba-ba" [Bonnye was performing "Snowflake," (Valerio et al., 1998)], they started going, "Stop-stop, stop-stop," changing the words. Let's see, "chicken" is the one I think they used today. "Chicken, chicken" using the same intonations up and down. . . . Joey actually did it [using the word "chicken"], until I stopped singing "ba-ba" and changed [to singing] the [other] songs he wanted to hear with the [the word] "ducks" yesterday. When I finally stopped singing "ducks," he quit [singing with me]. I was laughing at him [because he was cute]. He realized then that he was copying me. So Andy and all the rest of them started following him [singing].

Bonnye interpreted her observations:

> So they are a little older; they are closer to two. What they are doing is they are starting to realize that maybe this is [an imitation game], and I'll follow suit. I'll follow right behind them [imitating them] and [I] change it [the pattern] just a little and let them keep going. They realize they have a little bit of control. They have a little bit of power. They have discovered, "We can make them [the teachers] do what we want."

Communally, teachers and toddlers in each class performed many songs each day; however, those communal performances varied. Communal activities often began as private activities that attracted participants. The young toddlers were reliant most often on their classroom teachers or the music teacher to sing for them, as they occasionally joined in with movement and some vocalization as noted previously by Bonnye. In contrast, the older toddlers often performed familiar songs and movements in pairs, small groups, or large groups. They even held their own music classes in their classroom and outside with other classes on the playground. Salia stated, "I know the times they usually, will like, initiate music, at the lunch table, right before nap, when they know it's time to go to bed. And waking up from nap they usually sing it, and in the sand box together is when they usually like to initiate singing."

During the second focus group interview, Salia explained:

During our lunch-time is our free concert. Either while they are waiting for us to prepare the lunch or just kind of after they have their milk, that's when they'll sing their favorite, "Jump Over the Ocean"[Valerio et al., 1998], or they sing "Happy Birthday" or what's the other song they sing, Miss Marilyn? It's usually "Jump Over the Ocean." They will sing that all together or "[Here Is the] Beehive." Yesterday, they all sat at the table and raised their hands up, and had their hands going like this (demonstrating the finger-play movements for "Here Is the Beehive") all over the table, and we were like, "Okay." [Salia gave a look that indicated she was positively impressed.] So usually during our lunch, that's when they all, I guess, that's their way to be together, and I guess maybe they know they can talk and be kind of loud [and they think], "But Miss Salia and Miss Marilyn won't say anything [to make us stop], because we are doing music."

Salia added:

One person [child] will get started and everyone else will join in. Me and Miss Marilyn [sic] let them go. That way they aren't hitting each other. They aren't reaching on each other's plate. They are singing music, smiling, and engaging with each other. . . . And also they like the loft. They especially love the bottom part of the loft. That's where they sing the night-time songs because they have the pillows. They are all going to bed, lay [sic] down together, and sing the night-time songs. And then like the "Jumping" (or "Mama Pushes Me on the Swing" ["Swinging" (Valerio et al., 1998)], that's usually sung at the top of the loft. They will hold hands and swing each other in a circle or they all [jump when they chant] "Jump over the Ocean."

When asked if she was engaging in these music activities with the children, Salia answered:

No, me and Miss Marilyn [sic] are cleaning up somewhere or preparing to go outside, or maybe we are sitting on the blue carpet reading with some other children. Then the others leave us and go up there and start singing [with the children in the loft].

(5) *Toddlers share music with family members and friends.* As toddlers made music with their teachers and classmates, the teachers also noticed the toddlers sharing music with family members and friends. One mother stopped by the classroom when Kristen was working with the Toddler B group.

> There was a mother who came in to pick up her child. The little girl brought her mother over to the carpet where we were and said, "Sing, Mommy, sing!" The mom was laughing and said, "She sings these songs all the time at home. I don't know what she's singing, but I do my best, and I move with her." She [the mother] was great! She sang the swinging song where you swing with your mommy, and the little girl was just so excited to have her mom there and participating with her, and the mom was so supportive of what we were doing.

Salia observed her daughter, Kaylie, with family members:

> I experience that not only at school, but at home as well, because I have a two-year-old daughter, Kaylie, and she has been doing these [music activities] ever since she was six months [old]. So ever since then, she has my mother, my sisters, and my dad singing them, the "ba, ba," [songs and chants with neutral syllables], and I have to teach them the songs, because she makes them sing with her. And even at home, she will stand up and dance with her grandfather—he's an ex-pro football player and so he's really big. And it's so funny to see them dancing together in the living room, because she has to always dance. She will sing the songs by herself in the car, or just playing with her dolls she will sing. Or she will make them [the dolls] sit in a circle so she can sing to them. It's too funny!

On the playground, Marilyn often noticed the toddlers from her class involving toddlers from another toddler class in communal music-making.

> And they do it on the playground, too. . . . [When] Kaylie and her crew get together, whoever it is, [they] get on this little, little thing they've got there, a ledge thing, and they will get on top of there, and one will get started. . . . [It's] like a whole crew of them. They are doing this [music] all by themselves. We don't say anything, they just all of a sudden . . . [they start having music class together].

(6) *Music activities are beneficial for toddler language and social development.* As they observed the toddlers, the teachers noticed that music activities were beneficial for language and social development. The teachers noticed that music activities seemed to help most children develop language vocabulary and speech skills. Bonnye noticed:

As far as talking, we have a couple [of children] that haven't been here since they were infants, so they haven't had music play [experiences] since they were tiny. Suddenly when the music [play classes] started, Michael started talking, and Charlie started talking, making sounds that were recognizable words. They started to talk and then trying to sing. So it was like it helped jump-start their vocabulary, where the ones that had the music play since they were in the infant room, and then moved to toddlers, they were [already] talking. A lot of them [talked] early and a lot better than one-and-a-half-year-olds should be [talking]. It's like, it's helped improved their language, because they can sing before they'll speak.

Linda noticed that music activities were beneficial for one particular child who was new to the Toddler A group.

We've got Serena in our class. Bonnye and I have been wondering how to, kind of like, get to Serena. She's not walking or anything. We've noticed that when we start singing, or whatever—I was just singing this morning and I looked around and Serena was just bopping up and down. She was just having herself a good time, so we know that one thing that Serena really likes and one way we can really, really get to her, really is through music. We learned that this morning. [Linda said all of this with great joy.]

When asked to explain what she meant by "get to her," Linda added, "She [Serena] just started in the Toddler A room, and she has a long way to go, socially and walking and mingling with the other children and then mingling with the teachers too. But once we start singing, she, like, just joins right in."

Marilyn said:

I notice how fast they [the toddlers in her class] talk. . . . A lot of people were noticing this one girl [in our classroom]. [They were] saying, "Why is she talking like this? My goodness gracious! She's like a wild vocabulary!" I said, "No, it's because she loves music." They talk faster [when they participate in so many music activities].

With regard to social development, the teachers incorporate music into activities in order to shift inappropriate toddler behavior into appropriate toddler behavior. For instance, Bonnye explained:

Yesterday we played in the sand, and the kids started humming, and we started singing, "We're pouring the sand, we're pouring the sand, don't throw it at me, we're pouring the sand." I had two little boys throwing sand, and I'm trying to teach them to pour it instead of throwing it at me. They seem to respond better when they have a tune behind it. Just regular words, they tune out. The musical tune gets their attention, and then they hear the words, especially with the boys.

Kristen noticed social skill development, combined with language development, emerging among the older toddlers. She commented:

> There are times when they all want to hold on to my hand only when we perform "swinging," and I will ask them to find another partner. I'll say, "Find a friend you can swing with." And they will go and find a friend. Sometimes the other friend wants no part of it, and we [the toddlers] have to learn that that friend may not want to swing right now. So they are learning social skills. And in that they are also using vocabulary and words to express those results. Sometimes it is only a "No," but that's still developing language.

All classroom teachers commented on how shy children in their classrooms overcame their shyness during music activities. Moreover, Kristen was astonished to find out that Devin, an outgoing child in music class, was once considered to be shy by his classroom teachers. Linda began:

> What I've seen about our toddlers is that the ones that are kind of shy, they aren't shy to sing. I mean they just come out and start singing all on their own. . . . They sing all kinds of little stuff and just go about doing their little business or something, like it comes natural to them.

Salia added:

> I agree with Miss Linda. One of our children is Devin, and he's very shy— and very, scary shy. He won't talk to anybody. He will clam up, and it's like he's almost really scared to talk to someone. But with music, you'd never know. Miss Kristen is shaking her head now. [Kristen was shaking her head in amazement.] She was shocked that I even said he was shy, but he is. He is very shy. With music you would never know it, because he loves to sing. Of course, now that he's used to me and Miss Marilyn, he talks with us, no problem. But if someone new were to come in and try to talk to him, he would "Mm-mmm." [Salia closed her lips tightly to demonstrate Devin's becoming shy and withdrawn].

Q2: What common set of understandings do these teachers share with regard to toddler music development?

According to Blumer (1969) and Patton (2002), humans develop understandings as they interact with each other. Following are the common understandings that emerged from data analysis: (1) Teachers and toddlers love their musical experiences. (2) Teachers understand and respect toddlers' spontaneity, and responding to that spontaneity through music works well with their approach to toddler development. Finally, (3) Teachers and toddlers are co-musically dependent, independent, and interdependent.

(1) *Teachers and toddlers love their musical experiences.* All of the teachers who participated in this study expressed a love for music, what participation in music activities does for them and the children in their classrooms. Music activities are fun for the children and the teachers. Actively participating in music makes the children and teachers feel good, and it helps the teachers manage the classroom. Music also has a calming effect that the teachers and children appreciate. Linda said:

> I can tell you from being in Toddler A, when the children get a little anxious or a little rambunctious, we start singing. It doesn't matter what we are doing, all we have to do is just start singing. It is totally different. It's like they calm down automatically. Music really works. Thank God for music!

Marilyn asked Salia to talk about why she called music classes, music therapy. Salia explained:

> I call it music therapy, because it adds order to our room. . . . When the music friends [Kristen or the undergraduates in music education practicum] come in, they [the toddlers] are just calm. . . . As soon as we say, "Let's clean up, music [the music teacher] is coming," they automatically start singing. They go to the blue carpet and sit, and they just start their own music. . . . We [Marilyn and I] love when they come in, because we just get a moment of peace. . . . So we enjoy it.

(2) *Teachers understand and respect toddlers' spontaneity, and responding to that spontaneity through music works well with their approach to toddler development.* When using the PITC approach to toddler care and education and the Music Play approach to music activities, teachers are encouraged to respond to what may seem like spontaneous, and even random, movements and vocalizations made by young children. Doing so requires flexibility, imagination, and patience. When the children are allowed to sing at the table, they learn to communicate with each other, even though it may take them longer to finish their meals. Salia commented:

> Just by, for instance, at the lunch table. Yes, they may get loud [while] singing or they may be distracted from finishing their lunch, but me and Miss Marilyn [sic] recognize that that is the way they are engaging with each other. That's the way they are socializing, and as long as they're not singing and pulling each other's hair out, what's wrong with them singing at the table? I'm sure that in some of their families, they don't do that at home, but you know, this is school. They need some time to socialize and get along with each other, so we choose our battles. It's not hurting them to sing at the table.

Bonnye recognized that teachers and parents are not always comfortable with toddlers' spontaneous music-making. She is very thankful for parents who appreciate their toddler's spontaneity, and she likes responding to children spontaneously. Bonnye said:

> A lot of teachers [in general] don't like [responding to the children's spontaneity]. Their problem is their [toddlers'] parents are expecting certain things out of them [toddlers], and their parents don't realize that they [toddlers] should be spontaneous. For instance, Linda and I got very tickled with Joey's dad. He came in one Monday and said, "Y'all are not going to believe what Joey did in the middle of church yesterday. They were singing a hymn, and in the middle of the pianist playing, and nobody is really singing, he [Joey] pipes up and started singing "Five Little Ducks Going Out to Play" [Traditional]. He sings the whole song in the middle of church, and most of the people were looking at him like [Bonnye made an expression that indicated, "Oh, my gosh! What is that child doing?"]. [Joey's dad went on,] "We just let him finish because we figured he wanted to participate, and he knew the words."

Bonnye explained:

> He [Joey] didn't know the words they were singing in church. He understood that it was time to do music. I think it is a lot of having parents that are willing to be okay with things not being this, this, this [with her hands she indicated a strict list to be followed] every second. As a teacher, I've done it [music] with some of them [the parents] expecting everybody to be perfect, and then I've done it [music] this way, and I'd rather have this way. I like the spontaneity. It keeps—makes—every day not the same. It's a lot more fun when you don't know what's going to come out of them [the toddlers], especially on rainy days or cold days. You are stuck inside, and you don't know what they are going to come up with.

Bonnye reminded us about the PITC approach, "It is very big on individualized things, in letting . . . the kids direct the learning. And we have been taught to do that. If we do that, it's [the toddlers' development] natural."

Kristen wrote about following the child's lead during music play sessions. Often when she followed a child's lead, other children began to participate in music activities, even if they had been engaged in other activities. At other times, her following the child's lead increased that child's music or movement participation. Kristen wrote the following about the Toddler A group:

> When I walked outside to greet this class, they were scattered all over their play area. I began singing [a hello song] and noticed one boy skipping as I was singing. I took his cue, and began skipping as I sang. When the other children saw this, almost all of the children in the class joined us to skip around the play area. When we stopped skipping and I sang the assimilation patterns (Valerio et al., 1998), many of them stopped to sing. Some were only singing the sol-do pattern but a few were singing the assimilation patterns. After the hello

song, I performed "Stretch and Bounce." No one was chanting with me during the chant, but three boys joined me on the "shhh" at the end of the chant. Only one boy imitated my acculturation patterns after the chant. By this time, I lost my large entourage, and had only a few fans left to enjoy the show. I started singing "Swinging," and one boy was enthusiastically swinging as I sang. I copied his movements as I sang. When I did this, he would make his movements even larger and more dramatic. Another boy wandered over to swing with me. He held my fingers, and we were swinging as I sang. The enthusiastic young lad was the only person to perform my patterns. I attempted assimilation patterns. He was pretty accurate on most of the patterns.

With regard to the older toddlers, Kristen wrote about inserting children's vocalizations into familiar songs, letting children choose colors for their color song, and letting them suggest the animals they should pretend to be in their animal song. By following the children's lead, she was able to engage them in many music activities that allowed them to direct their learning.

This group was not very responsive at first. One boy initiated a sound of "pow." I used this sound in our dorian hello [song], and at the conclusion of the tune, one girl was not singing the song, but she performed the motion for the end of the song [patting the floor quickly and repeatedly with alternating hands]. When I began using the word "pow" in the song, all of the children began participating. This same boy was saying, "black," pointing to his shoe. I took his cue to begin our color song. I included his shoes and numerous other items of clothing on other children. After several performances of the song, I began leaving off the final pitch, the resting tone. After I looked directly at the instigator of the color song, he took the cue and sang the resting tone that I had omitted. After this song, many of the children began suggesting animals to be used in our animal song. After the animals, we were ready for a [pretend] nap. We performed "Ni, Nah, Noh" [Valerio et al., 1998] and "Wake Up" ["Snowflake" with the words "wake up" performed on the first two rhythm patterns (Valerio et al., 1998)], several times. At one point when I was taking too long to begin, the instigator of the day began singing "Ni, Nah, Noh" before I could begin. He was pretty accurate with the song. Immediately after this, he began the "Wake Up" chant. During "[Here Is the] Beehive," several children counted to five when I omitted that section of the song.

(3) *Teachers and toddlers are co-musically dependent, independent, and interdependent.* Children are initially dependent on the teachers for music contexts, and teachers are dependent on the toddlers for listening, movement, and vocal responses that they may interpret and respond to by making music. Teachers provide music contexts and then follow the child's lead, letting those leads direct the toddlers' learning. By doing this in the classroom setting, children's individual needs are met as they learn to participate in a community. As a community, they are musically dependent on each other. As the interplay of co-music dependence increases and deepens between

toddlers and their teachers, the teachers begin to notice the development of co-music independence.

Co-music independence may be observed when young toddlers begin saying, "More," after hearing a song they want to hear again. Though they depend on the teacher, toddlers independently request to hear specific songs. Bonnye remarked about the young toddlers, "Once we sit down and start, every time I stop a song, it's 'More, more.' If they can't say more, they are signing 'More.'" As they develop, toddlers begin to request specific songs and rhythm chants. Salia remarked, "Once you say, 'music,' they are ready [for music class]. They request certain songs. If they don't sing them, then they request them [again and again]." Soon, toddlers are independently leading music activities without the teachers' interaction, as previously described when the older toddlers were making music in pairs or small groups, or at the lunch table or on the playground as a large group.

According to the teachers, independent music leaders began to emerge, especially among older toddlers. The teachers were quick to recognize that these leaders were exercising their music independence, and the teachers co-musically supported that independence by letting the toddlers take the lead. Kristen remarked about Kaylie:

> In particular, when we would start "Ni, Nah, Noh," she knows the whole song and she could have led the class, and I was ready to walk out the door and let her continue. She can sing the entire song and take the kids through that process [of singing "Ni, Nah, Noh" and pretending to take a nap and then chanting "Wake Up" and pretending to wake up].

Kristen elaborated on the process of how the children pretend to take a nap while singing "Ni, Nah, Noh." Then they pretend to wake while performing a rhythm chant, "Wake Up." It is a routine the children learned from Kristen, and they perform it often during the day and during music class. They get pillows from the housekeeping center to make their pretend naps more realistic. Kristen said the following about Kaylie:

> She is [singing and] also doing the movements. She is lying down on the floor like she's taking a nap, and at the point where we do the "Wake Up" chant at the end, she is "waking up" and throwing her hands in the air.

On another day Kristen wrote:

> When we decided to take a nap, Kaylie began singing the song before I did. She performed the song accurately, though she omitted the final "nighty-night" on sol-do [a descending perfect fifth]. She followed the song with the "Wake Up" chant. We performed this three times, with Kaylie leading each time.

The classroom teachers noticed other children becoming music leaders. Moreover, the teachers discovered that the children liked to make music without the teachers. Marilyn noticed:

First it was Salia's daughter, Kaylie, who would be the only person that would start all of them [making music]. But I've seen Devin, . . . Sally, Kim— like little leaders—Maddie, [and] Curtis would do it. All of them are like little leaders now. They just say one thing to [children from other toddler classes] on the playground. If they hear those songs, they are all gathered around that one person, and we [the toddlers] are just going at it [performing their variations of music activities].

Salia added:

They [the toddlers] don't like for the teachers to come and get too involved [when they begin their own music activities on the playground]. As soon as you start walking off [toward them], they look at you like, "Don't come over here. We've got our own thing going on." So we kind of stand close to watch, but when the teacher comes, it doesn't go on for as long. They'll kind of be involved with the teacher, but they are like, "Why is she coming over here? We've got our own thing going, and here she comes." [Salia said this in a disgruntled tone.] They kind of scatter when the teachers come. But if you watch from a distance, they'll just go and go.

Kristen also noticed Kaylie, in particular, becoming more rhythmically independent as the study progressed. Kristen described a type of rhythm pattern conversation she had using improvisatory rhythm patterns with Kaylie. Midway through the study Kristen wrote the following in her journal.

During "Stretch and Bounce" there were many interesting occurrences: Another girl had joined the group by this time and she was filling in omissions along with the first girl. . . . Kaylie was creating her own acculturation patterns and I was repeating them. After I began imitation/assimilation patterns, she began creating one of her own, which she repeated several times. When I created a different pattern, she imitated [the new pattern].

At the end of the study, Kristen described how she was guiding Kaylie through a rhythm pattern conversation while performing the rhythm chant. Kristen explained:

From a musical standpoint, I was informally introducing same and different rhythm patterns. The interesting thing yesterday was that Kaylie was not only changing the words but also the rhythm pattern.

When asked what that meant to her, Kristen replied:

> That she [Kaylie] is starting to generalize some of the information that we have done. I don't know if she was completely conscious of the fact that it was a different pattern, but I was. I was excited about it! And again, on that social level, they are learning turn taking—my turn, your turn.

When asked how she thought Kaylie might have learned to converse with her in rhythm conversation, Kristen explained that she "asked one of the [classroom] teachers to model the difference. So we were using the [ideas of] scaffolding and working with the more knowledgeable partner and modeling it in that particular case." Using principles of scaffolding, modeling, and working with a more knowledgeable partner, as explained by Bruner (1983), de Vries (2005), Piaget (1926/2002), Piaget and Inhelder (1969/2000), Reynolds, Long, and Valerio (2007), and Vygotsky (1962, 1978), Kristen then demonstrated how she and a classroom teacher modeled being musically different.

In this study, the teachers and the toddlers they observed were interdependent music-makers, because they each brought unique and vital qualities to the dynamic, ever-changing world of toddler development. Without music context provided by the teachers, the toddlers would be left to invent music on their own. Without the children's responses to interpret, the teachers would have no need for making music together. By creating an environment that integrates music repetitiously in a variety of ways throughout each day, and by approaching toddler development as relationship-based, the teachers in this study could not imagine responding to toddlers without using music.

DISCUSSION AND RECOMMENDATIONS

The teachers in this study were keen observers of the toddlers they teach and of themselves. Their observations of how toddlers respond in the musical experience through listening, moving, and vocalizing corroborate the findings of previous researchers who observed children's music development in naturalistic settings (de Vries, 2005; Hicks, 1993; Moog, 1976; Moorhead & Pond, 1941/1978; Reynolds, 1995, 2006; Valerio, Seaman, Yap, Santucci, & Tu, 2006; Young, 2003; Young & Glover, 1998). Moreover, the teachers in this study observed themselves and the toddlers they teach as co-constructing meaning through music interactions for language, social, and music development as suggested by Reynolds, Long, and Valerio (2007). They also enjoy participating in those interactions, and they find music interaction processes to be a stimulating element of their life's work with toddlers. These teachers use music as a vital element of their lives. Even when they talked about their observations of toddler music activities in toddler classroom, the teachers in this study did not hesitate to make music to describe their interactions with children.

Through their observations of the musical experiences in their classrooms, the teachers were aware that they were bridging theories and practices of early childhood care and music development. Though the classroom teachers had limited exposure to professional development for using Music Play, they observed Kristen using that curriculum with the toddlers, and they astutely recognized the similarities between that approach to music development and the PITC approach they have adopted for infant and toddler development in their classrooms. The success of each approach lies in each teacher's ability to listen, watch, assess, and adapt her actions to meet each child's needs. Those abilities rely on each teacher's flexibility and willingness to respond to the spontaneity offered continuously by a classroom of toddlers.

Teachers in this study supported each other by creating responsive musical experiences in an environment that fostered relationships with the toddlers in their care. Moreover, the teachers enjoyed using music in their responsive practice with toddlers. Researchers should continue to involve teachers in the documentation of toddler music and social and cognitive development. By approaching music interactions as uniquely meaningful in and of themselves, researchers may further our understanding of music development and musical experience, while enhancing relationships, trust, independence, and community beyond the toddler years.

REFERENCES

Adachi, M. (1994). The role of the adult in the child's early musical socialization: A Vygotskian perspective. *The Quarterly Journal of Music Teaching and Learning, 5*(3), 25–26.

Blumer, H. (1969). *Symbolic interactionism: Perspective and method.* Englewood Cliffs, NJ: Prentice-Hall.

Bredekamp, S., & Copple, C. (Eds.). (1997). *Developmentally appropriate practice in early childhood programs from birth through age 8* (rev. ed.). Washington, DC: National Association for the Education of Young Children.

Bruner, J. S. (1983). *Child's talk: Learning to use language.* New York: Norton.

Creswell, J. W. (1998). *Qualitative inquiry and research design: Choosing among the five traditions.* Thousand Oaks, CA: Sage.

Creswell, J. W. (2003). *Research design: Qualitative, quantitative and mixed methods approaches* (2nd ed.). Thousand Oaks, CA: Sage.

de Vries, P. (2005). Lessons from home: Scaffolding vocal improvisation and song acquisition with a 2-year-old. *Early Childhood Education Journal, 32*(5), 307–312.

Gordon, E. E. (2003). *A music learning theory for newborn and young children*. Chicago: GIA.

Hicks, W. (1993). An investigation of the initial stages of preparatory audiation (Doctoral dissertation, Temple University, 1993). *Dissertation Abstracts International, 5404A*, 1277.

Lally, J. R. (1990). Creating nurturing relationships with infants and toddlers. In J. R. Lally (Ed.), *Infant/toddler caregiving: A guide to social-emotional growth and socialization*. Sacramento: California Department of Education.

Mangione, P. (2006). Creating responsive, reciprocal relationships with infants and toddlers. In J. R. Lally, P. L. Mangione, and D. Greenwald (Eds.), *Concepts for care: Essays on infant/toddler development and learning* (pp. 25–29). San Francisco: WestEd.

Moog, H. (1976). *The musical experience of the pre-school child*. London: Schott Music.

Moorhead, G. E., & Pond, D. (1941/1978). *Music of young children*. Santa Barbara, CA: Pillsbury Foundation for the Advancement of Music Education.

Patton, M. Q. (2002). *Qualitative research and evaluation methods*. Thousand Oaks, CA: Sage.

Piaget, J. (1926/2002). *The language and thought of the child* (M. Gabain & R. Gabain, Trans.). New York: Routledge.

Piaget, J., & Inhelder, B. (1969/2000). *The psychology of the child* (H. Weaver, Trans.). New York: Basic.

Reynolds, A. M. (1995). *An investigation of the movement responses performed by children 18 months to three years of age and their care-givers to rhythm chants in duple and triple meters*. Unpublished doctoral dissertation, Temple University.

Reynolds, A. M. (2006). Vocal interactions during informal early childhood music classes. *Bulletin of the Council for Research in Music Education 168*, 1–16.

Reynolds, A. M., Long, S., & Valerio, W. H. (2007). Language acquisition and music acquisition: Possible parallels. In K. Smithrim & R. Upitis (Eds.), *Research to practice: A biennial series: Vol. 3* (pp. 211–227). Waterloo, ON: Canadian Music Educators Association.

Valerio, W. H., Reynolds, A. M., Taggart, C. C., Bolton, B. B., & Gordon, E. E. (1998). *Music play*. Chicago: GIA.

Valerio, W. H., Seaman, M. A., Yap, C. C., Santucci, P. M., & Tu, M. (2006). Vocal evidence of toddler music syntax acquisition: A case study. *Bulletin of the Council for Research in Music Education, 170*, 33–46.

Vygotsky, L. (1962). *Thought and language*. Cambridge, MA: MIT Press.

Vygotsky, L. (1978). *Mind in society: The development of higher psychological processes*. Cambridge, MA: Harvard University Press.

WestEd. (1995). The Program for Infant/Toddler Caregivers *Trainer's manual, module I: Social-emotional growth and socialization*. Sacramento: California Department of Education.

WestEd. (2000). The Program for Infant/Toddler Caregivers *Trainer's manual, module II: Group care* (2nd ed.). Sacramento: California Department of Education.

Young, S. (2003). *Music with the under-fours*. New York: Routledge Falmer.

Young, S., & Glover, J. (1998). *Music in the early years*. Bristol, PA: Falmer Press.

3

A Community Music Program for Parents and Children with and without Special Needs

Marcia Earl Humpal

> Use what talents you possess—the woods would be very silent if no birds sang there except those that sang best.
>
> —Henry Van Dyke

This chapter focuses on a group of children between the ages of twenty and thirty months enrolled in a community music program that met one morning per week for forty-five minutes, over a six-week period. As a board-certified music therapist, I created the space for these children to experience music, with support from two early childhood developmental specialists and the caregivers accompanying each child. Additional specialists such as an occupational therapist, a physical therapist, and a speech/language pathologist visited the class occasionally and were available for consultations. In leading the adults and their children in activities such as simple songs, rhythmic games, movement, and musical stories, I provided participants with opportunities to play and make music together in order to meet both musical and extra-musical learning goals.

MUSIC THERAPY OR MUSIC EDUCATION?

Although they share many similarities, music therapy and music education are different. I use elements of both music education and music therapy in this community music program. Adamek and Darrow (2005) defined music therapy as using music as a tool to attain non-musical goals that address "students' development in cognitive, behavioral, physical, emotional, social, and communication domains. . . . While music therapists use the same media, namely music, as music educators, they use the music for a different purpose" (p. 103). Music therapy provides a unique variety of music experiences in an intentional and developmentally appropriate manner to effect changes in behavior and facilitate development of communication, social/emotional, sensory-motor, and/or cognitive skills. Since building social relationships is an integral part of successful music therapy, the elements of music are used to structure relationships, create a positive environment, and set the occasion for successful growth (Humpal, 2001). For additional information, see American Music Therapy Association (1999).

PURPOSE, PROCESS, AND BACKGROUND

The purpose of this chapter is to examine how the caregivers, toddlers, and music teacher/music therapist interacted, reacted, and responded to each other in a community music program. A secondary purpose is to investigate how music influenced these responses and reactions. My role was as teacher and facilitator of music experiences in this program, where I combined music education and music therapy interventions.

As a researcher, I utilized a variety of data collection methods, gathering data once per week for six weeks. After each class, I chronicled and reflected on the children's responses to others in the group about the music experience. I kept a journal of my feelings, interpretations, and reactions to the musical experiences. I also reviewed and reflected upon the videotapes and photographs taken during selected sessions. My two developmental specialist colleagues also compiled field notes throughout the six-week program. At the conclusion of the program, my colleagues and each caregiver wrote a narrative summary evaluation of their experiences in the program. I transcribed and analyzed all these forms of written and verbal data, focusing on the main areas of investigation in this chapter.

In the pages that follow, I describe how therapeutic and educational music experiences intertwined and influenced responses in the participants of the study. I seek to illuminate how young children and their caregivers grow and learn about one another within the music experience.

THE COMMUNITY MUSIC PROGRAM

The HarmoniKIDS music program is a collaborative effort between the Cuyahoga County (Ohio) Board of Mental Retardation and Developmental Disabilities (CCBMR/DD) and the Westshore YMCA. CCBMR/DD has a long tradition of providing inclusionary programming for young children and demonstrating its efficacy in helping children with special needs develop social interaction and acceptance skills (Humpal, 1991). The two agencies involved agreed to provide recreational and educational opportunities for families of children with and without disabilities in a community setting. The YMCA provided the space, equipment storage, and publicity for the class, and only families of children without disabilities paid a class registration fee. For many of the children, HarmoniKIDS represented their first experience in a structured group-learning situation.

The foundations of the class stressed the importance of family involvement, relationship building, and communication, starting with the adults' full participation in each of the children's musical adventures and providing musical experiences that everyone would enjoy. Specific goals were identified: To provide (1) parent training in the community and in an inclusive setting; (2) a time for parents to experience music with their children through singing, playing, moving, and listening; (3) a time for caregiver-child interaction; (4) a time for sharing and networking with other families; and (5) a time for learning songs and activities.

One of our extra-musical goals was to help children develop improved attention skills. We encouraged adults to use the free-play time at the beginning of class to make new friends or to interact with those they already knew, and to refrain from chatting during our circle time, as it became a distraction to participants. After class, staff were available to help families develop specific strategies to manage some of the challenges their children encountered in the session.

The Children and Their Caregivers

The children in the group were between the ages of twenty and thirty months. Tess, Reagan, and Zach came to class with their mothers. Grant was always accompanied by his grandpa. These four children were the typical peer models in our class—the ones without identifiable special needs. Tess was serious, quiet, and extremely observant. Reagan had a twin sister with Down syndrome who was hospitalized frequently, so Reagan rarely had her mother to herself. Reagan clung to her mother and rarely smiled. In contrast, Zach was self-assured, polite, and emerged as a leader. Grant was a very social boy who listened intently, moved effortlessly, and replicated music quite accurately.

Like their peers, the children with special needs were just as unique and complex. Katie, a charmer whose smile could light up the room, had Down syndrome. Her mother had high expectations for her and worked diligently with her both in and outside of class. Christopher was not able to move independently; he had cerebral palsy. He stiffened his body when he was distressed and cried uncontrollably at times. He was calmed by his mother's soft voice and gentle demeanor. His facial expressions made it clear that he had great affection for her. Angela had been in the hospital more than she had ever lived at home. She had DiGeorge syndrome, a genetic condition characterized by certain heart defects and a lack of or underdeveloped thymus and parathyroid glands (Hussain & Win, 2006). This condition also affected Angela's immune system and her speech, although she seemed able to comprehend things in the class. Her eyes seemed to be full of fear, and they rarely veered from her mother's face. Angela's long medical ordeal had been difficult for her mother, who often seemed on the verge of tears. On the other end of the spectrum were Will and his mother, Lillian. Will was born with one non-functioning kidney. His second kidney was failing, and he was on dialysis. His bones were fragile, and he was very weak. Nonetheless, Will talked incessantly and got around the room by scooting. He and his mother seemed resilient and amazingly positive.

The rest of the children in the class were suspected to have some type of autism spectrum disorder. Timmy never looked at anyone; he kept to himself and would not participate in any activity. His mother, too, stayed apart from other members of the group. Devonte was a beautiful boy with striking, big brown eyes and a great smile. He demonstrated boundless energy and little to no attention span. He lined up all the instruments in a categorization known only to him. His mother seemed exhausted at times and was desperately looking for ways to help Devonte make sense of his world. Drew was afraid of everything new and on occasion would burst into tears when his routine was interrupted. His parents took turns bringing him. His father seemed to be able to push Drew to take risks and try new things.

Curricular Approach

Our curriculum was both horizontal and vertical, subscribing to the premise that in the early years, children need to establish a strong foundation for supporting future higher-level skills (Meyerhoff, 2007). We attempted to design music experiences as a bridge to the children's next educational environment; this type of groundwork is especially important for children who require much preparation, repetition, and guidance to achieve success. We sought to engage children in higher levels of learning by expanding on our past musical activities.

For example, we introduced dynamics and then practiced the concept in different contexts in subsequent classes. First, the children listened to quiet music. We used our voices quietly by putting our fingers to our lips and vocalizing, "Sh, sh, sh, sh, sh, sh . . . quiet." We moved quietly by tiptoeing to quiet music. We played quietly on our little finger cymbals. Later, we expanded the children's experience and understanding of dynamics by adding the contrasting term, "loud."

I read Leslie Patricelli's (2003) book *Quiet LOUD*, demonstrating contrasting dynamic levels. At another session, the children helped me read by hitting a BIGmack® communicator (produced by AbelNet). Anything may be recorded directly into this powerful single-message tool. Pressing its large activation surface produces clear, single-message playback. My two BIGmacks® (one red, one yellow) are pre-programmed with my voice whispering, "Sh . . . quiet!" and shouting, "*Loud!*" Those who were able also joined in vocalizing the responses. Mixing up quiet and loud playing is always fun. Using the tune from the familiar children's song, "Johnny Works with One Hammer," I sang, "We can play our tambourines quietly, quietly, we can play our tambourines quietly now." "We can now play loudly, loudly, loudly, we can now play loudly, and then we *stop*." We sought to help them understand music by making music. Therefore, in every session we sang, chanted, played instruments, and responded physically to music.

We also adhered to the principles of Developmentally Appropriate Practice, advocated by the National Association for the Education of Young Children. This philosophy, based on the works of Piaget and Vygotsky, purports that play is fundamental and that children learn skills such as cooperation, problem solving, language, and mathematics, and develop curiosity, self-esteem, strength and coordination, self-direction, and values when we enrich their play (McCracken, 1997). Our sessions were built around developmentally appropriate experiences for young children, as well as age-appropriate and individually appropriate opportunities. Because of the special needs of many of our participants, we employed additional strategies that made these experiences meaningful.

Session Continued

For the children who have or are suspected of having autism spectrum disorder, we drew from an affect-based approach that employs both developmental and musical patterns, following many of the tenets of Stanley I. Greenspan and Serena Wieder's "Floortime," a developmental, individual-difference, relationship-based approach—or DIR™ (Weeks, 2004). Constructing this type of musical environment helps detect children's developmental patterns and then allows us to work with the caregivers, applying techniques to meet the individual needs of each child.

Our sessions reflected a blend of music education approaches and methods, carefully tailored to match or meet the needs of the members of the group. Many of our musical experiences demonstrate the general principles of Orff-Schulwerk, Kodály, and Dalcroze: (1) everyone is able to participate in music and (2) music is elemental in nature (integrating a variety of elements, e.g., speech, movement) (Colwell et al., 2004).

Window into a Session with Commentary

As children enter the room, they find and pick up a picture of themselves and then sign in by matching their pictures to duplicate images on the sign-in board. Background music of toddlers singing traditional early childhood songs plays as we bring out large, colorful balls used for therapy. Caregivers and staff help the children bounce atop the balls or push them around the open space, playing until everyone has arrived. *(This is an opportunity to work on large motor exercise and play, giving the children an opportunity for both spontaneous and facilitated.peer interaction.)* After approximately fifteen minutes, we improvise a melody to the words that provide instruction: "Balls away, balls away, balls are all done for today." Everyone joins in, singing until all the balls are put away.

Our music circle follows a model of guided group play; I lead the musical examples and the caregivers interact with their toddlers while helping them adhere to a general plan. We do not insist on any set response, and we may deviate from the initial intent and adapt our plans to follow the lead of the children. A gathering activity draws everyone into a circle setting. Recorded classical instrumental music plays as we congregate around a large transparent cloth with which we move to the music. *(The music helps calm the children and reduces the arousal level from the previous, more active playtime.)* Children listen and watch for directions. We move the cloth up and down; we let the cloth float; we shake the cloth; we move it fast or slowly. All of our directions are paired with demonstrations, words, signs or motions. Sometimes the children indicate the ways we should move by telling us via words, sounds, or by motions or movements. *(Multi-sensory opportunities accommodate the therapeutic needs of individual children; information that is processed in a variety of ways builds mental muscles.)* At the end of the song, the children are invited to go under the cloth. Giggles turn to hushed anticipation as the adults chant, "Jack-in-the-box, still as a mouse, hiding beneath his dark little house. Jack-in-the-box, quiet and still, won't you come out?" At this point, after a long and enticing pause, the cloth is pulled off their heads, and we finish the chant, "YES! I will!"

Commentary

Most caregivers find that the music and the structure of the musical experiences encourage children's on-task behavior and increase their ability to attend to routines and instructions. The importance of teaching the children how to follow directions is critical to their future classroom success; many of our young children need guidance and practice. Likewise, many of our caregivers need to understand that giving directions need not set the stage for a confrontation. Caregivers can learn to issue directives that go beyond motivating compliance. They can be encouraged and taught to give effective instructions that are simple, specific, non-threatening, and maybe even fun (Laus et al., 1999). Furthermore, adding music to directions demonstrates an effective strategy for structuring time and activity in our class environment, and consequently, in the home or extended environment.

Many publications have described ideas for helping children successfully transition from one daily activity to the next by singing familiar tunes with new words or by using music as a prompt for completing a task or following directions (Smythe, 2002; Zero to Three, 2002). Music therapists, music educators, and early childhood educators have described how music provides structure and cues for what is coming next in a routine (Humpal & Tweedle, 2006; Rubio, 2003; Moravcik, 2000) and how transition songs may be part of a team strategy for goal implementation (Humpal, 2002; Humpal & Wolf, 2003). Musical stimuli and interventions seem to support managing group behavior and reducing time off-task for children of a variety of ability levels (Register & Humpal, 2007). Therefore, we use transition songs throughout all phases of our classes.

Session Continued

The adults move a little closer to each other, tightening the circle, helping the little ones focus, while lessening the opportunity for them to escape. Now we introduce our tuffets. The tuffets are actually old phone books covered with duct tape. A song cue alerts the children to what is coming next: "Let's get our tuffets, our tuffets, our tuffets. Let's get our tuffets and bring them back here." At first, caregivers go with the children and help them carry the tuffets back to the circle, where they are placed in front of the caregiver. Picking up and carrying the heavy tuffets give excellent sensory input and help the children develop strength, move while carrying an object, and recognize their position in space. What song do we sing first, sitting on our tuffets? Why, *Little Miss Muffet*, of course! (*This song is yet another opportunity to practice movement and balance.*) Caregivers help children rock back and forth on their tuffets, "windmilling" and planting their hands first on one side, then the other. Both hands go in the air when the spider frightens Miss Muffet away. By now, the children are comfortable sitting in their own particular place in the circle. It is time to continue the class.

The routine hello song follows, with each receiving "high fives" and being recognized. As we move on to bounces, finger plays, and simple songs, teachers model the songs or rhythms for the children and caregivers. Bounces may vary in style—some children return to an adult's lap, while some bounce independently while sitting on their tuffets. Bounces help the children with beat awareness. Finger plays offer opportunities for vocal expression and fine motor practice. We introduce many kinds of instruments and equipment that will enhance children's musical experiences: bells, sticks, tambourines, small maracas, shaker eggs, and hand drums.

Commentary

Simple, repetitive songs expose children to the richness and patterns of the music and language. Speech sounds, rhyming words, rhythm, and syntax work their way into both the body and the mind. Pattern awareness is a necessary component for learning and developing memory and a precursor to understanding language and, later, to reading (Standley & Hughes, 1997). Making music together naturally fosters the social skills of sharing, waiting and taking turns, and participating in a group effort. Of course, making and hearing music gives children tactile and auditory stimuli and offers opportunities for active listening. Moreover, playing instruments awakens the sensori-motor systems to integrate unconscious information about weight, texture, shape, and relationships between cause and effect (Cave, 1998; Zero to Three, 2002).

"Parachute play" is introduced first as a sitting activity for shaking the edges of the parachute to music, then as a standing activity for shaking the parachute and walking, and finally, as a riding activity as the parachute is pulled around the room by the adults while the children sit on it. The children are able to experience their body moving in space. For some children, this may be their first time experiencing the freedom of unrestricted movement. (*Our movement examples help children develop their gross motor skills, including walking, running, marching, walking backwards, walking while holding or playing an instrument, or walking on tuffets.*) We transition to our story-time by singing a related movement song that directs us to sit back down.

"Row, row, row your boat . . . ," the caregivers sing as they help the little ones onto the tuffets that will become their "boats." Sitting in front of their children now, adults take hold of both hands of the children and push and pull, making the boats (and occupants) rock back and forth as they continue, " . . . life is but a dream . . . STOP!" Next, I chant, "Rock, rock, rock, rock . . ." while modeling once again the windmill type movement, bearing weight first on one hand and then the other. I continue, adding the familiar melody, " . . . rock your boat, gently down the stream. If you see a crocodile [at this point, I pull a crocodile puppet from the storage box behind me . . . and, with a big pause, silently move from child to child with my crocodile] . . . don't forget to . . . [I say, "Get ready. This will be LOUD!"] . . . SCREAM—EEEEEE!" I resume singing, "Row, row your boat, gently to the shore, if you see a . . ." [Next, I pull a lion puppet from the box] " . . . lion, don't forget to *roar!*" The movement ends, and the board book *Row, Row, Row Your Boat,* illustrated by Annie Kubler (2003) comes out of the music bags.

I sit within the circle formation, holding my copy of the book so that everyone can see it. The caregivers and I sing through the book, which illustrates the movements we have just performed and the words and sound effects we are singing. Finally, we sing the book again, pausing after the words "roar" and "scream." A Step-by-Step switch (produced by AbelNet) comes out. Similar to the BIGmack®, this device can be pre-programmed with a series of messages or words. Each touch of the 2.5-inch activation surface plays and advances messages in sequence. I move around the circle, singing the book and letting a child depress the surface of the switch, thus screaming or roaring. Some children readily use their voices and some sing when they press the switch. Others may not be able to use their voices or may not be able to process all of the words we use. However, because we have made adaptations to the book and the music, every child can respond in some way.

As the class draws to a close, the pace becomes slower and the music, often in triple meter, grows more tranquil. Caregivers rock their toddlers and sing quiet lullabies. This is often a favorite time, because children are given the opportunity to calm down while being held, hugged, or rocked by their loved ones. Lullabies promote melodic perception, a sense of beat, and most importantly, expressiveness (Feierabend, 1996). I cherish seeing the looks on the faces as the music ushers in relaxation and tenderness. After singing the lullaby several times as each child helps me accompany the group on the Q Chord (a digital songcard guitar, played like an autoharp), everyone joins in humming the tune. Finally, the children can be part of a duet by individually shaking shiny, silver chime egg shakers with me while our good-bye song incorporates their names.

Commentary

Because many of the children have special needs, we often adapt instruments, use picture cues or a picture schedule, or utilize augmentative switch devices to give each child an active "voice" and to facilitate successful music play for everyone. Furthermore, we recognize that we are teaching the adults as well as the children. Early childhood music educator Kenneth Guilmartin (1999) noted, "To take adults beyond the pleasure of proud observation into actual participation—even to the point where they, momentarily at least, get lost in the music and forget they are with a child—that is real success" (p. 15). As the weeks passed, I reflected on the caregivers and the children. I came to regard them as unique individuals as well as a fine-tuned ensemble, a group that evolved and became the embodiment of Guilmartin's definition of real success. I offer the following to illustrate my point.

The Social Unit

At first, our class did not feel like a cohesive social group. Instead, there were twelve toddlers and twelve caregivers. In some cases, there were dyads, but not all toddlers seemed connected to the adults who brought them to class. There were adult strangers, too—those of us who would lead the class and hopefully become friends to all. Some caregivers came to the group with a strong sense of musical confidence and ability, while others commented, "I know this probably will be good for my child, but please don't expect *me* to sing!" Initially, I sang, and my colleagues joined me. The children watched, as did many of the caregivers. One by one, the caregivers participated, because they knew that they were expected to do so. I purposefully sang without accompaniment, because I assumed the caregivers would not be using accompaniment instruments as they shared our songs with their children outside of our class setting. The adults were nervous, and many were not confident in their abilities to make music.

Over a six-week period of time, the group dynamic markedly changed. At the first session, many children cried as they entered the room. They were noticeably anxious and seemed afraid of this new situation and environment. Oh, but there were the balls! Grant left his grandpa's side and ran to push them. Zach immediately joined him. Will scooted over to them, and the three boys occasionally moved beyond their parallel play (a stage of play where two or more children play in close proximity to each other, but without interaction or shared intent). When a ball bounced off another child or off themselves, the children suddenly became aware of the others around them who were connected by the common theme of playing with balls. Meanwhile, the music played in the background. That is, until we sang "Balls Away." The same three boys became the leaders of the group, singing as they pushed (or in Will's case, rolled) the balls to the adults, who loaded them onto overhead racks.

Most of the other children seemed to fit into two categories—those who were quiet, overwhelmed, and totally attached to their caregiver, and those who were crying, screaming, or pulling on their caregiver while trying to leave the room. Christopher, however, slept in his mother's arms, and Angela buried her head against her mother while silent tears streamed down her face and her body shook.

By week three, most of the children recognized the meaning of the transition songs and were becoming aware of our routine, which had been reinforced by introducing a picture schedule. I had made a card with a picture or photographic representation for each main activity of our session. Before each class, I arranged the cards in sequential order from top to bottom on the schedule board. The board sat atop my supply box, in full view as the children entered the room. After our hello song, I referred to the Schedule Board and said, "This is what we will do today in HarmoniKIDS." Then, after each segment of the session, I removed the corresponding card from the board. I referred to each picture with words that expressed order (i.e., first, second, next, last). This helped the children, especially those on the autism spectrum, learn the class routine, to anticipate, and to wait. Because we reviewed songs previously learned, the children also gained a sense of comfort and familiarity. This was especially helpful for Devonte, Reagan, and Drew, but Angela and Timmy still seemed terrified and never extended their hands to touch an instrument, shake a cloth, or greet anyone. Their mothers were concerned, and they, too, isolated themselves from others. Meanwhile, some of the caregivers had made new friends and chatted enthusiastically before and after class. Some of the children also formed friendships. Katie watched Tess's every move and then pushed a ball to her. For Katie, this was a big step. Her usual play routine was one of solitude or of just watching and not participating. Tess had enticed Katie into a higher level of play and helped her begin to interact and take an interest in others.

By week four, the screaming had ceased. The children quieted immediately when it was time to move the transparent cloth to the rhythm of the recorded classical instrumental music. Christopher was awake on this day. His body relaxed in his mother's arms and a slight smile spread across his face. His mother helped him hold his hand on the cloth, as it gently moved up and down to the music. Angela now faced the group and, every now and then, extended one finger to touch the cloth or take her turn on the Q Chord. Will knew the words to every song and loudly sang along, commenting on each activity. Zach not only volunteered for a turn, he volunteered others, too, if they were hesitant. Drew and Reagan held on to the handles of the parachute and helped it shake. For the first time, Katie independently joined the rest of the children at the center of the parachute for a ride, with only an occasional glance upward to make sure her mother was still in the room. Timmy wandered away from the group with his mother following him, her eyes downcast. Later she shared her dismay over what she viewed as Timmy's opposition, and noted, "Most of the other children follow the directions, especially when they are presented in a musical way. I try to practice the music at home, but I'm afraid Timmy will never be able to respond like the other children do." However, Timmy had immediately stopped when the music stopped and walked again when it resumed.

At our final session, most of the caregivers seemed comfortable with each other. Lillian had even arranged for an informal reunion of the group. Grant's grandpa graciously bowed out of this future event, but thought that maybe his daughter might want to attend, since she had been hearing Grant sing in the car and at home and had heard the reports that he thoroughly enjoyed his time making music with his friends. Grandpa reported that Grant screeched with delight and clapped his hands each time their car turned into the driveway of the YMCA.

Many "firsts" happened at this final session. Angela patted her knees and extended her hand to greet me during our hello song. Katie signed along while Tess sang. Devonte did not leave the group. All the children listened and responded to the difference between music and silence. They either played instruments or moved to the music and alternately stopped when the music ceased. They all touched the Q Chord and quietly swayed to the beat of the lullaby. Unlike the first session, adults were not hesitant to raise their voices in song, and they sang effortlessly and joyously. Each adult and child was involved and immersed in making and sharing music together.

Then the moment that defined them as a group occurred. By this time, I no longer moved to each child for a turn to shake good-bye with the silver eggs, but incorporated into the song a chance for them to volunteer for a turn. Because of their limited mobility, I approached Angela and Christopher. Angela held out one hand, and Christopher slept (although I placed an egg in his hand and sang to him anyway). All the other children came to me for their turns. All, that is, except for Timmy. His head remained down, and tears filled his mother's eyes. Then, ever so slowly, his eyes sought mine, and he stood up. With a quick glance around the circle, he headed straight to me, extended his hands to me, and we musically said our mutual good-byes. At the end of our song, everyone clapped for Timmy and for his mother. Our twelve children and twelve caregivers no longer were separate entities but had melded into a musical support group.

Individual Change

Because I had time after our group ended to study and reflect on how the individuals and the group evolved and how they developed musically, I was afforded an additional benefit of being able to follow up on some of the families. Therefore, I can report on some recent developments.

Will is no longer scooting. He is running everywhere and is a healthy, curious little boy who may become the social organizer of every group of which he is a part. Lillian discovered that she was a match for Will's kidney transplant; he had the surgery and recovered with amazing speed. Lillian reports that Will still sings our hello song each morning.

Angela is enrolled in a toddler class for children with special needs. I am the music therapist for this class, so I have had the pleasure of watching Angela blossom and develop self-confidence. On her first day at school, both she and her mother were in tears. I brought out the transparent cloth, and the children gathered on the carpet to begin their music time. This was something familiar to Angela, so she and her mother joined us. A hint of a smile crossed Angela's face when my hands went in the air, indicating the start of "Golly, Golly, Golly Good Morning." Up went her hands. Since that time, her progress has been steady, and her confidence level grows daily. It has been fun to see a feisty side of her personality occasionally emerge. Unfortunately, her health continues to be erratic. She will soon be getting growth-hormone therapy. This is especially upsetting to her mother, who must administer the daily injections.

Drew's mother stopped by to see me, bringing with her a videotape that she had recorded while hiding behind a doorway at her house. Drew had set up a little pillow on the floor, sat on it, and turned into Miss Marcia. He led his imaginary group with amazing musical and structural accuracy. The clear tones of sol, mi, and la were evident in many of the songs he sang. He rhythmically played his tambourine, and he extended it to an imaginary friend. Music was now embedded in his repertoire of play skills.

Tess's mother sent me a note after she was awakened one morning by boisterous sounds coming from the baby monitor. Tess was singing and chanting to her teddy bear the songs she had learned in our class.

Grant reportedly sings "Balls away, balls away" with perfect sol-mi accuracy, when he cleans up his toys (which invariably include a variety of balls). He continues to add to his song repertoire and is a great lover of books that are read rhythmically.

PERSONAL REFLECTIONS AND CONCLUSION

I have learned to be comfortable with role release (relinquishing the direction of specific professional tasks and responsibilities to others) while teaching caregivers and colleagues how to use music to play effectively with their children. Caregivers have grasped pedagogical strategies demonstrated in class, such as musically guiding interactive play, developing multisensory opportunities for musical play, and composing songs to help their children make transitions.

I have wondered, though, if I am so concerned with using music as a tool to enhance non-musical goals that I sometimes neglect to recognize that music may simply provide joyful experiences that are important in and of themselves. An answer came to me in the often-quoted essay, "Welcome to Holland" (Kingsley, 1987), attached to a poignant note from Christopher's mother after our last session together. In the essay, a mother describes the journey of raising a child with disabilities. She likens the expectation and anticipation of a child's birth to the anticipation and anxiety that one might experience prior to taking a trip to a foreign destination. The day of the trip finally arrives, but the "travel destination" has changed—the traveler finds herself in Holland, not in Italy as expected. The destination is not better or worse, just different. Thus it is when parents bring a newborn child with disabilities into their lives—plans change, people grieve the loss of not having a "normal" child—yet life moves forward. The essay concludes with the parent encouraging other parents of children with special needs to seek the joys that are found during the "travel adventure" on which they find themselves.

Christopher and His Mother

In reviewing my notes and tapes of our classes, I had concerns about Christopher and his mom. There had been bright spots, the smile when the Q chord came closer to their place in the circle during week three and the relaxation of his hand as his mom or I helped him strum. At first Christopher cried, even when the music began. He startled and stiffened his body when the tambourines played, and seemed to use his eyes to communicate to his mother imploring her not to insist that he touch anything. Those eyes—how they came to gaze at the other children during free play. And finally, how they seemed to sparkle as his mom and he entered the room after a few weeks. But often, those eyes closed, and Christopher slept through many songs and musical experiences.

I have worked with countless children over the years and know that ability levels and lengths of responses vary greatly. However, I questioned just how much this child and this mom had gained from their time in the program. The answer came in the note that was penned beneath "Welcome to Holland." Through it, the voices of Christopher and his mother quietly sing and remind us that we cannot judge another's enjoyment or appreciation of music by our own limited observations, expectations, or frames of reference: "I know that Christopher enjoys music, even though he often sleeps through class (that only means he is happy, comfortable, and content!). I have thoroughly enjoyed your class, and often find myself singing 'Golly Good Morning.' Thank you for bringing us music and so much joy into our lives . . . and making Holland a more beautiful place."

MUSIC EXPERIENCE

Music experience has a unique power to affect people. It calms as well as energizes. It serves to bring groups of people and individuals together while still allowing them to reach deeply within themselves. Music experience adds order to our lives while allowing the creative and divergent sides of our selves to develop. I believe this to be true, yet I wonder if we take the time to value the power of music experience, and the impact that is more obvious in some than others.

Music experiences in our classes created opportunities. Simple melodic patterns invited responses, rhythmic patterns motivated movement, and silence brought quizzical looks, attentiveness, and anticipation. Meter and tempo both influenced how children and their caregivers moved and seemed to alter their states of arousal. Music experiences can ignite or awaken our need for music. The sounds and silences (i.e., music) were not solely responsible for the changes that took place in individuals and the group. How music was created and used (i.e., the music experience) was more important for inciting change. These experiences were key to the musical and extra-musical growth that we witnessed.

Several years ago, Martha Hallquist, then editor of *Early Childhood Connections: The Journal of Music- and Movement-Based Learning*, asked me to coordinate an issue focusing on music therapy in early childhood. As we reflected on the direction the issue would take, we recognized that music educators, early childhood educators, and music therapists have a responsibility to provide quality experience to young children and their families. Each of these professions has struggled with the need to differentiate between elementary and early childhood age levels and issues. It is to the benefit of all for us to collaborate and seek collegial endeavors. All of us, in our own ways, are striving to break down barriers. Hallquist (2001) acknowledged that there may be a continuing debate about the relevance of discussing the non-musical "by-products" of music education. Nevertheless, she stated:

> Readers will discover that the fields of early childhood music education and early childhood music therapy have many more similarities than differences. Let us therefore learn from one another so that as educators and therapists, we might meet the needs of children in our care. (p. 4)

Her comments continue to be relevant today. Let us not forget that we must strive to meet the needs of *all* young children. May our "woods" no longer be silent, but be filled with "birds" of all abilities, each singing his or her own special song.

REFERENCES

Adamek, M., & Darrow, A. (2005). *Music in special education*. Silver Spring, MD: American Music Therapy Association.

American Music Therapy Association. (1999). *Music therapy and young children fact sheet*. Silver Spring, MD: American Music Therapy Association.

Cave, C. (1998). Early language development: Music and movement make a difference. *Early Childhood Connections, 4*(3), 24–29.

Colwell, C., Achey, C., Gillmeister, G., and Woolrich, J. (2004). The Orff approach to music therapy. In A. Darrow (Ed.), *Introduction to approaches in music therapy* (pp. 3–14). Silver Spring, MD: American Music Therapy Association.

Feierabend, J. (1996). Music and movement for infants and toddlers: Naturally wonder-full. *Early Childhood Connections, 2*(4), 19–26.

Guilmartin, K. (1999). The adult is the real "student"! The challenge of involving parents in early childhood music. *Early Childhood Connections, 5*(2), 15–22.

Hallquist, M. (2001). From the editor. *Early Childhood Connections, 7*(2), 4.

Humpal, M. (1991). The effects of an integrated early childhood music program on social interaction among children with handicaps and their typical peers. *Journal of Music Therapy, 37*(3), 166–177.

Humpal, M. (2001). Music therapy and the young child. *Early Childhood Connections, 7*(2), 9–15.

Humpal, M. (2002). Music therapy for learners in an early childhood community interagency setting. In B. Wilson (Ed.), *Models of music therapy interventions in school settings* (pp. 389–424). Silver Spring, MD: American Music Therapy Association.

Humpal, M., & Tweedle, R. (2006). Learning through play: A method for reaching young children. In M. Humpal & C. Colwell (Eds.), *Effective clinical practice in music therapy: Early childhood and school age educational settings* (pp. 153–173). Silver Spring, MD: American Music Therapy Association.

Humpal, M., & Wolf, J. (2003). Music in the inclusive environment. *Young Children, 58*(2), 103–107.

Hussain, I., & Win, P. (2006). DiGeorge syndrome. E Medicine from WebMD. Retrieved October 1, 2007, from www.emedicine.com/med/fulltopic/topic567.htm#section~Introduction

Kingsley, E. (1987). *Welcome to Holland*. From *Kids like these* (TV movie). Retrieved May 18, 2007, from www.creativeparents.com/Holland.html

Kubler, A. (2003). *Row, row, row your boat*. Auburn, ME: Child's Play.

Laus, M., Danko, C., Lawry, J., Starin, P., & Smith, B. (1999). Following directions: Suggestions for facilitating success. *Young Exceptional Children, 2*(4), 2–8.

McCracken, J. (1997). *Play is fundamental*. Washington, DC: National Association for the Education of Young Children.

Meyerhoff, M. (2007). Helping parents understand and appreciate the power of play and music. *Perspectives, 2*(2), 3–4.

Moravcik, E. (2000). Music all the livelong day. *Young Children, 55*(4), 27–29.

Patricelli, L. (2003). *Quiet LOUD*. Cambridge, MA: Candlewick Press.

Register, D., & Humpal, M. (2007). Using musical transitions in early childhood classrooms: Three case examples. *Music Therapy Perspectives, 25*(1), 25–31.

Rubio, Y. (2003). Special children, the classroom, and music therapy. *Early Childhood Connections, 9*(3), 37–42.

Smythe, C. (2002). Preparing for smooth transitions. *Montessori Life, 14,* 42–45.

Standley, J., & Hughes, J. (1997). Evaluation of an early intervention music curriculum for enhancing prereading/writing skills. *Music Therapy Perspectives, 15*(2), 79–86.

Weeks, K. (2004). Merging Floortime with music: Exploring an affect-based approach that employs developmental and musical patterns. *Early Childhood Connections, 10*(2), 37–48.

Zero to Three. (2002). *Getting in tune: The powerful influence of music on young children's development.* Washington, DC: Zero to Three.

4

Musical Portraits, Musical Pathways: Stories of Meaning Making in the Lives of Six Families

Lori A. Custodero

Musical culture is a dynamic phenomenon, defined by multiple, evolving influences that connect experiences between disparate spaces and places, across time, and among groups of people. During our lifetime we experience a diverse number of musical styles, generated from our associations with gender, age, social class, ethnicity, geographical region, religion, or musical subculture (Cross, 2001). These affiliations constitute "sound groups" —a term Blacking (1995) used for persons linked by "a common musical language, together with common ideas about music and its use" (p. 232). Our musical culture is thereby an amalgamation of our cumulative experiences and present circumstance at a particular point in personal history.

A child's first sound group is the family, defined by the collective musical cultures of parents, siblings, and oftentimes, extended communities (Borthwick & Davidson, 2002). The salient influences of belonging to a musical culture are evident in the newborn's recognition of the mother's voice; responding to the familiar sound, the newborn invites further communication and begins to understand what it means to connect to another through a seemingly inherent reading of rhythm and tone (Dissanayake, 2000). Later, such sensitivities can be observed in the spontaneous music making of preschool-age children at play in homes, on playgrounds, and riding public transportation. Across cultures, they use music to express themselves in a variety of ways, including singing, moving, and tapping on available surfaces to create sound (e.g., Littleton, 2002; Moorhead & Pond, 1942/1978; Young & Gillen, 2007).

This chapter presents the stories of six families from a wide variety of backgrounds. Each family portrait involves a child who turned three years old during the four months of data collection. These snapshots of urban family lives depict distinctive ways music experience serves both parents and children vis-à-vis those aspects they identified as having value. The dynamic nature of music experience propels a brief cross-portrait analysis, which suggests three particular social pathways generated by the music making and provokes possibilities for applications in music educational settings.

Relationships observed among music, culture, and development led to three assumptions that guided the interpretation. First, both musical culture and family culture are defined by their societal and historical contexts (e.g., Stokes, 1994; Walsh, 2002). More specifically, what children experience as music education in families is informed by both the personal histories of parents and the current conditions of their own histories-in-the-making. Second, infants seem predisposed to musical proclivity inasmuch as they have well-developed sensitivities to culturally defined musical sounds at birth (Trehub, 2001). This means they can partner with adults in musical practices involving melodies, movement, and rhythms, constructing and co-constructing in culturally recognized and valued ways. Since evidence suggests adults develop parenting skills through attunement to their child (Bornstein, 2002), partnered musical engagement may be considered to have potential for influencing development of both parent and child (Custodero & Johnson-Green, 2003, 2008; Dissanayake, 2000; Miller & Goodnow, 1995; Shonkoff & Phillips, 2000; Trevarthen, 1999).

Third, musical practices may look and sound different in families socialized in diverse ways (Garcia Coll, Meyer, and Brillon, 1995). Although these portraits are not meant to be representative of a single social group, they are purposely chosen to demonstrate the broad range of possibilities around musical activity. Such breadth of responses and intersecting cultural identities created a meaningful context for inquiry into the function of music experience in families, and generated further questions about the implications for the multiplicities of cultural inheritance in more formalized music educational contexts.

FRAMEWORK AND METHOD

The process of inquiry is based upon a musical interpretation of the developmental niche framework (Harkness & Super, 2002), which offers a conception of the interface between child and culture considering the components of settings, practices, and parent characteristics. Super and Harkness (1986) write, "Homeostatic mechanisms tend to keep the three subsystems in harmony with each other and appropriate to the developmental level and individual characteristics of the child" (p. 545). In this study, musical experience may be viewed as contributing to such a mechanism—a parenting resource that brings disparate experiences together in a newly created shared collective. The individual and localized cultures of families create the need for what is called "independent routes of disequilibrium and change" (p. 545)—these are the pathways outlined in the stories portrayed here. In adopting the view of developmental change as learning and as resulting from interactions between the individual and context, the family can be interpreted as the local cultural unit. In this study, the family setting provided a context for viewing musical interactions that were anticipated to vary in form and function in terms of a range of characteristics including age, background, musical experience, ethnicity, and available economic and social resources.

In early 2003, my research team, including Elissa Johnson-Green and Faye Timmer, attempted to contact 138 New York City residents who had previously agreed to be part of a longitudinal study. Ten families agreed to participate, representing diversity in educational background, economic status, ethnicity, family composition, parent age, and neighborhood. Data included parent interviews, observations of children, parent diary entries of children's musical activities (in their choice of written or recorded form), and written researcher reflections. Questions for parents addressed their childhood memories of family music making, descriptions of current practices in their own homes, attitudes about musical traditions, and music making outside the home. Interviews were audiotaped and later transcribed; observations of children were recorded in field notes. A subsequent follow-up visit was scheduled, during which we asked for clarification on previous interview items and collected and discussed parents' diary entries.

Transcripts and audiotapes of interviews, parent diaries, and field notes were analyzed for each family. A process of thematic analysis involved repeated listening to and reading of the data; identifying and triangulating among research team members and across data sources, references to settings, practices, and parental characteristics; and then searching for coherent patterns of musical meaning making. Ultimately, a leitmotif was chosen (Holloway, Rambaud, Fuller, & Eggers-Pierola, 1995), which characterized the primary way music was being used. Interpretations were checked independently by three members of the research team and corroborated with participants. Six families were chosen for the purposes and space limitations of this chapter.

PORTRAITS OF MUSICAL PARENTING

The Rodriguez Family: Maintaining Homeland Connections

[We] must teach the children what background [they're] from—especially in the U.S. where there are so many different cultures and kinds of music.

Alicia Rodriguez is a thirty-two-year-old mother of two daughters, Danielle, eight, and Suzanna, three. Both she and her husband, Pedro, thirty-four, were born in the Dominican Republic and came to New York City when they were adolescents. Music, specifically dancing, is a valued component of their ethnic heritage. It plays a vital role in the transmission of cultural traditions within the immediate family context, regular family gatherings, and in larger community celebrations.

Alicia's childhood memories of music making in the Dominican Republic are firmly rooted in social relationships. Joined by her siblings, cousins, and neighbors, she creatively transformed found objects into musical instruments. She remembers the exciting rhythms called *perico ripia*, the "palo" drum, and dancing the merengue. Alicia has vivid memories of carnival-like parties lasting through the night, where music and dancing were central and hundreds of adults and children participated. Alicia describes the close community connections: "The neighbors . . . become part of your family and it's like you know them for years. . . . They come to your house like your brothers and sisters."

The Rodriguez's present community is predominately Dominican and because, according to Alicia, both music and relationships are extremely important in this culture, the tradition of community parties continues. She explains: "People go in the street, let's say after dinner . . . and they start dancing. . . . I came [to the U.S.] after I was twelve years old. . . . I can remember trying to keep on with [my] heritage, which is Spanish music." Alicia and her daughters share a passion for dancing; she notices that while the girls often enjoy making up their own movements, they also are beginning to imitate her, particularly the moves of the merengue. Music and dancing connect this family, allowing opportunities for parents, children, and significant others to engage in a cross-generational context.

It is important for these parents to maintain cultural traditions as they raise Danielle and Suzanna: "You always try to do the same things your parents did . . . [yet], I think the way [my children] think, it's differently. So we change a lot as we go. Music . . . you carry along, but the other things, . . . have changed, . . . changed a lot." Considering this inevitable cultural evolution, Alicia is aware that parenting strategies will also evolve as necessary to adapt to their current family situation. Juxtaposed with this, however, is the notion that the eternal qualities of heritage and music that transcend time and place and unite generations in a common experience, remain steadfast.

The Crane Family: Establishing Community

> Not only were we playing music, which we all loved, but we were best friends.

Gabe Crane, fifty, and wife Frances, thirty-four, have two sons: Harry, three years, and Holden, three months. Gabe's earliest musical memories are of singing in church. As an adult Gabe has consciously sought out similar experience. He has strong social bonds with the members of his church's male gospel group. This participation in music also gives him a sense of continuity between past and present traditions: "One reason I enjoy singing with the male choir as much as I do [is] because it's a different time but the same music." Through active participation in music, this African American family has forged vital connections to an extended community.

Through his parents' influence, Gabe formed an early interest in music that has stayed with him throughout adulthood: "We always had music around my house. My mother and father both sing. My father taught me to play the saxophone." This early introduction to music formed the basis for many of Gabe's closest peer relationships later on and identified him with a musical community. Gabe remembers:

Just about all of my friends played instruments. We organized dance bands that we were involved in from . . . sixth or seventh grade. When we went out to play at different functions the parents took all the equipment around in the cars— and the parents all knew each other. Not only were we playing music, which we all loved, but we were best friends.

Since Gabe's closest friendships have arisen from involvement in music, he encourages Harry to participate with him and acts as Harry's social and musical mentor. Gabe now brings Harry to the men's chorus rehearsals: "I'll take him on the choir stand with us and take him up when we sing." Harry is also one of the "charter members" of the Sunbeam Choir, the children's gospel chorus. As Gabe related, "[Harry] participated in the first performance that they had at the church [when] he was around a year and a half old. The main [reason why he joined so early] was for his socialization. He needed to be with other kids." At the beginning and end of each choir rehearsal, he stands with his peers of similar ages in a prayer circle holding hands. Harry has begun to form the social bonds through participation in community music making that Gabe formed early on and has regarded as fundamental through adulthood.

Frances also believes that the church musical community provides social opportunities for Harry and has encouraged him to participate, especially since Holden's birth. She also brings Harry's church experiences home: Their daily activity includes singing "Sunbeam songs" together. Frances noted, "He'll have one rehearsal and then he'll come back and go to the piano [we have at our house]. He starts playing and singing what they did at rehearsal, playing and singing the songs." Through music, Harry's tie to his family's church community has become part of daily life.

The O'Reilly Family: Creating Intimacy

> [Music] is a great avenue for silliness in the family, . . . you can all kind of let go.

Kerrie O'Reilly is a thirty-seven-year-old mother of three children: Mitchell, five; Kylie, three; and Catherine, two. She recently quit her job as an attorney in order to be a "full-time mom." Her husband, Tom, is also a lawyer. Both parents come from Irish-Catholic backgrounds. The family lives in an upscale area of New York City in a large apartment and has a weekend country home they visit regularly. The family lifestyle is driven by demanding professional responsibilities, the children's involvement in activities outside the home, and employment of a full-time nanny. For the O'Reilly's, music provides a source of intimacy between and among parents and children that is highly valued.

During our first interview, it was clear Kerrie didn't consider her family a musical one. She offered, "I've never really thought about music very much. It's not really a focus of our family life, I guess." Yet, when asked to describe any musical activity that goes on in her home, she spoke at length about several regular events that shape their daily experiences, including dancing to recorded music two or three times per week after dinner and reflecting on the emotional content of opera recordings.

The most prominent activity in their lives was singing, which was linked to the routines of family life. The weekly ritual of driving to their country home was accompanied by singing in the car with recordings; several journal entries recount these experiences. The most poignant and detailed descriptions involved the bedtime ritual. Both Kerrie and Tom sang songs to the children every night, honoring each child's preferences. Their repertoire ranged from patriotic songs to songs learned in church to songs they invented. Her descriptions of this singing ritual revealed not only the strengthening of parent-child bonds, but also bonds between the parents:

> I have to admit that it's sort of a romantic notion to imagine your kids remembering you sang them to sleep at night. I mean, that's kind of a nice thing to think of [laughs]. And my husband has a wonderful voice, so he does the singing at night a lot of times too. . . . Mitch asks him to sing "Danny Boy." . . . My husband does a nice rendition of it.

Part of the reticence to recognize the amount of music making that goes on in her family stemmed from Kerrie's definition of what music was. For her, music meant expertise, mostly in instrumental performance. This was evidenced both by explicit remarks about not playing instruments and by uncertainty around what constituted musical behaviors. The function of music as creating a sacred space where family members could express freely and connect with one another may be a hidden resource of which Kerrie and Tom were not consciously aware. In their family's world, with high expectations for professional achievement and conduct, music making provides an intimate mode of communication and expression that can be defined within the family, rather than measured by societal standards. Kerrie told us, "I like the release that music provides . . . like, when we do the dancing. You know you have to have that fun . . . acting silly as a parent, sort of standing up and dancing around with them and that kind of thing. I guess that's important to me."

The Levin/Botkin Family: Imparting Knowledge

  The purpose of art education is to give kids a better understanding of life.

Paul Levin, forty-six, and Joan Botkin, forty-seven, are married and have one child, Melanie, who is three years old. They are Jewish, of Eastern European descent. The presence and deep understanding of music plays a primary role in their child rearing, each parent assuming a uniquely strong yet compatible role. Both parents use music routinely, whether Joan's spontaneous music making or Paul's structured music time. They encourage active musical participation because they believe that knowledge of music will enrich Melanie's life.

  Joan is a full-time mother who also tutors outside her home. She appreciates music, using it with her daughter throughout their daily activity: "I just noticed during how much of the day music happens, like my mother used to do, a driving song, a waking up song, or just making up silly songs, nothing structured, . . . spontaneous music happens all through the day." Paul is a professional musician and music educator. His music making with Melanie includes structured piano time during which they play and sing the well-known folk tunes that permeated Paul's childhood. He and Melanie bond through this experience:

> Having a daughter, one of the things that I get the most pleasure out of is to share music with her, have our piano time together, or . . . sing songs with her. . . . It's a good part of our relationship, it's something we can really do together. And it's something she really seems to love so far. [I want Melanie] to be able to make [music] a part of herself.

Paul and Joan have combined their musical strengths in an effort to raise Melanie as a musical person: "[We] just want her to be a really good listener. [We'd] like her to have a deeper knowledge of the art form, to understand that [music] relates to everything."

The Bucci Family: Negotiating Identity

> I start remembering every piece of my life through some sort of music
> . . . I hope that it always stays like that.

Helena Bucci is a twenty-four-year-old mother with two children, Alison, three years, and Daniel, three months. Her husband, Marco, is twenty-seven and works at a music store; the family lives in the basement of his mother's home. As parents of two children, they are negotiating the transitions from youth to adulthood and parenthood using music as an important aspect of creating their family identity.

Helena's memories of her parents and of her youth are associated with particular songs: "Music's always been part of everything. . . . 'Saturday Night Fever' will make me think of my mom cleaning, and Billy Joel will make me think of my dad. . . . The Doors or the Beatles [make me] remember junior high school." For Helena, music continues to create associations and accompany the construction of parent-child relationships. She describes the significance of a song she and her daughter Alison share:

> While I was pregnant with her, I had seen the Tarzan Disney movie, and the song that Phil Collins sings, "You'll Be in My Heart," broke my heart, you know, I started crying. And I used to always rub my belly. And when she was born, I realized, when she was really acting up, that was the only song I could sing to her that would calm her down. And to this day, I sometimes sing it. . . . Now, I hear her singing it, because she's learning the words, and it makes me feel good. She [says], "Oh, Mommy, that Tarzan song," and I [say], "Yes, Tarzan, but it's yours and my song too."

Marco also makes connections between his past and current family situation. He has fond childhood memories of sitting with his grandfather and listening to recordings of Italian songs and operas. Recently, Marco discovered a CD of "Pepino, the Italian Mouse" and was excited to share his musical past with Helena and their children. Marco, a drummer, often meets with his brothers for jam sessions and extends this experience by taking Alison to the local music store, where they enjoy jamming on drums.

Even though Helena does not share her mother's appreciation for the Hispanic music of her homeland culture, she does use her mother's parenting strategy of listening, singing, and dancing to popular music while engaged in daily household chores and while caring for her children. Just as Marco's father used to play the guitar and sing to help him fall asleep at night, Marco now sings to Alison and Daniel to help calm and soothe them if they are upset or anxious.

Helena and Marco still enjoy listening to their music; yet, as parents, they know Alison needs to establish her own identity through music that is relevant to her. Marco said, "I think it's important that [children] have their own music. At least, when I was growing up, music was kind of a sense of who you were, you know. And [now] just watching Alison pick music . . . I like seeing her choices." As Alison negotiates her identity in the family as child, Helena noted that Alison incorporates music from her child's culture into her play environment: "Sometimes she'll be playing with her little people toys, and she'll start singing songs from *The Wizard of Oz.*" Occasionally, Alison sings songs to her younger brother that her mother had sung to her. In doing so, she connects her personal experience to the present situation and reflects parenting strategies as she plays "mom."

For this family, music is associated with identity over the course of time through interactions with grandparents, parents, friends, partners, and siblings. Marco and Helena continue to negotiate individual and family musical identities as they work to construct a meaningful family life.

The Parsons Family: Providing Coping Strategies

> I know what the benefit of music is.

Peggy Parsons, age thirty-five, has a rich musical background. In home, church, and school settings she recalls singing, dancing, and playing keyboards and drums. She is a teacher and mother of two children, Russell, four and a half, and Katie, three. Her husband, Sam, a firefighter, was working at the time of our visits. Through her descriptions, it was clear that music was central to Peggy's sense of self-efficacy and quality of life, and that she had a keen awareness of music's comforting and motivational potential for her family.

Peggy recounted several personal experiences with music and how they contributed to her resilience:

> I had a reading disability. So school, to me, was tumultuous; it was horrible. And I can remember coming home and putting on my *Hair* . . . soundtrack, and suddenly life was grand. Or, I would listen to whatever kind of record I had, . . . and life was transformed. Suddenly, my mood changed, I was happy, and then I would go outside and play with my friends. . . . [Even today] I can have a rotten . . . day and get in the car, and hear a song that I just love, and— it's gone. I think it's been my coping [strategy].

During her pregnancies, she reports being very ill and requiring hospitalization and remembers her unborn children responding to her favorite recordings. The joy experienced in that communal listening was "a tender moment when I could remember, ooh, you're in there, and you like this."

Peggy's awareness of music's coping function was evidenced in stories about her family members and how they used music to assist with learning and with life transitions. Katie has a speech disorder, and didn't demonstrate the typical word knowledge of a young toddler. It was through her responses to music—a song from the movie *Shrek* and Peggy's singing of "Edelweiss"—that Katie began using language by singing words to musical cues. In recalling her own childhood, Peggy spoke of her grandparents' love for big band music, and how it was part of the ritual of family visits. When her grandmother was nearing death, and was in and out of consciousness, Peggy asked that some Glenn Miller be played, and was amazed to hear her grandmother yell from the room, "And Benny Goodman!"

Peggy utilizes this motivating quality of music in her everyday parenting. She explained: "A song will come into my mind just to quickly get them out of fighting. [I'll say] 'Come on guys, sing with me.' And all of a sudden they have to stop and think about the song, so they're not like, fussing with each other." She played classical music for her children every day, which she believes has contributed to their general development as well as self-regulation. "It's the most amazing thing, the way it will take a completely hyper child and transform that child into a completely different mood."

The common ingredients that unite her childhood and adult experiences, specifically the transforming nature of music, have resulted in sustenance needed to cope with the emotional upheavals of family life:

> I kind of grew up in a family . . . that was not necessarily a happy family, and I think for my brother and I both, to go in our rooms and turn on the radio, and sort of escape it all, has definitely been a medium for me. But now, I should say, life is very happy, and so now it's just gravy, I guess, on Thanksgiving dinner.

POSITIONING PATHWAYS: MUSIC, CULTURE, AND FAMILY CONNECTIONS

Components of the developmental niche framework—the physical and social context of music making, the music practices, and the values reported by parents—all coalesced in idiosyncratic ways for each family. These pathways to musical meaning were based on interactions between personal history and local circumstance as well as the needs and responsive contributions of each family member. Looking across the portraits, there seem to be three directional positionings, or niches, that characterize families' use of music. Based on supporting relationships, these include (1) *inter*-connections, extending family to include additional support systems; (2) *intra*-connections, linking family members with one another; and (3) *inner*-connections, negotiating the external forces families encounter with a focus on individual growth.

For both the Rodriguez and Crane families, music making extends into a broader community of peers and family. An expanded sense of belonging manifests when musical practices are taken from the community into the home, linking the two settings. The music of these two families was especially specific and stylized. This focused repertoire was coupled with a sense of ownership linking the expanded membership in localized knowledge (Geertz, 2000). Interestingly, this extended family context is a long-standing tradition of both Hispanic and African American cultures (Greenfield, Quiroz, & Raeff, 2000). Such traditions honor the socializing influences of music and provide resources in terms of human capital. For both families this expanded community was a direct reflection on their own experiences as children and youth.

The O'Reillys and Buccis, who represent a polarity in economic and educational resources, are both struggling to create family unity. Instead of reaching out to enlarge their sound group, they have committed to defining their own household as the meaningful unit of musical knowledge. Within the sanctuary of their own home, the O'Reillys look to a socially sanctioned musical heritage to elevate routine activity and relieve the stress of daily living. For the Buccis, moments of musical connection are often spontaneous responses to popular media, and they also are making efforts to share individual musical experiences with one another. These families are negotiating identities (Frith, 1996)—the O'Reillys, through creating a context for shared experience between family members; the Buccis, through creating a new musical content based on contributions from each family member. Here the intra-connections that define them in terms of immediate associations with family are being strengthened through shared musical activity. Members of these families also discussed missed opportunities for learning music, yet this did not deter their enjoyment or even their informal engagement in singing and dancing. Variety in repertoire and more intimate social situations contrast with the inter-connected pathways, which had less variety in repertoire and more extended social circles.

Paul Levin and Joan Botkin both had histories that involved strong, playful childhood experiences in music. Dispositions toward the affordances available in musical activity are part of what each offers their daughter. Peggy Parsons also has very strong memories of music's role in her youthful struggles with family crises and personal challenges. Her need to use music as a way for coping with difficult times also established familial dispositions for musical activity. In these two families, music is purposeful and acknowledged for what it provides, which might be described as a family aesthetic, a musical lifestyle that spans musical lives. The resilience evident in the descriptions of Peggy Parsons and the personal satisfaction expressed by the Levin/Botkin family suggests that musical activity may be a positive factor in human development, one in which generational patterns can be both sustained and interrupted.

FINAL THOUGHTS

These portraits show how intersections of musical cultures create contexts for children's development. The leitmotifs chosen for each family reflect the most salient quality in their particular portrait. Not solely the representation of a single family, the various ways music was used seemed to be present in most of the portraits to some degree. Such presence across stories suggests there may be applicability in educational contexts in addition to families. Music is meaningful for children in the traditions shared in extended communities and in the intimacy of music making in small groups, creating bonds of mutuality and belonging (Dissanayake, 2000). Meaning may also be constructed in terms of negotiating multiple heritages through music and in providing a resource for comfort and cognition—for knowing the world, and for better knowing ourselves.

These findings illuminate the complexities, magnitude, and quality of children's musical backgrounds and offer implications for music education. The inter-, intra-, and inner pathways to musical meaning inform pedagogical connections, as classrooms of children, often gathered together by circumstance, collectively constitute a new culture with its own identity negotiated by its members. As peers and teachers mutually contribute to new sound groups, each individual has renewable opportunities for development of musical understanding and skill.

These family portraits offer lessons in possibility: Music teaching and learning are sources of continued development propelled by necessary adaptations to settings, practices, and characteristics transformed by collective contributions. Like a kaleidoscope, oftentimes the results are beyond what can be imagined, the musical pathway of each student and teacher landing for a moment alongside relative others, the interactions between qualities giving meaning. Through the shared experience, "what is" leads to new conceptions of "what could be."

REFERENCES

Blacking, J. (1995). *Music, culture, and experience: Selected papers of John Blacking.* Chicago: University of Chicago Press.

Bornstein, M. H. (Ed.). (2002). *Handbook of parenting* (2nd ed.). Mahwah, NJ: Erlbaum.

Borthwick, S. J., & Davidson, J. W. (2002). Developing a child's identity as a musician: A family "script" perspective. In R. Macdonald, D. Hargreaves, & D. Miell (Eds.), *Musical identities* (pp. 60–78). New York: Oxford University Press.

Cross, I. (2001). Music, cognition, culture, and evolution. In R. J. Zatorre & I. Peretz (Eds.), *The biological foundations of music* (pp. 28–42). New York: New York Academy of Sciences.

Custodero, L. A., & Johnson-Green, E. A. (2003). Passing the cultural torch: Musical experience and musical parenting of infants. *Journal of Research in Music Education, 51*(2), 102–114.

Custodero, L.A. & Johnson-Green, E. A. (2008). Caregiving in counterpoint: Reciprocal influences in the musical parenting of younger and older infants. *Early Childhood Development and Care, 178*(1), 15–39.

Dissanayake, E. (2000). *Art and intimacy: How the arts began.* Seattle: University of Washington Press.

Frith, S. (1996). Music and identity. In S. Hall & P. duGay (Eds.), *Questions of cultural identity* (pp. 108–127). London: Sage.

Garcia Coll, C. T., Meyer, E. C., & Brillon, L. (1995). Ethnic and minority parenting. In M. Bornstein (Ed.), *Handbook of parenting* (pp. 189–205). Mahwah, NJ: Erlbaum.

Geertz, C. (2000). *Local knowledge: Further essays in interpretive anthropology* (3rd ed.). New York: Basic.

Greenfield, P. M., Quiroz, P., & Raeff, C. (2000). Cross-cultural conflict and harmony in the social construction of the child. In S. Harkness, C. Raeff, & C. M. Super (Eds.), *Variability in the social construction of the child: Vol. 87* (pp. 93–108). San Francisco: Jossey-Bass.

Harkness, S., & Super, C. M. (2002). Culture and parenting. In M. H. Bornstein (Ed.), *Handbook of parenting: Vol. 2* (2nd ed.) (pp. 253–280). Mahwah, NJ: Erlbaum.

Holloway, S. D., Rambaud, M. F., Fuller, B., & Eggers-Pierola, C. (1995). What is "appropriate practice" at home and in child care? Low-income mothers' views on preparing their children for school. *Early Childhood Research Quarterly, 10,* 451–473.

Littleton, D. (2002). Music in the time of toddlers. *Journal of Zero to Three, 25*(1), 35–40.

Miller, P., & Goodnow, J. (1995). Cultural practices: Toward an integration of culture and development. In J. Goodnow (Ed.), *Cultural practices as contexts for development: Vol. 67* (pp. 5–16). San Francisco: Jossey-Bass Publishers.

Moorhead, G., & Pond, D. (1978). *Music of young children* (Reprinted from the 1941–1951 editions). Santa Barbara, CA: Pillsbury Foundation for the Advancement of Music Education.

Shonkoff, J. P., & Phillips, D. A. (Eds.). (2000). *From neurons to neighborhoods: The science of early childhood development.* Washington, DC: National Academy Press.

Stokes, M. (Ed.). (1994). *Ethnicity, identity and music: The musical construction of place.* Oxford, England: Berg.

Super, C. M., & Harkness, S. (1986). The developmental niche: A conceptualization at the interface between child and culture. *International Journal of Behavioral Development, 9,* 545–569.

Trehub, S. E. (2001). Musical predispositions in infancy. In R. J. Zatorre & I. Peretz (Eds.), *The biological foundations of music* (pp. 1–16). New York: New York Academy of Sciences.

Trevarthen, C. (1999). Musicality and the intrinsic motive pulse: Evidence from psychobiology and human communication. *Musicae Scientiae* [Special issue: Rhythm, musical narrative, and origins of human communication], 155–211.

Walsh, D. (2002). Constructing an artistic self: A cultural perspective. In L. Bresler & C. M. Thompson (Eds.), *The arts in children's lives* (pp. 101–111). Amsterdam: Kluwer.

Young, S., & Gillen, J. (2007). Toward a revised understanding of young children's musical activities: Reflections from the "day in the life" project. *Current Musicology, 84,* 79–99.

II

CHILDHOOD

5

Pulling the Curtain Back on Performance in the Elementary School

Carlos R. Abril

At some point in our lives, most of us have participated in or attended a school music performance. It may have been an experience as an audience member sitting on a metal folding chair, peering up at classmates or one's children singing or playing on a stage. It may have been an experience as a performer standing on stage with a group of peers, anxiously scanning the audience while awaiting the music teacher's signal to begin. The dichotomous roles—performer and audience member—connote a physical and psychological disconnect, akin to many Western performance events that maintain a veil of mystery around the performers' art (Small, 1998). While often structured to replicate such events, school music performances, serving a decidedly different purpose, might suggest a less disconnected relationship between performer and audience.

Is the goal of a school music performance to artistically stimulate or entertain an audience, much like a symphony concert or a musical? Considering that a school performance is a facet of schooling, should it not primarily serve as an opportunity for learning? Paxcia-Bibbins (1993) admitted that children's school performances may be entertaining but claimed they are, more importantly, a platform for children to demonstrate things they have learned in their classes. In her chapter describing the components of a quality school music program, Straub (2000) states, "School concerts are an outgrowth of instruction. They do not drive instruction. Demonstrations for parents are common, and whole-grade or whole-school project demonstrations often present the products of integrated units in which music plays an important part" (p. 36). Depending on the nature of the performance, she claims school performances can also showcase the ways multiple disciplines are dependent on one another. Further,

93

when framed as educational showcases or "informances," performances can serve as opportunities for the audience to recognize the need for and value of music in school (Abril & Gault, 2007). Successful music teachers in urban schools have reported that performances can make the music program visible to the school community, which helps to maintain or elevate its status in the community (Abril, 2006).

Some may dismiss an elementary school music performance as mere child's play, yet the literature points to the student learning that arises from such experiences. In a study of fifth-grade children, Feay-Shaw (2001) noted overall growth in students' musical abilities as a result of preparing for and performing a school musical. The author concluded that the performance motivated students to develop skills and learn music concepts. Similar results have been reported with children creating an opera (Raplenovich, 1996). Gotlib (2005) noted that children gain an improved sense of community and expanded awareness through the process of preparing for a performance. In a school where students from a regular elementary school were paired with students from a school for children with cerebral palsy for the purpose of performing a musical, regular students became more accepting of those who were different from them after the project period (Baisden, 1995). These musical and social learning outcomes arising from the process of preparing for and executing a performance point to its important contribution to student learning.

The purpose of this chapter is twofold. First, it seeks to deconstruct a school music performance at an urban elementary school. More specifically, it examines the expectations for and perceptions of a performance held by members of the school community and considers its effect on teachers' thinking about and implementation of a music curriculum. Second, it focuses on the impact of the performance—the idea, the actual performance, and the memories—on a group of children labeled at-risk. Presented in the form of a narrative, this chapter pulls the curtain back to bring into focus the things that happen before the first note is sounded on stage, the things children think and do during the performance, and the residual that lingers after the curtain falls.

SETTING THE STAGE

For three years, I have served as the director of an after-school program at Olympia Elementary School (OES), a public school in Chicago. I started the program to provide a group of children with additional opportunities to engage in music for one hour every week during the school year. I was assisted by graduate and undergraduate students at my university. Lessons, which were team planned and taught, were designed to provide the children with opportunities to experience music in a playful atmosphere that emphasized creativity through sound exploration, improvisation, and composition.

The program was open to those children who were thought to be in the greatest need of educational enrichment. Therefore, invitation letters were sent to the parents of all kindergarten children who had been labeled at-risk by the state. "At-risk" is a term commonly used in schools to describe students identified as having a higher than average probability of dropping out of school. While the process and criteria for determining if someone is at-risk varies among school systems (Taylor, Barry, & Walls, 1997), certain characteristics of students in U.S. schools are commonly used to make this determination, including low socioeconomic status, high absentee rate, limited English proficiency, and low school grades/achievement (Palas, 1989; Robinson, 2004). Fourteen children elected to enroll the first year.

OES is situated in a densely populated community just north of the Chicago city center, where busy streets and train lines noisily intersect. The three-story brick building, with terracotta decorations around its perimeter, stands tall among the local businesses, apartment buildings, and single-family dwellings. There was a full-time music specialist at OES—a luxury, given that the school district only partially funds any arts specialist. In this district, the decision to hire arts specialists resided in the hands of a school council. The after-school music program supplemented students' weekly school music classes.

Mr. Marshall, the school principal, described the meaning of this after-school program:

> This program is something we could not normally offer because there are no funds, and parents couldn't afford it if it was a private music program that they had to pay for. I think this program gives children who are in greatest need the opportunities others in more affluent areas might take for granted—taking lessons on an instrument, going to concerts, or getting small group instruction. I want these students to have an opportunity to know and do. This is important—no, critical—to the things we do in education.

As implied by the statement, most of the students attending OES come from families of limited economic means. In fact, over 95 percent of children in this school come from low-income households (Illinois State Board of Education, 2003). Were it not for the resident music specialist and the existence of this after-school program at OES, children would be unlikely to study music formally.

The Players and the Plan

This study focuses on the last four months of the second year of the program, when the children were between the ages of six and seven. The majority of the children who participated in the program during the first year also enrolled the second year. None of these children were enrolled in music or other arts activities outside of school. Except for one, all students were able to speak and comprehend English. Over half were native Spanish speakers. Alexia, a graduate student and experienced music teacher, planned and taught all the lessons with me. The resident music teacher, Ms. Castle, allowed us to use her classroom and served as a general facilitator. Mr. Marshall, the school principal, was supportive of the program from its inception. He also played a role in shaping its direction, as will later become clear.

I served as participant-observer, collecting field notes before, during, and after each visit (Glesne, 2006). Data were collected based on conversations and stories shared by faculty, staff, children, and parents; observations of behaviors, situations, and settings; and reflections on lessons, student progress, and observations. All sessions and the performance were video-recorded. Over time, I amassed a collection of artifacts including lesson plans, student work, programs, and handouts. I conducted a minimum of three interviews with each child in the program and two with selected members of the school community. Interviews with children were conducted before and immediately after the performance. As per the recommendations of Creswell (1998), the trustworthiness of the data was achieved through prolonged immersion in the field, triangulation, member checks, and reflections on my own subjectivity.

ACT I: BEFORE THE CURTAIN RISES

The idea of a performance had not crossed my mind when I began planning this after-school music program. I believed it was more important for children to have the opportunity to experience music in a number of playful and exploratory ways. The product of this program was learning that would arise from the music experiences themselves. This was grounded in the ideas of Piaget (1962) and Vygotsky (1978), who asserted that young children come to understand the world around them through play, where they can make sense of the objects, activities, and phenomena in a social atmosphere. In practice, I thought children should be provided with opportunities to sing, play instruments, listen to music, improvise, and compose. While there were no objections to these goals, the school community desired a staged performance.

I became aware of this desire in my first year at the school, when the children were in kindergarten. One afternoon, Ms. Castle, the school music teacher, asked, "Do you think you might have a performance at the end of the year? . . . We would like to have a performance so that everyone knows what we're doing." I tried to suppress my befuddlement, while admitting I had not given it any thought. I promised to consider how it might align with the curriculum I had mapped out for the year. The principal also made his thoughts known to me, stating that it would be a good idea to have a performance as a way to "sell the program and the school." Initially, I did not think a performance was appropriate for several reasons. First, I had created a curriculum designed to intrinsically motivate students through the process of creative sound explorations using instruments, their voices, props, stories, and listening stations. Second, I believed that preparing for a performance could have a deleterious impact on my being able to do the above. I preferred not to focus classroom efforts on children memorizing and polishing songs, dances, or musical pieces. As a compromise, I decided to extend an invitation to the school community to visit us during our lessons throughout the year—but no one did.

Not a month into the second year of the program, when the same children were in first grade, I was approached by various members of the school community, inquiring whether there would be a performance this year. Ms. Castle reminded me about having a performance and the need to set a date so it could be included in the academic calendar. In conversation with her, she alluded to the importance of being on stage because it would give the performance an added level of "formality and seriousness." A parent informed me that her daughter was wondering if there would be "a show" this year. In a lesson, I decided to talk with the children about performing on stage. They seemed excited about the idea, as evidenced by their wide eyes, smiles, and verbal outbursts (e.g., "cool," "yeah!"). Since Alexia was teaching with me that year, I discussed the issue with her on several occasions. We came to recognize that polishing a performance would conflict with the music experiences we strove to create, but after recognizing its importance to parents, children, and teachers, we decided to oblige.

Here are some of the perceptions of school performance I uncovered from various people in the school. Because she was the first to bring performance to my attention, I asked Ms. Castle to tell me about her desire for a performance as an outcome of our music program. In so doing, she likened it to standardized tests and other products of learning:

They [administrators and parents] always want a product from us [teachers]. For teachers it is the state test, for the art teacher it is her art show, and for music it is all in the performance. The principal expects the product from all of us. No matter what, he wants parents to have that. He wants to see a polished product. The parents also come to expect a performance, because it is related to music. . . . It's a way of sharing with the community . . . of letting them know what we are doing. . . . We want to keep them interested.

Mr. Marshall, the principal, believed that a school music performance is a "good indicator of the things that are happening in the classroom." When I asked him how he perceived the goals of a performance aligning with those of a given curriculum, he paused, acknowledging it was a good question for which he had no answer. He said, "The specialist [music teacher] should be the one to wrestle with that question because they know their discipline better than I."

Ms. Castle and Mr. Marshall agreed that performances served as ways of assessing any performing arts program. Curiously, neither of them explicitly described the performance as an important way for children to develop musically. In the minds of the principal and music teacher, it seemed that the music performance would help to validate the program, but not necessarily as evidence of music learning outcomes. I wondered what the danger was in measuring a program based on one or two performances every school year. How does or can performance serve as a way of assessing any type of learning, whether broad or specific? The children were unanimously positive about the idea of performing for an audience on the stage. They said: "It'd be fun"; "I like it. . . . My big brother was in the show last year"; "Cool!"

Rather than resist the idea, I decided to reposition my concept of school performance. Alexia and I would negotiate, reconcile, and come to embrace these seemingly conflicting values in order to respond to the larger context in which our curricular ideas and philosophies resided. As teachers, we would have to ensure the musical performance became an outgrowth of the curriculum. Having accepted the idea of staging a music performance, we set a date and proceeded as planned.

Putting It Together: Lessons

Steven was usually among the first to arrive in the classroom, moments after the dismissal bell rang. This day was no different. He peeked into the room, eyes wide in anticipation, obviously awaiting a signal from Alexia or me for permission to enter. I smiled and nodded; he skipped into the room, greeting us on his way to the end of the room where a drum circle had been set. Without hesitation, he started to play a drum. Initially, Steven's rhythms seemed random, beginning tenuously and soon erupting with a force strong enough to drown out the voices of the other children arriving, many of whom also gravitated toward the instruments. Steven was wrapped in the joy of playing the drum. As was typical in his and the other children's initial sound explorations of the day, it seemed to function as therapy, a physical release after a seven-hour school day.

After several minutes, I recognized he was playing the melodic rhythm from one of the songs we had sung the week before. I made my way toward him, sat at a drum, and imitated his rhythmic patterns as best I could. He stopped for a moment and looked up at me with a smile on his face, as if to say, "I know you are copying my rhythm." I engaged Steven in playing with those rhythms. I changed the dynamics, and after a few seconds, he matched my volume. He played faster, and I followed suit. Finally, I started singing the corresponding song as we played the rhythms at a more moderate tempo. As more children took notice of our musical play, they joined in—some singing the song as they walked into the room or sat by a drum, others playing the drums along with us. Eventually I invited everyone to join us as we reviewed the song "Hotaru koi," a Japanese folk song about a firefly. This was one of the images in the book around which we constructed our entire curriculum (and subsequent performance), *The Drums of Noto Hanto* (James, 1999). Steven's musical explorations became a springboard for the day's lesson.

This vignette describes the way our lessons often developed. Inspired by the seminal study of children's exploratory play on instruments (Moorhead & Pond, 1978), we purposely let the children play on the drums or other instruments to observe what they would and could do in an unstructured environment. As they played, we would observe, listen, and/or interact with them. These open spaces for play also provided Alexia and me opportunities to interact with individuals or small groups of children. Lessons would often develop from the children's music-making, as illustrated above.

Alexia and I also modeled playful behaviors. For example, when we first introduced the story of *Noto Hanto*, a storybook that would unify our curricular unit and performance, Alexia read the story to the children, adding dramatic pauses, characters' voices, and varied pitch inflection. As she read, I sat at the side of the room surrounded by an assortment of percussion instruments, which I used to enhance the story. The author of the book used words to imitate the sounds of drums, which Alexia read in rhythm. I echoed her rhythmic patterns on a drum, improvised melodic motifs on a xylophone and glockenspiel to represent certain characters in the book, and created soundscapes using instruments to represent the story's setting. Alexia noted, "They were so enthralled that they sat there transfixed as if waiting for the story to begin again."

We used various elements of the story—characters, images, emotions, culture—as themes to explore in music lessons. Since the story told the tale of a village using drums as a peaceful means of protecting themselves, every lesson included opportunities for students to drum. We helped children develop basic drumming skills. They learned to play specific rhythmic patterns that naturally arose from the words in the book through experiences of speaking the words in rhythm, echoing the rhythms on drums, arranging and rearranging the rhythms, and incorporating some of the rhythms in their musical improvisations. In addition, each lesson included opportunities for the children to play with the drums in less directive ways. For example, we paired the children and asked them to find new sounds to play on the drum and use them in call-and-responses.

The setting of the book is Noto Hanto, a coastal village in Japan, so we showed the children several pictures of waves crashing on rocky cliffs off the Sea of Japan, and asked them to use words to describe the scene. After additional explorations with sounds created to depict the images, we asked children to form groups of three or four in order to create a composition that reflected the images. The following week we asked them to return to their groups and replicate their pieces. Alexia and I helped the children make decisions, revise their work, and practice performing their compositions. This creative process was shaped by ideas on music composition discussed in the literature (Webster, 2003; Younker, 2003).

One question loomed large for me during teaching episodes such as these. How could playful, exploratory experiences with music propel the group toward preparing a performance? Alexia and I decided that we could continue to reinforce some of the things the children were learning (e.g., songs, compositions), such that they would be able to replicate them at a later time. We would think of ways to share the things they were doing in class through a performance. Alexia and I strove to maintain a playful approach in favor of a more efficient means of propelling the children toward a polished performance. We were, however, aware of changes in the way we engaged with the children. As the performance approached I became more directive and demanding in my teaching style. At other times, Alexia spent more time than usual perfecting a song, so that the words and melody were perfectly accurate. When we took the time to reflect and discuss our lessons from the prior week, we were able to re-calibrate our teaching style to remain playful and responsive to the children.

A Close-up

With cinnamon-colored skin, black wavy hair, and big bright eyes, Pedro was the oldest member of the group, having repeated kindergarten the year before. He was the only child in our group who rarely used words to communicate and did not speak during the interviews. When he did speak it was in muffled Spanish. Alexia and I were also unsure whether he could understand us in either Spanish or English. When we instructed the children to do something, he would usually look to his peers and copy what he saw them doing. This resulted in his being a step behind the others. His classroom teacher and a school counselor informed me that he was scheduled for evaluation to determine if a learning disability was hampering his ability to comprehend and communicate.

Pedro had great difficulty focusing on tasks and was slow in responding to teachers' and peers' musical, verbal, and non-verbal cues. His drumming echoes in response to a leader were often a fraction of a beat behind the rest of the children, and he had difficulty replicating rhythmic patterns he heard modeled by his teachers or peers. When the group stopped playing, he usually continued playing for few seconds, seemingly unaware that everyone else had stopped. While his peers seemed to improve as drummers and singers, Pedro's progress was not obvious.

Pedro sought opportunities to make his peers laugh through gestures and other non-verbal behaviors. On several occasions we found him running through the school hallways instead of coming directly to our room after school. When he played call-and-response games on the drums, Pedro's responses were usually loud, seemed to have no relation to the call, and seemed to cry for attention. At first, the other children laughed at his behavior, but as the performance time approached, his outbursts were ignored. However, his sister Maria, who was also in the program, was usually cognizant of Pedro's behavior. On several occasions she took responsibility, apologizing or claiming that she would provide her mother with a report of his inappropriate behavior.

On the stage

Alexia and I felt it was important for the children to experience being on the stage before the performance date, so we scheduled the last two lessons on the stage. The first lesson was like our typical music lessons but somewhat more teacher-directed. On that day we did not offer opportunities for free explorations, but instead reviewed the songs, movements, compositions, readings, and improvisations that would make up the performance— all the things they had learned in the last four months. Pedro was absent.

We used the last lesson to put all the pieces together on stage. They included various readings from the story, a dance with masks that children created, drumming patterns and pieces they had learned to play, compositions they had created, and improvisations yet to be realized. As we proceeded, we soon realized our presence on the stage had a major effect on Pedro. While the other children were more focused than we had ever seen them in the classroom, Pedro was unable to focus on one task for more than a minute. His drumming was completely unrelated to the music we were performing. When we started to sing, he moved to the back of the stage, running in circles. We hoped he would choose to refocus and return to task after a few minutes. At one point, some of the children became highly distracted by Pedro, so we sat him in a space on the side of the stage. I informed him he could join us when he was ready; he never did. The new atmosphere on the stage may have been too distracting to him and may have explained his behavior. After the lesson, I talked with him and his sister in Spanish to explain the reason he was needed for the performance and how important his contribution would be. I was hoping his mother would come to pick him up that afternoon, so I could speak with her. But alas, his fifth-grade brother arrived to accompany them home.

Alexia and I questioned whether we should allow Pedro to perform the next week. Our greatest concern was that it would detract and distract from the music experience the other children had prepared. Would Pedro make it more difficult for the other children to focus or perform? Would it take away from the other children's experience? Would his behavior affect the way the audience evaluated the program? Pedro may have needed a successful experience more than some of his peers. As Alexia and I parted ways, we had not resolved what to do about Pedro the next week. We decided to wait and see.

ACT II: THE CURTAIN RISES

A little before the dismissal bell sounded, the children came to the music classroom to prepare for their performance. The children were visibly excited, some literally jumping in place, with a mixture of controlled energy and anxiousness. Though not expressing much emotion on his face, Pedro appeared uncharacteristically focused, standing in line rather than running down the hall. Pedro seemed to understand the stakes. We acted as if nothing had happened the week before.

As the children lined up in the hallway to make their way to the stage the adults and older students behaved noticeably differently toward them. It was as if the children were seen as more important in light of their being performers. Some of the older students gave them high-fives; teachers who passed by wished them luck. Max, the security guard, appeared surprised that Pedro was one of the performers. He signaled toward Pedro with a flick of his head, a frown on his lips, and a smile in his eyes, as if to indicate his surprise that he was performing. I asked, "What do you think?" "Not bad, not bad," he said, while adding in a whisper, "I didn't think he could handle something like that." I never asked him, but was left wondering what he meant. Was he surprised that Pedro was on-task in general, chosen to perform, or doing something musical? As we arrived behind the stage door, we took inventory and realized they were ready.

The result of four months of work and play in the music curriculum would be celebrated today. We hoped that the experience would be a positive one for the children and one that was representative of our work together. The final performance was meant to be a window into our curricular unit based on the book. The performance consisted of songs and instrumental pieces learned; compositions, dances, and art created; and improvisations to be played, all woven into the story.

At one side of the stage sat three of the children. They started the performance with a piece they composed, inspired by the image of the Sea of Japan and the opening lines of the book. With triangle, ocean drum, and chimes in hand, they looked at their instruments and one another, reading the opening of the story in unison, "Noto Hanto points upward like a thumb in the Sea of Japan." Then they began to play their composition. The wind chimes gently played, followed by the rumblings of the ocean drum. On certain occasions, that sound carpet was punctuated by the flurry of sound from the triangle. They swelled in a crescendo and then faded away to nothing, ending with the wind chimes. They performed it much the same way they had creating it months earlier. The other children, sitting at their drums, seemed intrigued by the music. A few students briefly turned toward me as if to measure my reaction to their peers' performance.

Every time Alexia or I gave the children an indication of what they should prepare to play or do next, they were ready to go. While the children were mostly focused on their performance, there were some exceptions. During one group's drumming piece, Pedro stopped and turned in his seat to watch the audience for a few minutes. He may have been looking for or at family members in the audience. Although mostly on-task, during transitions Steven was distracted by the pictures of the book being projected on the back of the stage and oblivious to the audience or to the things happening on stage. Upon playing a dramatic rhythmic piece that swelled to a climax and ended with a boom, Maria, who sat with her back to the audience, looked over her shoulder to acknowledge the audience, or maybe to see their response as they applauded.

About eight minutes into the performance, the children were intensely focused on their tasks. The music teacher, sitting in the audience, even noticed it. ("I was astounded at how focused the children were. . . . They were focused on you and Alexia to lead them through it. . . . I couldn't believe that *these* first-graders could do it, but they really rose to the occasion.") One unexpected moment in the performance captured the essence of our teaching approach. It happened when I started to improvise on the drum in response to one of the plot turns in the story. When I finished, Shanequa responded with her own drummed improvisation, demonstrating both fluency and confidence. She maintained the tempo I chose, copied some of my rhythms, and added some of her own. Initially I was surprised but in an instant I decided to give every child an opportunity to share their own improvisation. I played a call and each child improvised a drummed response. When Lisandra played, she played the drum in a way no one had before her, sliding her hand smoothly over the drum head to create a soft, sustained sound. This was something she had experimented with in the classroom before. A big smile came upon her face at the end of her improvisation, seemingly taking pride in the originality of her music-making. Most of the children maintained the same tempo I set, made their answer as long as the question, and emulated some of the rhythmic or dynamic characteristics.

As we made our way around the circle, I could sense the anticipation as we arrived at Pedro. I noticed many of the children, especially Maria, looking at him to see how he would do. Once I finished my call, he struck his drum with all the force he could muster, producing two loud sounds. While not in tempo or the same length as the call, or particularly musical for that matter, it was played at the correct point in time. To the unknowing observer, this would have seemed unmusical or even incorrect; however, this was an accomplishment for Pedro because he was focused and demonstrated his understanding of musical call and response. The musicality of the children's responses varied and I was never sure of the intentions of their improvisations. Clearly some were thoughtful and built upon what they heard in the call; others may have been created to garner attention or incite laughter. Regardless, that spontaneous moment in the performance captured the playful and improvisatory nature of our music-making experiences the past four months.

We ended with a Japanese children's song, "Kuma San." The children sang and danced to it at the front of the stage. Upon conclusion, the audience enthusiastically applauded, and the children bowed as we had practiced the week before.

ACT III: THE CURTAIN FALLS

A great deal of effort and energy is exerted by teachers and students in preparing for and realizing a performance—but what happens once the curtain falls? To better understand the residual impact of the performance, I interviewed each child, as well as other members of the school community, a week after the performance.

When asked to describe how they felt while they were performing, the children were overwhelmingly positive. The most common term describing their feelings was "happy," yet other word choices such as "proud," "good," "loved it," "nice," and "excited" were quite frequent. They used the word "proud" to describe their feelings, both during and after the performance, and also applied it in reference to other people who attended or were informed about the performance.

When asked to pinpoint the part of the performance they liked most, the children overwhelmingly referred to their experiences in the large drum circle. It seemed that the social dimension of playing in collaboration with their peers, as well as the power of playing the drums together, in unison, left an impression on the children. They alluded to experiencing a general sense of joy and group cohesion. Steven said, "We all played it on the drums like this . . . loud and at the same time. . . . That's awesome!" Lisandra said, "It is because we do it all together, and it sounds good like that. I loved that part." Joshua noted, "I get into it. . . . I don't think about that much. . . . I'm just with everyone else." It was clearly the most memorable if not their favorite part of the performance. Research suggests that experiences connected with significant emotions may have a lasting impact on the memory (Sloboda, 2005). Performing the music on stage for others may have also contributed to a heightened emotional impact.

Research can offer some explanations for the children's affinity for group music-making activities. Prior research has suggested that communal music-making is a pleasurable human activity and might lead to increased levels of endorphins in participants' brains, which result in feelings of happiness (Dunbar, 1994). Mithen (2006) offers an evolutionary argument, stating that "those who make music together will mould their own minds and bodies into a shared emotional state, and with that will come a loss of self-identity and a concomitant increase in the ability to cooperate with others" (p. 215). Music education research has suggested that playing in ensembles helps students feel connected to their peers (Adderley, Kennedy, & Berz, 2003) and can contribute to one's musical identity (Abril, 2007; Lamont, 2002).

Alexander was the only child who did not mention the large group drumming, but instead focused on an improvisatory duo he and Shanequa performed at one point in the performance. He explained why, "It was just us, and everyone could hear what we were playing. Just us! . . . I got to show my mom all I could do." Alexander was a child who loved to play the drums but seemed confined (and would get off-task) when given strict guidelines or teacher-directed rhythms in class. However, when working on his own, with fewer boundaries and limitations on a drumming composition or improvisation activity, he flourished. Given more freedom, he would become engrossed in playing complex rhythmic patterns in mixed meters, rife with syncopations, until he felt they had been perfected. Alexander referred to himself as a drummer first and foremost, because he loved to do it and he felt he did it well. He was quite possibly the strongest drummer in the group, with the ability to play complex rhythms and draw out various timbres on the drums. When asked, he claimed there were no musical role models outside of school that were influencing him. This music program may have offered Alexander the opportunity to develop his individual musicality as a drummer.

While she attempted to give him independence, Maria was protective and keenly attuned to her brother Pedro's behavior. On several occasions I noticed her negatively reinforce Pedro for something inappropriate he did.

She also claimed to keep her mother informed of his behavior. In the last interview, I asked Maria what made her happiest while performing. Without hesitation, she said, "That Pedro was there with me. . . . I gave him a big hug . . . and so did my mom when it was over. I was proud of Pedro, because he behaved bad sometimes. . . . My mom said he had to do it . . . and he behaved good at the stage." Maria also thought about her own performance but again in terms of how she was viewed by others: "My mom was so proud of me that she gave me a big smile and a hug." Maria seemed disappointed that her father could not be in the audience, but she felt he was present in spirit. She said, "He was thinking about me. . . . He had to work."

In interviews, the children were keenly aware who did and who did not attend the performance. Many of them named all the people in their family. Others recognized that a family member could not be there because of other responsibilities (e.g., work, health). Some children claimed to recreate the performance for family members not in attendance, and others said they were rewarded by their families after the performance.

The things the children spoke about after the performance differed from those the interviewed adults discussed. I turned to the music teacher for her observations both during and after the performance because of her ongoing relationship with the children. She stated:

> They were sharing what they knew already and could do in your class . . . but I don't think the learning outcomes would have been the same without the performance. . . . The children needed that to be motivated to further their musicianship, . . . really pay attention in the lessons. It helped them build the confidence in their playing, their singing, and their ability to get up in front of a group of people. I saw it in your lessons and in them after the performance was over.

A year later, Ms. Castle recalled their coming together for the final performance:

> They rose to the occasion. . . . While the rehearsal the week before was out there, the day of the performance they were all there with a high level of attention and focus that I hadn't seen all year long. I could see you working on that, though, in every lesson. . . . These kids have such a hard time staying focused.

While we can never know for certain if it was the performance itself, the weekly lessons, or some combination of the two, we might view our performance as an integral component of the music program, not an artificial extension as I first conceived it.

When asked about his observations of the performance, the principal noted that the students appeared motivated and focused, which he believed led to their success. Other words that continued to arise during our conversation included "cooperation," "motivation," and "accomplishment." The principal said, "Teamwork is really important and something I saw in the performance—when they had to cooperate with one another, listen to your instructions, and move, sing, or play. It was impressive how they negotiated it all on the stage." A performance offers children opportunities to make music and share it with others, while also building upon broad educational goals that are of interest to all educational stakeholders.

ENCORE

In *The Culture of Education* (1996), Jerome Bruner asserted that education occurs within the larger context of the world in which it exists, with the microculture representing the demands of a cultural system affecting those who operate within it and the macroculture consisting of a series of "values, rights, exchanges, obligations, opportunities, and powers" that come from extended systems. All the participants in the after-school program played within a unique cultural operating system. While Alexia and I proceeded with our preconceived ideas for how that system should operate, we came to recognize and respond to the larger systems in which we were entrenched. In so doing, the fixed system in our mind became more responsive, more malleable.

Music teachers might design their programs (microcultures) with fixed ideas and philosophies, but should also consider how these matters affect and are affected by the milieu in which the programs reside. Our curriculum was shaped by our understanding that play is an important facet in the education of young children. Not only is it thought to help them understand the world around them (Vygotsky, 1978), it is considered to be a developmentally appropriate practice in their education (Bredekamp, 1987). Many studies have demonstrated the importance of play in helping children come to understand music (Andress, 1998; Campbell, 1998, pp. 178–180; Moorhead & Pond, 1978; Pond, 1981). Musical play provides learning experiences that cannot be obtained through more traditional classroom group activities (Littleton, 1991), yet they can support one another (Taggart, 2000). It may be possible that play and performance are mutually reinforcing, supporting entities.

We wanted the performance to be a window into our curricular unit where we were able to showcase some of the students' learning and demonstrate the musical play we considered to be a part of the music learning process for young children. This had been our hope all along. Ms. Castle noticed this, stating: "You seemed to be educating the audience, . . . letting them learn about the things you do as a teacher to get the children to learn music, . . . how and what you taught in the lessons. . . . I didn't think it was much different from the stuff that you did in the classroom every week." Music teachers might consider ways they can become more effective educational ambassadors of music education in their school community (Abril & Gault, 2007).

Initially I resisted the idea of the performance, but later negotiated a change in thinking, recognizing its importance in learning and building community. The performance people connect with one another—child to parent, child to teacher, teacher to parent, teacher to administrator—through music. It also became a celebration of learning, in which people outside the program felt compelled to participate. Sharing and celebrating learning through a performance can encourage outsiders of the program to peer in. It may also help others see the children in a different light—as "serious" makers of music.

School music performances serve a decidedly different function than do professional performances (e.g., symphony concerts, musicals). The audience and performers are closely connected with one another, emotionally, physically, and psychologically. This is in contrast to the disconnected relationship between an audience and performers in a formal concert setting (Small, 1998). The children in this study were keenly aware of the people for whom they were performing—loved ones and caregivers—as well as those who were visibly absent. Children in this program seemed to relish the opportunity to have loved ones present, where together they could celebrate their accomplishments. Working toward a common goal in a social atmosphere, such as a performance, may be especially important for at-risk children, who need opportunities to succeed and ways to help them become more closely connected to the school community and their peers (Abril, 2006; Jenlink, 1993; Shields, 2001; Taylor, Barry, & Walls, 1997).

The children in this program learned to produce various tones on the drum, play varied rhythmic patterns, sing on pitch, compose with understanding, and improvise on an instrument. The performance also helped motivate them to focus and solve problems. Prior research with fifth-grade children has shown how children become motivated to learn in the process of preparing for a school musical (Feay-Shaw, 2001). The current study demonstrated that this is much the same for these first-grade at-risk children in an urban context, as it was for a select group of fifth-grade children.

The opportunity to perform can help to make the everyday special. The sets, the curtains, and the applause may help to solidify the experience in the children's memories. Research has suggested that highly emotional life experiences in childhood are often carried into adulthood (McAdams, 1993; Sloboda, 2005). The experience of working cohesively toward a common music goal can be a powerful thing. School music experiences may be the only place that children have opportunities to engage in such important social experiences with the arts. Members of the school community behaved differently on the day of the performance, interacting with the children and even the teacher a little differently. People in this school community were supportive and encouraging as the children were about to enter the stage. Parents and loved ones helped children mark the occasion by celebrating in their own way after the performance. The ordinary school day was elevated to an extraordinary one through the performance.

In his book, *Musicking*, Christopher Small (1998) recognized the need for music educators to help *all* students develop their potential as makers of music. He states,

> In exploring we learn, from the sounds and from one another, the nature of the relationships; in affirming we teach one another about the relationships; and in celebrating we bring together the teaching and the learning in an act of social solidarity. (p. 218)

In the process of playing with the elements of music in a semi-structured learning environment in our after-school music program, this group of first-grade children explored music, learned music, and celebrated music. Pulling the curtain back revealed that the power of the performance came from connections made with music and people.

REFERENCES

Abril, C. R. (2006). Teaching music in urban landscapes: Three perspectives. In C. Frierson-Campbell (Ed.), *Teaching music in the urban classroom* (pp. 75–95). Lanham, MD: Rowman & Littlefield Education.

Abril, C. R. (2007). I have a voice but I just can't sing: A narrative investigation of singing and social anxiety. *Music Education Research, 9*, 1–15.

Abril, C. R., & Gault, B. M. (2007). Perspectives on the music program: Opening doors to the school community. *Music Educators Journal, 93*(5), 32–37.

Adderley, C., Kennedy, M., & Berz, W. (2003). A home away from home: The world of the high school music classroom. *Journal of Research in Music Education, 51*(3), 190–205.

Andress, B. (1998). *Music for young children.* New York: Harcourt Brace.

Baisden, C. (1995). Working together. *Teaching Theatre, 7*(1), 13–16.

Bredekamp, S. (Ed.). (1987). *Developmentally appropriate practice in early childhood programs serving children from birth through age 8.* Washington, DC: NAEYC.

Bruner, J. (1996). *The culture of education.* Cambridge, MA: Harvard University Press.

Campbell, P. S. (1998). *Songs in their heads.* New York: Oxford University Press.

Creswell, J. (1998). *Qualitative inquiry and research design: Choosing among five traditions.* Thousand Oaks, CA: Sage.

Dunbar, R. I. M. (1994). *The human story.* London: Faber and Faber.

Feay-Shaw, S. (2001). The view through the lunchroom window: An ethnography of a fifth-grade musical. *Bulletin of the Council for Research in Music Education, 150,* 37–51.

Glesne, C. (2006). *Becoming qualitative researchers* (3rd ed.). Boston: Pearson Education.

Gotlib, A. (2005). The show must go on. *Canadian Music Educator, 47*(2), 44–46.

Illinois State Board of Education. (2003). *Illinois school report card.* Retrieved April 11, 2005, from iirc.niu.edu

James, J. Alison. (1999). *Drums of Noto Hanto.* (Tsukushi, Illus.). New York: DK.

Jenlink, C. L. (1993). The relational aspects of a school, a music program, and at-risk student self-esteem: A qualitative study (Doctoral dissertation, University of Oklahoma). *Dissertation Abstracts International, 0524,* 9418710.

Lamont, A. (2002). Musical identities and the school environment. In R. MacDonald, D. J. Hargreaves, & D. Miell (Eds.), *Musical identities* (pp. 41–59). Oxford: Oxford University Press.

Littleton, D. (1991) *Influence of play settings on preschool children's music and play behaviors.* Unpublished doctoral dissertation, University of Texas at Austin.

McAdams, D. P. (1993). *The stories we live by: Personal myths and the making of the self.* New York: Morrow.

Mithen, S. (2006). *Singing neanderthals.* London: Weidenfeld & Nicolson.

Moorhead, G. E., & Pond, D. (1978). *Music of young children.* Santa Barbara, CA: Pillsbury Foundation.

Palas, A. (1989). Making schools more responsive to at-risk students. ERIC/CUE Digest No. 60 (ED316617).

Paxcia-Bibbins, N. (1993). More than music: A collaborative curriculum. *Music Educators Journal, 80*(1), 23–28.

Piaget, J. (1962). *Play, dreams, and imitation in childhood.* New York: Norton.

Pond, D. (1981). A composer's study of young children's innate musicality. *Council for Research in Music Education, 68,* 1–12.

Raplenovich, K. (1996). The magical place called opera. *Active Learning, 1*(1), 20–23.

Robinson, N. R. (2004). Who is "at risk" in the music classroom. *Music Educators Journal, 90*(4), 38–43.

Shields, C. (2001). Music education and mentoring as intervention for at-risk urban adolescents: Their self-perceptions, opinions, and attitudes. *Journal of Research in Music Education, 49*(3), 273–286.

Sloboda, J. (2005). *Exploring the musical mind.* New York: Oxford University Press.

Small, C. (1998). *Musicking: The meanings of performing and listening.* Hanover, NH: University Press of New England / Wesleyan University Press.

Straub, D. A. (2000). A snapshot of a quality K–12 music program. In B. Reimer (Ed.), *Performing with understanding* (pp. 33–44). Reston, VA: MENC.

Taggart, C. C. (2000). Developing musicianship through musical play. In *Spotlight on early childhood music education* (pp. 23–26). Reston, VA: MENC.

Taylor, J. A., Barry, N. H., and Walls, K. C. (1997). *Music and students at risk: Creative solutions for a national dilemma.* Reston, VA: MENC.

Vygotsky, L. S. (1978). *Mind in society: The development of higher psychological processes* (M. Cole, V. John-Steiner, S. Scribner, & E. Souberman, Eds.). Cambridge, MA: Harvard University Press.

Webster, P. R. (2003). "What do you mean, make my music different?" Encouraging revision and extension in children's music composition. In M. Hickey (Ed.), *Why and how to teach music composition* (pp. 55–65). Reston, VA: MENC.

Younker, B. A. (2003). The nature of feedback in a community of composing. In M. Hickey (Ed.), *Why and how to teach music composition* (pp. 233–242). Reston, VA: MENC.

6

"El Camaleon": The Musical Secrets of Mirella Valdez

Chee Hoo Lum and Patricia Shehan Campbell

One thrust of contemporary qualitative research in education is the advancement of democratic principles relative to social justice, the distribution of benefits, and the growth of understanding the "other" beyond the cultural mainstream (Denzin and Lincoln, 2008). By the late twentieth century, the decades-long dominance of value-free social science research was found to be unnatural, incorrect, and unsuitable, while qualitative modes of inquiry were developed to help democratize and celebrate hidden histories and cultural practices. The liberation movements, including civil rights and the rise of feminism, helped shape scholarship in ways that could contribute to economic justice and utopian cultural politics (Giroux, 2000). Then a surge of interest in the relationship of narrative inquiry to social change developed, with the realization that self-narration can lead to personal emancipation, and that *testimonios* may serve as "emergency narratives" that recognize problems of repression, poverty, and marginality (Beverley, 2000).

Giving voice to marginalized people and naming silenced lives are important goals of narrative research (McLaughlin & Tierney, 1993). It is our position, supported by those of Denzin & Lincoln (2008), Sandoval (2000), and Smith (1999), that marginalized groups deserving greater attention by music educators include children and the poor, rural, and ethnic minority populations. Thus we have created a narrative of a Mexican-American girl that emerged from a dialogue between her and one of us (Chee-Hoo Lum). We contextualize the events and characters that play out in this narrative and draw on the work of Denzin & Lincoln (2008), House (2008), and Richardson (2000) in shifting the meanings of narrative writing into the realm of creative analytic practice. This scholarly style encompasses conversations, personal reflections, layered texts, and music notation that blur the edges between text, representation, and criticism. It is our means of giving voice to one little girl, Mirella, and to the lives that surround her in one rural Mexican American community in the American West.

FULL-FRONTAL: MIRELLA'S FAMILY BAND

Lum: "If you were to draw a picture about music, what would it look like?"

Mirella: "I'll draw me and my friends singing hip-hop!"

Mirella had an alternative drawing (figure 6.1) to show me when I returned the following week. It was a full frontal view of Mirella, her father, older sister, younger brother, and her father's friends—all in the act of making music in the basement of her family home. In pencil and crayon, her depiction of music was an animated one, and the seven large and small figures appeared actively engaged and happy together.

Figure 6.1.   Mirella's father (singing), Miguel (accordion), Victor (bass guitar), Tony (drum set), Brenda and Alex (backup singers), and Mirella (miniature drum set). The black box next to Mirella was a sound mixer that had hook-ups to all the microphones placed in the sound studio (still under construction) that was housed in the basement of the family home.

SETTING THE SCENE

I (Lum) came to Viewcrest Elementary as a volunteer for a university-school collaboration called Music Alive! in the Valley. The year-long partnership was devised to provide a civic engagement of university music education students and faculty with townspeople, children, and teachers from a rural location in a Western state in the United States. It also sought to afford opportunities for positive social contact between communities via musical performances, participation, and training experiences, and to validate the diversity of musical expressions. In this manner, the lives of both university and community participants were expected to be enriched through discovery of each other in and through music by virtue of the involvement of undergraduate music education students in teaching, school performances, interactive sharing sessions, and short residencies of one day to one week (Soto, Lum, & Campbell, 2008).

As I was curious about the music experience in the lives of the Viewcrest Elementary School children, I approached some of the classroom teachers with a request to speak with children they felt were inclined to music. Mr. Mendoza, a third-grade teacher, spoke fondly of Mirella Valdez, stating that she possessed a keen sense of rhythm and participated actively during music lessons. Then he introduced us. In subsequent visits, Mirella and I spoke during recess and I visited her family home, intrigued by the musical activities she engaged in with her family members.

Viewcrest Elementary School is situated at the edge of an Indian reservation and in the heart of the valley of a major east-west river in the western United States. This fertile agricultural region is a place where apples, hops, grapes, apricots, and cherries grow. Within the school district are four elementary schools, one middle school, and one high school. The public school district serves three thousand students, 75 percent of whom are Mexican American, 18 percent Native American, and 7 percent Euro American; there is only a trace of Asian Americans (a dozen Filipino American families) in the region. With a large migrant population comprising the majority of Mexican American families in the district, over five hundred students leave school each year to follow their families in seasonal labor elsewhere in the western United States (Soto, Lum, & Campbell, 2008).

VIEWCREST GIRL

Mirella Valdez sat at the back of the class, next to the blind-covered windows of her third-grade classroom. She was staring out the windows into the silent rolling hills and wide expansive fields that formed the unmistakable landscape that surrounds her school, with its sprawl of brick and glass walls that angle upward to its red zinc roof. Mirella, age eight, had thick, dark, shoulder-length hair and appeared regularly at school wearing a pair of blue jeans and T-shirt that never seemed to fit. Her clothes tended to be too small and seemed like hand-me-downs, well worn with old stains that proved their age. Mirella exuded a passion for life through her sparkly brown eyes and expressive smile, and her cocky, confident air was evident in her tone of voice when we chatted in the cafeteria and school hallways.

Mirella journeyed to the United States from Mexico with her parents soon after she was born. She recalled her parents telling her about their trip, which she described in compressed time: "When my daddy was packing the stuff, and when they let us get out of the hospital, we came over." Her manner of speaking, in particular the use of "over," was her subtle (perhaps subconscious) reference to her family's crossing the international boundary line that separates her birthplace from her new home. Mirella's grandparents had already been in the United States for many years, working as apple-pickers in orchards of the valley. As Mirella stated boldly, "It's because my grandpa was here and he wanted them to come over, so we came over here." Mirella's parents entered the same occupation, whose location she noted: "It's inside this big building (apple warehouse where both parents worked), and they get the apples." Mirella resided with her parents, her eleven-year-old sister, Brenda, and her three-year-old brother, Alex. They lived in a quiet neighborhood about three miles from Viewcrest Elementary School, in a comfortable three-bedroom house with an extension basement, under construction during the time of my visits.

THE FAMILY BAND

When Mirella told me that her father had a band and they practiced almost every evening, I was eager to visit the family. The school administrator, who spoke on my behalf since I do not speak Spanish, asked the family permission for me to visit them. The parents agreed immediately and invited Ms. Soto (a colleague who served as a Spanish translator) and me to their house that evening.

The first thing I noticed when I stepped into the living room was a massive 40-inch television. Mirella, Brenda, Alex, and their mother were watching *Telenovela*, a Spanish drama series; Mirella's father emerged from the back of the house. I saw an old button-box accordion on a chair next to the black sofa and wondered if this was iconic of the Tex-Mex *conjunto*-style music that someone in the household might enjoy playing. This Tex-Mex genre had made its way from the Lone Star State along with the migrant workers who were drawn to the valley during the 1950s and 1960s for the steady agricultural work they could find.

After chatting with the family for several minutes, I heard live music (an amplified drum set and a bass guitar) streaming from the back of the house. The music reverberated throughout the house, and I felt the floor pulsate beneath my feet. I could not contain myself, so I asked to meet the band members. Mirella led me through a dark hallway to the back of the house, and I noticed unfinished woodwork in the doorways and where the walls met the floor. We arrived to a newly constructed basement made from cinder blocks, its electrical wiring still hanging from the ceiling. This was the practice studio or den. The band members greeted me as I stood in awe of a wondrous set-up: sound-mixer, 88-keyed synthesizer, drum set, accordion, bass guitar, and microphone set-up for the singer.

Approximately one year ago, Mirella's father had formed an ad hoc *conjunto* band with his close friends and relatives who lived in the neighborhood. There was Tony, Mirella's cousin, who played the drum set; Victor and Miguel, workmates of Mirella's father, who played the bass guitar and the accordion; a sound engineer who looked after the mixer and microphone equipment; and a lyricist who compiled lyrics of songs and wrote performance notes for the group members. None of the band members had had prior experience playing in a band. They had decided on instruments they might like to play, and by trial and error, they learned their notes by ear from the radio and on CD. They practiced almost five days a week for an hour or two in the early evenings. The band had successfully performed at several weddings and *Quinceañero* parties and planned to record a CD when the home studio was finally completed. (The *Quinceañero* is an important rite of passage in Latin and Caribbean cultures. Celebrations vary, but some families throw a large party for a daughter's fifteenth birthday.)

Mirella spoke with familiarity about how the band members learned their music: "They bought a radio [with a CD player] and if it's paused, they get a little bit, and then they push pause and then they write it." It was a learning process of imitation, listening intently to each musical phrase from CD tracks; writing the words; using idiosyncratic, invented ways of transcribing chords and melodic parts; and practicing individual instrumental parts by ear. On some occasions, Mirella's father worked out the parts before rehearsal and then taught them to his fellow band members.

Mirella, Alex, and Brenda were always in the den when the band practiced. Behind the band set-up was a small space housing a miniature drum set and miniature accordion. That was where Mirella, Alex, and Brenda hung out as the *conjunto* band played its music. The three siblings took turns playing the miniature instruments along with the band. Mirella adeptly played the miniature drum set, using the drumsticks with ease on the snare drum, hitting the bass drum to the beat of the songs with her foot pedal, and striking the cymbals at appropriate moments. Although the miniature accordion could only produce a single drone, young Alex, dressed in a cowboy hat and holding the

Figure 6.2. "El Camaleon"

accordion like a professional player, mimicked Miguel (on the accordion), moving and grooving to the band's amplified music. In addition to playing the drum set, Mirella started to learn the accordion and the bass guitar from her father and on her own, as these instruments were readily available in the studio for her to use when the band was not rehearsing.

The band's repertoire consisted mainly of regional *Tejano* music like that performed by the members' favorite three-man *conjunto* band, Los Diferentes de la Sierra (The Different Ones from Sierra). Mirella's father told me that they currently have about fifty songs in their repertoire. Of the many Mexican popular tunes that Mirella knew, her favorite was "El Camaleon" ("The Chameleon") by Los Diferentes de la Sierra. Many of her classmates knew this song as well. During the Cinco de Mayo celebration at school in early May, the invited DJ blasted "El Camaleon" on the speakers. Everywhere I turned, children, teachers, parents, grandparents, and toddlers sang and danced to the song. Mirella sang an excerpt of the song for me in the school hallways (figure 6.2), and I also heard the family band perform it in their home studio with Mirella's father as the lead singer.

JESUS SONGS

Going to church was a weekly affair for Mirella, Brenda, and Alex. Every Friday evening, their grandparents picked them up to stay for the weekend, and on Sunday mornings, they all went to church at Primera Iglesia Bautista (First Baptist Church), a thirty-minute drive down the highway from their home.

In church, Mirella, Brenda, and Alex attended Sunday school, where, as Mirella described:

> All the kids, we go to this little room and it has two tables and a bunch of chairs for all of us to sit and play. And we have like this guy, he is the one from the church. He teaches us songs of Jesus. He has like a big book, and every time like everything has to be of Jesus and so when we are finished with that, we go back over there (when we are finished with our notebook), we sing a little and then we go over there and sing more songs.

Mirella was thrilled that I wanted to hear some of the "Jesus music" she had learned in church. She asked if I wanted to see the movements that accompanied the song. She gleefully explained, "Sometimes you clap, sometimes you laugh, sometimes you stomp, or sometimes you say, 'Amen!'" (figure 6.3).

1. If you're truly saved, say Amen, Amen!
2. If you're truly saved, clap your hands;
3. If you're truly saved, march like this;
4. If you're truly saved, laugh out loud;
5. If you're truly saved, do all four.

Figure 6.3.   "Jesus Song I"

Figure 6.4. "Jesus Song II"

Hardly finishing the last phrase to the song, Mirella jumped with joy and proclaimed that she had to sing her other favorite "Jesus song" to me (figure 6.4). She explained the Spanish lyrics to me: "God likes people who are fat and skinny, tall and short ones."

> Christ loves all the little children—all the big ones and the small ones.
> Christ loves all the little children and he tells them come, come, come.
> Christ loves all the little children—all the fat ones and the skinny ones.
> Christ loves all the little children and he tells them come, come, come.
> Christ loves all the little children—all the pretty ones and the ugly ones.

Christ loves all the little children and he tells them come, come, come. During her weekend visits to her grandparents' home, Mirella entered a different musical world. In addition to the influence of the church, her grandparents listened to Spanish songs on cassette tapes, most of which were also religious in nature. As Mirella remarked, "Not hip-hop. Like sometimes they just hear whatever kind of music, but they don't like pop. . . . [Usually they listen to] songs of church." On occasion, the family gathered at Mirella's uncle's house to sing these religious songs, with one or more family members accompanying the group-sing on the guitar.

SMACK THAT: THE ONSLAUGHT OF POPULAR CULTURE

The rap and hip-hop culture had already left its distinctive imprint on Mirella's musical life. She shared this passion with her classmate and best friend, David. The two eight-year-olds wasted no time choosing their favorite pop songs—"Smack That" by Akon, featuring Eminem, and "Fergalicious" by Fergie.

Mirella and David had memorized the lyrics of "Fergalicious" and were eager to sing them for me. As Mirella sang, she was able to picture the instrumental interlude in her head: "And then they stop for a little while and they say, 'Four tres two uno, Freakalicious [Fergalicious]!'" After talking to Mirella and David about the many rap, hip-hop, and R&B songs they listened to, sang, and performed, it seemed to me that they were intrigued by the physicality of the songs. They were drawn to the potential of dancing to and even acting them out (as in the songs' video versions), instead of the explicit meaning of the songs' lyrics.

There were several factors that helped to sustain Mirella's constant exposure to the latest in popular music. Hot 99.7 FM was the local radio station that Mirella loved listening to every day at home as she did her homework during the late afternoon. The radio station featured local DJs like The Neighborhood, Foley-Licious, and Sean Tha Don that "always play 'the hottest hits' and the newest of today's music" (NewHot997, 2007). Mirella's interest in popular music had also been sparked by her older sister, Brenda. She recalled Brenda listening to the radio all the time and dancing in their shared bedroom: "I don't know [what songs they were] but my sister, she likes to dance them." Mirella, who did not dance with her sister, remarked: "Like every time she turns on the radio, she starts dancing. And I'm like, 'Brenda, stop it!' and she's like, 'I don't have to!'" But Mirella enjoyed dancing by herself when no one else was watching: "So I switch on the radio, and then I dance. I put my hand like that, and then I go like that." The two sisters shared a small collection of CDs that included singers Shakira, Daddy Yankee, Chris Brown, and Akon. Brenda had clearly influenced Mirella's taste in music.

The other source of popular culture influence for Mirella and David, along with many children I spoke to at Viewcrest Elementary School, was satellite TV (or "the dish"). In particular, Channel 838 (Mun2), drew the attention of second-, third-, and fourth-grade children. Mun2 (pronounced "moon dos") is a Spanish-language program on a national cable TV station that targets young Latinos in the United States. The channel has an informal, fresh, and hip focus with teen programming, variety shows, and movies.

Mirella and David spoke at length about the various dance moves they had learned from watching the variety programs on Mun2. They were also avid fans of MTV programs, as they described to me their current favorite hit, "Gasolina" by Daddy Yankee (a Puerto Rican reggaeton recording artist):

It's Spanish. It's like . . . It's this song that is about a bunch of people singing like that, huh. But on the video clip, they are on motorcycles singing. And racing . . .but on most of the videos, they have to have girls—like in "Gasolina," [a girl holds a machine gun] but she's not gonna shoot, just kind of like drive by, like the gangsters.

Both Mirella and David were enthusiastic about describing these music video sequences, and they talked about how they would dance to the videos at home. David candidly described, "You should have seen my sisters. When they sing, they put on big old fucking jackets! Like they run from each other's room and they crash!" Mirella related how she first started watching Mun2: "It's because [of] my sister. She's always singing and always turning on TV when I was small, and then that's where the songs happened." Mirella, Brenda, and Alex still enjoyed their time together as siblings, watching Mun2. As Mirella described, "Like we all listen to it together. . . . Sometimes me and my sister and my brother, sometimes we sing with them."

LESSONS LEARNED FROM MIRELLA

Mirella's eight-year-old musical world is filled with a myriad of contrasting genres, from the *Tejano* regional music of her father's influence to current popular Spanish-language hits, and from children's religious songs to the hard-core rap and hip-hop that radiates from the ubiquitous media. Technology is the main reason for the co-existence of these musical possibilities within Mirella's home and surroundings, and formed "an integral part of [her] auditory and visual environment" (Marsh, 1999, p. 2). It included MTV on the family television, Daddy Yankee and Akon on her sister's radio stations and CDs, her grandparents' Spanish religious songs on their cassette tape players, and the sound studio combination of mixer, synthesizer, and complete microphone set-up of the family band.

Technology is at the heart of Mirella's music enterprise, constantly defining and re-defining her musical identity. Technological devices are "extensions of children . . . both human and institutional—sometimes in concert, sometimes in tension—to bring about subtle and unpredictable change in children's opportunities for action through quite mundane processes" (Lee, 2001, p. 167). This technology also allows migrants like Mirella and her family to taste and immerse themselves in the musical cultures they knew so well in Mexico, creating "diasporic attachments . . . the doubled connection that mobile subjects have to localities, to their involvement in webs of cultural, political, and economic ties that encompass multiple national terrains" (Inda & Rosaldo, 2002, p. 18). It matters not that Mirella's family lives in a rural, agrarian community, in a small town removed from both Mexico and the urban locus of hip-hop, because the music is carried over the air waves and to the dish that serves the genres they enjoy.

Alan Merriam proposed ten functions of music in his classic text, *The Anthropology of Music* (1964), namely, the functions of emotional expression, aesthetic enjoyment, entertainment, communication, symbolic representation, physical response, enforcing conformity to social norms, validation of social institutions and religious rituals, contribution to the continuity and stability of culture, and contribution to the integration of society. He recommended the study of culture, including music, in order "to know not only what a thing is, but, more significantly, what it does for people and how it does it" (p. 209). In sharing her musical world, Mirella revealed some of these functions. By playing her miniature drum set behind the family band as they rehearsed, Mirella constantly absorbed the goings-on of the band members as they communicated with each other and expressed themselves through music. The band itself is significant as a musical-cultural symbol, with continuity through Mirella, her elder sister, and her younger brother as they immersed themselves and will eventually become part of the next generation of Tex-Mex *conjunto* musicians. The music played by the family band entertained not only the family members but also their surrounding community. They performed at weddings and parties where they provided people enjoyment. They also made money through these performances. It was clear that Mirella's music—at home, school, and in the community—was multifunctional, indicating that "the same performance, the same event, or the same music complex can serve a variety of functions" (Kaemmer, 1993, p. 143).

Mirella and her family are members of the growing Hispanic population in the United States. They live in a transported Mexican community developed from a transient home for migrants to a stabilizing place where families settle, raise children, and grow into their dual identities as American citizens with histories and a heritage in Mexico. They work seasonally in the fields and warehouses and in service jobs at fast-food restaurants at the highway exits and rest stops. Many are poor but do well in rural areas where housing costs, including rentals, are a fraction of urban housing, and groceries provide inexpensive pre-packaged food in bulk for far less than the fresh food of city stores. They live quietly. Even teachers of the children from these poor, rural, Mexican American families know little of their lives outside of school. Yet by listening to Mirella and through my interactions with her family and friends, it was possible to enter into a musical and social reality, alive and well beyond the cultural mainstream. Mirella's voice was heard loud and clear, and her commentary conveyed something of her own values and that of her community.

In music lessons at school, these children's wide-ranging encounters at home and "encounters with technology tend[ed] to be ignored along with the musical practices, primarily associated with popular culture" (Young, 2007, p. 340). Being cognizant of musical repertoire that is close to the hearts of the children—repertoire contextually significant and bearing meaning to their interactions with family, friends, and their community—would allow the classroom music teacher to plan for lessons that build and extend on their musical interests, tapping on their personal experiences and expertise. Musicians like Mirella's family band could be invited to play at school functions or during music lessons, allowing for an immediate connection between the school and community. This can extend to partnerships, where *conjunto* or even mariachi bands could be set up within the school, garnering support directly from parents and culture bearers within the community.

FADING OUT

I was thankful to Mirella for allowing me a glimpse of her rich musical life, as it filled me with hope that music is alive and well in the hearts of these Viewcrest Elementary School students, in their homes and with their friends. As a gesture of my appreciation, I scanned two hardboard copies of Mirella's drawing of her family band in action, adding a title, "Mirella Valdez—Aspiring Singer, Ballerina, and Nurse," and laminating them before presenting them to her. In subsequent visits to the school, I noticed Mirella had used one hardboard copy as a permanent cover to her school folder, while the other was displayed at the back of the classroom. She smiled and waved to me whenever I walked by the classroom. When I bumped into her at the cafeteria, I would ask her about the family band and the new songs she was singing with her best pal, David. As the university-school collaboration came to a close, I intentionally faded into the background, hopeful that perhaps this chance encounter with Mirella would spark her future endeavors in music making. It certainly enriched my horizons as a music educator interested in children's musical cultures.

REFERENCES

Beverley, J. (2000). *Testimonio*, subalternity, and narrative authority. In N. K. Denzin & Y. S. Lincoln (Eds.), *Handbook of qualitative research* (2nd ed., pp. 555–565). Thousand Oaks, CA: Sage.

Denzin, N. K., & Lincoln, Y. S. (2008). Introduction: The discipline and practice of qualitative research. In N. K. Denzin & Y. S. Lincoln (Eds.), *Collecting and interpreting qualitative materials* (3rd ed., pp. 1–43). Thousand Oaks, CA: Sage.

Giroux, H. (2000). *Impure acts: The practical politics of cultural studies*. New York: Routledge.

House, E. R. (2008). Qualitative evaluation and changing social policy. In N. K. Denzin & Y. S. Lincoln (Eds.), *Collecting and interpreting qualitative materials* (3rd ed., pp. 623–640). Thousand Oaks, CA: Sage.

Inda, J. X., & Rosaldo, R. (Eds.). (2002). *The anthropology of globalization: A reader*. Malden, MA: Blackwell.

Kaemmer, J. (1993). *Music in human life: Anthropological perspectives on music.* Austin: University of Texas Press.

Lee, N. (2001). The extensions of childhood: Technologies, children and independence. In I. Hutchby & J. Moran-Ellis (Eds.), *Children, technology and culture: The impacts of technologies in children's everyday lives* (pp. 153–169). New York: Routledge Falmer.

Marsh, K. (1999). Mediated orality: The role of popular music in the changing tradition of children's musical play. *Research Studies in Music Education, 13,* 2–11.

McLaughlin, D., & Tierney, W. G. (Eds.). (1993). *Naming silence lives: Personal narratives and processes of educational change.* New York: Routledge.

Merriam, A. P. (1964). *The anthropology of music.* Evanston, IL: Northwestern University Press.

NewHot997. (2007). Retrieved September 4, 2007, from www.newhot997.com

Richardson, L. (2000). Writing: A method of inquiry. In N. K. Denzin & Y. S. Lincoln (Eds.), *Handbook of qualitative research* (2nd ed., pp. 923–948). Thousand Oaks, CA: Sage.

Sandoval, C. (2000). *Methodology of the oppressed.* Minneapolis: University of Minnesota Press.

Smith, L. T. (1999). *Decolonizing methodologies: Research and indigenous peoples.* Dunedin, New Zealand: University of Otago Press.

Soto, A. C., Lum, C. H., & Campbell, P. S. (2008). *A university-school music partnership for music education majors in a culturally diverse community.* Manuscript submitted for publication.

Young, S. (2007). Digital technologies, young children, and music education practice. In K. Smithrim & R. Upitis (Eds.), *Listen to their voices: Research and practice in early childhood music* (pp. 330–343). Waterloo, Ontario, Canada: Canadian Music Educators' Association.

7

Improvisatory Musical Experiences in the Lives of Children with Severe Disabilities

Kimberly A. McCord

Large glass doors open automatically as the children arrive in the music classroom, where I sit for the first time as a guest and watchful observer. Some whiz by me on their motorized wheelchairs, two compete with one another to see who can enter faster, and others walk dutifully to their chairs. Personal aides accompany many of the children. Some children are missing limbs, others seem unable to control their bodily movements, one is drooling, and another is using a ventilator to breathe. That the children are present in this classroom is a major accomplishment facilitated by the people and mission of Vincent School, which empowers children to participate in formal education as fully as possible.

This was my first observation of the children I would be working with during a music teacher residency at Vincent School. Although I have taught children with disabilities for thirty years, I felt somewhat apprehensive, wondering how I would help students access the musicality they had inside. I had rarely worked with children with such severe physical disabilities. Nonetheless, I was committed to sharing my expertise in jazz and improvisation with these children, believing they were capable of enjoying and growing from these musical experiences.

I hoped to enhance the life and development of these children in some of the ways described in the literature. O'Brien (1987) identified five outcomes for lifestyle enhancement that encourage children with severe disabilities to develop competence through skill acquisition in ways that enhance their community presence, respect, and choice. Special educators recognize the importance of promoting self-determination by having children participate in planning what they will do and learn (Browder, 2001). Friend & Bursuck (2006) stated that "children need to be aware of their strengths and weaknesses, the potential impact of these strengths and weaknesses on their performance, the support they need to succeed, and the skills required to communicate their needs positively and assertively" (p. 357). I believed that providing musical experiences in playing and improvising could help the children reach these goals.

The purpose of this chapter is to describe my work in creating musical experiences for children with severe disabilities through instrumental performance and improvisation. In so doing, I plan to address the following questions: How can we recognize the impact of musical experiences on children with severe disabilities? How can they demonstrate their knowledge, skills, and understanding with such limited communication skills? How would these children respond to experiencing music through playing and improvisation?

PROCEDURES AND PARTICIPANTS

I collected data during my residency that included field notes, a journal, and audio recordings of selected performances and sessions. I also had many discussions with teachers and staff to gain greater insight into the children and to support or disprove my observations. Trustworthiness of the data was established through my extended immersion in the field and through triangulation of the multiple data sources. Data were entered into a qualitative research program to aid in discovering patterns indicative of changes in the children's musical experiences. Since the children had unique abilities and disabilities, I chose not to compare them to other students. Instead, I examined how children learned to express themselves as individuals through music.

TEACHING APPROACH AND ADAPTATIONS

Music educators and music therapists have used the Orff approach of teaching music with individuals and groups of children with disabilities with great success (McRae, 1982; Orff, 1980; Voigt, 2002). Voigt (2002) described the key concepts of Orff Music Therapy:

> The musical material used in Orff Music Therapy is influenced by four factors: music understood in the sense of musike [a total presentation in word, sound and movement], improvisation, the instruments used and the multi-sensory aspects of music (p. 170).

Gertrud Orff in *The Orff Music Therapy* (1980) explained further:

> Instruments, non-musical objects and body instruments can produce sound. Vo-
> calization, as well as complex verbalization, comprise the content of speech,
> which can be rhythmic or meditative. Movement in music therapy can range from
> a facial expression or a spontaneous motion of a part of the body to movement
> as a dance or inner movement (feelings—for example, to be moved by some-
> thing) . . . The idea of creative, spontaneous music making is central in Orff Mu-
> sic Therapy. Its purpose is to provide a creative stimulus for the child (p. 9).

I decided to use an Orff approach, because I believed it was an effective
way to meet the musical and extra-musical goals I had set for the residency.
I did have to adapt the traditional Orff approach because many children
were non-verbal and others had difficulty moving. The Orff approach was
the means through which I thought we could help each child play one instrument well enough to improvise deliberately and expressively.

INSTRUMENTS

During the music sessions, we used a variety of Orff and percussion instruments. Because many instruments required students to play with mallets, I
acquired adaptive mallets, which come with shortened sticks and built-up
grips or T-handles to give children better control. Some mallets had larger
heads or ones made of various materials including cork and rubber, which
helped prevent slippage. Some had large, yarn-wrapped heads to soften the
sound for children with uncontrolled movement or children who play the
instruments with too much force.

Other instruments included a ride cymbal, hi-hat cymbals, a drum controller, and a Soundbeam. The drum controller is a small device, about a
square foot and approximately an inch thick. There are sixteen small rubber
squares situated on the surface of the device, which are touch sensitive. Each
rubber square triggers a different drum sound. The drum controller is connected to my Macintosh laptop computer, and the sounds are accessed
through GarageBand, a software loop program for Macintosh computers. The
Soundbeam is an ultrasonic beam that senses movement and triggers a MIDI
or synthesized sound that is built into the Soundbeam hardware. It enables
people with disabilities to use any form of movement as a way to manipulate
pitch, volume, and vibrato. Adjustments can be made for it to respond to large
movements (a wheelchair moving around a room) and small movements
(eyebrow movement). It responds to any movement within an ultrasonic
beam. It can be programmed to play a variety of timbres.

THE CHILDREN

This chapter will focus on a few selected children, most of whom were age 9 or 10. Jessica walked with crutches and wore braces on her lower legs. She told me she loves to dance and showed me a few of her moves. Charlie was a ten-year-old with a body about the size of a 16-month-old toddler. He used a wheelchair to move, breathed with the assistance of a ventilator, and talked only in brief phrases. Rachel had underdeveloped arms and was learning to write using her feet. Kendra was a little person with arms that appeared twisted, with her palms facing up in their natural position instead of down. She also used a motorized wheelchair. Heather had spastic cerebral palsy and was non-verbal, but she communicated with a beautiful smile. Jeremy was non-verbal with cerebral palsy and used a motorized wheelchair. He often seemed angry and acted oppositional. Serena was a junior in high school who had no ability to move except for one eyebrow and one finger. She, too, was on a ventilator and had a medical aide who monitored the operation of the ventilator. Serena came to school in beautiful outfits, braided hair with colorful beads, and manicured nails with polish.

VENTURES IN IMPROVISATION: THE RESIDENCY

Initial Experiences

The first lesson focused on students selecting instruments and my adapting them according to each child's needs. All Orff instruments were on an adjustable table so that students could access them from their wheelchairs. Some children could hold regular mallets; others used adaptive mallets. Occupational therapists brought a variety of latex wraps, head pointers, and other materials to help children grip or access instruments. Teachers and staff helped adapt instruments as I helped students explore and determine the instruments they wanted to play.

Teachers and staff helped me comprehend that which the non-verbal students were trying to communicate. Their facial expressions, excited arm movements, and shrieking often meant the children desired to play an instrument. Students who did not want to play a particular instrument dropped their sticks, frowned, or shook their heads. Once we determined students' instrumental preferences, we provided the children with physically comfortable positions for playing their instruments.

Most students wanted to play the ride cymbal or drum controller. They were fascinated with the variety of drum sounds that the device offered, and their excitement about playing drums seemed typical for students this age.

Students with limited mobility in their hands or fingers and students who use head pointers were the best candidates for the drum controller. Students with weak muscle control could lightly tap the rubber squares and hear satisfyingly loud bass drum thumps and cymbal crashes. When the children made a sound for the first time on the instruments, they responded with stunned and surprised looks. Others laughed at the sound of the vibraslap. Children encouraged one another as they shared what they could play. They particularly enjoyed hearing the sounds of the drum controller. I had the device set to play jazz percussion sounds, and the children only needed a couple of minutes to orient themselves to the locations of the different sounds. I showed them where to find the ride and crash cymbal sounds and other drum sounds they could use in their improvised solos. It was a thrill for me to hear their shrieks of delight or to have them lift their heads to look at me with big smiles on their faces.

Kendra, a little person with small and disfigured hands and arms, wanted to play the xylophone and worked to find a way to play it with a mallet.

Kim: I have all of these different mallets that will work well on this instrument. Which ones do you want to use?

Kendra: I'll use the regular ones. I have this thing on my hand that I can stick it through. [She has a glove on her hand with a pocket to put a pen or pencil through].

I pushed the mallet through the pocket attached to her hand, but the end of it was stabbing her upper arm as she tried to play. She adjusted the grip and tried to make it work. She did not want any assistance from me. Kendra worked with the grip, and the occupational therapist made some suggestions and helped her take off the glove. She found a way to hold the stick without the hand support. Granted, she had difficulty controlling the mallet; she kept missing the xylophone bars. The occupational therapist continued to brainstorm with her. A few minutes later, Kendra played with a shorter adaptive mallet with one hand and a regular mallet with the other. The short mallet had a cork head, but she was not entirely satisfied with the sound, which was somewhat muffled.

Kim: What do you think? Will it work?

Kendra: Yeah, I guess so; let me try it for a while.

This example illustrates that children with disabilities need to learn to advocate for themselves and be active in decisions involving their learning. Some children are able to play instruments more easily and adapt more readily than others. Teachers might be too quick to assume that a child with disfigured arms and hands should sing rather than play an instrument.

However, that student might be agile in using her feet or a head pointer. I sought to give the children choices based on their instrumental preferences and opportunities to work independently on challenges associated with playing those instruments. The children asked for assistance only when needed.

Children with severe cognitive and physical disabilities are typically successful in making music with the Soundbeam (Ellis, 1994; Russell, 1996). Charlie quickly figured out how to play different pitches of chords by moving his wheelchair in three-foot increments. Later in the music sessions when the children improvised on the instruments, Charlie combined wheelchair movements with 360-degree spin and concluded by playing a bicycle bell mounted on his wheelchair. Everyone cheered. He seemed pleased with his effort and the attention.

A teacher asked Jeremy if he would like to play the Soundbeam, and he frowned and grunted while waving at the ride cymbal. During my first observation visit, however, he refused to participate in music class, which did not include children using instruments. The teacher positioned Jeremy in front of the ride cymbal. We handed him a stick, but his grip was so rigid that he could not coordinate hitting the stick on the cymbal. He succeeded in moving his arm up but could not move it down with enough control to hit the cymbal. Instead, he moved the stick into his body or dropped the stick while trying to make contact with the cymbal. One of the therapists increased the height of the cymbal, and Charlie played the cymbal by striking it underneath as he moved his arm upward. Sometimes he tipped over the cymbal, but he was determined to play it. He enjoyed the loud sounds and the sound of the cymbal crashing into his wheelchair as it fell.

I guided Jeremy toward the Soundbeam, because I knew he would be more successful working with it than the cymbal. Although I had programmed a cymbal sound into the Soundbeam, he remained uninterested in playing anything but the real cymbal. I was concerned with the constant disruption of the cymbal falling and worried about Jeremy getting hurt when his arm got caught in the cymbal. The other adults did not share my concerns; therefore, I learned to adjust my own teacher-instincts and allowed Jeremy the opportunity to become a cymbal player.

Another Day

In the second lesson, Charlie (who played the Soundbeam in the previous class) played the drum controller. He was able to play a bass drum sound consistently on beat two. Then he added cymbal and snare drum sounds to the bass drum sound. At first, he played patterns that were hip-hop-like, and then he shifted into a rock-style pattern. With his tiny fingers and hands, he managed to jump across several of the rubber pads to create syncopated dance rhythms that caused many in the class to nod their heads and to move in dance-like ways. Some children liked to experiment and play different instruments each day, while others preferred to play the same ones.

Rachel: Can I try this one today?

Nera [occupational therapist]: We have been working on writing with her feet. I think you can do this. What do you think, Rachel?

Rachel: Yeah, can I try it first?

Kim: Sure. [I offer her several mallets, and she nods at the regular mallet. I hand her a mallet that she takes with her toes.]

Nera helps Rachel position the instrument and adjust the mallet in her toes. I notice they add a mallet to the other foot, too. To play with both feet on the bass xylophone, Rachel must lift her feet quite high. She sits on an adjustable office chair, its seat adjusted as high as it can be. She frequently drops the mallet, so the occupational therapist works with her and adjusts the mallet so it is not too long. This helps, but she still struggles to play the bass xylophone with an accurate rhythm.

Rachel is playful, and she insists with a straight face that her real name is Paris Hilton. At the end of each class, she rushes to me and asks if I know of different pop singers and songs she likes. When I am not familiar with the singers, Rachel sings the songs for me. She also loves Broadway shows, and as she leaves the class she sings a song from *High School Musical*.

Both Charlie and Rachel are quite musical. Even with severe limitations, both are able to share their musical interests with their peers and me. Both are aware of the musical world around them. The school arranges field trips to take children to concerts and musicals as frequently as possible, but it is quite expensive to transport children with medical aides and assistive equipment. Many children come to school in ambulances and are simply too fragile to travel anywhere else. When they return home, most of their experiences are limited to what they see on television and out of the windows. Charlie has these types of limitations. Participating in music by singing and playing instruments can be incredibly meaningful for children with severe limitations because their musical experiences might otherwise remain passive.

Jessica's muscular dystrophy has progressed rapidly. She was in a wheelchair and no longer offered to dance for me. She was able to play the Orff instruments and used regular mallets, but now she played with slight coordination challenges, symptomatic of children with cerebral palsy. Even though Jessica does not have cerebral palsy, making her muscles respond by moving requires considerable concentration. I wondered how to create a "swing-feel" for children who play after the beat and not with the beat. I encouraged Jessica to play with one mallet so she could concentrate on moving only one hand. She put forth great effort and succeeded. Although it was never completely accurate, Jessica's rhythm improved with each repetition of the song.

Kendra was successful playing the xylophone. Her solos were inventive, going in and out of time with rolls, rests, and a sense of the form of the music we were creating. Eventually, she varied the bass ostinato part, adding stick clicks and harmonies. Her right arm, twisted at an angle, made playing difficult, but she adapted by positioning her body in her wheelchair so she could strike the bar from above rather than hitting the bar from the side. Kendra's friends, Carlos and Joe, also played creative instrumental improvisations with ease. At one point during Kendra's solo, all three engaged each other through music. They played brief responses to her improvisations. For example, Kendra played a roll on the tonic pitch of the song, and the others rolled on the tonic in higher octaves. Another time she clicked Joe's sticks to her left, and Carlos clicked her stick on the right (the side of her body with the more limited movement). I am not certain if they planned it, but it was a clever way to end Kendra's solo. Heather enjoyed hearing them and literally screamed with delight.

Heather eagerly played the Soundbeam by holding out her arms and pushing herself up and down in her wheelchair. She was not able to control the pitches but was thrilled nonetheless to create her own sounds. On the last note of the music, Heather became the soloist by sustaining the note, something Kendra called "the big ending." She made eye contact with me when she was ready to end the last note. Her wild and furious playing imitated a cadenza, and her facial expression indicated that she was satisfied with her creation. She knew exactly the type of improvisation to play just before we ended the song. She decided to do this without coaching from the teachers, and she had predetermined how long and fast she wanted to play. I recorded the performance, and the class listened to the recording. Heather's face showed excitement and anticipation, as the music approached her solo and her big ending. I wondered if she enjoyed listening because she had had a solo or if she was thinking about ideas for improving her subsequent solos.

Communication

Heather and I communicated through non-verbal means. She communicated through her facial affect, and I learned to interpret her facial gestures by observing her range of facial expressions. She was able to smile, frown, lift her eyebrows, squint her eyes, shake her head, shriek, and laugh. She seemed to also understand that we could communicate with each other about the music with our faces and eyes. When Heather wanted the instruments to play after her cadenza, her facial expression changed from squinting of her eyes and a slight frown to lifting her eyebrows and smiling as she made eye contact with me. She waited to laugh and shriek until the silence at the end, after I signaled for the other instruments to stop playing.

I found it especially challenging to understand Jeremy, however. His facial expressions consisted of frowns or empty stares. He became angry and screamed if we asked him to play anything except the ride cymbal. At least one aide had to help pick up the cymbal each time it fell over and re-position Jeremy's hand so that he could play the cymbal again. He patiently waited until it was his turn to play a solo, and then he threw his arm trying to hit the cymbal. Was Jeremy satisfied with the sound the cymbal made when he knocked it over, or did he want to be able to play it in more musical ways? He seemed to have three moods: anger, indifference, and great excitement. His teachers noted the same patterns throughout the day.

Playing with Eyebrows

At lunchtime, Serena worked on learning to manipulate the Soundbeam with her eyebrow movements. Of her entire body, she had the best range of movement in her eyebrows. She was unable to smile or talk, but she squinted her eyes when she was happy and smiling. Her occupational therapist said they were working on training her to access a computer by using eye movement. In her limited communications with the occupational therapist, Serena had expressed excitement about playing the Soundbeam and her ideas for making music. The occupational therapist came with her to the music room, and the three of us worked together to configure the Soundbeam. They continued working on using the Soundbeam after I left the room. When I returned the next day, she could play some of the Orff instrument parts and participate in musical improvisations during our class jams. When she raised her eyebrow, the Soundbeam pitch went higher, and when she pulled her eyebrow into a frown, the pitch became lower. She was even able to produce a pentatonic scale.

I tried programming various Soundbeam timbres for her to use, and she communicated with her eyes to let me know if she liked them by looking to the right for "yes," center for "okay," and left for "no." I listed all the sounds she liked, and the occupational therapist planned to make a board on which each sound was written. Then Serena could look at it, and we would know which sound she wanted to use.

Another Musical Experience

Charlie zipped into the classroom on the third day and maneuvered into the spot in front of the ride cymbal. His aide immediately helped him with the drumstick next to the cymbal stand. His open hand was about four inches long and three inches wide. His tiny fingers were not able to support the drumstick, and when he tried to use the stick he dropped it. An occupational therapist joined us in creating ways for Charlie to play the cymbal. She tried strapping the stick to his arm, but even then it was too heavy and caused him fatigue. I could see the disappointment on his face. We talked about other options for playing the cymbal:

Kim: Shall we try using this mallet instead? [I show Charlie an Orff mallet and how we could turn it around to play on the handle end instead of the head.]

Charlie [gives me a look that tells me he does not like the idea]: Isn't there a different drumstick?

Kim: These are the only ones we have here, but I could go to a music store on my way home and see if I can find a lighter one. [Charlie gives a big smile.]

Kim: I'll look and see what they have and we can try it tomorrow. In the meantime, how about you play with this mallet so you can practice with the rest of the class. [He agrees.]

Charlie came to class, and we showed him three different sticks. The occupational therapist worked with the lighter sticks, using an armrest she clamped to his wheelchair, positioning his arm so he could play the cymbal. He did not have to hold his arm up high, so it worked better than other methods. She also rigged a music stand on which to set the stick when he needed to rest.

That day I focused on improvised jazz solos. The children had worked with the jazz singer on a day prior to my residency at the school, and she had modeled and played recordings of improvised scat solos. They had also worked on producing call-and-response scat solos. We talked about what makes a good jazz solo, after we watched a videotape, recorded four months ago, of the class singing scat solos with the jazz singer. The singer used a Jamey Aebersold recording of a jazz rhythm section playing a blues progression. Children who were non-verbal hit a big switch button that had a pre-recorded short scat solo performed by the singer. The children laugh as they watched themselves and each other singing. Some solos were funny, but I interpreted the laughter as delight in seeing themselves perform, instead of laughing at how their solos sounded.

Kim: Can someone tell me what you liked best in the solos?

Kendra: I thought it was funny when Carlos put the word "dog" in his scat.

Others: Yeah! [Heather shrieks, and Jeremy bounces up and down in his wheelchair and vocalizes, "Ahhhhhh."]

Jessica: Why did you do that, Carlos?

Carlos: I couldn't think of any more scat sounds, but I think I saw a dog picture or something and it made me say it.

Jessica: Oh, I wondered why you did that.

Kim: Did anyone else have something they liked in a scat solo? What did you think of Kendra's solo?

Carlos: I thought it was good. When she clicked her sticks on mine, I was surprised. [He refers to the instrumental solo she played yesterday, not her scat solo.]

Kim: How come?

Carlos: I don't know; I guess I didn't expect her to do that, and she surprised me.

Kim: Did the clicking help to make her solo sound good?

Jessica: No!

Carlos: Yes!

[Heather and Jeremy bounce a bit in their wheelchairs.]

Kim: What do you think, Kendra?

Kendra: I thought it was all right, I think I could have made it better.

Kim: How?

Kendra: I liked the click, but I think it went on too long.

Kim: What would you have taken out to make it shorter?

Kendra: Maybe take out some of the slow hits, and then it could move faster.

Kim: Do you mean the rhythm was too slow in the part where you played a note and then waited awhile and played the next note?

Kendra: Yeah, it was funny at first, and then it just turned into boring.

We discussed how to make solos interesting and how to save the best ideas for the end of the solo. I showed them ways to make sounds on the instruments by playing the stick backwards or using fingertips on the Orff instruments and cymbals. We talked about ways to make solos interesting on the Soundbeam, and I used Heather to demonstrate.

Charlie: Twirl your wheelchair around really fast!

[Heather tries this, and the class laughs.]

Kendra: Do it in slow motion now!

[She spins in a slow circle.]

Jessica: Hey, the music sounds slower when she does that!

I asked them to experiment with finding different ways to produce sound on their instrument. Heather played *glissandi* by raising and lowering her arms in the beam while Jessica watched.

Jessica: Like this?

[She models the same idea to me on her soprano xylophone.]

Carlos: That sounds like the Soundbeam!

We performed our song—a brief, swing-style piece that I composed—and both boys played with concentration and control. Jeremy played a solo first that started in a relaxed manner. As he became more excited, however, his muscles tensed, and he began to play louder. This is common among individuals having the same form of cerebral palsy. As they become more excited, their muscles become spastic. Jeremy's stick became caught in his wheelchair, and he could not detach himself without an aide's assistance. Then he stopped playing. He looked down at the side of his wheelchair where the stick had been stuck. I could not tell if he was pleased or frustrated.

It was Charlie's turn, and he looked up to see if his peers were watching. He played seven or eight times and then put down the stick. The class continued to play the accompaniment, waiting for him to rest and then continue playing. He played another four notes, needed to rest again, and finally mouthed, "Okay," to me.

Rachel decided to play the hi-hat cymbals after struggling to hold mallets with her feet. She tried to play solos on the hi-hat, but could not figure out a way to make them sound different from the usual reverberant ringing or the sound of closing the cymbals.

Kendra played her solo on the alto xylophone, trying something new. She played intervallic thirds in brief patterns, using rests to fool us into thinking that she was finished. Then she played more thirds and made eye contact with Carlos who held up his stick. She ended with one triumphant click. Jessica began her solo, struggling to coordinate and play. The right stick became caught beneath the bars. She shrugged her shoulders and yelled, "I'm done!"

Heather waited patiently with her hand on her wheelchair control, ready to move when it was her turn. She waited until the end of the musical form to began her solo. She began by turning her chair in tight circles, so that the Soundbeam responded with a flurry of notes. Soon she slowed and when she came to the beam sensor, she moved her arms and her body up and down, looking at me with absolute glee. She knew the big ending was coming which meant everyone would hold the last note as she soloed on the Soundbeam. When I signaled the big ending, Kendra and Jessica played a roll (playing with two mallets alternating quickly), while Charlie tried to create a roll-like sound on the cymbal. Jeremy, who did not play, watched Heather. She and the others watched me for the final cut-off, and then they cheered. The adults in the room clapped and congratulated the children. Jeremy looked at us but did not make a sound or move.

Charlie exhibited signs of increased musicianship and sensitivity. Kendra learned to be thoughtful about her playing, improving her solo improvisations during each class session. Conversely, Jessica continued to struggle. While initially she was energetic and willing to try anything musically, she now seemed to give up easily. In my previous research on children with learning disabilities, I identified a behavior that is common among children with disabilities that was first described by Seligman as "learned helplessness" (as cited in McCord, 2004). In his description of learned helplessness, Seligman (1975) said, "Persistence is a byproduct of success, and if success is repeatedly out of reach of the student, he or she learns not to try" (p. 210). Children with disabilities often perceive success as being unattainable, and they eventually learn not to try (Seligman 1975; Peterson, Maier & Seligman 1993). "Students exhibit *learned helplessness* when there is not a good match between learning objectives and student attributes; therefore, one single set of standardized objectives cannot be expected to meet the unique learning abilities of individual students in inclusive classrooms" (Stainback & Stainback, 1996, p. 210).

Learned helplessness in the music classroom can appear as resistance in doing a task or the need for constant feedback from the teacher (McCord, 2004). Some children try to copy ideas from others, or they may give up and not even try to do the task. Jessica showed signs of learned helplessness. I asked the teachers about this possibility, and they related that she was declining physically. Her disability was a rapidly degenerative form of muscular dystrophy. There are forty-two forms of muscular dystrophy, and hers was unfortunately one of the more aggressive forms. What appeared to be her giving up was actually a sign of sheer exhaustion and side effects of the medication she took. Yet other caregivers and professionals agreed that in the past few months they had noticed Jessica giving up and possibly showing signs of learned helplessness.

Last Day of the Residency

On the last day of my residency, the class and I recorded the three songs we had polished, with improvisations from each student. On that day, Jessica decided we should have a name and suggested "The Rockin' Jazz Band." Others agreed. Jessica introduced the group and the song on the recording, I counted off the tempo, and then we began. Some improvisations were clearly in a jazz style, yet others were not but still reflected the students' personal accomplishments. For example, Jeremy's improvisation seemed to be more of an exercise in hitting the cymbal, than expressing himself in a jazz style. However, some did learn to play stylistically.

Charlie played with a plastic flute-cleaning rod, and it sounded better than the metal rod he had used on the previous day. The drum sticks were not manageable. He seemed to have a bit more physical stamina, too. Rachel played the hi-hat and maintained her performance on beats two and four. Kendra played a solo similar to the one she performed on the previous day, and Jessica used one mallet to play each note of a scale on the xylophone before she concluded. Sandra, a student who had missed the other classes, played a structured solo on the drum controller. She started out with a rock drum break, then a jazz-brushes solo between the snare drum and cymbal, and ended with thumping tom-toms and a cymbal crash. She did all of this with a head pointer attached to her baseball cap. She seemed highly satisfied with her solo, given her display of a big smile.

Jeremy switched to the Soundbeam on the final day. He rolled into the room and went directly to the Soundbeam. He began his solo by hopping up and down in his wheelchair. He pushed his torso up and moved his arms in the beam. As he did this, he grunted and smiled. This was the first time I had seen him smile.

I meet with Jeremy's educational team on the next day. The teachers noticed that when Jeremy returned to the classroom after music he seemed depressed and sleepy. The following conversation ensued.

Kim: Do you think Jeremy was frustrated by trying to play that soundbeam yesterday?

Julie [occupational therapist]: He was so excited! (Talking to the team) Have you ever seen him move that much?

Angie [aide]: No, he was a different kid; I couldn't believe it. He kept trying and wouldn't give up like he usually does. No fighting with us, either. He was cooperating and listening to me for once.

Carla [third-grade teacher]: Did you notice he slept all afternoon? I thought he was depressed [she had not attended the music class]. I couldn't get him to wake up; he was so tired.

Julie: You know why, don't you? That is the most physical I have seen him all year. I think it wore him out.

Despite the draining effects of the musical experience on Jeremy, his playing served as a motivator to get him to move. Voight (2002) explained further, "A child with a cerebral motor disability, such as cerebral palsy, may have great difficulty in moving at all, resulting in a lack of incentive to use his motor abilities to explore surroundings. This lack of stimulation can prevent him from having experiences necessary for positive social and emotional development and for the development of perceptual abilities" (p. 166). Playing a musical instrument can be an effective way to motivate a person to do things both musical and non-musical.

The last soloist was Heather, who played the Soundbeam using a combination of wheelchair twirls and arm movements. She tried at one point to get the Soundbeam to respond to her eyes blinking and mouth opening, but then switched to arm movements for her solo during the big ending. The children held their notes for the big ending, and we released the sounds together.

We listened to the recording of our performance, and for the most part, the children listened quietly (although moving in response to what they heard), until Heather's solo. When Heather heard herself playing, she made excited vocal sounds and moved joyously in her chair. The children enjoyed hearing their playing, as evidenced in their facial affect, gestures, outburst, and movements.

CONCLUSION

The musical goal of the residency was for these children with severe disabilities to learn to improvise expressively using a musical instrument. The different traditional and electronic instruments, along with the unique ways of playing them, gave the children multiple ways to express themselves and to be included in the music-making process. Children showed the ability to play rhythmically and melodically with a sense of phrasing. Depending on the part and instrument the student played, many were able to play in a characteristic jazz style.

Adapting instruments was critical to the children's success in the program. Had there not been an electronic instrument specially made to detect movement anywhere in the body, Serena might have never been able to partake in the improvisational experiences. Given the nature of Kendra's disability, we might have asked her to sing; however, she was able to teach herself (with adult assistance) to use the mallet on the instrument. This helped her to become an active agent in the teaching and learning process (Browder, 2001; Friend & Bursuck, 2006).

How can we recognize the impact of musical experiences on children with severe physical disabilities? Teachers must be aware of the unique strengths and limitations that accompany children with disabilities. Collaborating with special educators, parents, occupational therapists and other professionals helps music teachers come to this understanding. Learning to read facial expressions and body language, instead of relying only on speech, can guide teachers toward adapting instruction for individual children. Charlie and Rachel had significant physical disabilities that might have limited their participation in most music classrooms, yet they came to our class with a high level of desire to make music based on their experienced successes. Jeremy used all of the physical energy he had to play instruments in ways his teachers had never witnessed. Serena, who in some ways was a prisoner in her own body, was able to play an instrument, apparently for the first time in her life.

How can children demonstrate their knowledge, skills, and understanding with limited communication skills? Performance-based assessment has become a best practice assessment tool in the general music classroom. Heather clearly knew when and how to improvise over the final chord of the music. She also developed various techniques to play the Soundbeam. If I had expected her to play an ostinato on an Orff instrument as Kendra did, she would not have been successful. She contributed musically to the piece according to her own abilities, and each day she finessed her part or tried something new.

How would children with severe disabilities respond to experiencing music through playing instruments and improvisation? Children are usually fascinated with playing musical instruments. The children I worked with were no different. They came to class each time brimming with excitement about playing instruments—making music. At first, some were shy about playing their improvised solos, but as they grew more comfortable with their instrument and developed ideas they were enthusiastic about performing.

It was the immeasurable qualities that made musical meaning evident to me: Serena's eyes as she made music on the Soundbeam for the first time, Sandra playing the drum controller with her head pointer and then smiling as a way to communicate the joy she felt, Jeremy hopping up and down in his wheelchair and making sounds that communicated "*Yes!*" Yes, we all do have music inside us! Music teachers just need to create musical experiences that nurture and make accessible children's inner musicality.

REFERENCES

Browder, D. M. (2001). *Curriculum and assessment for students with moderate and severe disabilities*. New York: Guilford.

Ellis, P. (1994). *Special sounds for special needs: Toward the development of a sound therapy*. International Society for Music Education 1994 Conference.

Friend, M., & Bursuck, W. (2006). *Including students with special needs: A practical guide for classroom teachers*. Boston: Allyn & Bacon.

McCord, K. A. (2004). Moving beyond "That's all I can do": Encouraging musical creativity in children with learning disabilities. *Bulletin of the Council for Research in Music Education, 159*, 23–32.

McRae, S. W. (1982). The Orff connection: Reaching the special child. *Music Educators Journal, 68*, 32–34.

O'Brien, J. (1987). A guide to life-style planning. In B. Wilcox & G.T. Bellamy (Eds.), *A comprehensive guide to the activities catalog: An alternative curriculum for youth and adults with severe disabilities* (pp. 175–189). Baltimore: Paul H. Brookes.

Orff, G. (1980). *The Orff music therapy* (M. Murray, Trans.). New York: Schott Music Corp.

Peterson, C., Maier, S. F., & Seligman, M. E. P. (1993). *Learned helplessness: A theory for the age of personal control.* New York: Oxford University Press.

Russell, K. (1996). Imagining the music, exploring the movement: Soundbeam in the sunshine state. *Queensland Journal of Music Education, 4*(1), 41–48.

Seligman, M. (1975). *Helplessness: On depression, development and death.* San Francisco: W. H. Freeman.

Stainback, S., & Stainback, W. (Eds.). (1996). *Inclusion; A guide for educators.* Baltimore: Paul H. Brookes.

Voigt, M. (2002). Orff music therapy with multi-handicapped children. In T. Wigram & J. DeBacker (Eds.), *Clinical applications of music therapy in developmental disability: Pediatrics and neurology.* London: Jessica Kingsley.

8

Composing in the Classroom: The Journey of Five Children

Betty Anne Younker

There is a body of music education research that informs us about children's musical experiences in composition (Wiggins, 2001; Younker & Burnard, 2004), students' perceptions about composing (Younker, 2005), and effective ways to respond to students' compositions (Hickey, 2003; Reese, 2003). Within the area of students' experiences in group composition, research suggests that the observation of verbal and nonverbal behaviors can provide insight into what students find meaningful in music (Burnard & Younker, 2002; Dillon, 2004; Morgan, Hargreaves, & Joiner, 2000; Seddon & O'Neill, 2001) and how musical meaning at the individual and group levels is constructed and negotiated (Macdonald & Miell, 2000a, 2000b; Wiggins, 2003). This work furthers knowledge of mediating factors that contribute to the construction of musical meaning while composing, the level of musical meaning students can acquire through composition (Franca & Swanwick, 1999), and the role critical thinking can play throughout the process. By observing and listening to students as they compose within the musical experience, we can make inferences about possible benefits of composition and begin to examine the role critical thinking plays while composing. Identifying how, when, and why students explore, examine and negotiate possibilities, converge on solutions, and evaluate that which has been accepted during the process of composing can inform us about what is meaningful at the individual and group levels.

PURPOSE AND BACKGROUND

The purpose of this chapter is (1) to make explicit the power of music composition in the lives of a group of fifth-grade students as they create original music in group composition and (2) to identify aspects of their critical
thinking while they are engaged in group composition. Specifically, my inquiry focused on the nature of action and interaction among five boys and
the presence of critical thinking during composition tasks. Observing the
students' activities and thought processes led me to make inferences about
the children's understanding of music and its meaning to them.

The boys' experiences occurred within a fifth-grade music classroom in a
school that is ethnically and economically diverse and that offers regular
music classes from kindergarten to grade five, all of which are taught by a
certified music specialist. The story begins in the students' first composition
class of the year, where they reviewed, created, and performed ostinati patterns. This is followed by an in-depth account of one group of students—
five fifth-grade boys who were in those music classes. It details the creation
and performance of a composition, a process that unfolded during eight
sessions over the course of seven weeks. Following that is a snapshot of the
students' final performance, which occurred at the conclusion of the academic year. The chapter ends by providing questions for further consideration and investigation into composition-based music-making.

The initial motivation to spend time in this music classroom was my interest in music composition and the philosophical, pedagogical, and curricular questions related to its use in music classrooms, processes of composition, and the meaningfulness of these experiences. I chose this site
because of the music teacher's commitment to organizing the fifth-grade
curriculum around composition. Laura, the music teacher, believed
strongly that all her students deserved the opportunity to be actively involved in music, including being a part of a final concert. Before she came
to the school, the final concert was an auditioned event that resulted in a
few students having major roles, some students having minor roles, and
other students having minimal to no involvement.

Laura's fundamental reason for teaching music was to ensure that every
student was involved in musically meaningful ways, and she believed that
composition allowed that engagement to occur. The resultant experiences
included students being introduced to music concepts and then creating
and performing compositions in groups based on them. Such activities, interspersed with rehearsing and performing requisite school plays and as-
semblies, occurred between October and March. In March, students either
self-selected groups or were placed in groups by Laura. They participated in
eight to twelve lessons creating group compositions to perform in two May
concerts—one in the afternoon for the students and staff and one in the

evening for parents, family, and friends. The concerts were videotaped so that the students could view their performances later. Afterward, all of the students completed surveys inviting them to reflect upon their year of composing and performing.

COMPOSING IN THE CLASSROOM

October: First Lessons

As I walked into the music room, my first reaction was that it was a space for active music making—it gave me a sense of openness and engagement. There was not a desk to be found, and there were only three stools placed on the carpeted floor. A piano sat across from the door and a sound system with CDs on top and around it was against a wall. On, underneath, and beside tables were Orff instruments (e.g., xylophones, metallophones, glockenspiels); hand drums, Ghanian drums, rainsticks, cowbells, and buckets of mallets. There were shelves housing books, files, instruments, and music. Instruments found on the shelves included electric keyboards, containers of rhythm instruments, and African drums of varying sizes.

Approximately twenty-two students entered the room talking and laughing while finding a spot on the floor. Laura walked to the door to greet the students, and I remained by the piano. As it became apparent where Laura was actually going to sit (she chose one of the three stools placed around the perimeter of the room), the students shifted and, at times, moved from their original spaces to sit closer to friends. The atmosphere was relaxed, informal, and accessible, yet focused. The lesson began, and students shifted their attention to Laura. If a student did not "settle in," Laura or another student provided a behavioral reminder. After one or multiple reminders, Laura provided more direct and prescriptive behavioral remedies.

Laura began by outlining the activities for the sixty-minute class period: (1) review ostinati patterns, (2) create and practice multiple patterns in groups, (3) perform for each other, and (4) respond to each other's group compositions. Specifically, students were asked to work in groups to create multiple ostinati patterns they could perform as a group. They had to know what an ostinato pattern was and whether or not the ones they created fit together when they performed as a group. Laura utilized five physical spaces, each designated as a group's compositional area: (a) the music room, (b) the custodians' room, located across the hall, (c) a space at the end of the hallway from the music room behind a set of double doors, (d) a space down the hallway and around the corner from the music room at the bottom of a staircase, and (e) a space next to the music room behind a set of doors in a very short hallway.

The room became alive with energy as students selected instruments, experimented with different mallets, called out to each other as various instruments were explored, hunted for appropriate bars for the pitched instruments, and banged on the various drums. They asked Laura or me questions about mallets and/or places they could find the missing bars, made decisions about instruments they wanted to use, and informed each other when they were ready to meet in their designated space. It appeared the students needed time to set up their instruments and explore playing. Thus, what might have seemed chaotic was their settling into the task, becoming familiar with the instruments, and releasing their energies. Playing melodies or melodic motives, banging, or playing on drums filled all of the compositional areas, until someone in the group focused the members' attention and reminded them of the given task.

My entrance into any of the groups' designated spaces was either ignored or met with questions. I had observed Laura respond to students in the classroom and, therefore, had a context for their expectations of us as teachers. Often my initial desire was to take over and show the students how they could do better. My thoughts ranged from, "They need to be more focused" to "It would sound better if . . ." to "They aren't playing together." I had to continue working on being patient, listening, and offering suggestions only when requested. When students asked me questions, I helped with a problem (e.g., the togetherness of the ensemble, how to begin, how to transition, how it could be better) or defused an issue between students. As one would expect, when students are engaged in group activities, differences arise. This case was no different. Students became frustrated when instruments were first choices for multiple students, off-task behavior interrupted the compositional process, musical material was favored over other material, and the form could not be agreed upon. Even during times of dissonance, however, there was evidence of active learning and engaged participation as the assigned product was formed. The students were aware that they would soon perform their ostinati patterns for their peers; thus, some of their motivation was directed by the music teacher's expectations.

The students in this class responded in ways comparable to other students with whom I had worked in similar composition-based experiences. They played and explored sounds in a random fashion, but with a sense of purpose. Upon arriving at their designated space, the group members typically began as individuals, playing with and without patterned sounds on their chosen instruments. At times, they tried out their sounds on each others' instruments. Students would focus on each other by repeating the teacher's expectations for the task: "What are we going to do?" or "We have to get started!" or "Listen to this" (a tune, rhythmic or melodic pattern, or a sound).

The students' extensive musical exploration was reflected in their playing sounds, repeating patterns, responding musically to what a peer had just played, responding verbally to what a peer had just played, imitating what a peer had just played, verbally directing attention to what a student was playing (either self or other), returning to the music room, and observing others. Most often, students offered verbal suggestions to focus on something that emerged from their explorations. The students' prompts elicited responses from the other group members, which in turn led to the shaping of their compositions. Each group decided on patterns, choosing from those created and presented by individual members. Some groups decided to use two or three patterns that they would play simultaneously, while others layered the entrances of the ostinati patterns, focusing on the pulse to ensure that they played together. Some groups decided to have two sets of patterns and placed them in an ABA form. The decision to include the various sets of patterns (or two different single patterns) was sometimes based on wanting to include multiple patterns that were not compatible when played together. One solution was to have some patterns comprise the "A" section and others comprise the "B" section.

As Laura or I visited each group, we asked the students to play what they had created thus far. Subsequently, the students and teachers provided each other with musical descriptions of and questions about the emerging compositions. Often the students' descriptions included specifics about the music that revealed their conceptual understanding of the music. These descriptions included naming the form, pitches, rhythms, and tonalities and addressing the perceived suitability of an instrument for a certain motive or phrase of music, the perceived appropriateness of a phrase of music within a certain section, and the sense of ending or beginning and whether or not either was adequate.

Often, students reminded their peers that they soon had to perform for the other class members and that it was best to begin practicing. Practice typically included one student showing another student how to play the various parts. As Laura and I traveled around to the different groups to announce that their group time was ending, the students collected their instruments and returned to the music room. After each performance for the class, the students applauded, and Laura posed these questions: (1) "Did they do the composition?" or "Did they finish the assignment?" (2) if they did, "What worked, what was good about it?" and (3) if they didn't, "What could they change in order to make it work?"

March through May: Five Boys Composing

It is March, and the students have experienced a variety of classes during which they learned about composing within teacher-directed parameters: ostinato patterns, theme and variations, music to enhance or represent (in this case, music for a commercial or a children's poem), a melody that "takes you on a trip," and ABA form. Now was the time for students to create a piece of music that they would perform in the final May concert. Specifically, this task included (1) exploring and making decisions about sounds that would be organized into a composition, (2) making decisions about how to preserve what had been created from session to session, and (3) practicing what had been created in preparation for the performance. The instructions were to "create a piece of music and write down anything, if needed, to remember what you composed from week to week."

Up to this point, the teacher had given the students specific assignments, but now they were asked simply to create a piece of music. The debate about who decides the constraints and freedoms for children's compositions has been included in many studies. A recent study that focused on fourth-graders' perceptions of their compositional processes and products found that "the students seemed to prefer compositional experiences that allowed more opportunities for choice and control" (Pohl, 2005, p. 138) and that "choice is an important element in composition tasks" (p. 140). What occurred in this setting were experiences of structured and less structured activities, each allowing for choices to be made by the students. This final activity prompted students to make decisions about their composition. In all, students were encouraged to explore, converge on solutions, and assess what was chosen musically. They were also required to assess peers' products and provide reasons for what worked and did not work compositionally.

The focus group for this and the sections that follow comprised five boys: Ted, Edward, Nate, Colin, and Cole. I observed them over eight sessions, with the shortest lasting nine minutes and thirty-seven seconds and the longest lasting fifty-three minutes.

The students entered the room and found their space on the classroom floor. Laura reminded them of the task that was before them for the next eight weeks: to create a piece of music that they, the composers, would perform in mid-May. Laura formed the students' groups for this task. The group of Ted, Edward, Nate, Colin, and Cole began to make their way to the instruments, so that they could choose what to carry back to their designated compositional space. Edward and Nate conversed, examining mallets and their compatibility with the chosen instruments. As they had experienced in previous classes, the students understood that their choice of instruments would need to be reevaluated as the piece of music took shape; thus trips back to the music room were expected and accepted. With instruments in hand, the five boys walked out of the music room and found their assigned space.

These boys were now in the same fifth-grade class; Edward and Nate had been in a split fourth/fifth-grade class during the previous year, which had experienced the composition curriculum. Edward and Nate had been or currently were taking private piano lessons. Ted, a recent immigrant from Asia, had minimal knowledge of English. Cole was African American, did not have private lessons, and came from an economic background that differed from Nate and Edward. There had been times when Cole lived with his family in a car. The lack of clean, properly fitting clothes and the presence of dirt under his fingernails indicated a possible struggle with the necessary domestic resources. In addition, Cole's level of verbal ability appeared to be less developed than Nate's, Edward, and Colin, particularly that of Nate and Edward. Cole displayed a strong desire to belong and participate and, for the most part, he had a positive attitude. Colin was of the same economic status as Nate and Edward, but did not receive private piano instruction. His desire to participate appeared to be less than the other boys, and it was often difficult to get him to cooperate and be a part of the group. It was clear from the interactions, or lack thereof, that Edward and Nate, and Edward and Colin, knew each other. At times, I perceived Ted and Cole to be the social outsiders in this group.

The first session was short, since much of the sixty-minute class involved Laura detailing the content of the next eight classes. The boys' space was across the hall from the music room in the custodians' room, a large room with desks, chairs, a refrigerator in the back half, and an open space in the front half. Ted chose the soprano xylophone (which he later traded for the glockenspiel), Cole the snare drum, Colin the bass xylophone, Nate the alto metallophone, and Edward the bass metallophone. Time was spent as each student found a space to set up his instrument. During this time Edward and Colin talked with each other, and Nate set up the alto metallophone. Ted arranged the bars on the soprano xylophone, and Cole played the drum. The final setup included Nate and Edward facing each other, with Ted in the corner and Colin behind Edward. Cole sat adjacent to Ted.

The experimentation on instruments began. While Cole continued playing the drum, Colin sang a melody familiar to Edward, who attempted to play it on his instrument. Nate also attempted to play that same melody. He imitated Edward's version of the melody and then created extensions of the melodic material. The focus of the remaining minutes included Edward showing Colin how to play the melody Colin sang, Nate attempting to get Edward's attention, Cole playing on his own on the drum, and Ted fixing the bars on the soprano xylophone and playing notes. Colin sang a tune to Edward, who then attempted to play it as Colin watched.

Nate attempted to play the melody, imitating Edward, and then extending it into something else.

Nate to Edward: Did you make that up?

Colin: No, that's [inaudible] song.

Cole: I like it better than . . .

Nate: Edward, Edward. [He played a melody.]

Nate: Edward, Edward.

Edward showed Colin how to play the melody on the bass xylophone. Nate played the melody and then showed Edward.

Nate: Edward, how do you play that? [Edward played as Nate watched.]

What eventually emerged were two melodic motives, the one sung by Colin and played by Edward, and the one created and played by Nate. Nate, who was accepted by and included in the group, interrupted the interactions between Colin and Edward. Ted and Cole, however, remained as individuals throughout the session, each playing on his chosen instrument. The only interaction between either of them and the trio was when Nate asked Cole to stop his insistent playing on the drum. Nate and Edward each played their melodies while Colin watched. Nate showed Edward the high and low G and stated, "That could be the A."

The first decision! Word came via Laura that class time was ending, so the boys picked up their instruments and walked back to the music room.

Sessions 2–5

The next five sessions involved the boys creating, practicing, teaching, learning, applying, arguing, discussing, including, excluding, and exchanging and changing instruments. Nate identified the beginning, "That could be the A." It had emerged from Nate's exploration of a melodic idea that caught the attention of Edward's ears, who asked for it to be played again. Edward imitated it by listening and then playing what Nate had played. Then Edward extended the melodic material. This interplay became the centerpiece of how the entire composition was created.

Edward played a melody and then Nate corrected and modeled how it was to be played. He played again and then extended the melody.

Nate: That could be our A, and we would have to repeat it twice. [Nate played the melody.]

Edward: Then we need a B.

Edward: I think A should be . . . [He played the melody, comprised of an 'a' and a 'b' section. Then Nate played the first part of the melody but with a different ending.]

Edward: I think it should fit . . . [He started to play the melody.]

Nate [after playing the melody]: How about that?

Edward: Yeah, sure.

Edward and Nate interrupted the compositional process by asking Cole to stop playing on the drum, bass metallophone, or bass xylophone, while they moved from instrument to instrument to explore playing their created melodies with different timbres. Often during this movement and after questions were posed within the group and by the teachers, the boys changed specific notes of the composition. The decision to write the material in notation occurred when Nate asked, "Do you want to write it down?" In response to Edward's "Sure," Nate went to get pencil and paper. Between Nate and Edward the melodic content was written with standard notation and the names of the notes above the notation, so those who could not read music could follow what they wrote. The process of notating the material, exploring, and practicing solidified the material. While some students worked individually, others played for and responded to each other.

Edward: What can that be?

Nate: Well—ABA.

Edward: The only problem is . . .

Nate: Wait.

[Edward plays another melodic motive.]

Nate: Actually—when that happens. . . [He begins to play.] I hear a different one. [He plays again.] That could be our B.

Nate: We can play A and then repeat it and then B.

Edward: We could transpose it [A] to G and fit it into a B.

Edward: Has anyone come up with a B yet?

Nate: We have a B. We need a C.

There were multiple instances of Edward and Nate attempting to include the other boys, with questions like "Do you have any ideas?" but in the end, the two were clearly the teachers of the other group members and the main contributors to the composition. Cole clearly wanted to be part of the group, as he would repeat what Nate and Edward had said. He repeated, "That is the A." There were clear moments of inclusions for Cole, specifically during times when Nate asked, "Do you like it?" Interestingly enough, when Cole made a comment and was ignored, he reverted back to playing loudly on his chosen instrument at the time (drum and bass xylophone). This, of course, elicited a repeated "Stop!" from Nate and Edward. Often Nate responded to Cole's interruptions by asking, "Do you like it?" or one of the two boys took on the role of teacher, teaching Cole the part, to which Cole responded immediately. In another instance, Cole announced, "I'm going to play something random" and did so; he then stated, "Maybe this could be our B. Maybe, I said maybe," and then continued to play. Nate began to imitate Cole, and Edward joined him.

Nate: What part of the song are we talking about?

Edward: Maybe we can fit it into the B.

A poignant interaction occurred when Edward reminded Cole that the "B" part came from Cole's exploration. Cole was particularly touched as he exclaimed, "Cool. So you made up a part, and I made up a part, and you made up a part." It was clear that inclusion was important to him and that he attempted to find ways to be included.

Interactions between Ted and the other boys were largely non-existent, except for those directly related to the compositional task. Nate and Edward taught him the material; Nate, Edward, and Cole asked him to stop playing when repetitive passages occurred that included and did not include material of the composition. On occasion Nate asked Ted, "Do you like it?" after playing a certain portion of the composition. Ted made no attempt to interact or contribute to the group process. One would suspect it was due to his unfamiliarity with English. Ted delighted in the sounds he created with *glissandi* and playing random notes on the glockenspiel; he was intense as he practiced the melodies of the A and B sections. For the most part, he responded to directions, but at times appeared to ignore the pleas of the boys when they attempted to get him to stop what he was doing so he could be part of the group practice sessions.

Colin missed the second session, and with his re-entrance into the third session came a different group dynamic. The emerging relationship between Cole, Nate, and Edward appeared to be threatened because of Colin's unwillingness to cooperate and to focus.

Edward: How can I teach you if . . .

Cole: Stop. Play the right notes.

[There were clear instances of tension and confusion.]

Edward: Give us eight beats.

Colin: What?

Edward: Give us eight beats.

Cole: No, bass bar, you play first.

[Eight beats were given; all attempted to play. Edward attempted to direct them.]

Cole: No, I don't want to.

[Edward played the "A" melody multiple times.]

Cole: I don't want to play with him [meaning Colin].

It is difficult to ascertain why Colin adopted the role of tension-provider. Colin had missed one session and, in spite of successful interactions with one member of the group during the first session, might have sensed a solidification of the group in his absence. My perception was that Colin might have sensed all of this and was attempting to reestablish his place in the group. Whatever the reason, it took the boys countless attempts to play together, in addition to direct intervention provided by Laura, who might not have known the level of tension when she entered the room. Her immediate inclusion of Colin, however, appeared to settle things: "Okay, bass bar [Colin] is setting a good beat so . . ."

Laura adopted the role of facilitator and teacher by describing, asking questions, and responding to what was offered by the group.

Cole: We all go together.

Laura: You know how to count it off.

Edward: 1, 2, 3, 4. 2, 2, 3, 4.

[All played the "A" part.]

Laura: Cool!

Edward: We aren't done yet.

Laura: Okay so that was the A so now go on to the B.

Edward: We don't all know the B.

Laura: Okay.

Edward: We have to write it down.

Laura: Okay, good. Write it down. Who created what?

Edward: Nate and I created the A.

Laura: Yes, but remember, this is a group composition so . . .

Often, Laura's contributions merely focused the group, and I wondered whether or not the students needed a teacher in the room full-time. Would that have kept the compositional process moving at a more efficient pace? Would the effectiveness of their compositions have improved? This is part of a larger question that often is asked in response to support for group work. The critical question might be, what is gained from time for interactions that consist of what one might call off-task behavior? It was in the playfulness between the boys that inclusion occurred, relationships were formed, and tensions were resolved. And it was the boys who most often resolved the tensions and brought each other on- (and off-) task. This space allowed the relationships to form, the roles to be adopted, and personalities to emerge.

Nate: We have to practice.

Edward and Cole: Okay. [Nonetheless, they continued to play with their mallets in a sword fight.]

Cole: Move.

Nate: No.

Cole: Move.

Nate: No!

Cole: Then I'm not going to play.

[Ted played, and the conversation continued.]

Edward: Okay, we have to practice.

All counted: 1, 2, 3, 4, 5, 6, 7, 8.

The boys had a task, and most of them realized the need to focus as exhibited by statements like, "We need to practice" and "We are on stage next week." One needs to weigh the benefits of composing in small groups in light of the interactions that result from students being given a space in which to make music through composition and performance. In the larger picture, the sense of ownership exhibited during the process of creating is critical, and that level of ownership occurs, in part, because of the student-led interactions.

Roles

Nate and Edward adopted the roles of the main creators, deciders, and teachers. Initially Cole was a learner, and unbeknownst to him until the fifth session, a creator. There was one insertion by Cole, in session two, about what could be included in the composition. In the middle of Nate's and Edward's conversation about the content of the A section and the inclusion of the B section, Cole stated, "Let's play some kind of ostinato." Nate and Edward ignored this comment and continued their discussion (through talking and playing), but Nate consistently attempted to include Cole by asking, "Do you like it?" In another instance, Cole responded to something Edward played:

Nate: That was kind of a cool idea. We could do this on stage. Edward, we could do that on stage.

Cole affirmed: Edward, we could do that on stage. Do you know why? They are all the same size [the bars on the bass xylophone and bass metallophone].

The idea was not implemented, but Cole's offering indicated his desire to be included and his courage to contribute to the content of the piece of music.

There were instances of Cole adopting the role of teacher, particularly when Colin was not on task. As a learner, Cole figured out the melody, assessing and fixing as he reconstructed it. He learned parts of the composition from Nate and Edward. Throughout, he was consistent with practicing, even when he felt frustrated (e.g., "I get it. This is hard. This sucks."), but he always felt the urgency to know the music and showed excitement when he was successful (e.g., "I did it. Watch me.").

Ted and Colin did not contribute as creators or teachers, but they were learners throughout the process. Colin appeared to have little interest in the process but contributed by playing when asked, often repeatedly, by his peers to stay on task and to play with them. His job was to introduce the steady pulse at the beginning and throughout the transitions of the piece, and in the end, he was joined by Cole at Laura's suggestion.

Ted's role throughout all of the sessions was that of a learner. Others either taught him the melodies, or he taught himself after listening to the other boys practice. Ted was persistent, and it appeared that he wanted to be accurate in his performance. It also seemed important to Nate, Edward, and Cole that Ted knew his part, as all of them, particularly Edward, spent time teaching him the A and B melodies. Any other material that Ted played consisted of random notes, *glissandos*, and sounds from parts of the Orff instruments that did not include using the bars. It was as if he were curious about sounds that could be created from the sides of the barred instruments or the wooden parts on their top sides.

May: The Performance

The students excitedly headed to the performance space. The dress rehearsal and concerts were ahead of them, and time was of the essence. The students were asked to decide on titles for their pieces. Snippets of conversations revealed descriptions of their pieces (e.g., "How about . . . ?" "Our piece reminds us of . . . "), until a decision was made and recorded (e.g., "So the title is 'Rain.'"). Each group had time on stage for a dress rehearsal that involved making decisions about set-up, a performance run-through, responses from group members and the teacher, and, if necessary, a second run-through. If needed, the group was sent to rehearse or make decisions about specific aspects of the composition, with either the in-residence graduate composition student or me in the group's presence. Every year, Laura hired a graduate composition student to work with the students during the final few sessions. The role of this student was to listen and respond to the composition group; during the student's first visit, he or she talked to the fifth-graders about his or her experiences as a composer.

During the set-up and after the initial run-through, the teacher asked questions and relayed directions (e.g., "How did you guys feel about it?" "Oh—that's a good idea. Why don't you try that?"), and students continued to practice and guide each other (e.g., Edward and Cole shadow-practiced as the teacher talked with the group; Edward began to practice, while Cole watched him and corrected a wrong note). Final rehearsals and decisions occurred and preparations concluded for the concert.

Concert night arrived; the concert hall was ready with chairs arranged for parents, grandparents, siblings, aunts and uncles, and friends. House lights were lowered, stage lights were raised, and the particular light requested for the first number was set. There was a buzz in the air as students expressed nervousness and excitement. And, typical of this music program, the performance was a success.

The group of five—Nate, Edward, Cole, Colin, and Ted—appeared on stage wearing a variety of clothing styles. Nate and Edward wore golf-type shirts with pants; Cole had on a clean white T-shirt with dress jeans; Ted wore the same jacket and pants that he had worn during the school day; Colin was the most casual, wearing a T-shirt and pants that resembled his daily school attire. Cole appeared nervous.

The group of five boys had called their composition, "Rain," with a total playing time of one minute and thirty-eight seconds. As they began, Cole looked to Nate and Edward to begin, while Nate and Edward looked at each other in an effort to coordinate their beginning. Ted and Colin appeared to glance in the direction of Nate and Edward, particularly Edward, since he sat on the end of the group's instrumental configuration and was easily visible by others in the group. The performance was "amazing," as I wrote in my field notes. The A section went as planned with a smooth transition into the B section that fitted nicely into the whole of the composition. The tempo increased slightly during the B section (not as planned), but they continued to play together. After the transition back to the A section, Cole and Colin settled back into the original tempo. Cole was intent, while Colin appeared to be more *laissez-faire*. At the end of the performance, the boys appeared to realize that they had succeeded in performing their composition. Smiles, applause, and bows. Bravo!

The fifth-grade students' responses on the post-concert survey, distributed during the subsequent music class, reflected their thoughts about the experiences, including decisions made; interventions by the teacher, the in-residence graduate composition student, and me; and the concert. They wrote about what they learned and enjoyed, and about what could be done differently and what was helpful. The following is a sample of the class members' responses to the question, "What did you learn about music that you didn't know before?":

"I learned so much. I learned how to fit a piece of music together. I am very proud of what I learned."

"I learned a lot including I could make music."

"I learned ostinatos, APA, theme and variations, and tons more."

"I learned a lot of people don't do squat but if you set them in line they're like having two of you."

"I did a very good job."

"That new people produce different music."

"I learned that working in groups helped us go quicker and makes music sound better than I thought. I didn't think we could do that."

These words were a synthesis of the October through May composition experience. The students valued the opportunity to compose and perform their own works, work with new friends, and have time to explore. They understood the importance of asking questions in response to what they had created; the questions guided their decision-making and helped them find areas that needed work. And, finally, they appreciated the guidance of Laura, the graduate composition student, and me, which contributed to the quality of the composition and cohesiveness of the performance.

FINAL CONSIDERATIONS

The Nature of Action and Interaction between the Five Boys

The actions of and interactions among the students were fluid. Some changed and others remained constant. Insights into the students' decision-making came from their exchanges, questions, and decisions. Information about what the students valued from a musical perspective for their composition was gained by examining the boys' words, actions, and interactions (Burnard & Younker, 2002; Dillon, 2004; Morgan, Hargreaves, & Joiner, 2000; Seddon & O'Neill, 2001; Wiggins, 2001). Questions raised by Hickey (2003) and Reese (2003) in terms of how music teachers might respond to students' original compositions and what roles we should adopt continue to be asked. Specifically, is our role in helping students shape their interactions, or is there such a role? How could teacher interventions expedite positive interactions between Colin and the other boys, particularly when he was not cooperating? What might be done to include Ted in the decision-making processes when his focus was on practicing what he was taught? Should we be concerned about ensuring the same level of interaction and participation among the students in the group or step back and allow for the student to take the necessary time to feel ready for those interactions? It is clear that the boys needed time to negotiate their roles and levels of inclusion, and that over time, trust developed. If we had intervened, then perhaps the needed trust to work cohesively and safely would be thwarted.

The Role of Critical Thinking

What was the role of critical thinking in the students' experiences? Were they taught to think critically? Was it modeled and facilitated? We need to examine the assumption of roles adopted by the stakeholders in the learning environment and identify who does the thinking, learning, and teaching. To re-visit Dewey (1938) and Bruner (1996), we need to place learner and thinker on a continuum and view them through the lens of what it means to be a thinker (Lipman, 2003). What are the possible constructions of understanding and thinking through composition? What is the role of thinking critically in and about music and how is it facilitated? Perhaps rather than teach, the approach to music composition in our classrooms should be to set up an environment in which students are given the freedom to explore and experiment—an environment that creates *a need to know* how sounds can be organized, how they can be layered into multiple colors and textures, and how sounds just sound. Then, the role of the teacher is to move between teaching, facilitating, coaching, and learning (Reese, 2003). If the teacher shifts between these roles, the students will shift as well, and be required to negotiate problems, generate solutions, converge, and integrate the best solution for that moment. In essence their role and the teacher's role would alternate between learner and teacher, thus creating a community of learners (Bruner, 1996; Dewey, 1938).

The spaces afforded to the students in this situation allowed them to argue, negotiate, and mediate as decisions were made, which are all processes of thinking critically (Dewey, 1933/1991). It takes time for students to make musical decisions, whether as individuals or in groups, and while it may have appeared that students were sometimes off-task and wasting time, my observations and interactions with them revealed that time spent talking about things other than the music, or what appeared to be goofing off, was part of the process. I noted that much of the off-task interaction was crucial for the group cohesion and the students' ability to think collectively about choices made.

Students' survey responses reported that the teacher's and my role ranged from being helpful to being intrusive. Interestingly enough, students understand when they need our interjections and guided questions and when they do not. Perhaps a question like, "Do you need any help?" should suffice, before we talk and make assumptions about what they *need* to know.

As Reese (2003) reminded us, we should describe what we heard, ask them what they want an audience to hear, offer suggestions, and justify our input.

Inferences about the Boys' Understanding of Music

The boys reflected their musical understanding in interwoven threads of musical, verbal, and physical gestures (Macdonald & Miell, 2000a, 2000b; Wiggins, 2003). Some of the students' interactions began verbally and concluded with a musical phrase played on an instrument or sung. They gave descriptions about the music that, at times, were completed with musical gestures. A few questions linger in my mind: Does rehearsing, describing, debating, and performing reflect what they know about music, or must they be able to identify and describe with words in order to reveal what they know? Do we need to be explicit about assessing what students know through their actions and spoken and written words? Does knowing that a student's contribution was permanently incorporated into the composition provide him or her with a sense of personal investment in that product? Does that investment provide a student with a sense of meaning? Does it matter what is meaningful, or should we just "let it be"?

Involving students in musical experiences that provide choices, require decision-making processes, and strengthen the group and individuals are some of the strongest educational experiences that music teachers can provide. Allowing for less limits students' potential for meaningful experiences that matter. Involving students in communities of music-making and providing spaces for shifting roles can be empowering, a constant I have observed when students compose. The other constant is the ever-emerging questions that require me to continue my interactions with and observations of students' compositional journeys.

REFERENCES

Bruner, J. (1996). *The culture of education.* Cambridge, MA: Harvard University Press.

Burnard, P., & Younker, B. A. (2002). Mapping pathways: Fostering creativity in composition. *Music Education Research, 4*(2), 245–261.

Dewey, J. (1933/1991). *How we think.* Buffalo, NY: Prometheus Books.

Dewey, J. (1938). *Experience and education.* New York: Collier Books, Macmillan.

Dillon, T. (2004, April). *The role of new technologies and the influence of prior musical training and experience in young musicians' collaborations.* Paper presented at the Musical Collaboration Conference (SEMPRE), Keele, U.K.

Franca, C. C., & Swanwick, K. (1999). Composing, performing and audience-listening as indicators of musical understanding. *British Journal of Music Education, 16*(1), 5–19.

Hickey, M. (Ed.). (2003). *Composition in the schools: A new horizon for music education.* Reston, VA: MENC.

Lipman, M. (2003). *Thinking in education.* New York: Cambridge University Press.

Macdonald, R., & Miel, D. (2000a). Creativity and music education: The impact of social variables. *International Journal of Music Education, 36*(1), 58–68.

Macdonald, R., & Miel, D. (2000b). Musical conversations: Collaborating with a friend on creative tasks. In R. Joiner, K. Littleton, D. Faulkner, & D. Miell (Eds.), *Rethinking collaborative learning* (pp. 65–78). London: Free Association Books.

Morgan, L., Hargreaves, D., & Joiner, R. (2000). Children's collaborative music composition: Communication through music. In R. Joiner, K. Littleton, D. Faulkner, & D. Miell (Eds.), *Rethinking collaborative learning* (pp. 52–64). London: Free Association Books.

Pohl, A. (2005). *A comparison of fourth grade student perceptions of their compositional process and product for two different tasks.* Unpublished master's thesis, University of St. Thomas, Minnesota.

Reese, S. (2003). Responding to students' compositions. In M. Hickey (Ed.), *Music composition in the schools: A new horizon for music education* (pp. 211–232.). Reston, VA: MENC.

Seddon, F., & O'Neill, S. (2001). An evaluation study of computer-based compositions by children with and without prior experience of formal instrumental music tuition. *Psychology of Music, 29*(1), 4–19.

Wiggins, J. H. (2001). *Teaching for musical understanding.* New York: McGraw-Hill.

Wiggins, J. H. (2003). A frame for understanding children's compositional processes. In M. Hickey (Ed.), *Music composition in the schools: A new horizon for music education* (pp. 141–165). Reston, VA: MENC.

Younker, B. A. (2005). Fifth-graders' constructive musical understanding through composition: Reflections from a university- and school-based music educator. Paper presented at the biennial General Music Education Colloquium, Mountain Lake, VA.

Younker, B. A., & Burnard, P. (2004, August). The notion of collaboration in group composition: An analysis within and across young composers aged 10–12 years. In R. Ashley (Chair of SMPC), *Musical collaboration.* Symposium conducted at the International Conference on Music Perception and Cognition (ICMPC), Evanston, IL.

III

ADOLESCENCE

9

Strings Attached: The Reality Show

Margaret H. Berg

This chapter is an intrinsic case study (Stake, 1995) of the Thunder Ridge Middle School seventh-grade orchestra's first concert of the year, *Strings Attached: The Reality Show*. Although this narrative will only focus on the seventh-grade concert, this concert is held annually in the middle of October for grades six through eight. While the teacher predetermines the pieces, the order in which they are performed is determined by lottery. Other key aspects of the concert include three activities: students writing scripts read before the performance of each piece that explain features of and/or techniques needed to perform it; after-school set-up of the performance space by students; audience participation in some performance-related activities; and a volunteer beginner-parent demonstration following basic instruction by a student. The band room, where the concert is held, is a more intimate performance space than an auditorium, and the concert atmosphere is described by the orchestra teacher as "cozy" with a feeling of "controlled chaos."

Members of the seventh-grade orchestra represent a wide range of academic and musical backgrounds. Some students are quite advanced, having learned to play their instruments in an extracurricular Suzuki program. Others have played for only a year, with no private instruction. Still other orchestra members are new to the school and began playing their instrument at the beginning of the school year. The twenty-six-member orchestra also represents a diverse cultural spectrum.

Thunder Ridge Middle School is one of eight middle schools in the Cherry Creek School District of Denver, Colorado. While some schools are recognized as being the best in Colorado, schools that serve highly transient and diverse populations are not. The thirteen hundred students at Thunder

165

Ridge Middle School closely represent the district average for ethnic diversity, with approximately 10 percent of the school population being African American, Asian American, or Hispanic American, 70 percent Caucasian and 0.5 percent Native American. Approximately 13 percent of the students at the school qualify for free and reduced-price meals, which is slightly below the district average of 19 percent. Thunder Ridge Middle School, situated in the middle-class southern Denver suburb of Centennial, opened in 1991.

Ellen Ravnan has been the orchestra teacher at Thunder Ridge Middle School since the school opened. Her energetic approach to teaching, coupled with her attention to developing strong technical skills and musicianship in her students, often results in her being asked to adjudicate, give clinic presentations, and serve as a festival conductor throughout the state. Ms. Ravnan has given several clinic presentations at Colorado ASTA (American String Teachers Association) conferences. She devotes many hours to her teaching each week, and spends the majority of her time outside school as principal violist in the Arapahoe Philharmonic and performing at freelance jobs.

This chapter begins with vignettes of two pre-concert activities: writing a script to be read prior to the performance of a concert piece and setting up the performance space. Next, a lengthier narrative tells the story of the *Strings Attached* concert. The narratives were created based on field notes; informal interviews with the teacher and students were conducted to provide information on the program and participant backgrounds, and were used to verify the narratives. Field notes were coded using low-inference descriptors (LeCompte & Schensul, 1999) in order to help the author maintain a close connection between observed events and codes and to facilitate the writing of normative vignettes or "realist tales" (Van Maanen, 1988) and a theme-based analysis of narratives (Polkinghorne, 1995) of the concert and related events. The last part of the chapter contains discussion of key aspects of this concert with reference to salient sources.

WRITING A SCRIPT FOR *TRUMPET VOLUNTARY*

Amy, Jennifer, and Latisha come dashing into the orchestra room after school, as the dismissal bell rings.

"Do you guys have the blue paper of what we are supposed to talk about?" asks Latisha in reference to the table created by Ms. Ravnan of concert pieces and key concepts and/or skills the group should talk about in the script they create.

The girls look at the blue piece of paper and see that Ms. Ravnan had suggested they talk about hooked bowing and its challenges. Ms. Ravnan also suggested they "include some demonstration" as part of their script.

Amy begins the discussion about the script and offers to record their key ideas. "Alright . . . hooked bowing is when you . . ."

"Hook the bows, duh!" responds Latisha. "Anyway, guys, how else do we say something is hooked?"

"We can just play bar four together, right?" suggests Jennifer.

"Oh, and say that the two notes that are hooked are both going down bow, okay?" adds Amy.

The three girls nod their heads in agreement.

"Maybe we should look at a dictionary or something, just to find a different word to explain 'hooked,'" says Amy.

Latisha asks, "Ms. R., do you have a dictionary? I mean, what's another word for 'hooked' we could use in our script?"

Ms. Ravnan stands up from her desk and walks over to the group. "I have a dictionary of bowings. Do you want to look at that?"

Amy takes the dictionary, looks up the term "hooked bowing," and reads it out loud. The three girls then agree to add "going in the same direction" and "a space between the two hooked notes" to their script.

Amy then reads what they have written. "Okay, so we start with all playing bar four, then one of us explains that hooked bowing is when two notes in a row are down bow—I mean, go in the same direction—and there's a space between the two notes. How does that sound?"

Latisha and Jennifer nod their heads up and down, suggesting approval of what the group has written.

"Let's try it from the start!" says Latisha.

Amy counts off four beats, then the three girls play the first two beats of bar four in *Trumpet Voluntary* before laughing.

"Man, I was off!" says Latisha.

"You have to count it in your head, Tisha!" says Jennifer.

"Alright, alright calm down!" says Latisha.

"What if we start with the bar before, so we can get into it a little?" suggests Amy.

"Yeah, *that's* my problem!" says Latisha.

The three girls play again, beginning in measure three with Amy counting off for the group. Their performance of measure four, although not exactly in rhythmic unison, was much improved from their first attempt.

"Who's gonna talk to the audience about the definition?" asks Amy.

"You do it—you're the smart one," says Latisha.

Amy then recites the agreed-upon definition for hooked bowing.

"What are the challenges of hooked bowing?" asks Jennifer. "Ms. R. wants us to talk about that too."

The three girls look at each other for a few seconds, seeming at a loss for how to explain the challenges of a bowing they are able to play without much additional concentration.

"What about something like: when we first learned it, it was hard because we were used to doing everything down then up?" suggests Latisha.

"Okay, that's good," says Amy, as she writes down Latisha's comment.

From the back of the room Ms. Ravnan lifts her eyebrows and looks at me as if to say, "That's interesting; not exactly the depth of thinking I was looking for," then smiles.

"We got it! With time to spare. Let's go over it one time for Ms. R.," says Latisha. She continues, "Oh, Ms. R., we need you . . . Can you come here for a minute to see our *fabulous* talking about *Trumpet Voluntary*?"

The three girls smile, as if they realize with Latisha's comment, that their script is not only completed, but something of which they are proud.

THE GREAT EQUALIZER: SET-UP CREW

Ms. Ravnan enters the room and reviews the schedule with the students who have volunteered, with parental permission, to stay after school and set up for the concert this evening.

"Okay, folks. I expect you to work *quietly* on homework for the next hour. Then we'll do chair set-up and lottery and program set-up for about another hour. After that, we'll eat pizza and breadsticks, then quickly get dressed for the concert. The set-up time will go quickly, so make sure you've read the directions sheet first, *then* ask me any questions about what to do. It's up to you guys to get the band room set up right, with the right number of chairs and seat treats and lottery tickets in the envelopes taped underneath audience member chairs. Those of you who helped with this in sixth grade, you can help the ones that are doing this for the first time. Okay. Quietly take out your homework, grab a chair or spot on the floor, *then* come to the table by the cello lockers to get a snack."

The ten set-up crew members grab a music stand and chair or stake out a space on the floor as they pull materials from their backpacks.

"Ting, you're with me; we're setting up chairs," says Nick.

After fifty minutes, Ms. Ravnan asks the students to read the directions and then decide which group to join—chair set-up, stuffing envelopes with lottery cards and seat treats, or taping envelopes to chairs in the band room.

Jaymin, Alex, and Jin quickly approach Nick to volunteer to also help with chair set-up. Kenia and Skylar—stand partners in the second violin section—decide to help cut pre-printed strips of paper, one for each audience member's chair. The strips of paper read, "Thank you for coming to our orchestra concert tonight. Unfortunately this is not a winning card" or "Thank you for coming to our orchestra concert tonight. Congratulations! You are winner #_____" (a number from 1 to 12, with one number for each piece to be performed at the concert). Raven and Sebastian put seat treats in envelopes along with the paper strips and fold concert programs.

The students begin to work. The group in the band room cleans the space and brings in chairs, bass stools, and the piano from the orchestra room. Kenia and Skylar sit in the orchestra room cutting the lottery ticket strips; they also cut piece title paper strips and place them in a basket. Raven and Sebastian also sit in the orchestra room and stuff envelopes with the paper strips and a lifesaver, as well as fold programs. After an hour has passed, the students still need to tape the envelopes to the bottom of the audience chairs and put the concert programs next to the band room door on a music stand. Ms. Ravnan enters the band room and tosses a roll of masking tape to Nick.

"Nick, can you and some of the others help Raven and Sebastian (Seb) put a loop of tape under the seat of each chair? Then they can stick the envelopes onto the tape. We've only got about fifteen minutes until the pizza guy comes, so work together," says Ms. Ravnan.

The band room students pass the roll of tape to each other, tearing a long piece off, then making a loop and sticking it under the seat of each audience member's chair. Raven and Seb enter the band room and discuss which chairs to tape the twelve winning ticket envelopes to, then tape these envelopes to the selected chairs; the non-winning ticket envelopes are taped under the remaining chairs.

Kenia enters the band room with a music stand and the concert programs tucked under his arm. He places the music stand outside the band room door with the programs in an orderly pile on the stand.

After ten minutes have passed, Ms. Ravnan gathers all the students in the band room. She asks them to double-check the chair set-up so they are sure they have the correct number of chairs for the performers and audience members.

"Good job, guys!" exclaims Ms. Ravnan. "I hope you all sign up for set-up crew next year in eighth grade, because you are all pros! Let's go eat some pizza and get dressed."

The students and Ms. Ravnan leave the band room, with the students elbowing each other. Raven and Seb give each other a high-five, with Seb saying, "Way to go, amigo!"

IT'S SHOW TIME!

Parents, grandparents, and siblings of seventh-grade orchestra members take programs and then sit in the audience. The chairs are quickly filled and some siblings need to sit on a parent's lap. Audience members can be heard speaking various languages, including Japanese, Chinese, Spanish, Korean, and English, reflective of the various ethnic groups represented. It seems that the parents of some students alternate between speaking English and their native language, while others converse with family members using only their native language. While some parents appear to be in their early forties, others seem to be barely thirty years old.

The orchestra members sit in two rows with a music stand placed between every two chairs. Some students look at the concert program, while others whisper quietly to their neighbor. The atmosphere might be described as intimate, since the audience is seated near the performers. Due to the smaller-sized room and nearly eighty people present, there is a constant, although not excessive, hum from audience chattering. According to the orchestra director, the performance space, set-up, and concert format all contribute to the atmosphere of controlled chaos.

At seven p.m., Corina walks to the middle of the front row of performers. She welcomes the audience and explains the nature of the concert:

Welcome to Thunder Ridge Middle School's seventh-grade *Strings Attached: The Reality Show* concert. For those of you who were here last year, you know you are in for some fun! For those of you who weren't—don't worry. We won't be eating bugs or figuring out how to make a house like they do on those TV reality shows!

Aide continues introducing the concert to the audience. "You may have noticed in the program that the concert order will be determined by a lottery. All of you—moms, dads, grandmas, even little brothers—will help with the lottery. In a minute . . . but not yet . . . we will ask you to reach under your chair and remove the envelope. Some envelopes have winning cards and others don't. But don't worry; everyone gets a lifesaver seat treat. Okay. Are you ready to get your envelope? Okay, go!"

The audience members reach under their chairs and remove envelopes taped to the chairs by the set-up crew. The noise level is noticeably higher, and some surprised parents can be heard exclaiming, "I got one!" upon finding a winning ticket. This noise level contributes to the feeling of chaos, not typically an aspect of a traditional concert format.

Courtney conducts the concert order lottery. At the same time, Sarah, Cat, and LaQuisha walk to the dry-erase board near the back of the room to write down the concert order. The lottery begins.

"Okay, everyone," says Courtney. "Look at the ticket in your envelope. If your ticket reads 'Thank you for coming to our orchestra concert tonight. Congratulations! You are winner #1,' please come stand next to me."

A father in the first row stands up, pumps his right fist in the air, then walks toward Courtney. "Please read the piece of paper, Mr. . . . . Whose dad are you?" says Courtney. The father turns toward the orchestra, points to Nick, one of the bassists, and whispers his last name to Courtney.

The lottery continues until a list of twelve pieces is written on the dry-erase board. Laquisha then writes "Boogie Man Blues" and "Closing Remarks" below the last piece selected in the lottery, since Ms. Ravnan wanted to make sure that the orchestra ended the concert with one of the most well-liked pieces and a student thanked the parents for coming and reminded them about future orchestra concerts.

The concert begins. Ms. Ravnan describes the concert as a "kitchen fridge approach, since we play what we've got reasonably ready to play by the week before the concert." The repertoire is a mix of short method-book melodies from well-known orchestra pieces like "Ode to Joy" and "Carmen," a collection of three short folk songs, a popular movie melody, a grade-two orchestra piece that the group will play on their Winter concert, scales, short solos played by some of the students who take private lessons, and a beginner-parent demonstration. Each piece is preceded by one or more students reading a script they wrote that describes the piece, specific skills needed to play the piece, its difficulty level, and how the piece compares with other pieces being performed.

The concert begins with the performance of "William Tell," followed by the beginner-parent demonstration. The beginner-parents' demonstration is treated as the highlight of the concert. For ten minutes preceding the beginner demonstration, a parent and his or her child, a beginning student, go to the hallway, where additional instruments have been set up for parent use. The orchestra student is referred to as the "student teacher." In some cases, like this evening, a parent is unable to attend the concert due to his or her work schedule or is unwilling to perform. Prior to the concert, Ms. Ravnan solicited Jennifer's mother to serve as a parent volunteer substitute for Lady's mother, who had to work.

During the ten-minute session, the student teacher shows the parent how to stand, hold the instrument and bow, and play the open string part to "Skip to My Lou." Some student teachers use a guide written by Ms. Ravnan that contains key questions ("How do they hold their instrument?"), suggestions ("Jaw in chinrest), and notated and non-notated musical parts for the piece. Prior to the concert, Ms. Ravnan had told the students that their parents' instrument and bow holds would not be perfect. Yet, some of the student teachers make suggestions to their parents, reminding them to "keep your violin parallel to the ground" or "make sure your bow is halfway between the bridge and fingerboard" during the beginner demonstration performance.

As the parent volunteers prepare to leave the band room, the noise level increases from some audience members asking each other about the next concert event. I overhear a young elementary-aged boy, sitting on his mother's lap, ask, "Why are those people leaving? Is it (the concert) over?"

After the student teachers and parent volunteers leave the band room, three boys—Chase, Denzel, and Nick—stand up and demonstrate correct body position and instrument and bow hold for the violin, cello, and bass. The boys use key phrases taught to them by Ms. Ravnan (e.g., "nose, string, elbow, foot") in their demonstrations. Nick ends the demonstration with a humorous challenge for the audience: "Now, audience, your job is to see if our new parent beginners are keeping their nose, string, elbow, and foot in the right place. If one of them doesn't, raise your hand, and I'll throw you a snake! The person who raises their hand first gets a snake. Hopefully we won't need too many snakes!"

Some parents laugh; others lean over to ask another adult about why Nick would throw a snake. Mr. Janus, a popular life science teacher at Thunder Ridge, is known to keep several live and stuffed snakes in his classroom. Periodically, Mr. Janus throws stuffed snakes at students who appear to be daydreaming.

The audience and other performers talk quietly while waiting in the band room for the return of the student teachers and beginner-parents. Three minutes later, the group walks into the band room, as the performers and audience clap and cheer loudly. The seated performers view the accompaniment part to "Skip to My Lou," while the beginner-parents and student teachers stand in front of the orchestra. The student teachers help the parents get their instruments and bows in proper playing position. Some student teachers whisper into their parents' ears before playing, perhaps reminding them about their position or the number of times to play each note. Nick introduces the piece to the audience.

"And now for the highlight of the evening, our beginner demonstration of 'Skip to My Lou.'"

He looks at the audience and winks while pretending to hold a violin with proper position.

After a pause, one parent raises her hand, followed quickly by three other parents and one sibling. Nick throws a stuffed snake to the parent who raised her hand first. At about the same time, he throws the snake, the student teacher of the parent whose elbow had begun to move toward the left whispers into her mother's ear. The mother quickly fixes the position of her elbow.

Nick encourages the audience to clap at the conclusion of the piece. Some adults and children give the performers a standing ovation, a gesture of extra support for the performers. While some parents seem hesitant to look at the audience, one father takes a large bow while two mothers give their student teachers a high-five.

Ms. Ravnan comes to the front of the performance space and signals to the students to be quiet. The speakers for the next piece, "Carmen," come to the front of the performance space to briefly describe the meaning of the piece and how it differs from "Boogie Man," the final piece on the concert.

The concert continues with the orchestra performing "Anasazi", a grade-two orchestra piece that the group will perform again on the winter concert. After playing six measures, Ms. Ravnan stops the orchestra and turns to the audience.

"Sometimes, we don't begin together or some of us are thinking of playing a piece at the same tempo or speed as the piece we just played. Let's just try that again!"

Ms. Ravnan signals to the orchestra to pay attention, and the orchestra begins again. The ensemble is much more together, although it seems that not all students are confident of the notes or bowings in the piece.

Next, the orchestra performs three scales, followed by three folk songs—"Mozart Melody" (more commonly known as "Twinkle, Twinkle Little Star"), "French Folk Song," and "Lightly Row." These pieces are played by six students new to orchestra this year and their second-year stand partner performance buddies who play a harmony part on the repeat of each folk song. The speakers for the folk songs address what they learned from each piece and which piece was easiest and hardest to learn. Following the performance, the second-year stand partners and audience clap for the beginners in a clear demonstration of support.

The second half of the concert includes two piano and two cello solos interspersed with the remaining full group pieces. Two students, Jordan (a first-year orchestra student) and Zach, serve as speakers for the soloists, sharing information about the composer and title of the piece as well as the name of the performer's private teacher and how long the performer has been taking private lessons.

At approximately eight p.m., the students come to the last piece written on the dry-erase board, "Boogie Man Blues." Jennifer reads the prepared script for the piece. First, she introduces the soloist for the piece and then talks about "swinging the eighth-notes." Finally, she talks about why the orchestra likes this piece.

The students perform the piece with obvious enthusiasm for this style of music, swaying as they play the eighth notes. When the piece is finished, the audience cheers loudly as orchestra members stand up and bow. LaQuisha comes to the front of the room for the closing remarks, thanking the audience for attending and reminding them to see the back of their programs for future concert dates.

As Ms. Ravnan exits the band room, she sees Sebastian's father, a beginner-parent demonstration parent volunteer, waiting for his son in the hallway. Ms. Ravnan approaches him and asks him what he thought about learning to play "Skip to My Lou."

"I don't know, Ms. Ravnan, how they do it!" says Sebastian's father. "I mean, it's a lot to think about, keeping my hands in the right shape, the instrument up, and holding the bow right! Sebastian sure looks better than I do holding the violin."

"You had a good teacher there. . . . It can take a little while to get comfortable holding the violin," says Ms. Ravnan, as she smiles.

Sebastian then smiles back at Ms. Ravnan. "Yeah, it's harder than it looks—at least at first!" he says to Ms. Ravnan and his father.

Just then, Daniel's father approaches Ms. Ravnan.

"Thank you for giving him the chance to play a solo. I think it was good for him to play the Bach ["Prelude" from *Cello Suite no. 1*] for an audience," he comments.

"Yes, it's always good to get the chance to play, and it can be motivating for the other kids and parents. . . . Maybe some of the other cellos will want to take private lessons now after hearing Daniel play!" comments Ms. Ravnan.

At that moment, Daniel appears, and Ms. Ravnan compliments him on his performance.

"Great job, Daniel! What do you think about how it went?"

"Okay, I guess! I think I started it a little slow, but everyone seemed to like it anyway!"

Ms. Ravnan and Daniel's father nod their heads in agreement with Daniel's second comment.

Just then, two male students quickly walk by me, with one student humming the melody of the final concert selection, "Boogie Man Blues." The other student joins in. As indicated by their enthusiasm, it seems both students enjoyed playing this piece as well as participating in the concert.

As I walk to my car, I begin thinking about former students of mine from the years I was a public school orchestra teacher. I am reminded of Shawn, who like Nick, was a student with a passion for dirt-bike racing and a keen sense of humor. I also think about Randy, whose mother, like Lady's mother, was the sole breadwinner for the family and would have been one of the parents who could not attend the concert due to her nighttime job. Lisa, Randy's mother, wanted her son to be involved in orchestra because "he likes violin and it will keep him out of trouble." I wonder if these students, given their personalities and/or financial challenges, continued to play in orchestra after I left the school district to begin work on a doctoral degree. I also wonder if their school orchestra experiences contributed to long-term adult musical involvement, whether it be through performance activities—playing in a community orchestra or chamber ensemble—or attending professional orchestra concerts.

Then I remember Alexandra. A first-born child with strong perfectionist tendencies, Alexandra left the stage in tears after having a small memory slip during our annual solo recital. My mind then shifts to thinking about some of the other young beginners I taught, dressed in their finest church clothes sitting on a parent's lap as they listened to an older student play a movement of a concerto near the end of the hour-long solo recital.

I am concerned when I think about how all of these students most likely had gifts that I could have recognized had they had the opportunity to participate in a *Strings Attached* concert. I also think about the stress, much of it coming from self, on a student like Alex who might have thrived as a performance buddy for a beginner and might have chosen to *not* play a solo, if she had had the choice. Finally, I think about the message that was subtly sent to students at the annual solo recital about student skill in relation to when they performed on the program—beginning, middle, or end.

And then I realize that, based on my experiences as a performer and teacher, I wish to share the alternative *Strings Attached* concert model with practicing and pre-service teachers and encourage them to consider the opportunities this model provides. It challenges the messages conveyed using a traditional orchestra concert format, places value on individual students' strengths, and builds group cohesion.

DISCUSSION

Ms. Ravnan perceives orchestra teachers, generally, to be fairly conservative with respect to implementing alternative concert formats, since "they don't know there *is* another way (to present a concert)." On the other hand, she is a model of a teacher who questions the status quo and creates a new vision of a school orchestra program through alternative concert formats, since "no individual is bound to accept unquestioningly the way [reality] is constructed. Musicking, being exploration as well as affirmation and celebration, is one way in which the question [of who we are] can be asked" (Small, 1998, p. 134).

The *Strings Attached* model is based on several features that distinguish it both from a traditional concert format as well as from the informance model that is being used more frequently by instrumental teachers (Burton, 2004) for the first concert of the year. These features include having the flow or concert order being determined by the lottery drawing at the start of the concert and creating a plan that allows for the unexpected as it happens among students, parents, and audience. The atmosphere of controlled chaos and the close proximity of audience and performers contribute to the uniqueness of this concert.

We might consider the impact of this alternative concert format on the students and teacher. Although the lottery-determined concert order provides for a different and unpredictable concert format, it also subtly promotes equality rather than hierarchical ranking and relationships among orchestra students. For instance, beginners and advanced students perform the same number of pieces. Also, advanced students may perform at any time during the concert rather than near the end of the concert, as is typical in a traditional concert or solo recital program. At the same time, advanced players are recognized through solo performances and/or playing more challenging parts on some pieces. However, their skills also contribute to the *ensemble* by encouraging others to take private lessons and embellishing the orchestra's performance with additional harmonic material.

The *Strings Attached* concert model also provides opportunities for expanded student self-definitions through participation as scriptwriters, speakers, blackboard scribes, teachers, peer performance buddies, and set-up crew members. During more traditional orchestra concerts, individual performance-related skills are apparent and sometimes highlighted. This focus often results in the creation of dichotomous self-definitions of musician or non-musician, particularly if these performance experiences are negative (Abril, 2007; Lamont, 2002). Conversely, the *Strings Attached* model offers an opportunity for other skills to be recognized and utilized, thus enabling students to broaden their definition of who they are in relation to other orchestra members. It is possible that orchestra program retention is aided by the opportunities this concert format provides individuals for using a variety of skills as well as creating self-definition that encompasses their unique interests and abilities.

Some of the repertoire performed and the specific skills needed to perform pieces serve as the teacher's informal assessment of the students' work. Atypical repertoire performed during this concert includes scales and an orchestra piece that is still being learned. Some repertoire requires technical skill development like shifting and vibrato. Ms. Ravnan likens these features of the concert as "teaching to the test" since "I have to teach the students the skills I want them to practice rather than giving up on or not getting around teaching them." Ms. Ravnan draws a connection between her role, students' approach to practice, and the repertoire performed at the concert:

> Since a majority of the kids don't take private lessons, I am a teacher and not just an orchestra conductor. Also, I can understand that these kids can't see ahead to May or high school when they'll need these skills. They will take seriously and practice what's going to be on the concert . . . so I have scales, shifting, and vibrato on the concert.

While Ms. Ravnan believes this concert has many benefits, she also recognizes the challenges associated with the format and content of this concert. Ms. Ravnan describes her background and current musical endeavors as performance-oriented. Therefore, she notes that "I feel some tension" when the orchestra has to stop playing and begin a less-polished piece again. She also notes, "You have to keep the faith in students to follow through on tasks and to write not only entertaining but informative scripts for this concert."

Who Gets Attached?

The first words in the title of the concert—*Strings Attached*—encourage us to explore how this concert results in multiple attachments being formed between students and other students; parents and students, and by extension parents and the orchestra program; teacher and students; and students and the teacher. This concert provides several opportunities for students to build relationships both between students from intact social groups that exist outside of orchestra as well as between students with varied musical, academic, racial, and socioeconomic backgrounds. By writing a script, sharing speaking or blackboard scribe responsibilities, working together on the set-up crew, and functioning as performance buddies, relationships are formed or strengthened between students who might not have the same opportunity during rehearsals or a more traditional orchestra concert.

In fact, these aforementioned activities serve an equalizing function since students with less musical skill, as is the case with Nick, can assume a leadership role. Sometimes, relationships are formed between a more experienced or confident student and less confident or shy student. Since the *Strings Attached* concert occurs near the beginning of the school year in October, it helps to establish group cohesion and friendships, thus contributing to the integration of society (Merriam, 1964), while providing another subculture in which the adolescents can participate (Adderley, Kennedy, & Berz, 2003; Morrison, 2001).

Sloboda (2005) suggested music can be a "ready source of conflict between people" (p. 329), as is the case with the hierarchical configuration of concert order and repertoire performed at traditional orchestra concerts, chair seating, family musical background, and availability of resources to take private lessons. However, in the case of the *Strings Attached* concert, these differences between students are mitigated, thus fostering group membership and cohesion.

Because of their hands-on performance experience, parents might extend support for their child's musical growth and thereby contribute to the quality of the orchestra program by paying for private lessons. However, for those parents who do not wish to participate in the beginner demonstration, a barrier might still exist, since the parent chooses not to take a risk by performing in front of a group. Perhaps this parent had negative experiences as a student or perceives of orchestra concerts as opportunities for only those with talent who represent a privileged form of musicking (Small, 1998, p. 134) to perform.

The *Strings Attached* concert also fosters attachment between the teacher and students. Ms. Ravnan describes her creation of the concert as a manifestation of "how I learned to love the ones I'm with." The performance format helps her to appreciate students' different strengths, since "they don't

walk into my room as a group, they walk in as individuals." In fact, Ms. Ravnan realizes that, if it were not for this concert, "I probably never would
have known who was a writer, who had good handwriting, and who had
good wit." While features of the concert result in the integration of literacy
into the music classroom while also differentiating instruction (Northey,
2005; Tomlinson, 2004), most importantly, this concert enables the teacher
to "make a virtue of the diversity of student skills" rather than diversity being problematic.

Finally, this concert results in the students and teacher becoming attached
through the teacher respecting students' need for independence, and consequently, giving them some independence. While Ms. Ravnan provides
guidelines for setting up the performance space, key concepts to include in
a script, and important aspects of posture and instrument position to teach
to a beginner-parent, she "let(s) them run the show" by "helping with the
plan but letting the students do it." By allowing students to be more involved in the concert preparation and program, she provides a safer way for
students to exert their independence rather than some peer group music activities that may lead to increased defiance and alienation (Zillman & Gan,
1997).

The bond I observed between teacher and students as a result of this
concert and the concert-related activities adds to the extant research on
orchestra student retention. Global factors (such as student attitude toward the teacher, socioeconomic status, academic achievement, and various motivational factors including parental indifference and perceived
cost of participation) influence retention (Hurley, 1992; Klinedinst,
1991; Martignetti, 1965; Morehouse, 1987; Perkins, 1998). This case
study provides a view of how the teacher can impact, and in some cases,
mitigate the negative influences of these factors through the concert format and social interactions. For instance, the playful banter between the
teacher and students ("You're the sixteenth-note gals!"), teacher trust
("It's up to you guys to get the band room set up right"), and support for
the students ("I hope you all sign up for set-up crew next year in eighth
grade because you are all pros!") provide examples of how a teacher can
promote positive student attitudes toward the teacher and orchestra experience. Also, the teacher's behind-the-scenes action of securing a substitute parent prior to the concert to replace a parent who is unwilling or
unable to participate in the beginning-parent demonstration provides an
example of how a teacher can mitigate the potential negative impact of
parental indifference.

Furthermore, students become attached to the orchestra program
through enculturation, including direct instruction from the orchestra
teacher, playing such cultural exemplars as "Ode to Joy" and "Trumpet
Tune," and having multiple opportunities for and a variety of interactions

with other students through scriptwriting, set-up crew, blackboard scribe, and performance buddy activities (Tishman, Jay, & Perkins, 1993).

What Is Reality?

The title of the concert, *Strings Attached: The Reality Show* causes me to not only ask, "Who gets attached?" as a result of concert participation, but also, "What is reality?" On the surface, reality is the seventh-grade orchestra at Thunder Ridge Middle School, which includes students with varied musical skills from diverse cultural, socioeconomic, academic, and musical backgrounds. Reality, as reflected in concert repertoire, consists of the orchestra pieces, short folk songs, and scales students are able to play near the beginning of the school year in October.

However, if I consider the question "What is reality?" on a deeper level, I realize that this concert questions, shapes, and transforms participants' (students, the teacher, and parents) definitions and experiences of the reality of what occurs at standard public school orchestra concerts, the goals of orchestra concerts, and the reasons for student participation in a school orchestra program. Determining the concert order by lottery, providing equivalent performance opportunities for beginning and advanced students, utilizing the diverse skills and interests of students, and fostering an atmosphere of controlled chaos result in expanded student and parent conceptions of orchestra concerts and orchestra program involvement.

For audience members, an orchestra concert becomes accessible by their participation in activities including the lottery and seat treats, beginner-parent demonstration, and encouragement of audience feedback and response to student humor during the concert. Coupling these activities with an intimate setting can dissolve the barrier that often exists at traditional orchestra concerts between the audience and performers (Davidson, 1997). In fact, this type of concert questions a commonly accepted assumption in literate societies—that performers and audience members are members of two distinct groups, one consisting of gifted performing artists and the other of detached, passive audience members whose function is to consume and evaluate rather than participate (Merriam, 1964; Small, 1998). Since the silent and passive audience is a more recent phenomenon compared with eighteenth-century concerts, where audience comments and non-verbal responses were viewed as an element of the performance (Small, 1998), in a sense, *Strings Attached: The Reality Show* encourages the audience and performers to go back in time to a past reality.

Strings Attached: The Reality Show is a model for instrumental music teachers to consider as they reflect on the multiple functions and goals of concerts. While concerts are a common instrumental program activity, they can be used to shape and perhaps transform student, teacher, and parent perceptions of public school orchestra programs. Furthermore, this concert model can help adolescent students form important relationships with peers from diverse backgrounds. At the same time, this concert model can also help individuals form identities based not only on musical skills, but also on unique abilities and interests that truly are valued and contribute to the ensemble program.

REFERENCES

Abril, C. R. (2007). I have a voice but I just can't sing: A narrative investigation of singing and social anxiety. *Music Education Research, 9*, 1–15.

Adderley, C., Kennedy, M., & Berz, W. (2003). "A home away from home": The world of the high school music classroom. *Journal of Research in Music Education, 51*(3), 190–205.

Burton, S. L. (2004). Educate our advocates. *Music Educators Journal, 90*(5), 17–21.

Davidson, J. W. (1997). The social in musical performance. In D. J. Hargreaves & A. C. North (Eds.), *The social psychology of music* (pp. 209–228). New York: Oxford University Press.

Hurley, C. G. (1992). Student motivations for beginning and continuing/discontinuing string music instruction: A preliminary investigation (Doctoral dissertation, University of Wisconsin, Madison). *Dissertation Abstracts International, 53*, 2727A.

Klinedinst, R. E. (1991). Predicting performance achievement and retention of fifth-grade instrumental students. *Journal of Research in Music Education, 39*(3), 225–238.

Lamont, A. (2002). Musical identities and the school environment. In R. MacDonald, D. J. Hargreaves, & D. Miell (Eds.), *Musical identities* (pp. 41–59). Oxford: Oxford University Press.

LeCompte, M., & Schensul, J. J. (1999). *Analyzing and interpreting ethnographic data.* Walnut Creek, CA: Altamira Press.

Martignetti, A. J. (1965). Causes of elementary instrumental music dropouts. *Journal of Research in Music Education, 13*(3), 177–183.

Merriam, A. P. (1964). *The anthropology of music.* Evanston, IL: Northwestern University Press.

Mithen, S. (2005). *Singing neanderthals: The origins of music, language, mind and body.* London: Weidenfeld & Nicolson.

Morehouse, T. L. (1987). The relationship of selected attitudinal factors to dropout and retention in beginning string students (Doctoral dissertation, University of Houston). *Dissertation Abstracts International, 49*, 0757A.

Morrison, S. J. (2001). The school ensemble: A culture of our own. *Music Educators Journal, 88*, 24–28.

Northey, S. S. (2005). *Handbook on differentiated instruction for middle and high schools.* Larchmont, NY: Eye on Education.

Perkins, D. L. (1998). Factors relating to student participation in public school string programs (Doctoral dissertation, University of North Texas). *Dissertation Abstracts International, 59*, 4388A.

Polkinghorne, D.E. (1995). Narrative Configuration in qualitative analysis. *Qualitative Studies in Education, 8,* 5–23.

Sloboda, J. (2005). *Exploring the musical mind.* Oxford: Oxford University Press.

Small, C. (1998). *Musicking: The meanings of performing and listening.* Hanover, NH: University Press of New England / Wesleyan University Press.

Stake, R. (1995). *The art of case study research.* Thousand Oaks, CA: Sage.

Tishman, S., Jay, E., & Perkins, D. N. (1993). Teaching thinking dispositions: From transmission to enculturation. *Theory into Practice, 32,* 147–153.

Tomlinson, C. A. (2004). *How to differentiate instruction in mixed ability classrooms* (2nd ed.). Alexandria, VA: ASCD.

Van Maanen, J. (1988). *Tales of the field: On writing ethnography.* Chicago: University of Chicago Press.

Zillman, D., & Gan, S. (1997). Musical taste in adolescence. In D. J. Hargreaves & A. C. North (Eds.), *The social psychology of music* (pp. 161–187). New York: Oxford University Press.

10

Drawing Middle-Schoolers' Attention to Music

Jody L. Kerchner

Welcome to Langston Middle School! Late in July, the superintendent of schools approached me about teaching a middle-school general music class that had never existed and that did not have equipment, a music teacher, or a curriculum. Working with middle-school students fills me with excitement. Yet, despite seven years of successfully teaching elementary- and middle-school general and vocal music in the public schools with my own students in my own classrooms, and nine years teaching in middle-school general music laboratory settings, I was anxious about teaching these particular sixth-, seventh-, and eighth-graders at Langston Middle School.

What follows in this chapter is an intrinsic case study (Stake, 1995) of a single entity. This case study is comprised of episodic classroom narratives that occurred during five months in the Music Workshop at Langston Middle School. Considered together as one story, the cluster of narratives will give the reader a sense of the broader picture of the students' music listening experiences, their small-group work, and their interactions with their peers and me (the teacher).

Throughout my professional career, one of my primary research areas has been investigating children's music listening experiences, particularly their verbal, visual, and kinesthetic responses to music (Kerchner, 1996, 2001, 2005). Listening is integral to every musical behavior—composing, improvising, singing, playing an instrument, moving, participating as an audience member, critiquing, and reading some form of notation. Therefore, the Music Workshop students' music listening experiences and their visual music listening maps, as individuals and as members of small groups, were of interest to me. Bresler (1995) suggested that action researchers "study and aim to improve . . . their understandings of their own educational practices, their understandings of these practices and the institutions in which they operate" (pp. 10–11). While I had used mapping to investigate individuals' music listening experiences and as tools to rehearse musical ensembles, I had never used student-generated listening maps in a group setting to investigate middle-school students' music listening experiences, group dynamics, or means for co-creating shared musical meaning. Thus, my teaching situation enabled me to conduct a study based on elements of action research practices, in order to understand my own teaching and the students' music listening experiences individually and in small groups.

The confluence of the students' musical, social, and academic abilities, along with their classroom verbal and non-verbal interactions, is integral to relaying the tales of the students' music listening experiences, decision making and problem solving, and interactions with one another and with me as the teacher. Key questions of this case study are:

- What features of the music do the students choose to depict on their visual listening maps?
- What is the nature of the students' performance of their music listening maps?
- What is the dynamic of the students' small-group work, as they create and perform their music listening maps?

Two or three times per week from the end of August through January, I listened, observed, videotaped, reviewed, analyzed, transcribed, and reflected on the events in the Music Workshop at Langston Middle School. Admittedly, I did not know what I would find as a result of collecting and analyzing copious field observation notes, journal entries, written video teaching reflections, interview transcriptions with students and faculty, and student portfolios that contained their Music Workshop projects, but I did look for possible trends.

Early in the journey of viewing and reviewing the students' written journals and my videotapes of the classes, I noticed that these teens were musical, inquisitive, sensitive participants willing to engage in music experiences, especially those involving music listening and movement. They also responded positively to the visual stimuli (e.g., exploring sound sources on indigenous instruments, viewing PowerPoint presentations with pictures, following listening representations/symbols) that accompanied music listening lessons. However, they complained loudly when asked to read standard music notation.

THE FIRST WEEK

Approximately forty-five students were enrolled in the middle school's Music Workshop. Students were constantly enrolling in and then dropping out of the class, having been suspended from school or having moved to a different town to live with another parent or guardian. Of the forty-five students, only four were girls. Only a few students actually elected to be a part of this newly offered course. The others needed one-on-one supervised learning within the school. My students were not in the band, chorus, or orchestra. The school's special services personnel labeled many of the students as academically, socially, and/or behaviorally challenged, yet a handful of these students were considered gifted. Others were simply students who had no interest in being in an ensemble. Some spoke English as a second language. Regardless of the reason, the Music Workshop was offered for students who had nowhere else to go during the beginning periods of the school day. Our Music Workshop class was where the students belonged.

The general music curriculum I sketched suddenly seemed less important than making a connection with each student and learning about his or her musical preferences and the types of music listened to outside of school. Our musical conversations were starting points for trusting and learning about each other, "dialoging together in order to name [our] worlds and better understand [our] realities" (Jorgensen, 1995, p. 80). I recorded all of the students' responses to questions on a dry-erase board, such as "What type of music do you listen to when you're not in school?" "What do you like about that music?" "Where do you listen to music?" Most of the students were eager to tell me about their listening to rock, rap, gospel, jazz, hip-hop, and country music. "Me, too!" I said. A strange connection, but it was there, much to our mutual surprise. The students told me they listened to music on their iPods, in the car, at home in their bedrooms, and at church.

BOBBY AND THE *BAD NEWS BEARS*

At the beginning of September, I introduced mapping to the students. Listening maps are drawn, invented notations of what one hears, thinks about, and/or feels while listening to music. These impressions typically take the form of pictures, words, invented symbols, graphs, standard musical notation, or any combination thereof. Since the students seemed to enjoy moving to music and viewing video clips, I thought mapping might be an effective teaching tool. I also thought mapping might be a way of getting them into creating and reading musical notation.

Before looking at the actual music listening map, we explored types of symbols that would be found on road maps and world maps, as well as the purposes for using maps. The first mapping experience was primarily teacher-directed. I drew a music listening map of the overture ("Prélude") from Bizet's *Carmen* and presented it to the students.

J.L.K.: Take a look at this map. This is a music listening map. On it, I've included some features of the music that might guide your ears as you listen to it. Looking at this music listening map, what do you expect the music to sound like? [Silence.]

J.L.K.: Okay, let me try again. If your ears were following this map of rhythms, melodies, instruments, harmonies, dynamics, and the musical mood, what information might these drawings show you about the musical sounds? [We had just studied the basic elements of music.]

Michael: Squiggly.

J.L.K.: What about the music might be squiggly?

Michael: The way the pitches go up and down, just like this. [He stands and points to the symbols projected on the wall.]

J.L.K.: Let's remember that and see if that's how the melody does move.

Christian: I think there're lots of repeated notes, because there are repeated drawings on the map.

J.L.K.: Like where on the map?

Christian: [He stands and points to the listening map.] This part keeps repeating.

J.L.K.: Let's remember that idea, too, as we listen to the music. Any other ideas?

T.S. (alias "Cupcake"): There are different parts of the music. See these different areas? I think each part will sound different.

J.L.K.: Hmm . . . interesting observation, T.S. Let's see if that happens in the music. Now, as I "perform" this map by pointing to the markings, try to figure out what is happening in the music. Let's see if the music sounds as you thought it might sound, when I point to those particular symbols.

Surprisingly, the students were captivated as I performed the listening map. Upon the completion, they applauded, and I curtsied. Then we compared their expectations for the musical sound prior to the listening to how they actually heard it. There was repetition, and there were different themes in the music that were represented by different markings on the map. The students wanted to see the map performed again.

Next, the mapping experience focused on the students' individual listening experiences. I distributed copies of my map, copied onto overhead transparencies, to each student. Their task was to try to point to my map as I pointed to the map on my overhead transparency. Most of the students attempted to point to the map as we listened to the music once more.

> J.L.K.: What did you hear in the music that is not included on my listening map? Think about it and this time, decide what you would like to add onto my original map and how you will represent that feature of the music. You might have several features of the music that you choose to add.

We listened to the overture repeatedly over the course of the next fifteen minutes. Each time the music ended, someone restarted the track on the CD. Scott, in his unchanged boy-voice, stated, "The music moves by so fast! I need to keep hearing it, and I need to figure out where on this thing [map] my drawings belong. There's so much to think about!" During this "additive mapping" session, some of the students tried to be a bit silly as they sang parts of the overture, yet they always returned to the task. Some students sang the theme to the movie, *Bad News Bears* (Bizet's *Carmen* "Prélude"), into pretend microphones. One student, however, had put his head down in his arms, covering his face and removing himself from the activity.

J.L.K.: Bobby, are you feeling okay?

B: Yeah.

J.L.K.: Are you finished adding onto your map?

B: No.

J.L.K.: May I help you with anything?

B: No. I can't do this. The music plays so quickly, and I can't do music.

J.L.K.: What do you mean?

B: I can't play an instrument, and I can't read music.

J.L.K.: That's fine, because for this mapping activity, you don't need to do either.

B: But I can't do the fast music, because I'm slow.

J.L.K.: What do you mean, Bobby?

B: I'm a really slow learner in all my classes, and the music goes too fast for me.

J.L.K.: Can you tell me how the music sounds to you? Anything. In any words or drawings or movement that you want to use to describe it.

B: (shrugging his shoulders) Everyone learns faster than I do. I don't want to do this.

J.L.K.: There is no right or wrong way to do a map. That's one of the neat things about mapping. What's important is that you show what you heard as the music played. Will you please try to add at least one thing to the map?

I stepped away from Bobby to give him space to think, although I kept my eyes on him for the remaining mapping time.

Soon it was time for the students to perform their maps. Each student, some reluctantly, approached the overhead projector to perform his or her listening map and its additions. To my original listening map, the students had added words and pictures to describe specific instruments, crescendo and decrescendo symbols, words to describe the tempo of the music, and words or pictures to describe the mood of the piece. A few students used different shapes (i.e., circles, squares, and triangles) to show repeated musical sections and phrases. We applauded each person's performance. Some seemed relatively accurate in coordinating the music with the mapping representations. Other students began to map accurately and then appeared lost, but they eventually found their way back on the music listening mapping path.

Bobby did not volunteer to perform his map, but, by default, it was his turn at the end of the class. He refused to get out of his seat. I had decided that he would somehow participate in the mapping performance experience, so I asked him if he would perform the listening map from his seat. He nodded yes. He called me to his seat. He said, "I want you to point, too." I told him that I would. I placed Bobby's map on the overhead projector. With his marker, he had merely traced the same markings I had made to represent the music. The music began. I pointed to the map on the overhead transparency, while Bobby unenthusiastically pointed in the air from the opposite side of the room. "You have to go back to the beginning!" I had made a mistake that Bobby had promptly corrected. At the conclusion of the music, Bobby and I looked at each other, and he smiled. His classmates applauded. Yes, Bobby had participated in the mapping process, but more importantly, he experienced being successful in class. I wondered what happens to students like Bobby in our educational system if they continually receive the message that they are slow or incapable of learning. How do teachers' low expectations of students, based on their academic achievement and not their other talents, nurture students to become emotionally healthy adults? Although Bobby did not add new markings to the map, he traced the symbols I had placed on the original map. He also performed the map, thereby demonstrating his understanding of the order of the musical events. By taking the risk to perform, Bobby and his peers created success on their own terms.

FANFARES AND UNCOMMON SMALL-GROUP MAPPING EXPERIENCES

I began to wonder why the students were drawn to the mapping experience. Why did the students choose to participate? Did the maps coincide with their learning preferences? Did the fact that the task was a non-verbal one appeal to them? How might their mapping experience change as a result of working in small groups instead of working individually?

Usually, the most active students were the sixth-graders, the hyperactive and verbally impulsive students I teach in the Music Workshop. Over the course of four days in mid-January, we met in the middle-school cafeteria, a small space with long rectangular tables. It was much larger than the crowded room in which we normally met. The walls were covered with large posters of famous sports and entertainment stars talking about determination, self-respect, self-esteem, and achievement. Holding class in the familiar cafeteria was initially disorienting to the students. During the first five minutes of the class meeting, I wondered why I had ventured onto this new turf. Many of the students repeatedly ran from one side of the cafeteria to the other; they yelled, dropped to the floor and rolled, and spit into the large plastic garbage receptacles. Today these students found group work and maintaining focus nearly impossible. No one seemed to care about learning or listening to music. Although I had two additional teacher assistants in the cafeteria with me, there was no sense of an established learning environment.

At a loss for what to do next, I played a recording of Mozart's *"Jupiter" Symphony, Third Movement,* and began pointing to a music listening map originally created by Mary Helen Richards (1980). One by one, the students began to approach where I was standing, perhaps out of sheer curiosity, perhaps feeling obligated to attend to my action. Eventually, after I repeatedly played the music and pointed to my map, the students sat on the benches attached to the cafeteria tables and watched my activity. When everyone was seated and settled, I asked the students to tell me what about the music was represented on my map. Remarkably, the students willingly responded and even asked about my process of performing the map (i.e., "How did you know when to point to each marking? Did you practice at home?"). The official tribal meeting had begun.

Given the students' impetuous behavior at the beginning of class, I was apprehensive about facilitating a group mapping activity, but I was committed to having the students create group listening maps. I provided directions for the task and asked them to create a map of Copland's *Fanfare for the Common Man* in small groups. They would determine their own groups, of three or four students each, and create symbols, words, pictures, graphs, markings of anything they heard, thought about, or felt as they listened to the two-minute *Fanfare* excerpt. On the first two days, the groups would create a rough draft in pencil on 11″ x 14″ white paper. On day three, they would transfer their maps onto 4′ x 3′ pieces of plastic banquet-table covering, using colored markers. After practicing, on the last day of the project they would perform their maps for each other and a few guest audience members.

The task began. The students had no difficulty self-selecting their groups. One eighth-grader, two seventh-graders, and two sixth-graders decided that they did not want to be in a group; they preferred to work alone. I honored their requests without asking questions or trying to change their decisions. The students were responsible for pushing the replay button on the CD player when they wanted to listen to the music. I videotaped and assisted the groups, but only if assistance was requested. We listened repeatedly to the *Fanfare* for forty minutes on each of the three days of class.

Before most groups began drawing, the students focused their attention on three issues: (1) who would be the first to draw the map, (2) who could hold pretend mallets in their hands and play the bass drum opening of the *Fanfare*, and (3) who could create the most interesting body gestures to accompany the music. Students began to sing the trumpet theme, while others pretended to play a trumpet. Still others counted the number of times the bass drum and gong were struck. Some students put their heads on the table, seemingly uninvolved. When I asked those students if they intended to participate, they responded, "It's not my turn to draw now, so I don't need to listen." Occasionally, I provided task and behavioral expectation reminders to individual groups or students, but for the most part the students were cooperative, self-monitoring, and engaged.

Observing the students transfer their movements, singing, and pretend instrumental playing to the rough draft of the map, I noted that some had started drawing their maps at the upper left edge of the paper and progressed linearly to the right side of the paper—an observation also found in Upitis's (1992) investigation of children's invented notations. As one student reached the right edge of the paper, another took the pencil and began another line under the first person's markings. Interestingly, these students captured the linear progression of the musical events—the pervasive opening rhythmic figure, the melodic contour of the solo trumpet line, the repeated rhythmic figure, the gong, and the melodic contour of the ensuing trumpet duet. Some students made a few marks on their maps and then wanted to listen to the music while pointing to their marks to test their accuracy.

Except for the eighth-grader, the students working individually created pictures of instruments, people playing instruments, or an entire map filled with graphic representations of melodic contour. Often these maps were non-linear representations of the music, and they did not follow the left-to-right positioning of the symbols on the paper. For the students who drew the graphs, my key to understanding their listening experience was watching them practice pointing to the music as they listened to it. From those observations, I inferred the relationship of the symbols to the musical events. While it was not necessarily obvious from the symbols, the students performed the map following the melodic and rhythmic contour of the music. "My hand just feels the music, so I follow the lines," said Steve, a seventh-grader who stated that he "can't learn when there is too much noise around" him. He told me that that was why he chose to work alone on the mapping project. Mindy told me that her map was "flexible," because even though she might not follow her map exactly the same way each time she heard the music, she could "make it up by following the lines as she heard it differently each time."

After two classes creating rough drafts of their listening maps, the students transferred their representations onto the plastic table coverings. Scott, Cody, and Darius were reluctant to place their penciled rough draft onto the larger plastic in permanent marker. They were in the midst of a disagreement that resulted in a flurry of erasures, grabbing the pencil from each other, and disagreeing about the melodic contour and how to represent it. Even when Scott began drawing the final map, Cody and Darius continued to change the markings on the draft map. Among the groups, the person who drew the markings on the rough draft also assumed the responsibility for drawing those same symbols on the final map. The students reminded each other verbally, and with an occasional shove, when it was their turn to draw. Being responsible for owning specific representations on the map became a recurrent theme.

On Thursday, the students taped their maps onto the cafeteria walls and practiced performing them. They decided where they would stand to perform, the order in which they would perform, whether or not they would use a pencil or other object to point to the map, which order the groups would perform their maps, and who would be the stereo and video operators. At one point, I noticed David, a quiet, blonde-haired eighth-grader looking frustrated. He told me that he did not have enough hands to perform his map; therefore, he asked permission to have Mr. Wolf, their regular Music Workshop teacher, perform the percussion part. David's map contained many markings—dots, larger circles with smaller dots inside them, and curvy lines to depict the melodic contour. I told him that he needed to coach Mr. Wolf on his part of the performance and that they needed to practice performing together.

Typically one person in each group emerged as the organizer of the performance. Students seemed comfortable assisting those who did not point accurately to the group's map. Denise simply stood beside Malcolm and showed him where to point. Every so often, I overheard her say, "Now move to the next one [representation on the map]." Alexis, who chose to work alone, told me that she would not perform by herself. When I asked her how I could assist, she said that I could stand beside her while she performed her map. "This is embarrassing." She also told me she needed no help performing. Still other students continued to revise their final maps. One group threw away their final map and asked for a clean piece of plastic so they could begin again.

Before the class ended, we discussed concert etiquette and performance process. Reflecting on this lesson strategy, I wondered if our chat about performance instilled undue anxiety in the students. I wanted them to understand that their listening map performances would be a special event for them and their audience, but I may have promulgated stereotypes of how performers and audiences behave, at least in most classical, on-stage performances.

The day of the listening map performances at the Langston Middle School arrived. Usually students slowly trickled into class as the announcements began. On this day, however, most students arrived to tape their map to their spot on the cafeteria walls and to organize the group prior to the performance. Denise, an eighth-grader who frequently reminded me of her gratitude for my being female, told me that she set her alarm clock "extra early this morning. I needed to find a vision for my hairstyle today. I mean, I'm going to be videotaped and performing and all." Tyler, an eighth-grader who played football and worked on a farm, grumpily stated, "We can't do our map today. Christian is not here." I told him that someone else would have to cover for Christian. "We can't do that! This whole line on our map is Christian's! He drew it, and he has to perform it." I encouraged Tyler to do his best and to try to figure it out during the practice performance session before the performance.

The principal, assistant principal, and superintendent of schools entered the performance area. I invited them, because I wanted the students to have an audience of the school's important people and the opportunity to demonstrate their co-constructed meaning of the music they had mapped. Surprisingly, three other teachers entered the cafeteria—those whom the students had invited. During the performances, visitors, drawn by the loud sound of the repeated Copland music, stopped into the cafeteria to watch.

Before each performance, I asked the group members to describe "what about the music" they had captured on their map. This task was met with generalizations such as "the instruments," "the ups and downs," "the way the music moved," "what we heard," and "I don't know." Yet during the mapping performances, the students were quite decisive in pointing to the symbols they had created.

In some cases, the maps consisted of stacked, vertical representations that required two or three students to perform the map simultaneously. For example, David and Mr. Wolf performed a mapping duet—the former pointing to the map as the percussion played, the latter artistically following the melodic and rhythmic contour of the music. David prefaced the performance with, "I don't read music, so I don't know how this will go." When the melody moved upward with notes of short duration, his finger moved in that same direction, coinciding with the markings on his map. Without words he indicated his understanding of beat, subdivision of beat, note duration and rhythmic contour, phrasing, melodic contour, and dynamics. Others, like Cody, Colby, and Dusty, clumped together pointing to representations simultaneously occurring in the music.

Other maps were linear, so the students took turns pointing to the markings they had created. Tyler reluctantly performed his own and the absent Christian's portions of their group's linear map. Although his finger completed the map before the musical excerpt ended, Tyler found a place on the map that seemed to represent the melodic contour of what he heard in the moment. Although he said that he became lost, Tyler improvised, so the map's representations fit his music listening experience.

Marcus's group (he elected himself the leader) also created a linear listening map, but they used different colored markers to indicate phrases and different instruments. Marcus was a young man who spoke few words, yet when he did speak, his comments were insightful, direct, and emphatic. When it was his turn to complete his group's performance of the map, Marcus decided to exaggerate his performance gestures—anything to get a laugh. What resulted, however, was a ballet performance of his portion of the map. When the trumpet fanfare melody moved by step or leap, Marcus hopped in place or stepped away from the map to leap. When the music moved upward, his motions became larger and higher, and his facial expressions became purposeful smiles. The opposite occurred when the music moved downward, and he lay on the floor when the music reached cadential points. Although his peers laughed and his performance appeared out of control, I was fascinated by his coordinated full-body movements, which reflected the musical nuances.

Justin, Taylor, and Tyree offered an unexpected addition. Before the music began, Taylor announced that their map would be accompanied by a theatrical play. He pointed to linear (melodic contour lines) and non-linear (people playing drums, gongs, flute) representations on their map. Simultaneously, Justin and Tyree pretended to be at war, pretending to shoot guns during the percussion, firing cannons when the gong played, and writhing on the ground when the trumpets played. Justin fired his gun during the solo trumpet fanfare section, and Tyree fired his gun when the duo trumpet section occurred. Marcus, taking a turn videotaping the performance, stopped the camera and shouted, "Wait, that's where the music stopped for the other groups, but his map ain't finished yet." I responded, "That's right, Marcus, but they captured a longer piece of the music than some of the other groups. Please turn on the video again." He retorted, "Now why they go do that for?" The play and the mapping continued, until Tyree won the war.

The performances lasted until the final minutes of class. The students were engaged, focused, and pleased with their accomplishments. Bobby and his group took turns performing their linear melodic contour map. Although Alexis never made eye contact with her map or her peers, she performed her map while I stood at her side. Steve was the final person to perform his solo map, which consisted of overlapping swirling lines and curves in perpetual motion. Steve pointed at the lines and curves at the top center of his map, when the music began to play. After about fifteen seconds, he told me to stop the music so he could begin again. Steve pointed at the same lines and curves, and once again, seemed to get lost. He continued to follow his map with obvious uncertainty. At one point, he dropped his hand from the map, looked at me, and shrugged his shoulders. The class bell rang. Our performance time had ended, but the music continued. Steve's eyes filled with tears.

J.L.K.: Steve, which class do you have after this one?

Steve: Reading.

J.L.K.: Would you like to stay here in the cafeteria to perform your map?

Steve: Yes, please.

Justin: Hey, Steve, I'll stay, too, to be your audience.

Scott: Yeah, me, too, Steve.

J.L.K.: Okay, you let me know when you want the music to begin, Steve.

Steve nodded for the music to begin. Yet once more, he pointed to the lines and curves at the top center of his map. His finger moved over and under the markings. At times, I thought he would stop again, but he did not. Steve made the map work, coming to its conclusion when then music stopped. When he turned around, his audience applauded. He smiled and gave us a thumbs-up signal. He said, "I did it! Can I take my map with me to Reading?" Steve pulled the map from the wall, and the three boys hurried from the cafeteria to their next class.

INTERPRETATIONS

The following section presents lessons learned from my interactions with the middle-schoolers and their mapping processes and performances. Stake

(1995), reflecting on the nature of qualitative researchers' interpretations of case study data, offered, "We draw from understandings deep within us, understandings whose derivation may be some hidden mix of personal experience, scholarship, [and] assertions of other researchers" (p. 12).

One of the most important lessons at Langston Middle Schools was the transformations that occurred in the middle-schoolers, the relationships between the students and me, and in me as a teacher. I began to trust the at-risk adolescents in the Music Workshop. I learned to put away my fears of losing control of the class and of potential external judges (e.g., the superintendent, the principal, the Oberlin teachers, my dean, the students) and their perceptions of the professor as a music teacher in a real-life teaching situation. In turn, the students learned to put away their fears of being perceived as inadequate in the eyes of an adult—their teacher—and of being scolded for their social interactions.

Although initially skeptical, the students became comfortable sharing what they were thinking, hearing, or creating in class. They seemed stunned when I genuinely wanted to know their opinion or when I did not know the answers to questions they raised. It was difficult for many of them to understand that I had no single expectation for how their music listening maps should be created and performed. Perhaps they were eager to participate in the mapping experience because "when students begin to understand that creativity is valued, they begin to feel motivated to participate" (McAnally, 2006, p. 103). I wondered how many times in their schooling these adolescents would encounter situations that invited creative problem solving and in which their unique solutions would be accepted and celebrated because they were meaningful to them, instead of fitting a construct imposed by a teacher.

One of my goals for this class was for the middle-schoolers to become aware of diversified musical soundscapes that would leave new imprints and forge new connections in their internal cognitive notebooks (John-Steiner, 1997). Through the mapping experiences, the students used sophisticated problem-solving skills to decipher and construct meaning from all types of music. Although they encountered a variety of folk, world, and popular musics in class, their maps depicted their understanding, using their own terms and methods of representation, of specific classical music excerpts. "Relatively few people, especially children and young people, choose to listen to classical music. People are not usually enculturated into classical music with anything like the same intensity as they are into popular music" (Green, 2001, p. 187). Yet, the Music Workshop students demonstrated a willingness to sample "my" music, maybe because I sought to validate their musical tastes and values and to understand how they were formulated. Giving students appropriate learning tools empowers them to discover and build musical meaning of any style of music in the context of their past and present musical and life experiences.

The music listening mapping procedure was an effective pedagogical tool for drawing students' attention to specific musical events, even in the small-group mapping experiences. Bamberger (1991) suggested that musical representations/invented notations "hold still so that children can reflect on [them]. In a conversation back and forth between playing on the paper and looking back at the trace left behind, the children can learn about their own knowledge, their functioning knowledge, which ordinarily escapes scrutiny as it passes by in action and through time" (p. 52). I observed students refine and edit their mapping representations, discuss musical events, and rely on their collective musical memory in order to compare musical sections and discover musical patterns. Mastery of the music listening mapping tool, while it lifts some of the usual academic expressive constraints, also imposes others. Musical events still move by in time and space, and musical nuance and emotional import often elude description, whether by word or visual representation.

Because the students provided sparse verbal descriptions of their maps, I had to infer much of the meaning by watching the students point to their maps while speculating how the representations corresponded to the musical sound. I viewed the maps as externalizations of portions of their music listening experience—what they heard, felt, and thought about as they listened. They chose what to include on their maps; therefore, I did not assume that the markings symbolized an exhaustive view of their experiences.

Similar to my other music listening studies (Kerchner 1996, 2001), the groups' listening maps tended to include pictures of musical instruments or people playing instruments, sectional form, repetition and contrast, texture (solo/duo trumpets), melodic and rhythmic contour, beat and beat subdivision, figural metric groupings—counted and grouped notes indicating some durational values (Upitis, 1985, 1992)—and pictures of musical associations (Civil War).

Some students' mapping performances (e.g., how they pointed to the representations, especially the connected linear lines) indicated their sensitivity to musical nuance and style (Kerchner, 1996, 2001, 2005). Mapping seemed to capture the intuitive knowledge (e.g., Steve, Mindy, Marcus) gained through the senses during music listening. Thus, the students grouped notes as they heard them, instead of how they might be grouped in standard musical notation learned during formal musical training.

The students' performances surprised me, because the students became personally attached to their mapping contributions. They owned the process of drawing and transferring their representations onto the final listening map, subsequently performing those same markings as they heard them in the music. While student organizers/leaders emerged in the groups, no single student performed the entirety of a group's map. Each person individually took a turn performing or simultaneously performing the map with other group members. Furthermore, the performances consisted of more than pointing to mapping symbols. They included kinesthetic/gestural expression, singing, and drama, minus anything spoken.

As students listened to the music and performed their maps, they often said, "This isn't right," or "Oh, that [symbol] is not yet in the music." Following the listening maps was challenging, especially for those who drew curvy, connected, non-linear graphic maps. Although they might have become temporarily lost, the students had obvious aural anchor points in the music and on the map that eventually brought them back on track. Sometimes the students got ahead of themselves while pointing to the maps, because, at one point or another, they too quickly anticipated musical events. Eventually, however, they reconnected their map, pointer finger or pencil, and the music.

The small groups represented small communities of learners (Wenger, 1998). The students had no difficulty selecting their group members, who were mostly their closest friends. There were leaders within the group, and students who kept others on task by stating that it was their turn to draw on the map. There was clear division of labor. David pointed to the trumpets, and Mr. Wolf pointed to the percussion. Each person had mapping representations that he or she performed. The group members helped each other practice and perform as accurately as possible. Most group members were invested in the mapping process and product. Not only did the group support its own members, but they also supported other students who had worked alone.

Vygotsky's premises suggest that the internalized processes of learning are not performed in isolation, but rather in the context of interacting with peers, adults, cultural artifacts, and past and present experiences (Vygotsky, 1978). The Music Workshop students worked together in peer groups to create a shared meaning of the Copland *Fanfare*. The mapping project demonstrated their self-teaching and peer-teaching strategies, learning, and reflection in a manner representative of popular musicians' learning practices (Green, 2005)—rather than learning from a sole adult authority who imposed external assessment. The students' interactions affected their mapping and performance of the music; conversely, their mapping and performance affected their understanding of the music.

We are challenged to find strategies for teaching and learning that (1) are enjoyable and informative; (2) capitalize on the social nature of teens by offering group work and individual work opportunities; (3) are active, hands-on experiences (even during music listening)—imperative for active and energetic teens; (4) are student-directed, without fear of impending evaluation of their work by the teacher; and (5) foster mutual respect and trust between teacher and students. What, then, looks promising for the future of general music in our secondary schools, whether urban, suburban, or rural, based on this study? Wenger (1998) suggested that change can occur by finding "inventive ways of engaging students in meaningful practices, of providing access to resources that enhance their participation, of opening their horizons so they can put themselves on learning trajectories they can identify with, and involving them in actions, discussions, and reflections that make a difference to the communities that they value" (p. 10).

REFERENCES

Bamberger, J. (1991). *The mind behind the musical ear: How children develop musical intelligence.* Cambridge, MA: Harvard University Press.

Bresler, L. (1995). Ethnography, phenomenology and action research in music education. *The Quarterly Journal of Music Teaching and Learning, 6*(3), 4–15.

Green, L. (2001). *How popular musicians learn.* Aldershot, U.K.: Ashgate Publishing Limited.

Green, L. (2005). The music curriculum as lived experience: Children's "natural" music-learning processes. *Music Educators Journal, 91*(4), 27–32.

John-Steiner, V. (1997). *Notebooks of the mind: Explorations of thinking.* New York: Oxford University Press.

Jorgensen, E. (1995). Music education as community. *Journal of Aesthetic Education, 29*(3), 71–84.

Kerchner, J. L. (1996). *Perceptual and affective components of music listening experience as manifested in children's verbal, visual, and kinesthetic representations.* Unpublished doctoral dissertation, Northwestern University.

Kerchner, J. L. (2001). Children's verbal, visual, and kinesthetic responses: Insight into their music listening experience. *Bulletin for the Council of Research in Music Education, 146,* 35–51.

Kerchner, J. L. (2005). A world of sound to know and feel: Exploring children's verbal, visual, and kinesthetic responses to music (pp. 21–33). In M. Mans & B. W. Leung (Eds.), *Music in schools for all children: From research to effective practice.* Granada, Spain: University of Granada.

McAnally, E. A. (2006). Motivating urban music students. In C. Frierson-Campbell (Ed.), *Teaching music in the urban classroom* (pp. 177–183). Lanham, MD: Rowman & Littlefield Education.

Richards, M. H. (1980). *Aesthetic foundations for thinking: Part 3—The ETM process.* Portola Valley, CA: Richards Institute of Music Education and Research.

Stake, R. E. (1995). *The art of case study research.* Thousand Oaks, CA: Sage.

Upitis, R. (1985). *Children's understanding of rhythm: The relationship between development and music training.* Unpublished doctoral dissertation, Harvard University.

Upitis, R. (1992). *Can I play you my song?* Portsmouth, NH: Heinemann.

Vygotsky, L. S. (1978). *Mind in society.* Cambridge, MA: Harvard University Press.

Wenger, E. (1998). *Communities of practice: Learning, meaning, and identity.* New York: Cambridge University Press.

11

At-Risk Teens: Making Sense of Life through Music Composition

Maud Hickey

It was a few minutes before six p.m. when Jonathon and Myles entered. My assistant and I had just finished setting up nine computer/music stations for students in the first of our weekly music composition sessions. Though I knew that these two were the oldest boys in the group (ages nineteen and eighteen, respectively), they seemed older and more mature than I had expected. They had a quiet demeanor and carried themselves in a polite manner during our brief introductory conversation. Our chat was abruptly halted by a flurry of energy as George (age eleven), Antwoin (fourteen), Tee (thirteen), and Roger (thirteen) came bounding into the room. Tee, the smallest guy, was wearing an oversized basketball jersey and waffle-type long underwear hanging out from beneath his oversized basketball shorts. Seemingly disinterested, he sat down at the closest computer station and laid his head down on the desk. Roger, George, and Antwoin, on the other hand, were excited—running about the room trying to find a computer station and admiring the shiny hardware.

On this first night, our goal was to teach the basics of operating the music sequencing software. Because the software and hardware did not always work, we spent much of our time running around to problem-solve the technical issues. The personalities and learning styles of the young men began to emerge. For instance, while almost everyone seemed to catch on quickly, George struggled and begged for attention. Tee did not want to be bothered and focused deliberately while he worked; Myles often sang as he played. Roger had a sense of humor—I could tell by the smile in his eyes—and he swayed and patted his head in a habitual manner as he concentrated. Antwoin seemed charming and affable. I sensed that his peers might challenge George, the youngest and neediest of the group.

By end of the first session, George had already fallen behind. He wanted to write everything in his notebook before leaving and ran out of time to put away his materials before zooming out of the room to catch up with the others on their way to a local college basketball game. He left a tangle of wires and cords at his computer station, while the others were careful to clean up and leave the stations as they found them. When they all had left, my assistant and I were excited and relieved that the class had a decent start and looked forward to the next few months of learning as we navigated the world of music composition with these eager young men.

THE STORY

The vignette above describes the beginning of a six-month series of classes in which my assistant (a doctoral student) and I taught music composition to a small group of African American young men at a long-term residential facility in Chicago. They had been placed in the facility for a variety of reasons, most often related to problems in their homes or with their families. They were labeled at-risk. My assistant and I provided this voluntary music program for ninety minutes on Thursday evenings from January to June. We used a sequencing software program called *Traction* on Macintosh Power-Book computers for composing music. Each computer was connected to a Korg X5D synthesizer via a small mixer. Besides the multiple sounds available for recording from the Korg synthesizers, students also had the option of using a microphone to record their voices in their compositions. The sequencing software *Traction* was chosen specifically because it kept a digital trace of anything recorded, even if students ultimately deleted material. This feature allowed me to retrace the music that students generated as they worked (referred to as their "digital scraps" hereafter). In addition, the software allowed the students to compose music without the need to read or write traditional music notation.

While I was not certain what to expect, my goals were clear. The first was to study the effectiveness of music composition as a tool for providing at-risk adolescents a positive and creative outlet in their lives. The second was to study the feasibility of using music technology to facilitate teaching music composition to students who had little or no training in music. The third goal was to test a music composition curriculum (Hickey, 2005). At that moment, I did not know how much I would learn or how my goals would transform into new approaches to teaching music composition.

I continue this story by rewinding to the beginning, when I began to plan for and make decisions about the structure of the class. I provide detailed narratives of three of the youngest men—Antwoin, George, and Tee—and share the group's concluding activities with the group. Finally, I provide conclusions about my findings.

The research design for this study was an instrumental case study in which I examined the issue of compositional identity with at-risk students. The data I collected and analyzed included field notes, transcriptions of videotaped lessons and audio interviews with the students and counselor, students' digital scraps and music compositions, and text from e-mail correspondence with the counselor. The data collected, especially the musical compositions, served as field texts to help tell the story of these students' lives not only while they were with us in this music composition class, but also outside of their classes. My role was as participant/observer.

BACKGROUND

I had been searching for a place in which to teach music composition in order to explore the possibilities of composition with at-risk teens when I stumbled upon this particular residential facility. Nearly a year in advance, I visited the facility several times and met with various administrators to explore the possibilities of a music composition class with the residents. Once all parties agreed to the terms of the class, the activities director queried the various homes in the facility to look for volunteers. Nine residents signed up, and I vividly remember sitting in the office of the activities director when she presented me with the names of the students. At the time, they were just names. "Do you want to know more about why they are here?" she asked. I hesitated for a moment. I had not thought about that, and the question caught me off guard. "No, I don't think so," I replied cautiously, because I did not want to be biased in constructing my opinions of the students with whom I would be working.

We walked through the century-old building and then to its newer annex, looking for a suitable place to set up and use synthesizer keyboards, laptop computers, and mixers. We also had to consider storage. We settled upon a room tucked away on the third floor in the old building. The marble floors, wide brick block walls, smells, echoes, and chill of the hallway and wide stairwell brought back memories of my own childhood parochial school days.

The room was not a conventional classroom space. It was rather small—approximately sixteen by twenty-four feet—with a large, long table in the middle and a few small tables around the sides. With a spaghetti-like mess of extension cords and power strips, we set up six stations around the large table and three on the side tables. The room was suitable for our needs, for the students had space to work at their own stations. My assistant and I could walk around comfortably, and we were close enough to interact with all of the students.

The logistics were finalized. Every Thursday evening the boys would arrive from their homes around six p.m. Six boys would attend class regularly, and two or three others would join us from time to time. A counselor was assigned to accompany the boys to class, assist in class as needed, and monitor their behavior. During our Thursday sessions, the counselor was content to find a chair in the corner of the room and catch up on work. More often than not, the young men paid no attention to him. However, sometimes the boys called him over to listen to their compositions or assist. At first I was grateful to have a resident counselor in the room in case I needed assistance, but soon after the program started, I barely noticed he was there.

The curriculum that I used was one I had been working on and modifying for several years (Hickey, 2005). The final goal was for students to compose music they would record on their own CDs and to compose a piece for the annual end-of-year awards banquet for all residents in the facility. I allowed the flow of sessions, feedback from the students, and personal reflections after each session to determine subsequence sessions, using my curriculum model as a scaffold. Consequently I did not cover the entire curricular scheme and will reflect on the reasons for this at the end of this chapter. The fourteen sessions followed this organization:

Sessions 1–3:	Listen and explore
Sessions 4–9:	Form
Session 10:	Musical elements: chords
Sessions 11–14:	Work to finish compositions

BEGINNING STAGES: GETTING TO KNOW EACH OTHER

The youngest boys in the group frequently came to class bounding up the stairs, racing and out of breath, while the older ones arrived a bit later, with a calm, slow, and cool demeanor. I learned about the lives of these young men during our pre-class conversations: the importance of family visits and heartbreak of not being visited, girlfriends, music, missing fathers, the difficulty of school, and the things that made them laugh.

The weekly pre-class conversations allowed us not only to gain the students' trust and get to know them better, but also to customize our music teaching to their unique needs and personalities. Because music composition is such a personal endeavor, a trusting and safe atmosphere had to be established in order for these at-risk students to feel comfortable enough to express themselves creatively and honestly (Appleton Gootman, 2002; De-

Carlo & Hockman, 2003; Eccles & Appleton Gootman, 2002; Heath & Smyth, 1999; Tyson, 2004).

During the first few sessions, the students used tutorials I had created to help them navigate the computer software and synthesizer. In addition, I wanted them to spend time exploring the vast array of interesting sounds on the synthesizer as a part of the listen-and-explore stage of the curriculum model. They seemed focused and intrigued by the multitude and variety of sound possibilities on the synthesizers, and they also used the computers to listen to recorded music they brought to the sessions.

After about forty minutes of focused exploration at their computer stations during the third session, Antwoin reminded me it was his turn to play his music. He handed me a bootlegged CD with the name Eminem written on the scratched-up plastic sleeve. The song Antwoin wanted me to play is called "Hailie's Song." In this song, Eminem tells the story of the pressure of being a single father and watching his young daughter grow, including the battle over custody and his anger toward the girl's mother.

As the five-minute-long song played, Antwoin lip-synced the words, George looked intensely sad, and the rest of them were completely silent. After it finished I commented on how sad the story seemed. "I like it," I let them know. I also acknowledged that it was music that I hadn't heard previously. After an unusual moment of silence, there was a sudden clamor for who would bring in music next week.

For the second half of the class I gave an assignment to compose a piece that depicted any place they were familiar with, using any of the sounds available to them in the software or on the synthesizer. I used this musical scenery assignment because it opens up many possibilities, has no strict rules, and prompts exploration of sound possibilities. It also engages the listening imagination as students think about the many sounds in the different places they go in their lives (e.g., the cafeteria, the beach, or the city streets at night). After about forty-five minutes, I stopped them in order to use the last twenty minutes of the session to play their musical sceneries for each other.

Before we began, I gave the requisite speech about listening as polite critics; that is, not being negative about each other's music but giving constructive criticism and positive feedback instead. They all shook their heads in agreement, with seeming sincerity, but probably more so because they just wanted to play their music for each other.

Roger was first with his piece, titled "Ry-Ry's Jam." "It's at home," he explained. Before the music began, I asked Roger for specific information about his composition. "What do your sounds depict? What were you thinking of at this point?" Tee interrupted me and suggested wisely, "Why don't you find out all that stuff at the end?" I smiled and agreed to his proposition. "Okay, Tee, that's one of your suggestions that I'll take from you." Myles laughed at that. Roger explained that his music described his home while he watched TV. "The loud part is Mom yelling," he offered. The music sounded to me like a free-flowing exploration of many different sounds on the synthesizer, one randomly after another. Nice applause from the others when his music ended after two minutes. At that point, I felt growing anticipation from others as they waved their hands in the air hoping to be next to share their compositions.

Tee was next. His composition, "MC," was seven minutes and forty-one seconds long. He explained, "This is when we are at McDonald's," and the other guys laughed. The composition describes, through sounds and lyrics, an experience of visiting McDonald's and ordering food. Under Tee's rhythmic, rapping voice are loud, pounding electronic sounds—a mix of timbres that pulsate rhythmically.

"MC"

I walk into McDonald's in a happy MOOOOD. I love it, I like it, I want my food. I want everything I have . . . they have.
Sorry for saying that.
But . . . it's gonna work out. I want everything; double cheeseburger, Mc-Chicken, fish filet-o, triple cheeseburger with cheeeese . . . quarter pounder . . . and soft drink. That's about fifty minutes long to drink. [pause]
I want an extra, extra, extra large, triple large, FRY.
On the side. [pause]
Yea, triple large fry.
This is how it's going to work.
I'm gonna max it out all night; it ain't gonna take but five minutes.
I'm gonna keep ordering the same thing. WO! I like it.
So I'm orderin', I'm waitin', waitin', I'm orderin', orderin', I'm waitin'. I like it. Wow. Cool.
They give me a letter; they give me a number on my receipt. 110! I'm mad. Yay. yay. yay! I'm sorry.
But [sings] love this [back to talk]
Okay.
This is where I get my food back. I enjoy it so much. Wooo! Woooooo!
Like it. Do you?
I wish you could taste it.
I'm enjoying it so much, my stomach is just rumblin'. Rorrroorrraugh.
I know every food that's gonna come out, so I get it before I hit the stores.
I love it! My stomach. Woooo!
It's just . . . I feel like I'm in heaven, I feel so good, I feel so fine, I feel so . . . wooooooo!
So. This is where I love it.

The big chicken. The Mc . . . I taste the McChicken first. Oh!
It feels so good. It feels so good. Feels so fine. Feels so great.
I wish I could I could feel more. Wooo.
You wanna taste this? Wooo! I'm sorry!
Psyche.
I wanna stuff myself feelin' good. Alright.
Yay.

The lyrics last for the first two minutes and thirty-three seconds of the composition, after which the music moves into a loud mixture of pounding synthesized electronic sounds that seem to wander until the end, a full five minutes later. I could not play the entire composition because of the class time ending, so I jumped to the end, and everybody applauded. "Tee didn't just write a song, he wrote an entire opera!" I exclaimed. He accepted this comment with great pride. Later, upon listening to the digital scraps that led up to Tee's "MC," I discovered one file that contained a gruesome description of a gangster going into a McDonald's and murdering the workers, with graphic detail of stabbing and shooting. Because this digital scrap never ended up in his composition, it seemed that Tee either knew what was appropriate for this class or felt respectful enough of the teachers to spare us the gruesome lyrics. Perhaps our interactive rather than authoritative role garnered his respect (DeCarlo & Hockman, 2003).

Antwoin was next. The others were starting to get antsy because of the length of time devoted to this listening exercise, but I kept going. Antwoin's piece was set in a funeral home and was titled "Lil Tipsy." His composition used a typical funeral home organ timbre, and he played a single line melodic improvisation for the song's duration (four minutes). It seemed to last too long, and I sensed the others were starting to lose focus. The subject of this music should have created a serious classroom atmosphere, but it was starting to get noisy.

Finally, with barely enough time left, it was young George's turn. When I suggested we start with him next week, he complained loudly. He really wanted to share on this night. I gave in and asked, "Okay, George, what does your musical scenery depict?" He simply pointed to a logo on his T-shirt that read, "Anti-Cruelty Society" (a group of boys volunteered weekly at the Anti-Cruelty Society.) The music began with a piano motive that sounded much like the beginning motive in the Temptations' song, "Lean on Me." After wandering with this chordal motive, he ended with a simple rock drum beat. While not particularly musically interesting to me because of its lack of musical development, the look of pride on George's face convinced me to refrain from judging him. My personal stance has always been to refrain from negative criticism in a public forum when working with young composers. Literature supports the importance of a non-judgmental stance, especially with at-risk youth and creative art making (Block, Harris, & Laing, 2005; Canino, 1995; DeCarlo & Hockman, 2003; Tyson, 2004). George was beaming with happiness that his music was played for his peers, and I wasn't about to squash that.

At this point, we had gone over the allotted class time. The students were getting antsy and new features of their personalities began to emerge as we ended the session. With that charming smile on his face, Tee used his synthesizer stand as a gun, making an imaginary cocking motion and shooting it toward me. George, Antwoin, and Roger moved to one side of the room to write on the dry-erase board. The counselor asked them to stop several times, and finally calmly offered, "You've lost your privileges." Roger, at that point, hid behind the door. George especially surprised me in his mischievousness—almost transforming into a different person—a more aggressive young man than I knew from observing him sit and ask questions innocently from his computer station.

With some extra effort, we sent the students home. My feeling about their first compositions was that they were too long, too mono-timbral, and more like impromptu improvisations than carefully-planned and developed compositions. Many questions raced through my mind that evening: Was my musical training aesthetic getting in the way of accepting these compositions? The students themselves seemed to love the music and demonstrated such pride in sharing. How do (or should) I approach quality and aesthetic in composing? How can/should I help make their compositions better? The solution to this issue (determining standards of quality) is central to successful music composition with children, and one that I believe might also be the greatest impediment.

I left that evening feeling discouraged in my role as composition teacher. However, after I sat down later and listened to all of the compositions and the digital scraps the students had composed during that session (ones I had not had the opportunity to listen to during class), I was pleasantly surprised. The students had composed more than just their musical scenery assignment. They had composed some pleasant music. Though most of the music was simple, it was organized and seemed intentional. This discovery inspired me to write each student a letter about the music compositions that they had created so far. In the personal letters, I commented on their progress and compositions in a positive manner. I wanted them to feel a sense of progress while encouraging them to explore more possibilities.

MIDDLE SESSIONS: COMPOSING THINGS THEY KNOW

By session six, we had established a comfortable routine. Upon arrival, students said their hellos and shared stories from their day, then sat down, put on their headphones, and began working. After twenty minutes, I stopped them and we listened to music, or I offered ideas for future compositions. Then, back to work. Most of the technological problems were solved, and my personal letters seemed to have given them extra motivation, feelings of pride, and goals toward which to work. As we moved into these middle sessions, I felt as though there was no time to teach. At times I felt guilty when I asked the students to stop working and listen to me talk. However, they were always compliant, quiet, and polite, and they gave me time to act as the knower. I finished each lesson by playing some music that I guessed they had not heard before, and then they eagerly jumped back into their work. The counselor noticed the concentration the students displayed during the sessions when they were simply working on their compositions. He said, "I've rarely seen them do anything for ninety minutes straight, except for sleep and play[ing] video games." The power of this creative outlet on their intrinsic motivation made an impression on me as I realized how powerful the act of creative composition could be as a positive force in their lives.

Three of the middle composition sessions were dedicated to the second section of the curriculum—learning about musical form. We talked specifically about beginning and ending, looping, and song form. I played music by Steve Reich, Aaron Copland, and Rufus Thomas to illustrate these concepts. The students were intrigued by the music I played. It was different from music they liked or were accustomed to hearing. They listened quietly and attentively, but they were also eager to share with me the music they listened to. The students' work was clearly influenced by a wide variety of musics. In these middle sessions, I began to wonder about the source of their musical inspirations. At times they wanted to replicate somebody's music. Other times the influence was more subtle, but still present, in their compositions.

In the following paragraphs I focus on George, Antwoin, and Tee as they worked on their compositions during the middle sessions. Instances where their music was influenced by music they listened to in and outside of class are highlighted.

George

"Nice but Deadly"
[words accompanied by loud, sustained synthetic guitar-like timbres]
Yes, this is what I'm talking about.
Everybody know when I walkin' about.
Everybody see me and then I just wanna shout.
I'm the next Slim Shady, ya better believe it.
Everybody know me as a great an', achievin' it.

I am the one, the one and the only;
You will know me as the only Kobe.
I play basketball, I play football, I play any sport you want me to
Just because I'm AMAAAAAAZING
There we go.

George was overweight for his age, but he carried himself lightheartedly. Vying for attention with his big, sweet eyes and silly sense of humor, he posed more of a challenge than the rest. While the others worked steadily and without much guidance, eleven-year-old George often sought attention by interrupting the other guys or by asking the teachers to listen to his music or to assist him with a technical matter. George was also very moody. One night, he wrote a piece titled, "I Quit," upset over his claim that he had lost his work on the computer. The result was a short pounding snippet: do-re-mi, do-re-mi. However, upon listening to his digital scraps, I noticed he had practiced that evening, tried playing the blues scale (learned in another class), and experimented with some fascinating chords influenced by blues. George seemed to get frustrated with his perceived lack of progress, hence his "I Quit" composition.

George adored the music of composer/performer Ray Charles. He learned how to play the boogie-woogie piano part from Charles's song, "Hit the Road, Jack" from the music therapy teacher who visited the facility on Fridays. George was keen to the potential problems of emulating somebody who had troubles in his life. "I don't want to be exactly like Ray Charles, 'cause he was on drugs and stuff like that," he confided after playing for me his composition titled, "Ray." "Ray" contained a boogie-woogie piano riff that accompanied George's singing, "Hit the road, Jack, don't you come back no more, no more, no more, no more . . . what cho say?" repeatedly (for a full three minutes!). It ended with George singing unaccompanied and enthusiastically the final words, "Hit the road, Jack!"

George also showed ability for including variation and humor in his compositional style. While most of George's music favored the piano timbre, one evening he discovered the timbre, "snow," on the synthesizer that intrigued him. It was an electronic sound that, when sustained, echoed continuously with soft, scattered electronic sounds. The piece he composed with this timbre was titled, "Love in Snow." It was a bit uncharacteristic for George, because it was very slow, patient, and mysterious. He loved playing it for the teachers. I asked him if he wanted to add an introduction. "An introduction? What's that?" I was a bit frustrated that he did not recall our session in which I discussed this concept. "You know," I explained, "A beginning to set up the music." "But I like my beginning," he responded. "Okay, then how about adding a filter?" I asked. "What's that?" I showed him how to add echo and delay filter with the software. He liked it and added it to each track. Then as we listened together to the new effects rendition, he suddenly banged out a loud cluster on the keyboard and enjoyed the effect that it caused—that is, my jumping three feet in the air. "Why don't we add this in as a surprise?" I asked after catching my breath. He liked that idea, and I helped him set up an additional track to record into. He listened carefully and waited until just the right moment, and then he added the surprise crash in the middle of the otherwise serene music.

George's wonderful sense of humor appeared in his other compositions as well. When he announced, "I'm composing 'Whisper Song,'" it drew chuckles from the other guys. I immediately guessed that I was not supposed to know about this song. For George, it turned out only to be the title of a silly composition he wrote about mad cow disease. After some research on my own, I learned that there is indeed a song titled "Wait (The Whisper Song)" by the Ying Yang twins, a sexually explicit hip-hop/rap tune that was very popular among African American adolescents. After listening to the real "Whisper Song," I understood why the title elicited giggles from the guys, and also why they didn't want me to know about this song. George's "Whisper Song," however, was a silly composition that alternated between his yelling about losing his leg in a high voice, sounds of bombs going off in the background, repeated laughter, and cows mooing. It was an amusing and cleverly crafted mix of recorded loops to tell a story. George seemed surprised that I thought it was so funny. He described the music by saying, "The guy is trying to get somebody to help him, because he has mad cow disease. So the cows have gone crazy (they're laughing) and taken over, and they're trying to hurt somebody, and there are bombs going off. Ha, ha, ha. Oooh ya, can't get enough of that!" Though George was in need of our attention, his good moods and silliness were infectious to us.

Antwoin

Antwoin was a confident young man with a carefree sense of humor and charming personality. Every week when he arrived, he politely asked us how we were doing in a most mature and sincere manner. He did not seem to have a care in the world. Each evening he came into the room with a smile, sat down at his computer station, and began to work. Antwoin composed the following unaccompanied spoken piece titled, "Baby Brother," in one of our middle sessions. The speaking is rhythmic, and each repeated phrase is spoken to sound a like an echo response.

"Baby Brother"

Hello? Hello?
Who is it? Who is it?

This is Matthew. This is Matthew.
Don't play with me. Don't play with me.
Yea maybe. Yea maybe.
I know you're an idiot, but what are you? I know you're an idiot, but what are you?
What are you? What are you?
[mumbled] I'm an a**hole. I'm an a**hole.
You totally freak me out. [shouting] YOU TOTALLY FREAK ME OUT.
[softer] It's totally cool—you freak me out. It's totally cool—you freak me out.

One particular evening, Antwoin earnestly summoned the counselor over from his usually peaceful resting spot in the corner of the room. Antwoin had been trying to pluck out the melody to a familiar Beethoven piano piece, "Für Elise," and wanted his help. Neither of them knew the title at that moment, but Antwoin sang the tune anyway. The counselor recognized it, and, having had some piano background himself, played the melody for Antwoin on the piano. Antwoin was thrilled. "Teach me how to play it! Please!" Antwoin begged. The counselor tried several methods, but finally wrote the letter names on a piece of paper inside Antwoin's notebook, with an attempt at writing the musical notation on the reverse side of the page. Antwoin wrote "Beethoven's 5th" at the top of that particular scrap of paper. Finally, the counselor took a permanent black marker and wrote the letter names on the synthesizer keys so that Antwoin would be able to connect the letter names on the paper to the letter names on the keys. Despite the written letter names, it was clear Antwoin picked up the melody by ear, thus not needing the notation or letter reminders.

As Antwoin continued learning the melody, my assistant walked over to see what he was doing. "What are you trying to play?" she asked as she put on a pair of headphones to listen. "Ah! Beethoven's 'Für Elise.'" She recognized the melody as Antwoin struggled to get it under his fingertips. "And where did you hear it before?" "I heard it in Target," he responded. "And I was thinking about it the last time I was here, but I couldn't think how to play it. And we have music therapy on Fridays, and I heard the music therapy guy playing it, plus it's programmed in this computer." My assistant probed, "What do you like about it?" "It's relaxing," he responded as he continued to get the notes under his fingertips. Antwoin's ultimate composition using the "Für Elise" melody was a creative "techno" version. It used an electronic timbre with a pulsating beat below the melody. It repeated several times, until it finally faded out at the end.

Antwoin continued his quest to learn familiar tunes. Another composition, titled "Q," mixed the melodies of "Ode to Joy" with the holiday version of "Joy to the World" in a seemingly random manner. He worked relentlessly in one class to play "Joy to the World." The digital scraps of his work showed twenty-eight different attempts to learn the melody, before he recorded it for his composition. Antwoin also showed a curious interest in Beethoven. During one session, I offered the students several CDs to listen to. Antwoin quickly grabbed my Beethoven CD and listened for several minutes. Antwoin composed a total of twelve compositions, each demonstrating great variety in style and compositional approach.

Tee

Tee, age 12, was the second youngest and the shortest student in class. He had a large mischievous smile and loved to tease. He appeared tough and worldly for his age, always hanging around the older Myles and Jonathan.

One evening Tee composed a song titled "Police." Everyone in the room noticed his loud voice in the microphone and the animation he demonstrated as he pounded the table to mimic the sound of knocking on the door. We learned that Tee witnessed the story of his lyrics while living in urban housing projects when he was nine years old. He described the music as being "about police coming into this man's house, because he murdered a girl." He continued in a factual manner, "We had police around our house every day, 'cause we used to live in the projects."

"Police"

Come on out.
Your time . . . Time is over, come out.
Shouldn't have murdered that girl.
I know you shouldn't a did that.
Open up the door! Open up the door!
We'll give ya a fat chance, just open up the door.
Open up the door, man.
Man, just open it up the door.
Open up the door!! Open up the door.
Come on now, open up the door. Ya need it.
Open up the door, man, I told you open up the door!!!
I said, oh now, you gonna make me start shootin' in here!!
Future style, with the lasers. I'm gonna burn your heart out.
[Rap style]
I'm walkin' down the street; you shouldn't a murdered that girl.
You wanna smoke some weed? You might as well be a crackhead.
[End rap]
Oh, snaps! You all did run, now I gotta chase her!
Get out of the bathroom right now!!! You ain't gotta pee; get out!
Uh oh, uh oh, I'm gonna shoot, shoot, shoot, shoot!
(sounds of getting shot)
I'm shootin', mmm hmm, mmm.
[inaudible]
Stop.

The composition, which describes police chasing and then killing a drug dealer, contains a mix of sounds including a helicopter, gunshots, pounding, and a bit of a rap rhythm beat in the middle. Despite the sadness and horror of the story, Tee was very excited about this composition. When I asked him why most of his music was loud, he responded with a shrug and said, "I grew up in a loud house." I wondered if Tee's inspiration to compose "Police" came from my lecture that evening on Steve Reich. I had played Reich's 1966 composition, "Come Out," composed for the benefit of six boys arrested for murder during the Harlem riots of 1964. The voice of a teenager in the looped music describes a beating that took place in Harlem's Twenty-eighth Precinct police station. The young men in the class were spellbound by this piece, and perhaps it was the inspiration for Tee's "Police."

Of his twenty-four compositions, one was noticeably different from Tee's other works. He composed it on the evening he was expelled from school. At first I thought Tee was teasing Antwoin when he came in bragging about his expulsion and complaining that it was Antwoin's fault. Tee acted tough and said, "I didn't like that school anyway" and "I hated the uniforms." He bragged that he was going to go to a different Catholic school on the South Side of Chicago. Tee was in a hurry to compose that night. He worked quickly and intensely.

The resulting composition, "Expel," provided a side of Tee we had never seen nor heard before that moment or since. It consisted of Tee singing in a soft, sweet unaccompanied voice lamenting the fact that he had to leave his school. The style and mood of his composition felt like a musical confession.

"Expel"
I don't know what I did to get kicked right out of school.
It felt so hard.
I don't know why I did. It felt so hard to say good-bye to my school.
[This line, and the following similar one, is sung in a melody reminiscent of
   "It's So Hard to Say Goodbye to Yesterday" by Boyz II Men.]
My school was Queen of Peace.
I don't know why I do these things,
'Cause I let somebody make me laugh, and I get into so much trouble today.
Wooooo.
It's just so hard to say good-bye to my school.
[Spoken] Yea.
I know what I did to get kicked out—
I punched this boy.
I cussed at my teacher.
It's so, so hard to get out of my school.
I left my friends.

I left my teacher.
I left my principal.
I left everybody that was my friend.
[Spoken] Yea, okay.

"Expel" impressed upon me the power that music has in the lives of these young men. Tee used this musical outlet to be emotional, sweet, and sad, whereas his identity had to be tough and nonchalant around his friends. In an interview at the end of our sessions, and while reviewing his musical output, Tee did not want to talk about "Expel." He told me he didn't like it and did not want to see it in his list of compositions. Yet it was something he created, because he had the opportunity to do so. The trust nurtured in our environment gave Tee this outlet to express himself openly.

Despite missing two sessions for bad behavior in the facility, Tee composed more music during the ninety minutes than any of the other young men. His demeanor was a pleasant front to the life woes that sometimes poured out through his music. He was charming and dismissed his music as no big deal, though he seemed to love composing, listening to music, and learning about music. When asked where his ideas came from, he paused, then thoughtfully replied, "From the past. All my stuff is true, except for the McDonald's stuff."

CONCLUSION: NEW QUESTIONS AND DISCOVERIES

What does it mean to teach composition? As music teachers, we are naturally concerned with knowing exactly how to plan, setting our goals and objectives with clearly defined outcomes. This is, after all, the culture of schools in the twenty-first century. In addition, music composition poses a challenge, because we ourselves have not been taught how to compose in our traditional musical education or teacher training. Our lack of training induces an even greater need for control, and we may use carefully defined objectives and rules to ensure success in getting students to a final product that can be assessed. The lesson I learned through this experience was that rather than controlling the compositional process, I simply needed to allow the students to play, to experiment, and to create with sound. As Burnard stated, "Our aim as music educators should be to facilitate a form of music education that focuses on genuine experiences of children being improvisers and composers rather than acting out a pre-defined model" (2000, p. 21).

The fine line between direct teaching and facilitating must be carefully examined and then balanced in a music composition class. To actually create from nothing in order to express oneself through sound is what makes the compositional process a unique pursuit. Further, composition has the potential to be more powerful than other musical activities students experience in schools. Composition gives students a chance to express their thoughts and emotions without having to explain anything to anybody. Children, especially at-risk children, gain from the experience of expressing themselves through artistic forms. With these students, an atmosphere of openness and trust is especially important (Appleton Gootman, 2002; De-Carlo & Hockman, 2003; Eccles & Appleton Gootman, 2002; Heath & Smyth, 1999; Tyson, 2004). Music composition supports individual development of ownership, autonomy, and authority that emerge as students become more competent and confident and recognize the knowledge associated with composing as problem solving (Berkley, 2004).

What about the compositions? At first I questioned the quality of the compositions, and I was discouraged. But as the class progressed, I learned that my aesthetic and theirs was different, and that we could learn from each other. I learned about Eminem, the Ying Yang twins, and Ludacris, and they learned about Steve Reich, Aaron Copland, and Beethoven. The development of quality in a music composition is a long, slow process. I have also learned not to judge quickly when I hear students' compositions. Rather, I ask questions and suggest potential changes, which they may or may not incorporate into the composition edits. The questioning critique (as opposed to telling critique), by themselves, their peers, and me, may help to develop students' abilities as lifelong critical thinkers and self-assessors. We might examine work of our peers in the visual arts and creative writing (e.g., Calkins, Hartman, & White, 2005; Reese, 2003; Soep, 1996) for guidance in our own understanding of how students develop such skills in music.

Finally, I learned that the soundscapes of these students and of all students' lives are pervasively and unconsciously influential in their compositions. And events as well as soundscapes inspire their music compositions. This has influenced me to add the prompt, "What inspires?" to my music curriculum. The students were inspired by the music they listened to daily, or heard in a local store, or heard on a CD I played for them. The inspiration must be there, and while it is naturally a part of their lives, it is the teacher's duty to help students discover and fuel the flame.

Music surrounded them, and they integrated it into their lives in the most creative ways by composing it themselves. My teaching was not central, but rather peripheral, to the time they had for sound exploration and experimentation. The approach to music composition in our classrooms might be more effective if we were to set up an environment in which students were given the freedom to explore and experiment—an environment that creates a need to know with the new sounds and ideas they learn—without our constant interruption. Our teaching environments should expose children to the widest variety of music—our own favorites as well as theirs. The muse only needs to be inspired through exposure to new ideas and new musics.

REFERENCES

Appleton Gootman, J. (Ed.). (2002). *After-school programs to promote child and adolescent development: Summary of a workshop.* Washington, DC: National Academy Press.

Berkley, R. (2004). Teaching composing as creative problem solving: Conceptualising composing pedagogy. *British Journal of Music Education, 21*(3), 239–263.

Block, D. H., Harris, T., & Laing, S. (2005). Open studio process as a model of social action: A program for at-risk youth. *Art Therapy: Journal of the American Art Therapy Association, 22*(1), 32–38.

Burnard, P. (2000). How children ascribe meaning to improvisation and composition: Rethinking pedagogy in music education. *Music Education Research, 2*(1), 7–23.

Calkins, L. M., Hartman, A., & White, Z. R. (2005). *One to one: The art of conferring with young writers.* Portsmouth, NH: Heinemann.

Canino, I. A. (1995). Coping with stress through art: A program for urban minority children. In H. W. Harris, H. C. Blue, & E. E. H. Griffith (Eds.), *Racial and ethnic identity: Psychological development and creative expression* (pp. 115–134). New York: Routledge.

DeCarlo, A., & Hockman, E. (2003). Rap therapy: A group work intervention method for urban adolescents. *Social Work with Groups, 26*(3), 45–59.

Eccles, J., & Appleton Gootman, J. (2002). *Community programs to promote youth development.* Washington, DC: National Academy Press.

Heath, S. B., & Smyth, L. (1999). *ArtsShow: Youth and community development.* Washington, DC: Partners for Livable Communities.

Hickey, M. (2005). *The results of a field-test study of a curriculum model for teaching music composition to children.* Paper presented at the Fourth International Research in Music Education Conference, April 5–9, 2005. University of Exeter, U. K.

Reese, S. (2003). Responding to student compositions. In M. Hickey (Ed.), *Music composition in the schools: A new horizon for music education* (pp. 211–232). Reston, VA: MENC.

Soep, E. M. (1996). An art in itself: Youth development through critique. *New Designs for Youth Development, 12*(4), 42–46.

Tyson, E. H. (2004). Hip hop therapy: An exploratory study of a rap music intervention with at-risk and delinquent youth. *Journal of Poetry Therapy, 15*(3), 131–144.

12

Boys' Voices:
Inside and Outside Choral Music

Patrick K. Freer

Yeah, it's been a rite of passage, all right.

—Clark, age fifteen

There is a long history of empirical research and practitioner-based literature noting a decline in the number of adolescent males who participate in choral music as they progress through middle school and into high school. Studies indicate that boys withdraw from choral singing during secondary school because of a lack of male role models (Van Camp, 1988), the changing voice and choral music's relevance to career goals (Phillips, 1988), and issues surrounding male identity (Demorest, 2000). The three profiles in this chapter represent one way of listening to the words of adolescent boys about their experiences in choral music (Freer, 2006b, 2007).

To fully understand the boys' experience in choral music, we need to listen to stories from multiple perspectives. At least three groups of boys have stories to relate that are integral to our understanding of the adolescent choral experience: boys who continuously sing in choral music ensembles, those who withdraw, and those who feel marginalized from the process because they do not see a connection between choral music and their lives or abilities (Freer, 2006b). The narratives contained in this chapter represent these three unique perspectives.

The following chapter contains the stories of boys enrolled in a school in the southeastern United States that I will call Holtz Academy. The two choral teachers at Holtz Academy are former graduate students of mine, and I have had frequent opportunities to work with the choral ensembles at the school. I met with the teachers to discuss the goals of this project, and they then selected the boys who participated. A total of six boys were interviewed, and the three youngest boys are profiled in this chapter. After the requisite permissions and consent were secured, each boy was interviewed on three occasions, with each session lasting approximately thirty minutes. The initial interviews were introductory in nature, and subsequent interviews built upon previous conversations. At the conclusion of each session, the boys were informed of the topics to be discussed in the following interview(s) and were encouraged to bring notes to the interviews as reminders of thoughts they might like to relate. Each boy brought notes to the interviews at one point or another. The boys were asked about such issues as the relationship of school music to their daily lives, their musical lives outside of school, effective instructional practices, peer support and/or pressure, and role models for continued musical involvement.

The semi-structured interviews were videotaped, transcribed, and coded using HyperRESEARCH qualitative analysis software. The boys had opportunities to review the transcripts for accuracy, which resulted in several clarifications of wording and intent. The boys took great pleasure in selecting their pseudonyms, and all other identifying markers of the school, teachers, and boys have been similarly altered for representation within this chapter. During a group meeting prior to the interviews, the boys collectively expressed the desire that their comments not reflect negatively upon their teachers. Though I agreed to omit any words that might be of concern, this subsequently proved to be unnecessary. The quotations appearing here are presented exactly as stated by the boys. Any researcher-generated clarifications are indicated within brackets.

Holtz Academy, a K–12 private school, is particularly interesting because the choral music program has been historically uneven: a relatively weak elementary program, a strong middle-school program, and a high-school program that has attracted only a minimal number of boys. Holtz Academy has recently employed a new high-school chorus teacher who has enrolled a large number of boys through the "football choir"—a beginning men's ensemble specially designed to fill the arts requirement for the school's athletes.

When reading their words, it is important to note how these boys describe their experiences and perceptions, particularly with regard to self-efficacy, autonomy, and musical ability. Research indicates that adolescent student musicians attribute their success or failure to their individual abilities (e.g., Schmidt, 1995; Legette, 1998), and that the perception of individual ability determines continued participation in musical practice (e.g., Ruddock & Leong, 2005). It is hoped that these stories will spark thoughts and conversations about how we might better attract, engage, and retain adolescent boys in secondary-school choral programs.

DANNY

Well, my name is Danny, and I have been at this school for nine years. I'm fourteen years old, and I'm in eighth grade. I started here in kindergarten. I've been here quite a long time. I started participating in the chorus here, starting in the fifth grade, and I really fell in love with it. I really enjoy singing. I like to perform. I really love to make people smile, make them laugh, and just make them feel good by being a performer.

Danny, whose interests in music are somewhat eclectic, stated:

Honestly, I cannot stand rap or hip-hop, or any of the other stuff that the rest of the world likes, it seems. I like classic rock, Queen, the Eagles, Elvis, stuff like that. I actually had to do a paper on rock 'n' roll and I found out a bunch of stuff. Rock 'n' roll, it seems to me, was the first music to come together by just combining stuff, like Elvis Presley made rock by combining blues, gospel, jazz, and he got rock. And, it's a perfect mix, to me, of all really good music, because rock can be anything from fast songs like "Life in the Fast Lane" by the Eagles, or it can be slow, like parts of "Bohemian Rhapsody."

Danny's interviews showed him to be an enthusiastic, optimistic member of both his middle-school chorus and several ensembles outside of school. He is a tall, lean boy with a tousle of blonde hair. He speaks using pitches lower than what might be comfortable, perhaps because he knows he is being interviewed about his experiences as a vocalist. He eagerly offered:

We've done musicals, and I've gotten some pretty good lead roles in those, and I'd like to say it's because of chorus because it's improved my singing. It started off with "Hey, singing might be fun" to "Hey, singing in front of a bunch of people onstage might be fun" and then it just evolved from there. It's affected me in lots of ways.

Speaking about his singing voice, Danny said:

I've had people tell me that I'm good. I've gotten a solo every now and then in chorus. I wouldn't say that I'm the best, but I think I'm not bad. I feel that I'm a good singer, but it's not really up to me to decide.

Danny was asked how his voice was different than other boys his age. He replied:

You can tell that they haven't sung much, because when everyone sings and we sound good, you can look over and just instantly pick out the ones that aren't singing. Mine's different, because I keep singing. I keep training it. I practice it, I pay attention, I rehearse, and they really don't. I think this is apparent, but I really love music. I enjoy music. To me it seems like I've improved, and it just seems like a talent that I can keep going with.

He continued:

When I was in fifth grade, the fifth-grade boys and girls would sing basically the same thing. There might be one kid whose voice started changing early, and someone might make a comment about that, and they'll laugh, and the teacher would just go, "All right, just sing it the best you can, but try to sing it right." But, I was not one of those kids. I was one of the kids who went [using a high-pitched voice], "Oh, oh, pick me, pick me. I want to sing the high part." But, now, I sing more in the baritone-ish, lower bass, low-baritone, high bass sort of stuff. And, it seems like I'm remembering back, "Geez, I used to be able to hit that note. What happened?" 'Cause I actually started off this year being put in the tenors and my voice has gotten deeper since the beginning of the school year.

Danny kept singing through the voice change, because:

I sorta felt that singing, just continuing to sing through it helped my voice keep a good range. The thought going through my mind was, "If I keep singing, if I just keep trying to hit those notes, those notes might not go away, and I might be able to still go into the low notes and keep some of the higher notes." But I definitely believe that a lot of guys drop out of choirs because of their changing voice. They can go from hitting a high A or something, and all of a sudden they can't come anywhere close to it; or if they're in the middle of the voice change, their voice sounds really weird. They're unsure about how their voice is; they don't trust their voice enough.

Danny did not sing in his elementary chorus:

because there were only about three or four guys in there. It ranged from the first grade to the fourth grade, and there were about twenty or thirty girls in there—a large amount of girls and just a couple of guys.

When he was in fifth grade, the middle-school chorus teacher personally asked Danny to join. Part of the appeal was:

being with some older kids, but it was mostly because I thought it would be fun, and if I didn't like it, I could always change classes the next year. I started coming just 'cause a bunch of my friends were doing it and when we started out, our chorus was a very small group, but as it sort of went on, as we entered the sixth and seventh grade, our chorus grew enormously, to a hundred from about twenty people, just from us getting better and us telling our friends how fun it was. And a lot of that growth came from guys coming in there with their friends.

Danny referred to Clark, another boy profiled in this chapter, as he recalled:

When I was in fifth- and sixth-grade chorus, there was one guy in the seventh- and eighth-grade chorus.

Danny stressed that the biggest recruitment factor for boys was the influence of other boys:

The guys brought the guys in. I'm already thinking about trying to get more people because I know that our chorus, as it is, it's a good size, but it could be bigger and better. I also feel that I've been a pretty good role model for the boys that are younger than me, like our sixth-graders.

Although Danny had not worked with a male chorus teacher, he felt that boys might be more inclined to join if there were:

a guy chorus teacher because he might be a little bit easier to relate to. If he's like my age, then every now and again his voice might crack while he's singing. The guy chorus teacher, he can relate to that. He can go, "Hey, I can remember that."

Teachers might make chorus more appealing to boys by allowing them some autonomy with regard to repertoire selection. Danny suggested:

If they're given old, slow songs, they're probably going to be, "Oh, it's boring, I don't want to do this." If you give them a good selection of music, if you let them choose what they'd like to sing—that they want to sing—then they can pay special attention to staying on the right part, and it would help them remember to prepare, to put the right attitude with the song, to put the right feeling into the song, to put the right notes in the song.

For Danny, repertoire is central to the attraction of choral music for boys:

It wouldn't surprise me if a bunch of guys started thinking, "This chorus stuff, it's not real music, it's like school music, it's the nice stuff that your mom and dad want to hear, the stuff that old people go to the concert halls to hear. It's not the stuff that is fun to listen to, the stuff that's cool to listen to." One of the things that really strikes me as a not very fun song is if it's really, r-e-a-l-l-y s-l-o-w and just sort of feels like the song drones on and on forever when we're singing it. But, if it were slow and then it got really fast and then had some change, that'd be a fun song.

Appropriate repertoire would likewise assist boys dealing with their changing voices. Danny stated:

Maybe pick songs, or have them sing parts that are a lot easier on their voice, things that they know that they can sing that aren't like totally like having to stretch for it, if you understand what I mean.

Danny believed that the rehearsal process itself might be a barrier for middle-school boys:

A lot of the guys just think it's the same thing, over and over again.

For Danny, repetitious rehearsal procedures lowered the challenge level, causing boys to become bored. He gave an example of:

a kid who has been in All-State [choir] a couple times, and I don't know if he's doing chorus next year, because he's one of the guys who goofs off, even though he really is good. He's a really good singer, but he was getting bored. It's like, "I've done everything I can in chorus, I've done really well, and it's boring now, there's nothing else to learn."

Danny said that middle-school choral programs ought to be structured to involve boys of varying experience levels:

I think there are guys that probably would want to be in chorus next year, but they aren't very confident in their voice. They sing it well, but they just sorta sing soft. A beginning men's ensemble would be a good choice for a guy that wants to sing but isn't really confident in his voice. But for the guy that feels chorus is boring because he's really good, he should tell the director, "It seems like I know a lot of this stuff, could we do something challenging, something harder?"

In Danny's view, there are three groups of students:

the ones that have loved it right off, the ones that have learned to love it, and the ones that won't. It's really just that simple. The teacher needs to pay attention to those kids in the middle—the kids who are interested enough to step in the door, but aren't quite sure about it.

It bothered Danny when other boys did not share his enthusiasm for choral music. He wondered:

Wow, how could someone come to a chorus class and not enjoy it and not find it fun? More important, how could someone come to a chorus class and not sing? They're actually getting better at singing, but they don't want to acknowledge the fact that this could be a cool thing to do. They will enjoy making class not about singing, but about them. They express the need for attention during class when they goof off; whenever the teacher turns the back, they start doing something stupid.

In response, Danny related:

I've actually thought about that before. What would I do to make things better? 'Cause I always go, "Well, we should do something to get them involved." But I keep thinking, "How can I do that?"

The options known to Danny were few, but they revolved around personal accountability, drawing boys into the experience by highlighting the positive changes in their vocal development:

> I feel like that would probably bring them to pay attention a bit more; it would probably give them the drive to improve. These guys, you can tell they want to, but they're limited by their peers, by their friends.

The notion of separating boys from girls during the middle-school years was strongly endorsed by Danny:

> If a guy tries to sing something, if he can't quite hit it, sometimes a girl might laugh at him and he might be, "Oh, I got laughed at by a girl." But if it's a bunch of guys that can sort of pal around, they can be a little on the silly side and probably still sound pretty decent. But then the girls' choir can do their thing, and the guys' choir will probably be a little bit less self-conscious about their own voices. And the songs might even be a bit more open, like the right kind of songs, like an all-guys type of song might have a bit better range, maybe. Then the guys can be guys and still be in choir; they can still hang out with their friends and they don't have to worry so much about their own voice, and the girls can do their thing.

Danny enjoyed being drawn into the context of the music being rehearsed. He said:

> We did "Walking in Memphis," and we were talking about, like, "What does this mean?" I happened to really like that song and I explained something about it, and the teacher went, "Oh, yeah, this means that and that and that." So if you can sort of get a feel for what the song means and you really grasp the whole concept of the song, then it makes it a lot easier to get into the song and get out a good feeling for the song. If you just randomly spout some information—"This means this, the composer makes it like this"—it will sorta go in one ear and out the other.

Within the rehearsal itself, Danny liked:

> when there's a bit of a diversity. What happens sometimes is she'll get us in a circle and she'll get us so we can hear all the different parts. We can hear what it actually sounds like. I like it when, to practice one part, she'll separate us off into different parts of the room.

One of Danny's first tasks as a high-school student was to enroll in the choral program. He had admired the high-school men's choir, because:

> the teacher gives them more of a choice in what they have to sing, and you hear their songs, and they get to sing the stuff that they can hit, like the really low, rich, bassey stuff. If they have to do something that's like a school song they'll

put like an edge on it, they'll make it really cool, they'll have fun with it. And you can tell that they actually like chorus.

Though Danny will sing instead with the elite mixed chamber choir, he's:

very excited about the fact that, more so than our middle-school chorus, we're going to have guys that actually want to sing, we're going to have a bunch of people that really want to be in the chorus, . . . they'll want to sing and have fun.

CLARK

Clark is a fifteen-year-old tenth-grader who sang in chorus throughout middle school but is no longer singing. Clark plays the baritone saxophone in the high-school band, is an avid theater student, plays sports with his friends, and loves math. Clark's interest in band began with a single year of saxophone lessons in fourth grade. He was initially intrigued by a visit of the high-school band to his school when he was a third-grader. However, Clark quit the band after just one year, because:

I guess I just didn't like having to practice.

When he enrolled at Holtz Academy in sixth grade, Clark related:

I don't think I got a chance to sign up for band; nobody ever said anything about it.

In grade eight, he decided to join the marching band as a way to make friends. Asked how he could recall enough about the saxophone to pick it up after a three-year absence, he replied:

I probably should have practiced more than I did, but I had a pretty great teacher in fourth grade.

For Clark, joining the band meant the chance to:

go to the games, get a free entrance. Most of my friends are in band; the people in it are lots of fun.

That sense of fun and friendship was demonstrated when the high-school marching band:

had a middle-school band night, and one of my friends was there, and I just hung around with him and really enjoyed the atmosphere of a Friday game.

Clark joined chorus as an extracurricular course offered during sixth grade and enrolled formally in grades seven and eight. He joined the sixth-grade chorus because:

I had just moved to this school, and I was sort of looking for friends. And that part didn't really work out, because I was the only sixth-grade boy doing chorus. But I just sorta liked chorus and liked singing.

Clark added:

I sing at church, not with a group, but I like singing at church, and we have chapel here every Friday. And, I enjoy singing at that. I actually annoy my family because if a song I like comes up on the radio, I sing along to it very loud and boisterously. I don't really have the kind of voice that, you know, modern singers have today. When I sing, I think I'm more of a bass. And most male singers today are in between a tenor and an alto, and I can't really sing that high. I scream very, very loudly at marching band games, and that's sorta killed my voice. I don't look at myself as a very good singer now.

Clark spoke haltingly during his interviews, expressing annoyance at the frequent "cracking" of his voice as his speaking pitch abruptly changed from low to high. Clark is a rather heavy-set young man with the beginnings of facial hair along his chin and upper lip. He initially described his voice change as:

very gradual, along my seventh- and eighth-grade year but then added, "I didn't really take care of my voice, you know, like a singer would, so it just sort of dropped. Now when I try to sing higher notes, it either doesn't come out or it comes out an octave too high.

Clark mentioned that he would be interested in knowing more about the physical process of vocal change, so that he could understand why his voice kept cracking. His lower speaking pitch means that Clark is often:

mistaken for my dad versus being mistaken for my sister on the phone. Yeah, it's been a rite of passage, all right.

The changing voice was the topic of a mentoring relationship between older and younger boys in Clark's previous school system. He recalled:

I remember that we had students from the high school in their senior year, some of them would come down to the lower school and actually intern almost, sorta being a teacher's aide. And I remember when they came to our chorus class; we were all really impressed. We asked them a lot of questions about changing voices, and it was pretty fun.

There was one boy in particular who served as a role model for Clark:

> I can't really remember his name, but of the three, he was the best singer, and I thought it was really cool just to be able to have fun with singing.

Clark was the only male member of his sixth-grade chorus. He continued to participate because:

> I just enjoyed it. I enjoyed taking the class, learning a bit of music theory as well as singing. Plus, I just don't like to disappoint people. But, the other part of it is that my teacher's a very vibrant, very captivating person, and being one of the only guys, I sort of developed a relationship with her that was a lot of fun. She moved pretty quickly. It was like, middle-schoolers don't have much of an attention span, so it was not a lot of staying too much on one thing for too long. And then, I think a lot of the trips to competitions were really fun for me, getting graded on what we had done.

His two best friends joined him in the seventh-grade chorus:

> partly since I was doing it and partly because they decided to try something new. It was just fun because we could work on stuff together. During down times we could talk to each other about guy stuff.

Clark once again found himself the sole male member of his chorus in eighth grade. He recalled:

> I actually sorta made fun of my friends for dropping out. I put up a wall, I guess. I just went to chorus, sang, and then left chorus. But I just didn't really talk that much to other people. It wasn't a very social thing for me in eighth grade. So I dropped out in ninth grade, because most of my friends were doing band, and I couldn't do both band and chorus at the same time. I think if I'd had the opportunity to do both chorus and band at the high school, I think I would. Because there's just as many people saying, "Ha, ha, band geek" as there are saying "Ha, ha, chorus kid."

At least during grades six and eight, Clark's choral experience was rather solitary, which was, as he said:

> ironic, because chorus is supposed to be a group activity. . . . It was positive in the sense that I stood out, and I was important. I got to basically hold my section together. I got to shine, which, you know, helps with the ego. But, it was also a not-positive thing during rehearsals. Girls would be chatty, and I couldn't really join them. In eighth grade, I sort of felt awkward, just because at the time all four grades were singing as one choir, because the seventh- and eighth-[grade] choruses were so small. There were a good amount of boys in the fifth and sixth grades. And, so, I was the only person singing like tenor, sort

of bass. But, not much has changed. I'm the only one on my instrument in band now, and then I'm only one of two people in my grade who does theater, so it's sort of the same thing.

Clark had some advice for teachers working with small numbers of boys in their choruses:

I think it's sort of a fine line between treating them special for being the only boys and then treating them too differently. Like, I would just advise them to just sort of treat the boys like all the rest of the members of the chorus. Not to single them out too much, but it also does help to give them rewards for sticking with chorus. I know this is very conflicting, but treat them differently but not too differently. There was a time when we were designing our chorus logo, and we had four different things, our school mascot, something else, a flag, and then my chorus teacher said we should put a bass clef on the fourth thing in honor of me. I wasn't sure whether it was a joke or not, but it sort of felt awkward, feeling sort of singled out.

Holtz Academy's choral program did not seem to provide a good opportunity for Clark to become involved as a ninth-grader. He said:

The high-school men's chorus was sort of a joke last year; they didn't really take it seriously. I wasn't good enough for the Chamber Choir, so I couldn't sing there, and I didn't want to sing with the not-serious guys in the men's choir. So there wasn't a place for me. But our top choir is actually very good. That's sorta what I wish I had really done, you know, stuck with it, gone through with it, and done the top choir. I really want to try to get my voice back in shape. I would like to go to a college where I could audition for an *a cappella* group.

I asked Clark if it would make a difference having a male choral teacher. He replied:

I think it's not really the gender, but how gender influences the teaching style. As a singing model, it all depends on the teacher's ability, but I don't think that it would be all that much different than getting the note from the piano or the female teacher trying to sing lower. My chorus teacher was a soprano, so she couldn't really sing low. At first she would try, but then it became a joke. She played on the piano or sang an octave up.

In Clark's view, issues of the changing voice and masculinity are central to why middle-school boys do not participate in chorus. He related:

It's very embarrassing to have a changing voice. It's very embarrassing in chorus class to have notes that you can hit sometimes and that you can't hit other times. It's very frustrating, and I think that's a very good reason why people drop out. When you become a seventh-grader, you're trying to be a man. Guys are trying to do manly stuff which they think is real life, and they don't see a lot of the teamwork values of chorus, the relationships that chorus provides as a lesson for real life. They don't realize that it's helping them; they don't really see the value. They used to sing just for fun, and now that they're becoming adults, they want to do something constructive, and they don't see chorus as constructive.

Clark continued:

I think sorta the perception of chorus is sort of a girly, fruity thing, I guess. Middle-schoolers, especially guys, are afraid to express emotions, and I think that's a big part of what chorus should be. It's like dedicating yourself to the song, in a sense, not just going up there and mouthing the words to a pitch, but actually trying hard on the song. I'm not sure how to put it, but it's like there's a difference between saying the right words and saying the right pitch versus really singing a song. And I think really singing a song expresses emotion, and I think that's what middle-school boys are afraid to do, to step out of their comfort zone.

Once boys join, Clark believed many drop out:

because of how their friends pester at them for doing chorus. "Ha, ha, you're the chorus kid." It's sort of hard to stand up to that.

After making those comments at the end of one interview session, Clark began the next session saying:

I thought a little bit about how music teachers could retain more students. I would guess just do a lot of different styles of music. Don't just do classical stuff, but don't shy away from it. Do a good mix of fun, Disney songs and stuff like "Ave Maria" or classical, beautiful chorus pieces. Now, to get more students, showcase your chorus in front of the student body, show them how much fun it can be. Like when my teacher gave us boys input on what songs we wanted, it would be more manly songs versus more girly songs. I think you do need to have some school music, but I think a lot of it should be fun music, getting people energized, getting the singers energized, getting the crowd energized, and just having fun.

For Clark, the ultimate goal of participating in choir was the satisfaction of being involved in making music that sounded good. That was reflected when we discussed the possibility of having separate male and female choruses in middle school. Clark said:

I think—this is just my opinion—that if you do a middle-school boys' choir, it's not going to sound as good as a middle-school girls' choir because of the changing voices and the difficulty of finding the right music for, you know, a seventh- and eighth-grade boys' choir. And, I think that not sounding as good will frustrate a lot of boys like me.

BILLY

Billy is a lean, tall, fourteen-year-old eighth-grader with a broad shock of blond hair. He is a rather quiet boy who uses few words when conversing. Billy is extremely interested in baseball, football, swimming, and golf. He would one day like to be an Air Force pilot. He played trumpet in band from fifth through eighth grades until a scheduling conflict forced him to give up band in favor of drama. Billy reported that he never sang much in elementary school:

> We just kinda sang a little bit, but we just kept the beat on stuff and did little maracas.

Billy likes to listen to "rock, classic rock, rap, and country." He stated:

> Well, my Dad won't listen to anything except country, so when you're in his car, you're going to listen to country. And then he kinda likes classical rock, too, so we listen to some of that. And rap, a lot of kids at school listen to it, and I've listened to it a couple times, and I like it.

Billy wanted to play guitar and put together a garage band:

> I used to play guitar, but it was when I was like eight, but I guess I gave up on it.

Billy described his voice change as gradual, with a change process "probably a little bit smoother" than that of his friends. He related that he knew what muscles are involved in his sports activities and knew what he could do physically to improve specific athletic skills. When asked if he would be interested in knowing about his own vocal anatomy, he replied, "That would be super interesting!"

Billy's involvement in band was sparked when he attended a fourth-grade assembly during which:

> the middle-school band actually came down to the lower school and performed for us and let us try out the instruments, so that was pretty cool. I don't really remember the chorus doing that. And everybody did band in fifth grade, so I guess that might be why I joined. Plus, I was impressed by the trumpet 'cause it was pretty loud and had the main parts of the songs.

Billy responded to the older students serving as role models for the younger students:

> It seemed really cool to do it since they were doing it. There's a kid who played on my baseball team when he was in sixth grade and I was in fourth grade, and he played the trumpet, so I guess he had an effect on me.

Billy's family sings in church, but only as part of the congregation. He was asked to pay attention to his family's singing as part of this project and reported that he could hear his dad singing softly. Billy inquired about his father's singing experience, stating:

> He looked kinda surprised 'cause he was just walking by and I asked him why didn't he sing louder. And he really didn't answer. He probably just doesn't want to talk about it.

His sister, a sixth-grader, was a member of the middle-school chorus at Holtz Academy, but:

> she doesn't sing. She stands there like this [imitates a bored stance] and goes like this [moves mouth silently]. I think her friends were doing it, and she thought it would be fun, but then she found out that she didn't like to sing.

The night before one of our interviews, Billy attended his sister's chorus performance. He recalled:

> She was kinda excited, 'cause I guess they got to dance during one of the choruses of the song. I think she thought it was pretty fun, but she still didn't sing!

Though Billy thought that he was unlikely to sing in a chorus ("I think it's too late for me"), future participation with group singing held some appeal, particularly:

> if my friends did—maybe if I met somebody who was really nice and he was doing the chorus and he kinda motivated me to do it, I would. If there was [sic] other guys beginning to sing, probably it'd be good, it'd be fun. I just don't like singing alone. Singing in a group would be a lot better.

When asked why he did not feel self-conscious playing baseball, he said the difference was:

> 'cause I know I can do it. But I don't know if I can sing. I have confidence in baseball but not in chorus.

For Billy, singing was:

fun if you're good at it, but I'm not a really good singer. I just don't sound good.

Billy described his voice as "kinda low when I'm talking to people, but when I'm yelling it's kinda high" and that it had begun getting lower "when I got into middle school." He related:

Me and my friend, we like to have a karaoke night, when we sing one song on Friday night. Last Friday we videotaped, oh, what was it?—oh—"Beer for My Horses" by Willie Nelson and Toby Keith.

He laughed and exclaimed, "*No!*" when I asked if he sounded good. But when I asked why he made the videotape, he responded:

It was probably just fun, because nobody else was listening to us, so I guess we weren't scared to do anything.

I asked Billy if anyone had ever asked him to join chorus, to which he responded by shaking his head "no." But if a teacher had complimented his voice and invited him to join chorus, Billy commented that he "might have done it, yeah. If I started early. Yeah, totally." According to Billy, other students:

think chorus is fun in our grade. And I was going to do it, but some of my friends talked me out of it. We were all getting out of band, because we didn't like it anymore, and we heard chorus was kinda easy because there was no homework or anything, and all you did was kinda sing, but my friend's mom didn't want him to do it, so he talked me out of it. Maybe she just wanted him to be challenged more.

Still, Billy believed that the chorus was:

pretty good. My sister's in chorus, so I come to some of the performances and everybody has a good voice, but sometimes I don't like the songs they sing. They sound kinda weird. I think the songs are supposed to be funny. Maybe if I was in fifth grade I would like them.

Billy stated that school choruses would be more appealing if they sang:

songs that everybody knows, or if they sang about stuff I like, that'd be good, too. Maybe adventurous songs would be cool. Maybe hiking in the mountains, going off to some new place. They did some TV shows and Beach Boys, so I guess they did make it a lot better for this year.

Billy's experiences in the middle-school arts curriculum prompted him to enroll in an art course during his freshman year in high school. He said:

I like sculpting, you know, pots and animals. But the school schedule does not allow him to enroll in more than one arts course. I asked him why he dropped out of band after seventh grade. Billy said, "We had to practice ninety minutes a week. Plus, I just didn't like the trumpet anymore. I wanted to play percussion.

I asked if he could have switched instruments, and he said it wouldn't have mattered since:

I just didn't like it anymore. Our teacher was kinda mean. Like, we couldn't really talk at all if she was working with somebody else, we couldn't just talk with the person next to us. And she wouldn't let us sit anywhere. I had a clarinet friend, and I was the trumpet, and we tried to sit next to each other one day 'cause the trumpet section and clarinet section sat next to each other, but she didn't like that. So she made us move. Probably because she thought we'd be disruptive.

I asked if sitting elsewhere would have helped Billy concentrate. He responded with a broad grin:

More. Well, I mean, it depends on when you're talking to him. If you're talking when we're not doing anything, then, yeah. But if you're talking to him when we're, like, doing the piece, then no. In English, we can pretty much sit where we want to, but we have to sit towards the front. And, history, too. I think the teachers should kinda go in with the impression that the students are gonna do the right thing rather than the bad thing.

For Billy, time to interact with friends would have increased his enjoyment and his motivation within school classes.
Billy related that in band:

I wasn't the best trumpet player, but I was one of the top two. And, I guess it was kinda getting a lot easier. If I got really good, I'd have stayed in there. But I was just, you know, average, so I guess if she would have challenged me a little bit more, I might have stayed in longer. Our band teacher really didn't push you to be better. She just expected you to get better.

I asked Billy to explain the difference between pushing and expecting, and he replied:

Well, giving encouraging words and motivating them to be better rather than just saying, "Just go home and practice this and then you'll be better." Like, our coaches encourage you when you do something great; they give you compliments. But, then they'll also push you if, like, you've got something wrong with your swing in baseball, they'll push you to get better. Our band teacher just expected us to get better. No pushing or compliments. Another thing, when math is hard, if you don't get it at first, but once somebody explains it to you, it's like, "Wow, that's easy" Music should be like that.

DISCUSSION

Optimal Experiences

The words of these boys clearly indicate that choral music experiences provide valuable opportunities to develop musical skills, heighten spiritual expression, communicate with an audience, collaborate with others, and achieve artistic growth (Hylton, 1981). It is particularly interesting to note that Danny described his choral experience as transformative and unlike other experiences in school. Danny wondered, "Wow, how could someone come to a chorus class and not enjoy it and not find it fun?"

Csikszentmihalyi (1990) identified such instances when experience moves beyond the mundane and becomes infused with certain conditions that cause people to seek repetition of these experiences. These "flow" experiences are characterized by high levels of both perceived challenge and perceived skill, a clarity of goals, deep personal involvement and concentration, self-directedness, self-awareness, the receiving of immediate feedback, and a lack of awareness concerning time constraints. These optimal experiences have been identified in students during music instruction, including during middle-school choral rehearsals (Bloom and Skutnick-Henley, 2005; Custodero, 2002; Freer, 2008). Danny and Clark described many of these flow characteristics in their stories. Clark commented, "I stood out and I was important. . . . I got to shine, which, you know, helps with the ego," and Danny wanted to continually increase the challenge level: "What would I do to make things better. . . . How can I do that?"

The Importance of Relationships

A theme that emerges from these stories is the importance of relationships. Sometimes the important relationship is between student and teacher (Danny and Clark), while family members play positive or negative roles in the musical lives of other boys (Billy). Friendships can also tie boys to chorus. It is perhaps no coincidence that Billy did not have any friends in chorus and that he was the only boy who had never sung in choir. A lack of peer support eventually drew Clark to withdraw from choir, though he persevered for two years as the only male member of his chorus. Students who exhibit high levels of social skills during the middle-school years are generally those who have strong, enduring friendships. Strong friendships provide support through the transitions to and from middle school and enhance positive feelings about school and learning (Aikins, Bierman, & Parker, 2005; Godfrey, 2003).

For the singers I profiled, the goal of musical excellence was prominent, but only when it was achieved with friends and comrades. They appreciated teachers who allowed for those friendships to take hold during rehearsal time and concert preparation.

A Sense of Belonging

These boys desired opportunities for autonomy, chances to interact with peers, personal attention from their teacher, activity-based learning experiences, and the expectation of high musical standards (Freer, 2008; Jackson & Davis, 2000). A sense of ownership and belongingness pervades the stories of those boys most successful in school, whether or not they are members of the choral program. Foreshadowing current thoughts about adolescent identity development, Sullivan (1953) emphasized that a sense of belongingness was key to the formation of a healthy self-concept during adolescence. Each boy spoke of this belongingness in terms of sports and music, primary contexts in which boys gain peer acceptance (Daniels & Leaper, 2006). The strong relationship between sports and music exhibited by these boys is no doubt influenced by the culture of the particular school they attend. Research indicates that students have higher educational expectations and achievement when they are involved in both athletics and music than when only involved in athletics (Feldman & Matjasko, 2007; Snyder & Spreitzer, 1977).

The boys interviewed for this chapter did not always agree on the reasons for boys withdrawing from chorus. Danny and Clark concurred that frustration with the changing voice has the potential to drive even the most interested boys away from chorus. Billy and Clark suggested that teachers could ameliorate this problem by providing specific information about vocal physiology and development so that boys can know what to expect. These boys did not have much experience with male choral teachers, and they were reluctant to suggest that male teachers would have more of a positive impact on adolescent boys than female teachers. But, they did emphasize the importance of creating opportunities for older boys to mentor younger boys. Only one boy, Clark, raised the possibility that singing could be perceived as "girly" or "fruity."

THE PERSONAL EXPERIENCE OF CHORAL MUSIC

As the stories of these boys indicate, the choral experience of adolescent boys is deeply personal. The making of choral music is collectively experienced with peers, but it is the individual experience that seems to determine the persistence and transition of boys through the elementary years, young adolescence, and later adolescent choral experiences during high school. That experience might be changed, and possibly improved, through the creation of separate experiences for boys and girls (Freer, 2006a), attention to the unique needs of male adolescent changing voices (Cooksey, 2000), and focused conversations between teachers about pedagogical techniques that specifically meet the needs of adolescent male singers (Barham, 2002; Freer, 2005; McClung, 2006).

These boys had a vision of what choral music should be and what their choruses could become. The biggest disappointment, however, was found within Clark's statement, "I really want to try to get my voice back in shape. I would like to go to a college where I could audition for an *a cappella* group." Behind those words was a disheartened boy who blamed himself for giving up on chorus, even though he had persevered as the only boy in the chorus for two years. When he tried to find a place for himself in the high-school choral program, there was nothing that seemed to suit his needs. Clark had a concept of his "possible self" as a singer, and he was planning ways to encourage that possible self to become a reality (Markus & Nurius, 1986; Sharp, Coatsworth, Darling, Cumsille, & Ranieri, 2007). Possible selves are a person's impressions of who they might become, who they would like to become, and who they fear becoming. The current emphasis on narrative within music education research makes this an opportune moment to consider what the theory of possible selves might contribute to our understanding of adolescent boys, voice change, and singing (Packard & Conway, 2006). Listening to the stories of boys regarding their "possible musical selves" may encourage further conversation about the experience of boys in choral music.

REFERENCES

Aikins, J. W., Bierman, K. L, & Parker, J. G. (2005). Navigating the transition to junior high school: The influence of pre-transition friendship and self-system characteristics. *Social Development, 14*(1), 42–60.

Barham, T. (2002). *Strategies for teaching junior high and middle school male singers: Master teachers speak.* Santa Barbara, CA: Santa Barbara Music Publishing.

Bloom, A. J., & Skutnick-Henley, P. (2005). Facilitating flow experiences among musicians. *The American Music Teacher, 54*(5), 24–28.

Cooksey, J. (2000). Voice transformation in male adolescents. In L. Thurman & G. Welch (Eds.), *Bodymind and voice: Foundations of lifespan voice education, Vol. 4: Lifespan voice development* (pp. 718–738). Iowa City, IO : National Center for Voice and Speech.

Csikszentmihalyi, M. (1990). *Flow: The psychology of optimal experience*. New York: Harper & Row.

Custodero, L. A. (2002). Seeking challenge, finding skill: Flow experience and music education. *Arts Education Policy Review, 103*(3), 3–10.

Daniels, E., & Leaper, C. (2006). A longitudinal investigation of sport participation, peer acceptance, and self-esteem among adolescent girls and boys. *Sex Roles, 55*(11–12), 875–880.

Demorest, S. M. (2000). Encouraging male participation in chorus. *Music Educators Journal, 86*(4), 39.

Feldman, A. F., & Matjasko, J. L. (2007). Profiles and portfolios of adolescent school-based extracurricular activity participation. *Journal of Adolescence, 30*(2), 313–332.

Freer, P. K. (2005). *Success for adolescent singers: Unlocking the potential in middle school choirs* [Video series]. Waitsfield, VT: Choral Excellence Press.

Freer, P. K. (2006a). Adapt, build, and challenge: Three keys to effective choral rehearsals for young adolescents. *Choral Journal, 47*(5), 48–55.

Freer, P. K. (2006b). Hearing the voices of adolescent boys in choral music: A self-story. *Research Studies in Music Education, 27*(1), 69–81.

Freer, P. K. (2007). Between research and practice: How choral music loses boys in the "middle." *Music Educators Journal, 94*(2), 28–34.

Freer, P. K. (2008). Teacher instructional language and student experience in middle school choral rehearsals. *Music Education Research, 10*(1), 107–124.

Godfrey, P.K. (2003). *Listening to students' and teachers' voices: An ecological case study investigating the transition from elementary to middle school*. Unpublished doctoral dissertation, North Carolina State University at Raleigh.

Hylton, J. B. (1981). Dimensionality in high school student participants' perception of the meaning of choral singing experience. *Journal of Research in Music Education, 29*(4), 287–304.

Jackson, A. S., & Davis, G. A. (2000). *Turning points: Educating adolescents in the twenty-first century*. New York: Teachers College Press.

Legette, R. M. (1998). Causal beliefs of public school students about success and failure in music. *Journal of Research in Music Education, 46*(1), 102–111.

Markus, H., & Nurius, P. (1986). Possible selves. *American Psychologist, 41*(9), 954–969.

McClung, A. (2006). Master teachers in middle-level choral music: Pedagogical insights and practices. *Choral Journal, 47*(5), 6–26.

Packard, B. W., & Conway, P. F. (2006). Methodological choice and its consequences for possible selves research. *Identity, 6*(3), 251–271.

Phillips, K. H. (1988). Choral music comes of age. *Music Educators Journal, 75*(4), 25.

Ruddock, E., & Leong, S. (2005). "I am unmusical!": The verdict of self-judgment. *International Journal of Music Education, 23*(1), 9–22.

Schmidt, C. P. (1995). Attributions of success, grade level, and gender as factors in choral students' perceptions of teacher feedback. *Journal of Research in Music Education, 43*(4), 313–329.

Sharp, E. H., Coatsworth, J. D., Darling, N., Cumsille, P., & Ranieri, S. (2007). Gender differences in the self-defining activities and identity experiences of adolescents and emerging adults. *Journal of Adolescence, 30*(2), 251–269.

Snyder, E. E., & Spreitzer, E. A. (1977). Participation in sport as related to educational expectations among high school girls. *Sociology of Education, 40*(1), 47–55.

Sullivan, H. (1953). *The interpersonal theory of psychiatry.* New York: Norton.

Van Camp, L. (1988). Current status of U.S. secondary and college/university groups and male participation; Part II, analysis and suggestions. *Choral Journal, 29*(5), 5–13.

13

Music in Motion: An Overture to the Student Experience in the High-School Marching Band

Cecil Adderley

Cara, a clarinetist in her suburban high school's marching band, claims that being in that musical group helped her connect socially with others. She says, "We've become a family." Her experience in marching band also helped her to recognize that in some organizations individuals have to work as a team to achieve common goals. In high school, students who are involved in the marching band often begin practicing before the school year has resumed, participating in summer band camps. These experiences may help students recognize the role of each player in relation to the larger ensemble. With the assistance of strategic instruction, insight, patience, and repetition—all integral components of the teaching and learning strategies of meaningful marching-band experiences—students may begin to experience the differences between making music as individuals versus the benefits of making music as an ensemble.

Unlike other school music ensembles, such as concert band and choir, marching-band instruction is typically scheduled before or after school hours. In effect, it is an extracurricular school activity. The marching band might be viewed as being entertainment or a service, especially since rehearsals occur outside of the school day and outside of the school building itself, and performances primarily occur at football games, outdoor competitions, or parades. The colorful uniforms, the physical movements on a football field, and the popular music that is often programmed can overshadow a marching-band's musical, pedagogical, and social worth. Ensembles, regardless of the music or venue in which they practice or perform, can provide learning opportunities for their participants. My investigation into the outdoor music ensemble supports the view that "much of an instrumentalist's musical development takes place in ensemble settings, where young musicians have the opportunity to develop personal expertise and integrate their skills by rehearsing and performing with other musicians" (Matthews & Kitsantas, 2007, p. 6).

PURPOSE AND METHODOLOGY

The purpose of this chapter is to investigate the high-school marching-band experience primarily from the participants' perspectives. I present information gleaned from marching-band students' verbal responses to questions that I posed in interviews about their decisions to become members of the marching band, their reasons for participating throughout their high school careers, their perceptions of skills acquired through their participation in marching band, and the general social climate of the ensemble. Specific questions included:

1. How are marching bands supported in the school community?
2. How are marching bands believed to develop student leadership skills?
3. How has marching band helped students become problem solvers?
4. How has this experience helped individuals work with others toward a common goal?
5. How are students of diverse backgrounds accommodated or facilitated as members of the marching band?
6. How does the marching-band experience inspire members to continue performing music after graduation?

I conducted the interviews at two public high schools over the course of several days after the marching-band season had concluded. The material found in quotations, unless otherwise noted, is excerpted from students' survey responses. For the purposes of this chapter, I did not compare students' race, gender, or grade level.

I selected the two high schools based on my professional relationships with the ensemble directors, when I was a marching-band festival evaluator and/or observer of their rehearsals during marching-band season. One high school, having a majority of black students, was located in the center of a large city (urban high school—UHS); the other, having a majority of white students, was located in a suburban area (suburban high school—SHS), near a large East Coast metropolitan center. I thought it important to include responses from members of each band, regardless of the school's geographic location, because of the different visual and musical performance traditions embraced by the two marching bands. In this case, the suburban band's performance emulated that of the drum and bugle corps tradition, while the urban band's performance emulated that of the show marching bands found at many historically black colleges and universities.

I interviewed a total of thirty-one high-school students (fourteen at UHS and seventeen at SHS) who currently participated in their high school marching band. At the conclusion of each survey, I probed students further, engaging them in informal conversation that was also audio-recorded. Additionally, I spoke with the ensemble directors concerning their students' participation. Throughout this chapter, I will highlight select marching-band students' comments that illuminate the meaning they constructed from their experience in an outdoor music ensemble.

As I compiled and reviewed the marching-band members' responses, several themes emerged from the data. The first theme was the issue of becoming a leader within the marching band. Other themes included developing trust and self-respect, developing sensitivity to people different from self, and changes in self as described by the marching-band students. To conclude this chapter, I present the students' perceptions of marching band support offered by their peers, parents, and schools.

DEVELOPING LEADERSHIP AND TEAM SKILLS

The marching-band ensembles in this study seemed to provide an environment that enabled participants to "learn a lot of things other than music," such as responsibility, leadership skills, teaching others, team-building skills, and interacting with diverse members of a group.

A trombonist named Evan (SHS) agreed with Cara (SHS) about team-building effects of the marching-band experience: "We all strive to do our best . . . to work together." Yet another marching-band member remarked that the more they focused on themselves as "individuals, the more it [the band's music-making effort] fell apart." Evan believed that those who were interested in becoming student leaders displayed the necessary skills to nurture other learners and to provide guidance that others needed to succeed during rehearsals and performances. According to Evan, the leaders in marching band tended to help those who were not learning the material at the same rate as others, because of differences in ability levels or effort expended. Those in leadership positions held other members accountable for knowing their music and learning the maneuvers (routine and/or drill). The student leaders modeled the musical material and drills so that other members had a reference for how a phrase should be played or a step should be executed.

Darlene, an enthusiastic flautist (UHS), revealed that the marching-band experience helped not only to refine required skills for working well with others, but also those necessary to build confident leaders. "I'm in ROTC

[Reserve Officer Training Corps] and serve as a leader in my unit. The skills learned in marching band, like those we have learned to complete the band drill maneuvers on the field, apply to the different coordinates we use to fulfill ROTC drills. Even though we are using a compass, pencil, and paper to figure out our location during ROTC exercises, the experience of leading others through the process to success is the same [as in marching band]."

Fred, another trumpet player (UHS), responded that, as a leader, "You have to show respect, and that you can help" the other members of the marching band. Sometimes that might include writing out music parts from a score, assisting with teaching the music, or even assisting with discipline. "It's not uncommon for some of the students to want to play around, but you have to encourage them to take marching band seriously if they want to perform well. If we work together, we come out with a better sound, a better [band] family."

Based on my conversations with the students, it appeared that many believed the respect, discipline, and willingness to help others displayed by those in leadership positions enabled many of the other students (section members) to follow the directions of the student leaders. These "outdoor music ensemble" members "stepped up to help make the performance better," not just for themselves as the leaders, but for all involved in the group.

One trombonist, Alvin, mentioned that marching band "builds teamwork," efforts that might not consistently be supported in classes during which students are not involved in hands-on group activities. "You really have to listen if you are going to be successful in marching band, because each musical role is dependent on the other," Alvin stated. He also noted that members' experiences in the school marching band helped his peers work as a group. Jennifer (SHS) stated that the process of negotiating the large-group marching-band setting provided her a sense of empowerment where she and others learned to "work with people." Learning to work with others develops over time and is tested and retested as each member embraces successes and failures as a team. If these learners work together, they come to believe that they will reach new heights musically, socially, and emotionally and will also bond with students they might not have otherwise encountered in their schools. The marching unit, with its many sub-groups within the ensemble, provides opportunities for both the musician and non-musician alike, something not usually found in the other concert ensembles.

The marching-band experiences for most of those surveyed elicited responses similar to the ones highlighted in this chapter. Music research provides accounts of potential student benefits by participating in marching-band ensembles, primarily in that the ensembles build smaller communities (band, sections of the band) within larger ones (grade levels, schools), groupings that allow individuals to learn from each other and feel comfortable as they continue to learn (Adderley, Kennedy, & Berz, 2003;

Cusick, 1973). These students are like many others who tend to seek an environment where they "are intellectually, psychologically, emotionally, socially and musically nurtured by membership in performing ensembles" (Adderley et al., 2003, p. 204).

Many of the students believed that "people skills" would be beneficial to them throughout their life journeys. Frank (SHS) and others believed they were learning life skills through firsthand experience that would help them navigate the challenges of high school and beyond. These students stated they had acquired life skills that others might take for granted, such as "not giv[ing] excuses, to be on time, [and] conduct[ing] yourself" in a respectable manner.

Leadership and team-building skills were not limited to the band field or the military unit in this school setting. George (UHS) mentioned that he not only tries to motivate others in the trumpet section, but also the members of the school's basketball team, of which he is a member. He believes that the ensemble experiences, coupled with opportunities outside of the music class, have enabled him to refine his leadership skills. "I've learned a lot [as trumpet section leader, but] I could be better. . . . I've acted the fool, but got the work done." George also incorporated some of the management skills he developed through his work as a junior missionary for his church into his marching-band roles at the school. He stated that one complements the other. "I used to be a follower, and after this . . . I'm a leader."

Allen's (UHS) comments reinforced other participants' statements about the leadership opportunities that lay the groundwork for future success in music and outside of the marching-band classes. Calvin (UHS) also commented on the opportunities to apply what he has learned through his experience in the marching band as a section leader. He mentioned that leading others has helped him develop better coping skills, as well as the ability to listen to the others in a class and realize the value of their opinions. This was apparent in his En-glish class during a discussion of Shakespeare's *MacBeth*. Even though he believed that his stated ideas were great, he understood the need to listen to the group and to learn the cooperation, consideration, and compassion that allow a group of people to work together. He has also learned that a leader does not always need to be forceful when providing the structure a group may need, and that outlining a plan may work better with certain groups than others.

The students' comments about developing leadership and interpersonal skills as a result of their participation in marching band supports Temmerman's (2005) statement that

> arts educational experiences are often organized around problems, issues or themes derived from varied real-life situations, in which priority is given to

active (rather than passive) learning and meaning-making transferable and connected to authentic everyday life circumstances. The focus is not on finding the one "right" answer, but rather on discovering various means to solve a single problem and taking and managing "risks" along the way (pp. 36–37).

Observing these students in the marching-band environment, I wondered if students enrolled in concert ensembles were as focused and dedicated as the participants of the marching bands. What social and musical skills might be transferable between concert and marching bands? How do concert band members' view of participation compare to marching-band members' views?

DEVELOPING SENSITIVITY TO DIVERSITY

Indicative of ideal communities, marching-band ensembles can offer members a range of musical, organizational, leadership, or behind-the-scenes opportunities to participate according to the students' strengths and interests. In both the urban and suburban settings, the marching-band members believed that their directors had made overt efforts to include all students who wanted to participate in the band, regardless of physical or other type of learning challenge that might otherwise prevent a potential member from full participation. Most of the students mentioned that the directors often found other jobs for those students who were challenged in some form, but who wanted to participate in the marching band. Several students recalled that students with special needs provided the voice-over for a performance or were members of the percussion section's front ensemble. Henry's (UHS) and Calvin's (UHS) responses focused on the director: "They [the students] might not be able to do everything, but our director isn't going to turn them away," and "Yeah, they have open arms for these people. . . . They will find something for them to do." In other words, marching-band participation is not contingent on a person's musical abilities.

Participating in a marching band also requires its members to interact with people of diverse intellectual and musical abilities in order to work together as an ensemble. Evan, a trombonist (SHS), exclaimed, "We take kids who've never played and teach them how!" According to Frank, one of the tenor sax players (SHS), the students needed "to work toward making the weakest member stronger by leading them, and working at it together." "Oh, yeah, you really have to work as a team to make the forms, [and] music," stated Aaron, a clarinetist. He felt that it was his individual responsibility to help others, so that they, too, could make a contribution to the larger group.

Ensemble members generally believed that they would be provided the guidance they needed to improve musically and to fit in to the marching-band community. Once this level of trust was established, some of the students who initially may have appeared immature and unfocused began to develop the stability they needed in order to modify their own behavior. Building trust, fitting in as new members, and connecting with others who would assist them as they learned the material were common concerns of many of the students. Barbara (SHS) explained, "You have to trust the others to do their job. . . ." Building trust and camaraderie encourages students to learn to cooperate within the larger-group setting, as they work together toward the ensemble's goals. As music educators, how might we prepare culturally responsible students, even in a marching-band setting?

GROWING UP

Some of the student leaders noticed moderate changes in the level of maturity of many members of the marching band and drastic changes in a few of the members. Debra (UHS), noticed a substantial change in one young man. She stated, "He was really bad [behaviorally], but this year the marching band kept him occupied." This young man observed others in leadership positions and realized he could assume such responsibilities if he were to change his behavior. Consequently, this student changed his behavior because he loved being in band. He realized that it helped him to improve, both musically and as a person. He even planned to audition to be drum major of the marching band.

Debra told me about this student, not because she wanted to be critical of the young man, but because she knew that people could change, as she had, in part because of the opportunities presented to them in the marching band. "I was a problem child, too, and my home was not the type of home you wanted to go home to." Marching band provided the structure she sought. Whenever practice was canceled, Debra mentioned that it was difficult to go home, because she really wanted to rehearse. It helped her focus, learn to cooperate with others, and forget about the home life she had experienced.

As students became more comfortable during the interviews, I inquired about their perceptions of which experiences led to nurturing student leaders. Each member of the marching band was considered to be a leader in her or his own right. The students noted, however, that those they identified as leaders were active in several activities within the larger school setting, and they played a number of the roles within the marching band, such as section leaders or drum majors. Several of the students stated that those enrolled in ROTC, student council, their local churches, or other structured groups benefited from the guidance they received in these settings and that they often applied those skills to other events in their daily lives. Many of the students remarked about the need for patience in their journey of acquiring leadership skills, as they worked with others in the marching band. They recognized the need to be fair, respect themselves and others, and communicate effectively in order to be viewed as strong leaders within the ensemble. Only a few marching-band students mentioned that these characteristics were positively reinforced by their church leaders, who praised them for being active and participating in positive activities as students.

I recognized the students' maturity in their ability to recognize and comment on unity within the marching band. They reported that as they worked more closely together, they began to accept the fact that if one person was incorrect musically or with their movements, then the others perceived that they were all incorrect. Collectively, the students came to the conclusion that they needed not only to correct the individual, but also understand their responsibility to the group effort. The ability to self-correct enabled them to internalize how music and motion contributed to the overall effect perceived by an audience. Individuals were aware of their responsibility to the group and to their audiences. One of the drum majors, Irene (UHS), summarized: "People are focused on 'I' versus 'us' . . . and we're trying to teach others to think of 'us' and [to] help them remember that there isn't an 'I' in [the word] 'team.'" The other drum major stated, "If it wasn't for band, I wouldn't be here [in school]. . . . I would be in trouble. . . . I would probably be doing something that I shouldn't be doing. . . . This provides me the structure to stay out of trouble . . . and that helps, too."

The SHS and UHS marching bands both focused on developing student leaders within their organizations; many of the skills were often used in environments outside of the music setting. The one difference between the two marching bands that I noted during the interviews was the incorporation of a specific leadership instructional component offered as part of the music classes at the suburban high school. The program is designed to take student musicians interested in serving as ensemble leaders through a series of exercises and experiences that the directors believe could produce better band leaders. They discuss the qualities of effective leaders, public speaking, and communication skills, as well as mentoring and serving as a role model for others.

The directors (SHS) stated that the marching-band experience "provides a society and family to which all band students can belong." This confirmed results of an earlier study in which "students enjoyed playing and said that 'the band was something you wanted to be in,'" and that they "welcomed the opportunity to 'feel part of something' . . ." (Adderley et al., p. 195). These (SHS) directors also stated that band "is a place where they learn values and standards, where they can learn to depend on one another in their pursuit of excellence. They learn about responsibility, doing their fair share, and sticking to a common goal. They learn to value people, respect their peers and not make superficial judgments. They frequently acquire[d] a stronger base for their adult life than any other avenue open to them." These statements summarize the value of participation in the school's marching band in developing students' leadership, musicianship, and interpersonal skills. In fact, these values are posted on the SHS marching band's website.

Barbara (SHS), a student, gave a strong statement in favor of the school's providing leadership training, noting that this training begins as a requirement for each freshman during his or her music experience. "Oh, definitely, they teach us leadership. . . . [The instructors] make sure we can see how the leadership courses can be used." The instruction provided to these students incorporates situations inside and outside of the band class so that the members can see the effectiveness of the skills and strategies in various settings. Similar comments were made by Diego (SHS), who believed that "we have learned how to react to people, how to get to your goal, and [how to] help people to follow you. . . . You can't lead others until you lead yourself."

Both of these students were pleased with the opportunities to role-play teaching others by providing constructive criticism to peers, offering to lead as appropriate models, not only for the students whom they might lead, but for themselves as they master new skills. Creating this type of learning environment speaks to the band directors' vision for their students not only to strive for excellence but also to provide models so that others may better understand the goals they are attempting to reach as an ensemble. These learning environments further support Lautzenheiser's (1992) statement that the students' "sense of discipline and persistence offer them some certain tools for success as they assume the responsibilities of their life" (p. 131).

It appears that some of the students also used these leadership classes as an opportunity to build self-confidence. Garrett (SHS) stated that he "came into the program as a timid person, but through leadership classes, I've become more extroverted . . . [and] gained a lot of ability to talk in front of people [like] talking to a crowd, organization, [and] time management." Ingrid, who is a member of the color guard/visual ensemble "didn't want to be a leader . . . [but] now . . . really want[s] to be a part of the leadership committee." She stated that "these are the best people to be around . . . my true friends . . . [and] supportive. . . . I love these people; [they] are extremely friendly."

DEFINING ROLES IN THE ENSEMBLE

The UHS and SHS settings provided the marching-band participants with opportunities for self-discovery and growth. This growth began by assigning students specific responsibilities and providing structured activities so that each member began to move gradually from one who follows to one who leads. The traditional leadership positions included drum major (field conductor), section leaders (those who provide instruction to the individual instrumental groupings), as well as equipment managers, music librarians, squad leaders (those who helped to set the exact drill coordinates), and other positions with lesser authority but valuable to the success of the unit. The directors seemed to select the older, more experienced band members for leadership roles within the organization. Many of these positions, such as drum major or section leaders, were assigned as the result of an audition; other roles were appointed.

It does not appear that either school's marching-band directors forced ensemble members to assume roles for which they were not prepared. However, some students observed their older peers holding positions of responsibility, so subsequently tended to gravitate to those specific leadership positions. The need to assume new roles within a larger group is not much different from the process many adults encounter in their career paths as they assume new levels of accountability in the workplace.

Each of these students developed skills that provided them not only with a focus, but also the confidence to attempt tasks that they might not have ever experienced if they had not participated in marching band. Temmerman (2005) reminded us that students must

> engage in a host of leadership behaviors. These include possessing a measure of empathy towards others, which extends to listening to and acknowledging other people's perspectives, being able to instill trust and trusting others and treating others with respect. On some occasions it calls for a shared goal to be arrived at through input from all 'players,' whereas at other times, it calls for someone to stand up and set the direction" (p. 37).

Do we as educators provide guidance to students who need structure to become effective leaders and followers? Do we create appropriate settings for students who have difficulty learning in traditional music education settings?

PERCEPTIONS OF SUPPORT FOR MARCHING BAND

The marching-band students who were interviewed for this study held interesting views on the schools' administration and the general community members' perceptions of the marching band and its membership. The UHS students' comments tended to vary; however, many participants contended that the administration considered the marching band to (1) provide a service to the school and greater community and (2) act as a positive activity for those students who chose to enroll. The students also seemed to think that band was not one of the administration's top school-funding priorities. Xavier (UHS) mentioned that "when you look at the equipment we have" it appeared that the administration had not done everything in their power to locate the financial resources for musical instruments needed for the students to perform up to their potential.

Bruce's (UHS) remarks reflected his notion of the administration's support for the marching band, because it provided school spirit at athletic games. He stated that the administration seemed to find funds to send the group to athletic events, but not to care for and replace uniforms and other musical and non-musical marching-band equipment. Bruce and his peers viewed the administration's decisions not as student support, but rather as schoolwide support. Many of the band members appreciated the administration's drive to fund campus beautification projects, yet they believed that other funding could be directed toward the items (e.g., marching-band equipment) that would affect the students themselves.

Allison (UHS) felt that it was not fair that other schools' administrative leadership teams had found financial means to provide better equipment for their marching-band members, yet their own ensemble used items that had been "taped together." Even though this member thought the members of the band took care of the equipment assigned to them, she believed they could perform at a higher level if they were provided appropriate monetary resources for much more durable and/or newer equipment. She stated that "we even borrow [equipment] from other schools," when their own was in poor repair.

It was apparent from the students' responses that the administration, parents of marching-band members, and the greater community of UHS were supportive of the marching band when they performed at football games. Most of the students mentioned that they believed everyone thought highly of the band. It provided football game entertainment and focus for school spirit, and it served as ambassadors that represented the best of the school. Bruce stated, "They come to the games to see the band. . . . They like us . . . and think that we're the best. . . . They like the group." One of the communities within the urban school district's zoning actually hosts a parade for the marching band to "show them off" to the community members. Most of the students wished that more of the administrators, parents, and other community members would attend the marching band's non-athletic performances occurring throughout the state and region.

The UHS and the SHS administrations gave noticeably different support to the marching bands. The SHS administrators appeared to make themselves available to the students on a regular basis. Many of these administrators attended not only athletic events, but also the rehearsals of the marching band, the competitions, and any event that provided additional visibility to the program membership and the school. Aaron, who plays the clarinet (SHS) stated, "The assistant principal is always there . . . at the competitions and games, even the practices. . . . They love us. . . . They build us up . . . talk with us, telling us how great we are, . . . to do your best, and have a good time. . . . [They] are really helpful."

Betty (SHS) conveyed that both principals established a model for other teachers in the school by supporting student activities. She stated that the visibility of the administrators at non-athletic event performances, such as the grand national championships, encouraged support from the SHS teachers, who in most cases provided the students with their assignments prior to a long trip when students would be absent from class. Other students suggested that some of the teachers could be a little more accommodating. One of the only negative comments concerning the administrative team dealt with financial support. Many of the students (SHS) stated that the administration could provide additional funding so that the parent organization would not have to raise as much money to support the band program as they currently did.

Program funding appeared to be a challenge for all school activities regardless of setting—urban or suburban. The biggest differences, according to the students' reports, appear to be the financial resources available to support professional musician contacts (marching-band clinicians who may provide additional educational commentary and suggestions for achieving excellence with the visual, musical, and movement components of the marching-band program) and time for parents to raise money as determined by their work schedules. The students recognized that their families wanted the best for their children who were enrolled in the marching band, and the parents often provided financial assistance beyond that which the local school districts budgeted for these programs.

Many SHS marching-band students indicated that the community supported the band program by providing donations. Patrons were actively involved at concerts and family nights that directly supported the music program. Several band members suggested that the mere number of fund-raising activities reflected the financial resources that would ultimately be available to their respective marching bands.

BEYOND THE BAND

The band students' (UHS and SHS) responses about their plans to participate in the arts, particularly music, after completing high school varied. The differences in their opinions could be due to the age differences among those whom I interviewed. It was not surprising that many of those who applied to institutions of higher education mentioned they would seek opportunities to continue to play their instrument(s), but not necessarily in marching band because of conflicting time demands between ensemble playing and their selected programs of study. Students who were undecided about their future plans wanted to pursue various musical activities unavailable to them in high school. Some dreamed of learning more about writing music, recording, producing, and other fields within the larger music industry. Their responses were as varied as the instruments they played or the band-front [guard] equipment they used in marching band.

CONCLUSION

The purpose of this chapter was to investigate the high school marching band from its members' perspective. As the members opened their worlds to me, I began to understand the value of the ensemble from their points of view. The dialogue that resulted from these interviews provided insight into their experiences and the benefits they received from their participation in the ensemble. Further, I explored students' perceptions of the support the marching bands received from the schools' teachers, administrators, and community members. Both urban and suburban high-school students desired to reach common goals as performers through the pageantry of the performance group. The students believed in the goals of their respective marching bands and recognized them as popular and meaningful opportunities in their high school experience.

To summarize, I found the students cognizant of the life lessons they learned, including the leadership skills they developed and which other students emulated. Many of these students matured, in part, because of working with these marching bands. Some students practiced their newly acquired or refined skills in non-musical school activities and in the larger communities in which they lived. The social bonding within the marching-band community also played an important role in the students' overall marching-band experience. Students developed friendships with other students that they might not have otherwise. The marching-band community brought together a diverse membership. Even though the bands were popular within the school setting, particularly at athletic events, the students still strove for additional opportunities to display their musical and movement talents.

Regardless of the geographic location and demographic description, the two high-school marching bands that participated in this study put their music in motion and provided students with experiences like few others in their schools or communities. Though the ensembles had specific performance goals, including those related to athletic events or competitions, it seemed that the directors provided ample opportunity for students to learn life skills that ultimately foster growth socially, psychologically, musically, and physically. Both ensembles appeared to focus on education, that is, music (and life) instruction through rehearsals, performance, and shared responsibility. While music education is a key component, the instruction seemed to go far beyond it.

The learners were aware of some of the many challenges they might face in their futures, musically and non-musically. That the urban and suburban band directors were concerned about their marching bands being positive student learning experiences is a step in the direction that Blocher (2001) described:

> Providing a music education for students through performance in band requires band conductors to make decisions about what to teach, how to teach, how to know if students understood the "it" that they were trying to teach and, perhaps most importantly, why band students should know or be able to do anything special with music (p. 8).

Additional areas for study might include investigating the roles and responsibilities many marching-band students assume after they complete high school, looking specifically at the number of students who continue to participate in the arts or take on leadership roles in their communities. Music educators need to focus on what students want to take away from their experiences as participants in our ensembles, including the marching band as viable instructional ground. Temmerman's (2005) statement provides us with a clue:

> The challenge for teachers is to create classrooms that support students' acquisition of the life and leadership skills that will help them do well in a progressively more complicated world and future. The arts possess the capability to perform a valuable role in meeting this challenge (p. 39).

As I observed these ensembles in rehearsal and/or in competition, it was clear that structure and routine had been established within the marching-band communities. The students memorized the routines and, accordingly, fulfilled duties that complemented the ensemble as a whole. As individuals and as a group, members completed a formula for moving from point A to point B onto a football field; psychologically, physically, and musically preparing for a performance; and exiting the field. They functioned as a unit, as a community. In discussing the experience of great art, Langer (1953) provided a statement that might pertain to the ideals of a meaningful marching-band experience: It is "a source of experience not essentially different from the experiences of daily life—a stimulus to one's active feelings, and perhaps a means of communication between persons or groups, promoting mutual appreciation" (p. 36).

REFERENCES

Adderley, C., Kennedy, M., & Berz, W. (2003). A home away from home: The world of the high school music classroom. *Journal of Research in Music Education, 51*(3), 190–205.

Blocher, L. (2001). Beginning with the end in mind: A personal perspective for teaching music through performance in band. In R. Miles & T. Dvorak (Eds.), *Teaching music through performance in beginning band* (pp. 3–11). Chicago: GIA.

Cusick, P. A. (1973). *Inside high school: The student's world*. New York: Holt, Rinehart and Winston.

Langer, S. (1953). *Feeling and form*. New York: Scribner.

Lautzenheiser, T. (1992). *The art of successful teaching: A blend of content and context*. Chicago: GIA.

Matthews, W. K., & Kitsantas, A. (2007). Group cohesion, collective efficacy, and motivational climate as predictors of conductor support in music ensembles. *Journal of Research in Music Education, 55*(1), 6–17.

Temmerman, N. (2005). The role of arts education in advancing leadership life skills for young people. *Australian Journal of Music Education, 1*, 33–39.w

14

The Violin and the Fiddle: Narratives of Music and Musician in a High-School Setting

Matthew D. Thibeault

During the second week of a year-long study of the musical experiences of high-school students, I visited the beginning improvisation class for string players. With about ten minutes left, their teacher, Mr. Marquis, asked them to improvise over a pentatonic scale while he accompanied them with a basic pattern on the piano. Most had no experience with improvisation; their playing consisted of timid and simple explorations of scales. Mr. Marquis asked one girl to come to the front to help demonstrate. She stood up, looking a bit shy as she shifted from side to side, her denim overalls setting her apart from the rest of the class.

As soon as she stood next to the piano, she was transformed. Her feet planted firmly, an intense look came upon her face as Mr. Marquis begin to play. Starting with simple explorations, telltale signs of bluegrass music crept into her playing—slides, double stops, and rhythmically rich syncopated patterns. She confidently built to a musical climax high on the neck of the fiddle of furious rhythm and dynamic expression, quickly finishing. The class applauded as she smiled self-consciously and shyly sat down. This first experience left me anxious to learn more about this Bay Area bluegrass fiddler.

This chapter presents two narratives centered on that student, one of six I followed for a study of students at Arts High, a public high school focused on teaching the arts. Eva Kikuchi is a high-school senior whose passion is bluegrass. Her stories are dominated by tensions: between classical and bluegrass music, between written music and aural folk traditions, and between a guided curriculum and development through her own musical explorations. These tensions are rooted in particular dilemmas inherent in contemporary music education, but they also reflect deeper educational problems and dilemmas. Exposing the tensions inherent in these narratives will show what the terms "music" and "musician" mean to students like Eva.

The first narrative presents how Eva came to be a musician and the tension in navigating one physical instrument with two identities: the violin and the fiddle. These identities, between school/classical/violin and home/bluegrass/fiddle, frame her biography and experiences and ground her conceptions of music and musician. The second narrative examines the school-sanctioned bluegrass lessons Eva gave to accomplished violin but beginning fiddle students at her school.

From a curricular standpoint, Eva's experiences raise important questions. What happens when the school's conception of the subject conflicts with the student's conception? What happens when a school tries to support or incorporate a vision of music not normally taught? The transformation of Eva's curriculum in teaching students over the course of the year provides a perspective on the challenges faced by music education in attempting to teach music outside the Western European tradition.

A few days after I first heard Eva in that strings class, we met for our first interview. Reticent, she asked that I not record our conversation. My notes record that we talked about her origins as a bluegrass player, straddling classical and bluegrass music, learning from playing in jam sessions, and the variety of groups she played with outside school. By the end of the conversation, she had warmed to the idea of talking, telling me, "This was fun. Nobody has ever asked me about any of this stuff, and I've never talked about these things or thought about them." After that first interview, Eva was comfortable with my recording our conversations. Propelled by what I saw on that first day, I set out to learn about Eva's life as a musician. In addition to observing her in class, I eventually spent dozens of hours at rehearsals, concerts, in extended one-on-one interviews, and finally jamming with her.

THE WORK CONCEPT, MUSICKING, AND EXPERIENCE

This study rests on three conceptions about the nature of music and musical experiences. The first is the work concept (Goehr, 1992), the idea that composers create "works" that have a unique status in ways that would not have been considered previously. Goehr persuasively argues that Bach would not have thought that way about what he was doing. She documents the transition from Bach's worldview to the emergence of the work concept. During the nineteenth century, this resulted in the idea of absolute music, in which the supreme reality of music was considered to be the isolated, self-contained work (Dahlhaus, 1989). Whereas a musician in

Mozart's time would have been educated as a performer, composer, improviser, multi-instrumentalist, and conductor, today's music programs train specialist performers to realize works under the direction of a conductor who "plays" the students (MENC & Choate, 1968; Palisca, 1964). This study examines the implications for music education of Goehr's statement that if music once existed for musicians, musicians now exist for music.

A second conception is Christopher Small's notion of musicking. Small's work conceives of music as if it were a verb, not a noun (Small, 1977, 1998). Critiquing the work concept, he restores an expansive sense of music as something that is done, and this existence within action is central to the way that I have approached the subject of music within education for this study.

Finally, students' own experiences with music and their interactions with music form the core of the educational analysis. Following Dewey's *Art as Experience*, I treat "what the work does with and in experience" (Dewey, 1934/1980, p. 1) as the actual work of art, rather than the object itself. This translates into attending to the actual experiences that students have with music, rather than focusing upon the quality of performances they produce, and allows for a different evaluation of a rehearsal for Eva's group.

These three concepts can be used to map a continuum of music education experiences. On one end, music education can be viewed as focusing upon the musical work as an object in a written fixed form and its performance; on the other, it focuses on the musician, the act of *making* music, and the quality of those experiences for students. Goehr presents the historical precedent of music existing for musicians within the Western tradition. It is apparent that much of the world outside American music education still functions with this orientation, without scores or predetermined notions of how a particular performance will sound, and often without a sense that there is a musical work at the center—be it jazz, bluegrass, African drumming, or hip-hop. Dewey's work constantly reminds us that our attention should remain focused on the interactions and transactions between the folks and the notes.

IN SEARCH OF A USEFUL DICHOTOMY: SCORE AND SETTING

Much of the profession currently uses terms such as "classical" or "Western European" versus "popular" or "vernacular." Odam and Leong have used "ear-bound" and "eye-bound" (Leong & Odam, 2002), but the inherent suggestion that the traditional eye-bound musician does not listen is problematic. I have attempted "work-centered" and "activity-centered," but here "work" lacks clarity in referring both to the object and Dewey's notion of the work as "what the product does with and in experience" (Dewey,

1934/1980, p. 1). One alternative formulation productive for this study is "score-centered" and "setting-centered." Throughout this study, the score (whether an explicit written musical score, or a memorized piece that had a fixed form) was at the heart of the experience regulating organization and behavior, particularly within a high-school ensemble or a chamber group's rehearsal. Alternately, for much of my work with Eva, the setting organized the behavior and the musical work, with the tunes giving way and collapsing or expanding to accommodate those who came to play, their talents and dispositions, and the audience. The terms "score-centered" and "setting-centered" are used throughout.

FIRST NARRATIVE: LEARNING TO PLAY ONE INSTRUMENT WITH TWO IDENTITIES

The Violin

In our early interviews Eva and I discussed how she became a violinist. When she was five, her parents enrolled her in violin lessons in the Suzuki style, a method that begins by teaching students to play songs by ear and from memory, later moving on to reading standard Western musical notation (Suzuki, 1969). Eva continued with her Suzuki teacher throughout our work together, only stopping during my follow-up interview period when she was away at college.

Eva also played with the orchestra in middle school and high school. Until eleventh grade, Eva did not play bluegrass or find others to play with. She also did not try to get involved with any jazz bands or other improvising groups that might have been closer to bluegrass stylistically. When she auditioned for Arts High, she did so as a member of the orchestra. By her sophomore year, Eva was in the first chair of the second violins, leading that section in rehearsals and making decisions regarding bowings for the section. She sounded like many of the students I spoke to when she told me,

> Like, once in freshman year, I remember, I probably don't practice classical music as much as I should, but freshman year, or sophomore year I was section leader of the second violins, and I was in advanced orchestra, but the numbers of the violins just worked out for me to be in the second violins because I wasn't even, I'm not that good, so. So I thought that was a lot of pressure on me, so I practiced my part a lot, and then I got really into it, and I thought, I think I was moving around a lot more, and I was more relaxed. We played *Night on Bald Mountain*, I think, and I thought it was so fun, and it was great because I practiced my part because, I thought, well, they're going to be following me, so I have to know what I'm doing. So that was a really fun year.

Eva's education had given her the skills to play well and enjoy herself as a violinist, in many ways not different from the rest of the string students at Arts High. In interviews, Eva located her own musicianship as beginning with her paternal grandmother, a violinist herself. It was an important moment when she gave her violin to Eva as she carried on the family tradition.

The Fiddle

Eva was a good violinist, but she was an amazing fiddle player, and this section outlines how she became a musician on the fiddle. These two words, "violin" and "fiddle," describe the same physical instrument, but carry critically different meanings. Eva made a point of this on stage during a concert when introduced to the audience as a guest with the Latin Ensemble at Arts High:

José: And we're going to invite Eva, on violin.

Eva: Fiddle.

José: Oh, on fiddle.

Eva identified strongly as a fiddle player. Although her grandmother had been a violinist who loved classical music concerts, her father had rebelled by falling in love with bluegrass music. Eva's home life was filled almost entirely with bluegrass music. Her father's listening and playing habits meant that she heard bluegrass music every day. She did not hear much popular music or anything else outside bluegrass, save occasional traditional Japanese music from her mother, or during her visits to Japan to visit her grandparents. Although she admitted curiosity about all kinds of music, throughout our time together Eva recognized almost none of the references I made, admitting that she had heard almost no rock, blues, hip-hop, or jazz.

Growing up in a bluegrass environment included more than simply listening to the music, it meant attending festivals. For all Eva's life, her family regularly attended bluegrass and Old Time festivals. Large gatherings, usually held at a campground or other outdoor venue, were filled with enthusiasts who went to play, jam, and listen. Throughout the grounds, musicians held informal jams around campfires or under trees. When she was young, Eva attended these festivals but she did not play, as she was still learning solely in a Suzuki style. But when I conducted our first follow-up interview, one of the things she felt most important in terms of her musical development was her attendance at these festivals:

MT: What do you think have been the most important influences in you becoming a musician?

Eva: Classical, bluegrass, or anything?

MT: Anything.

Eva: My parents.

Eva: And they'd take me to festivals. I wasn't into jamming when I was young—
I'd rather hang out with my friends, from when I was a little kid until when I
was twelve—but I loved the festivals because I had no curfew, and I could play
with my friends. Then I found out that music was very fun.

The connection between her listening and her playing came when Eva
was twelve. She brought her violin to a jam and was encouraged to play. She
was hooked. She told her parents that she wanted to learn bluegrass, and
they found a teacher who offered lessons. These lessons were like standard
jazz lessons; she was taught tunes, as well as the theory behind them
and the chords and scales that could fit. She memorized scales and patterns
and played with her teacher during most lessons. Still, she was not satisfied.
Though she felt that these lessons had some importance, when asked where
she learned bluegrass, Eva didn't mention these lessons until deep in our
conversations, and then often critically as when she said, "I didn't get it, because it seemed like work, not fun. He taught modes and scales." For Eva,
learning bluegrass was best accomplished through something other than
lessons.

Eva learned by playing with other musicians. From that first solo break,
Eva continued to find herself invited to play with other musicians. Many of
them made time to play with Eva, and the best description of her growth as
a bluegrass musician is to say that she spent eight years or so moving from
the edge of the jamming circle to the front of the feature stage at festivals.
This is hardly unique, and in my experiences with Eva, I continually saw
musicians inviting other musicians of various ages and abilities onto the
stage to play together. This community of learners fits well with the descriptions offered by researches such as Chaiklin and Lave (1993), as well
as by other researchers of improvised music, such as jazz (Berliner, 1994)
and popular music (Green, 2002; Rodriguez, 2004).

Bluegrass music has been called "the bebop of country music"
(C. Shahin, personal communication, September 14, 2004). Like bebop,
bluegrass prizes intricate improvisations and instrumental songs. The genre
had its start in Appalachia and was brought to national prominence during
the 1950s through the recordings of Bill Monroe.

Bluegrass music is like bebop in other ways, too. Both styles have a rich
history whose recordings, compositions, and famous performers can be
both a source of inspiration and a daunting presence. Contemporary performing musicians invite comparisons to the stylistic conventions estab-

lished by Monroe and others, and there is also pressure to carefully preserve tradition while still innovating.

NAVIGATING FIDDLE AND VIOLIN: THE BOW GRIP

Eva often spoke about the balance between her training on violin and her experiences on the fiddle. For instance, the way she held her bow is the result of her early Suzuki training, the standard bow grip of a classical musician. Classical technique for holding a bow is very different from the technique of a bluegrass musician, where the grip is quite loose and further from the frog of the bow. This loose grip and "dirty sound" may have originated because musicians were untrained, but over time this sound, enshrined in recordings of Monroe and others, became the sound of authentic bluegrass and the standard by which new generations of musicians were measured. The challenge for Eva was to find a way to negotiate the technical demands of both the violin and the fiddle grip, since each resulted in a different tone. Eva tended toward a sound a bit in the middle, too clean for bluegrass and on the gypsy end of the spectrum for classical music. We spoke about this tension between the fiddle and violin in Eva's own playing, and how her classical training could be an impediment to her bluegrass accomplishments:

> Eva: I think it really depends on taste because, lots of, some old-time musicians, like, there've been terribly scratchy-sounding fiddles, and you can just tell by listening that their bow's going all over the place, like over the fingerboard. But people have called them the best old-time musicians because they play in the style, and they play with a lot of feeling, so I think it really depends on taste.

> MT: Yeah, and it could even . . .

> Eva: How much you would let the bad technique get to you, or whether you call it bad technique at all.

> MT: Yeah, I was going to say it sounds like maybe even, those sounds become part of what's accepted and expected as the right sound.

> Eva: Yeah, right. Yeah, some people have told me that I don't play dirty enough, or that I'm too clean.

> MT: Mm-hmm, that's what they mean.

> Eva: Yeah, exactly. So, to them I'm not a very good musician, as opposed to someone who has never taken classical training and they sound a lot dirtier, but that's what they're supposed to do in the style.

> MT: It sounds like, I would guess that playing dirty is not just being uneducated, but like knowing that there's a certain kind of sound that you want to

get, and finding a way to get it, and maybe having a whole different set of ideals that you're striving for.

Eva: Right. It's hard, because the music is really traditional, and lots of people, like the best dirty musicians are old-time people who are usually completely self-taught. Or, I guess a lot of them are self-taught.

MT: Or, not formally taught.

Eva: Yeah

MT: Because I imagine that most of them probably grew up playing with people, seeing things, having more of a kind of apprenticeship than going to lessons.

Eva: Yeah. Yeah, and it's weird because, if you're classically trained, you'd think that it's easy to do that, like, 'they're not very good, I can do that any time,' you know, but, it's strange because you think you can do it and you're classically trained, and you've got techniques, but you don't have what they have, you didn't grow up the way they did and you don't know exactly how they learned to play. And it's like, you can't really go back and see what they did, because you already have your foundation set. I don't know, it's weird.

Eva's words speak to the bias that exists in much music education, where styles and techniques outside the classical tradition are seen as lesser achievements. She evokes an imaginary interlocutor, a classically trained musician who views the bluegrass musician as uneducated and untrained. But Eva's unusual vantage point, encompassing both the violin and the fiddle, responds to this interlocutor, "You don't have what they have." Eva also experienced how her Suzuki training could actually be an impediment to achieving a proper sound for the fiddle.

Eva kept her violin and fiddle lives separate for many years, but they eventually came together. Arriving as a freshman at Arts High, she intentionally hid her bluegrass interests. During her junior year, though, she brought a mandolin to a non-music class as part of a report where she would talk about bluegrass music. Two other students who liked bluegrass, Bob and Nate, spotted the instrument and asked her if she played. Eva confessed, and at this point they started jamming, eventually formalizing a group, Old Blind Clarence.

SETTING-CENTERED PRACTICES: OLD BLIND CLARENCE REHEARSES

The flexibility that distinguishes what I am calling setting-centered practices was apparent throughout my work with Eva and exemplified during the rehearsals of Old Blind Clarence that I observed. On October 22, 2003, I listened to a rehearsal. Eva was playing with Bob (guitar) and Nate (mandolin) in the band room. Bob began playing the tune "Arkansas Traveler," one the group had not worked on before.

Several things immediately distinguished the setting-centered rehearsals of Old Blind Clarence from rehearsals of score-centered groups I observed at Arts High. First, there were no music stands or sheet music. Unlike the Arts High band, the musicians came together and played in many combinations, guitar and fiddle, maybe with the addition of mandolin, and finally with a bass player. Regardless of who showed up, Old Blind Clarence could viably perform as an ensemble. The choice of material also was important in other ways. Whereas, for instance, a clarinet and piano duo observed for this study got together to practice only a specific piece and didn't work on any other music when they were together, Old Blind Clarence got together to work from a slowly evolving and changing set of tunes in a more casual way. Over time, I came to understand that perfecting the tunes was less the object of the rehearsal than development of communication between the group members.

Figure 14.1 attempts to represent the richness of setting-centered practices, a richness that might be hard to otherwise appreciate, by depicting three minutes of Old Blind Clarence's rehearsal. In the center of the figure is a graphic depiction of the actual sound recording from that rehearsal, which serves as a time key for the overall diagram. On the top of the diagram, the overall excerpt is blocked off into five sections: the first twenty seconds, where the group settles on which key they'll play in; an attempt to perform the tune; a regrouping where they experiment with different chord progressions; another attempt at performing the tune; and a final section where Bob and Nate practice the tune and solo breaks.

Between the top of the diagram and the graphic depiction of time, each of the three performers is tracked to show when they play, and what role they take on. In most bluegrass rehearsals, there are three common roles: playing or singing the tune, accompanying the tune with chords, and playing a solo break. The depiction of these three roles in figure 14.1 makes obvious one of the biggest differences between score-centered and setting-centered practice, namely, that each member flexibly moves among roles. Bob, Eva, and Nate take on each role at least once during these three minutes, although in a final performance it will likely be the case that only one of them plays the melody, followed by breaks by some or all the players. In contrast, although not discussed in this paper, depictions and analyses of score-centered rehearsals in school, whether large ensemble or small student-led chamber groups, did not uncover any instances of the kinds of role switching and communal composing found in Figure 14.1.

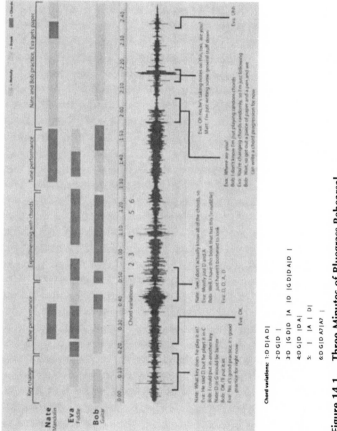

Figure 14.1.   Three Minutes of Bluegrass Rehearsal

Immediately below the time graph in Figure 14.1, a transcript of the discussion during the rehearsal is shown. The members stopped to talk when problems arose. The bottom of Figure 14.1 maps out the six variations on the chords for the tune the group tried. These are also located directly on the time graphic using numbers. When playing the tune more slowly, Bob inserts more secondary chords, such as in variations two and four, but when the tempo is quicker, they stick to fewer harmonic changes, such as variations one and three. Variations five and six are mostly an attempt to work on the final chords of the first period of the tune, and Bob ends version six with an A7 chord that he uses as a segue into a performance of the tune.

Tendencies in Setting-Centered Practices

This moment illustrates the basic tendencies of a setting-centered practice. The work is allowed maximum flexibility in several respects: the piece can be played slowly or quickly; it can be played by any number of players; it can be sung, hummed, or played wordlessly on an instrument. In addition, the chords used to accompany the melody are adjusted depending on what sounds best; at a slower tempo the musicians explore richer harmonies than sound good at a quicker tempo. In fact, the final part of their rehearsal has Bob playing a richer set of chords, while Eva and Nate stick to a simpler set of chords.

Setting-centered practice puts music in service to the musicians. The music is shaped to provide the optimal experience for the musicians. If there are more performers in the ensemble, they may play a longer version to accommodate more breaks. They will choose to play the piece in a key that is familiar and comfortable to the largest number of players, changing it when needed, such as when a singer needs a new key to give the tune a more comfortable range. When there are lyrics, they will sing, inserting instrumental breaks when desired. They may also choose to sing only a few verses, or sing them in a different order, or sing one verse several times between breaks, or harmonize them, or have different singers sing different verses. Over many observations, I could not find a musical dimension that was off limits to creative work in a bluegrass rehearsal, and much of the creative work came from testing, exploring, and talking about these dimensions.

The playing rarely stopped during setting-centered rehearsals. As indicated in Figure 14.1, although attempts to perform the piece start and stop, one of the musicians is always playing. Playing between coordinated takes often took the form of reattempting a break, trying to play something that someone else had played, or working on the melody. This productive disorder contrasts sharply with the etiquette of setting-centered rehearsals, something Eva dealt with when she began teaching violinists to play the fiddle.

SECOND NARRATIVE: TEACHING BLUEGRASS

Early in her senior year, Mr. Marquis, the orchestra director and Eva's teacher at Arts High, proposed that Eva teach bluegrass to the freshman string players. Each senior at Arts High fulfills a service learning commitment, and when I spoke to Mr. Marquis he said that he hoped Eva could loosen up the beginning students, who he felt were often somewhat inhibited. He thought that, especially coming from a peer, they might open up to this style of music. It was also important to Mr. Marquis that this was a style of improvised music that was often authentically associated with string instruments.

I learned about Eva's assignment during our first interview and was present at the first lesson she taught. Each lesson followed the same format: Eva would arrive for the Tuesday beginning strings class, go into the soundproof practice room in the back of the room, and students would come in groups of two or three for fifteen to thirty minutes each. For the rest of the year, I attended each of the meetings (which happened many weeks but not every week, as the school had a schedule filled with guest artists, student performances, and other events). By chance, Eva was often free after the lesson, and we used that time to discuss how the lesson went and generally talk about the changes in her musical life.

This teaching setting was perfect for learning about Eva's conception of music as well as examining the growing pains that accompany attempts to bring bluegrass to more traditional strings students. Eva had to explain things about her teaching, and in talking to other students, she revealed what she valued most in bluegrass, including how she learned and what she thought about composing solos.

The first lesson Eva taught began with ancillary questions and a general sense of what bluegrass is:

Shehime: What's on your bridge?

Eva: Oh, this? This is a pickup. I use it—I hardly ever use it. Sometimes I play gigs and it's really loud, like in bars.

Vina: Do they let you play in bars?

Eva: If I'm an entertainer, then I can go in. So I can't be in the audience, and I can't drink anything, but I can play. But I don't drink anyway, because you can't stay up all night and you can't play music. Soooo . . . So, do you guys know what bluegrass music is?

Shehime and Vina: yes

Eva: Yea, I like bluegrass a lot because it, um, you, instead of, you learn the melody first, and then you get to do things on it. So, like, um, when I couldn't improvise, I just learned the melodies and that's all I could play, so I'd learn like [plays a melody] but when you get, when you start hearing a lot of people, then you can hear different ideas, so you can, you hear like "Oh, that sounds cool" but I still didn't know how to improvise, so I'd just copy them. So, I'd hear like, "I don't think this was in the melody before" [she plays a short passage]. I'm not sure what the exact original melody is, because it's so old, so I think I heard someone do it and I want to do it because I thought it sounded cool. So I played it like that, so I'm saying "Oh, that's the melody now."

The students started with "Salt Creek," a simple traditional tune with A and B sections. She played for the students, then started to teach them the tune. Similar to other bluegrass music, she did not give them sheet music, instead teaching the song by rote. Toward the end of the lesson, Vina asked about this:

Vina: Do you learn most of your melodies off sheet music?

Eva: [laugh] Never off sheet music. By ear—like, I can't remember a time when I learned an entire melody off of sheet music.

[Mr. Marquis walks in, asks if they will come out and play something for the class, and the girls say, "Nooo!"]

Eva: Hmmm, what else? Oh yeah, I usually learn everything by ear and it's usually, I get a friend to teach me, but I can't remember a time when I learned off sheet music, but I pick up tunes pretty much any place I go, like festivals. Or, I did have fiddle lessons for a couple years, so my teacher taught me a lot. Right now I'm learning most of my stuff from the mandolin player in my band because I don't have a fiddle teacher right now, so I'm just learning tunes wherever. But I like learning by ear a lot better because you can hear feeling in the music, and then you can have an idea what you want it to sound like. And, I know you guys can probably sight-read better than me, I'm not a very good sight-reader.

Vina: Neither am I.

Eva: So when I have a sheet of music in front of me I never saw before, it's, I can look at the forte, pianissimo, but it's so much easier if I hear the piece just once, or if I just hear the orchestra play it at least once, but if you gave me a piece to practice by myself, then it's really hard for me to know what, you know, what the composer wants. But if you hear something, you can say "This is a cool tune" or "This one's kind of serious" or I don't know, maybe there's a boring tune somewhere but, yeah, that's why I like learning by ear better.

This exchange is emblematic of Eva's discussions with students. She promoted a casual atmosphere in the lessons and chose her own direction in the absence of guidance or restrictions by Mr. Marquis. Her teaching style was encouraging, and she gently but insistently prodded students through the beginning steps of learning by rote, then improvising. The students asked many questions, something that was absent from the larger classroom, and discussed aspects of bluegrass during their lessons.

In the lessons after the initial one, Eva gave them standard bluegrass phrases to ornament the melody. This was an intermediate step on the way to actually improvising a break. Not surprisingly, these early improvisations were met with resistance:

Eva: So, I think today, you guys are ready to start improvising on it ["Salt Creek"] yourselves.

Shehime: Noooo, noo, nooo.

Eva: Yeah, you are, you've been play—, you know it, you know, you've memorized it. So, okay, my point is, once you know a tune, you can start, okay, so you have your foundation, okay, you've got your melody. And I gave you a bunch of ideas, and, um, variations to start on, so that can, you can get ideas from those variations [they play the variations]. So like, in bluegrass usually, um, people take breaks, instead of everyone playing it together. So we can do that, I'll, um, I can back you guys up, and each of you can take a break. Just do something a little bit different. You don't have to go far from the melody, it's actually better if you stay close to the melody and tweak it a little bit.

"Do You Have Any Music for This at All?"

In January, Mr. Marquis decided to have Eva teach a lesson to the whole class, including himself. On a few previous occasions in class, he had asked them to play "Salt Creek" as an ensemble. I had observed him teach them about improvisation over that tune, both times when Eva wasn't present. His lessons used a subject logic approach (Choksy, Abramson, Gillespie, & Woods, 1986). Just like Eva's private teacher, Mr. Marquis talked about the key, the scale or mode that was appropriate, and asked the students to play. Often, he set up the activity in such a way that the students felt that they were simply being asked to play notes within the scale, but that any notes would be okay.

This approach contrasted markedly with Eva's. Her conception was reinforced by demonstration, the way she taught the tune, and her answers to student questions remained focused on the tune as a fundamental organic unit. First the tune was learned, then ornamented and played with, then solos were developed in mini–jam sessions where the group played breaks while Eva played backing chords. The tune was always present, central, and the central point of reference. In one lesson Eva talked about playing chords for backing, but at no time did she talk about chords when trying to tell her students how to solo. Instead, she stayed close to the tune.

Mr. Marquis asked Eva to teach the group because he had noticed that many of them had trouble with the rhythm at the opening of the B section. It started on the downbeat, but since the melody moved from *sol* to *do*, it sounded like the first note is a pickup. Half the students started before the others, and pretty soon the whole group was rhythmically tangled. Mr. Marquis spoke with Eva in front of the class:

Mr. Marquis: Okay, I think only one violinist has it, ahh, and that's about it. Uhm, go over the second part, just the second part slowly, play.

Eva: They all had it a little before, but then we only meet for an hour a week.

Mr. Marquis: I know, so what we need to do is focus a little bit more on, now, do you have, do you have any music for this at all?

Eva: No, I want them to play it by ear,

Mr. Marquis: Alright, I want them to play it by ear, but it's, but it's not enough time.

Eva: They have it, but it's hard to, I had it taped for them [inaudible].

Mr. Marquis: You have it taped?

Eva: Not on me now,

Mr. Marquis: No, what I mean is I can duplicate the tape, and then they can . . .

Eva: Or I can record myself,

Mr. Marquis: That's fine.

Eva: playing it, at two or three speeds.

Mr. Marquis: Just one speed is fine, okay, at a slower speed. Okay, do the second part, do the second part.

Then the students worked on the second part of the tune. Mr. Marquis led the charge and set the stage pedagogically:

Mr. Marquis: Okay, alright, now, I know most of you cannot do that, okay? I know most of you can't do it, so what I want you to do is just listen to the first two bars, the first two bars of it, then play. [to Eva] Do the first two bars. [Eva begins playing those two bars. She stops at the end of beat three, which musically ends the motive.]

Mr. Marquis: Okay, that much, try and do it. Ready? One two ready go. [They play that much and sound okay, although they had this fine before.]

Mr. Marquis: Again, one two ready go. [They play again.]

Mr. Marquis: Okay, alright, that's how you're going to learn the rest of this section. You're going to go into ensembles now, and I'm going to have Eva basically take the cellos first, cause they don't know anything, okay? So you're going to work with the cellos first, each group only ten minutes, ten minutes, ten minutes, ten minutes.

Despite Mr. Marquis's request that Eva work on improvisation, he focused his time on the work as exemplified in correctly performing the melody of "Salt Creek." His question, "Do you have any music for this at all?" suggests an underlying orientation toward score-centered practice. By asking this question, he reveals the disjunction between setting-centered and score-centered practice. If there is no sheet music available, then there is no music. Not merely that it might be more efficient or professional to teach the tune by means of a score, but the lack of sheet music indicates a lack of music in a more profound way. The music is in the score, and if you want to teach a tune, you should use a score. Eva remained steadfast in the face of this question by relaying her own pedagogic stance. She valued learning by ear. Just as there is no sheet music in bluegrass practice, Eva wanted to teach fiddle tunes authentically, by ear, not by sight. Eva also bridges the gap between her approach and Mr. Marquis's by mentioning that she had a tape of the tune and that she could bring in a tape or record herself playing the piece. Recordings hold a middle space in bluegrass music for Eva. They assist learning, and the work is defined by the act of recording (a certain break Bill Monroe recorded will always sound the same on playback), but it stays away from paper, where sounds are depicted in standard Western notation, rarely used for improvisational music. Even with a tune like "Salt Creek," Eva wants to preserve the notion that there is no one way to play it, and that impulse and a set of ears attuned to a context will always bring something fresh. As Dewey noted,

> In quality, the good is never twice alike. It never copies itself. It is new every morning, fresh every evening. It is unique in its every presentation. For it marks the resolution of a distinctive complication of competing habits and impulses which can never repeat itself (Dewey, 1922/1988, p. 146).

As Eva's work continued, her teaching evolved as her students' abilities improved. First, she had them back up each other during practice. Later, she tried to mix the ensembles up, making sure that she had a cello or bass who could play a bass line, and that there would be a more complete jam session experience. In later lessons, they talked more about what they had tried to do in their solo breaks, and there was a lot more playing in general. The students played well enough to perform a public bluegrass performance for parents as part of a concert in the spring, and all considered Eva's work a success, if an uneasy fit that wouldn't be replicated after Eva graduated.

CONCLUDING THOUGHTS

Revisiting Score-Centered and Setting-Centered Practices

Although there are not many bluegrass musicians at most schools, there are plenty of students like Eva. In the larger study (Thibeault, 2007), three of the six students I worked with could be defined as primarily setting-centered, the other three as score-centered. I found that the school music program at Arts High used only score-centered work. There are several reasons for this, including that learning in setting-centered situations is poorly understood by the music education profession. I believe teachers could reevaluate whether or not this ought to be the case. In this section, I incorporate findings more broadly from the entire dissertation.

From the teacher's standpoint, certainty of the score provides great comfort. Certified classic and high-quality works make for a curriculum that is defensible, an important consideration given music education's expendability within the general curriculum. These works also allow for amazing achievements of coordination, as when 200 people create a performance of Beethoven's Ninth Symphony. Music education that brings these experiences to students is a great educational service.

The drawbacks in the large ensemble tradition, however, are also substantial. In working with scores, we miss out on the rich environment that setting-centered work, as depicted in Figure 14.1, often encourages. These include opportunities to pick the key, choose the tune, evaluate the structure, play with the tempo, and make significant alterations simply for the pleasure of hearing them. During one group interview, several students at Arts High told me that they often felt like auto mechanics just there to do a job. This is possible when we invite students to a classroom where they rehearse without discussing, and ask them to play without a voice or choice in what is played or how things sound. A visiting conductor to Arts High summed this situation up. In complimenting the students after a rehearsal, he told them,

> Thank you so much for your work. You've really risen to the challenge. You're a great band. You watch closely, and I can do anything I want—I can play faster, I can play slower, I can shape the phrase and you're there with me. This is really what playing in band is about. You're the instrument, and I'm the performer.

Because how things should sound is known (admittedly, with some flexibility on the part of the director), what must be done physically and musically can be fixed and decided, leaving a clear path for musicians to go from where they are toward the goal. In contrast, the setting-centered musical object is, by definition, largely unfixed, undecided, and much more open to negotiation in a way that invites conversations of musical meaning and can promote the formation of musical judgment, the very kinds of discussions and goals music educators strive to foster in their classrooms.

THE POSSIBILITIES FOR SETTING-CENTERED WORK IN MUSIC EDUCATION

Eva's work teaching bluegrass shows that an alternative to commonly found music education practice is possible in a public high school. Students can engage in music education in a setting-centered situation. This work can bring a different set of emphases, and can invite and allow performers to engage in conversations that seem to have ended by the time a score usually reaches them.

In fact, Goehr reminds us that setting-centered practices have a long history in music. Music education might view the inclusion of these practices as a reintroduction after a long hiatus. For most of history, across most of the world, people gathered to make music by putting their own abilities, limitations, and interests above the musical work or composition. Indeed, often the music could only exist in the performance, as improvisation was expected and impossible to predetermine. This was true not only for musicians in India. It was true when composers provided a figured bass to be extemporized over by musicians, or when composers provided melodies without specifying which instrument would play. The move in Western music to notate everything had more to do with elevating the musician to the level of a romantic artist and the creator than it did with education (Goehr, 1992). It may well be the case that this set of affairs pushed music education to a stance that could be described as one where brilliant works are prepared so that performers have only to be in tune and on time, all else being stipulated by the score and by common practice.

Another aspect that ought to be addressed is the focus upon large ensembles. The performance of Beethoven's Ninth may be life-changing for the audience, and it should be a transformative experience for the musicians. But the limitations of this model are gaining attention. The aim of the San Francisco Symphony is to enchant the audience, not to liberate the performers. I argue that an educational program should aim for both, and observation of many rehearsals at Arts High and elsewhere does not provide much evidence this is happening. Questioning large-ensemble, performance-driven curriculum is not new (Mercer, 1972; Palisca, 1964), but there is renewed interest in considering alternative pedagogy (Green, 2002), as well as philosophical accounts that question music education practices (Elliott, 1995; Reimer, 2003; Woodford, 2005). Broadening the curriculum has also received attention from various policy documents, from the National Standards (MENC, 1994) to MENC's Housewright Declaration (Madsen, 2000), to volumes that document Bennett Reimer's Northwestern University Music Education Leadership Seminars (Hickey, 2003; Rodriguez, 2004). These volumes promote a more inclusive vision, while acknowledging the challenges and difficulties that always accompany changes in practice.

This orientation toward music, with the musician controlling and having a say in the music at nearly every level, was articulated by Eva. We were talking about why she always saw the good in performances while the score-centered students always picked out the shortcomings. She said, in describing the music she loved:

Eva: And I call it, I heard this term from a friend. It's people music, what bluegrass and Old Time are at least. It started off that a thing that people did that was a part of their lives and part of their entire community. And the non-musicians would come and dance and sing, and they all worked together during the day. It was a fun thing, a recreational time, not something to stress about and perfect things. A time of gathering and closeness. That's the way I think of it. All the jams, the bluegrass jams, even if you don't play you're still invited. I think that having fun is one of the most important things. I think that if I stressed about all the things I do—I don't believe in perfection. I think that if all your mind is set on is perfection, that it's a lot harder to enjoy music and you also become a lot more competitive against people, but it's also a drawback to your enjoyment of music.

MT: And so, your idea of music is of recreation, even though it's still about the sound, and about doing things that are musically interesting, but the concept is rooted in one that is embedded in life.

Eva: Yeah, the kind of music that I play, is, um, began as a recreational thing.

MT: It wasn't about putting on your best dress, and sitting quietly in a concert and . . .

Eva: Not at all.

REFERENCES

Berliner, P. F. (1994). *Thinking in jazz: The infinite art of improvisation.* Chicago: University of Chicago Press.

Chaiklin, S., & Lave, J. (1993). *Understanding practice: Perspectives on activity and context.* New York: Cambridge University Press.

Choksy, L., Abramson, R. M., Gillespie, A. E., & Woods, D. (1986). *Teaching music in the twentieth century.* Englewood Cliffs, NJ: Prentice-Hall.

Dahlhaus, C. (1989). *The idea of absolute music.* Chicago: University of Chicago Press.

Dewey, J. (1922/1988). *Human nature and conduct.* Carbondale: Southern Illinois University Press.

Dewey, J. (1934/1980). *Art as experience.* New York: Perigee Books.

Elliott, D. (1995). *Music matters: A new philosophy of music education.* Oxford: Oxford University Press.

Emerson, K. (2005). *Always magic in the air: The bomp and brilliance of the brill building era.* New York: Penguin Group.

Goehr, L. (1992). *The imaginary museum of musical works: An essay in the philosophy of music.* New York: Clarendon.

Green, L. (2002). *How popular musicians learn: A way ahead for music education.* Cornwall, England: Ashgate.

Hickey, M. (Ed.). (2003). *Why and how to teach music composition: A new horizon for music education.* Lanham, MD: Rowman & Littlefield Education.

Leong, S., & Odam, G. (2002). Music, technology, traditions and pedagogy: Working together at play. In M. Espeland (Ed.), *International Society for Music Education Conference Proceedings* (pp. 41–49). Bergen, Norway: International Society for Music Education.

Madsen, C. K. (Ed.). (2000). *Vision 2020: The Housewright symposium on the future of music education*. Reston, VA: MENC.

MENC. (1994). *The school music program: A new vision: The K–12 national standards, preK standards, and what they mean to music educators*. Reston, VA: Author.

MENC, & Choate, R. A. (1968). *Music in American society: Documentary report of the Tanglewood Symposium*. Washington, DC: MENC.

Mercer, R. J. (1972). Is the curriculum the score: Or more? *Music Educators Journal, 58*(6), 51–53.

Palisca, C. V. (1964). *Music in our schools: A search for improvement (report on the Yale Seminar on Music Education)*. Washington, DC: U.S. Government Printing Office.

Reimer, B. (2003). *A philosophy of music education: Advancing the vision* (3rd ed.). Upper Saddle River, NJ: Prentice Hall.

Rodriguez, C. X. (Ed.). (2004). *Bridging the gap: Popular music and music education*. Reston, VA: MENC.

Shahin, C. (2005). (personal communication, September 15, 2005).

Small, C. (1977). *Music, society, education: A radical examination of the prophetic function of music in Western, Eastern and African cultures with its impact on society and its use in education*. London: Calder.

Small, C. (1998). *Musicking: The meanings of performing and listening*. Hanover, NH: University Press of New England / Wesleyan University Press.

Suzuki, S. (1969). *Nurtured by love: A new approach to education* (W. Suzuki, Trans.). New York: Exposition Press.

Thibeault, M. D. (2007). *Music making lives: Score and setting in the musical experiences of high school students*. Unpublished doctoral dissertation, Stanford University.

Woodford, P. (2005). *Democracy and music education: Liberalism, ethics, and the politics of practice*. Bloomington: Indiana University Press.

IV

ADULTHOOD AND OLDER ADULTHOOD

15

Creation to Performance: The Journey of an African American Community Gospel-Jazz Ensemble

Marvelene C. Moore

This chapter chronicles the evolution and journey of a community gospel-jazz ensemble, Shades of Gospel, from its inception to the present. The journey is documented through stories that unveil the experiences of four African American members in the ensemble, interspersed with my perspective on events and my personal experiences as the founder and leader of the ensemble. References to the principles of teaching and learning within the African American culture are examined through a review of the function of music; the process of transmitting, acquiring, and engaging in music; and a historical survey of African traditions and their carryover to the African American culture. Experience as the source of musical, spiritual, and interpersonal teaching is paramount.

SHADES OF GOSPEL

The importance of cumulative experience to human beings is as natural and necessary as breathing is to life. Without living through situations, we cannot fully know, comprehend, or understand. Further, we cannot adequately pass on to others what we have not encountered, manipulated, or resolved through experience. This necessity of experience is reflected in the writings of John Dewey. He contended that in order for an individual and a society to learn, actual life experience is required, because "experience arouses curiosity, strengthens initiative and sets up desires and purposes" (Dewey, 1938, p. 31). Dewey understood that in order for an individual or a society to grow, develop, communicate, and make significant contributions to culture, community, nation, and the world, personal and communal experiences are imperative. In the case of music, the significance and benefits of experience to teaching and learning should be obvious due to the character of the medium. However, the type of experience in music varies in form depending on social, cultural, and environmental factors in the lives of the individual, culture, or community.

In this chapter, I present themes that emerged from interviews I conducted with select singers in Shades of Gospel, an African American gospel-jazz ensemble. Specifically, I will explore the relationship between (1) the function of music in the lives of the gospel-jazz ensemble members and (2) the nature of transmission, acquisition, and engagement in African American gospel-jazz music within the sociocultural context of the African American culture. These factors are highlighted through the narratives of several ensemble members as they responded to questions and talked about their affiliation with and musical participation in the group.

Two males and two females ranging in age from twenty-six to fifty-seven participated in the interviews for this chapter. They were selected based on the length of time they had been affiliated with the ensemble. Teresa Hodges, soprano, was the first member to join, and she and I sang as a duo for approximately one year. Our rehearsals were held at my house until the group increased in size, after which we acquired a place to rehearse at a local Methodist church. Francis Harshaw, tenor, joined the group the following year, and we formed a trio (typical gospel voicing) and sang for another two years. During the third year, I became acquainted with a graduate student in music education, Quinton Rayford, a baritone, at the University of Tennessee, and after his graduation I asked him to join the ensemble. Though typically gospel groups are voiced as soprano, alto, tenor (SAT), gospel jazz ensembles may be three to four vocal parts, like our quartet. Several other individuals joined the group in the interim. Erica Wilkerson, soprano, who joined us in 2007, was the last singer to become a member.

The name Shades of Gospel was derived from the differences in church affiliations among the members of the ensemble. The singers belong to various Protestant denominations, although one member is a former member of the Catholic Church. They represent the Baptist, Methodist, and Presbyterian denominations and non-denominational churches as well. When I received the call from God to form the ministry ensemble, I sought singers from different churches who had a strong belief in God, thus the name Shades of Gospel.

Regardless of their age, the people whom I interviewed expressed similar views on the influence or experience of their music in their lives, their perceived mission of the gospel-jazz group, and their reasons for becoming members. They viewed their mission as a union between (1) sharing the love of God for all people, (2) communicating the message of love through performance/ministry of gospel-jazz music, and (3) receiving religious and social benefits in the rehearsals and performances, which enhance their spiritual and personal growth. They considered the ensemble's mission being essential to living, based on their beliefs about God, a challenge both personally and as a group, and evidence of deliverance.

FUNCTION OF MUSIC

Gioia (2006) compared the function of music to the purpose of rooms in a house. He stated that in a typical house, the rooms are organized on the basis of how they are used and furnished dependent on the activities that take place. Consequently, a bed does not belong in a living room nor a dining table in a bedroom. Gioia determined that "such is the defining stamp of the uses to which we put things" (p. x), particularly music. He labeled his research in this area of music as the "House of Music." He further concluded that a house may have all the technical workings in it and may be labeled as beautiful, ugly, sublime, or ridiculous; however, in the final analysis, these qualities cannot be divorced from the way humans use it. Therefore, function becomes as important in music as are all of the technical, inner workings of the art.

In the African American culture, music permeates every facet of life, as it does in the cultures of West Africa, its ethnic ancestor. It functions similar to Gioia's House of Music. Whenever there is a gathering, appropriate music and dance may be performed. Consequently, when African Americans gather for worship, whether in church, a concert hall, a home, or the street corner of a community, singing and movement (dance) are a part. When available and depending on the venue, instruments become a part of the performance (Nketia, 1974, p. 31). Otherwise, the body provides the instrumental accompaniment through polyrhythmic hand-clapping and foot-stomping.

From my own experience in the southeastern United States, I have observed that participation in gospel-jazz music serves many functions for the African American whether in sacred or secular environments. Because it is Christian in nature, music functions as a means of communication to recount the tests and trials of life, to confess hope for deliverance, and to glorify and praise God for His role in people's lives. During these expressions, the individual is often transported to a different place where he or she is released from the real, physical world, after which he or she usually has a different perspective on life. In some instances, participation in gospel-jazz brings about healing, especially when the text of songs is based on the Christian belief in the scriptures that state, "But He was wounded for our transgressions, He was bruised for our iniquities; the chastisement for our peace was upon Him, and by His stripes we are healed," Isaiah 53:5 (Thompson, 1964). In the performance ministry of the music, people who unite in belief and in Spirit gather together, thus creating a religious identity and assisting each other in understanding who they are and what they can accomplish with the help of an all-powerful and all-knowing God. Finally, from this knowledge and assurance of God's help, individuals prepare to face the world, feeling confident of who they are and believing that everything will be all right. Music teachers' understanding this concept is important to instruction because for some students religion plays a major role in their lives.

TRANSMISSION, ACQUISITION AND ENGAGEMENT IN MUSIC

Sharing in a music experience, whether transmitting, receiving (acquiring), or engaging in its performance, is largely determined by sociocultural context. In other words, musical participation depends on the historical perspective of the culture, acceptable behavior within the culture, and the purpose for which the music is performed. Small (1998) underscored the importance of this belief by relating that the fulfillment music brings to individuals occurs only when they understand what people do when they engage in it. This suggests that engaging in music is action oriented, which Small further labeled as "musicking" and Campbell referred to as "rhythmicking" (Campbell, 1998, p. 69). Thus, musicking and rhythmicking are necessary actions when members of a culture *transmit* music, whether deliberately or incidentally; *acquire* music, whether knowingly or by chance; or *engage* in music in formal or informal manners.

Transmission of music in the African American tradition may occur when very young children are brought to choir rehearsals, seated in the church pews or rehearsal area and doing their homework or playing quietly with toys as the music is being rehearsed. Here the sounds are transmitted to the children quite naturally, and the evidence of the love of God for all people (mission 1) is presented informally through the message of the text and music and in the demonstration of love they observe incidentally by the interactions of the choir members. This is reminiscent of the West African practice of including children in all areas of life (Nketia, 1974), particularly in music where they actively participate, thus reflecting the practice of musicking and rhythmicking of adults.

Later, African American children and other individuals experience music in formal church services, where they acquire a deeper meaning of the music and the message of the love of God through performance and ministry (mission 2). Further, participants acquire a deeper understanding of the message through the linkage of song, dance, and instrumental accompaniment performed simultaneously in the service, which is another characteristic of West African music. However, to really understand the message and receive the ultimate personal and spiritual benefits (mission 3), participants must actively engage in the music and the worship. According to Sloboda (2005), participants are brought into a relationship with others when they actively engage in music-making and reflect human solidarity in their worship. Hand-clapping, foot-stomping, hand-raising, singing, and shouting affirmations to musicians are a few ways that participants become involved in the music ministry and worship.

TRADITIONS IN AFRICAN AND AFRICAN AMERICAN MUSIC

In order to acquire greater insight into the cultural context of gospel-jazz music, it is necessary to review briefly some characteristics of African music and discuss their cultural and musical connections to African American traditions. By doing so, we find that many African music features are also found in African American gospel-jazz music and that a direct relationship exists in the acceptable performance practice and response to the music associated with both cultures. In particular, the music of West Africa—Congo Republic, Cameroon, Dahomey, Gabon, Gambia, Ghana, Guinea, Ivory Coast, Liberia, Nigeria, Senegal, Sierre Leone (Southern, 1971)—and Africa-America (1) exhibit unique features of rhythm and melody; (2) link song, dance, and instruments together in performance; (3) display specific musical structure and form; and (4) promote a particular performance practice (Adzinyah, Maraire, & Cook Tucker, 1987; Bebey, 1975; Bowdich, 1873; Brooks, 1984; Equiano, 1789/2003; Nketia, 1974; Southern, 1971).

Music of Africa follows an oral tradition. Every village has one or two bards who are responsible for memorizing the history of the tribe, transmitting it orally, and engaging the villagers in "musicking." Like West African music, African American gospel-jazz is transmitted orally and learned aurally. The parallel to the African bard is the choir/ensemble director who typically listens to recorded music, memorizes the vocal parts, and teaches them to the singers by rote. The director must be able not only to hear and remember the parts, but also to sing them. The members follow a process of learning the music by listening to the director sing a phrase, after which they sing the phrase in each vocal part; soprano, alto, tenor (SAT). After each section of the group (SAT) has learned the first phrase, the choir sings the phrase together; they use the same procedure to learn the remaining phrases of the song.

West African and African American music is frequently polyrhythmic and polymetric with accents occurring on the off-beats, setting up extensive use of syncopation. The melodies tend to emphasize pentatonicism (Brooks, 1984), although the melodies from some African tribes may also be centered on the heptatonic scale. West African melodies may be harmonized with parallel thirds, fifths, or sixths above the melodic line (Adzinyah et.al., 1987) and with added swoops, slurs, and vocables. African American melodies are further harmonized with six-four (second-inversion) chords in series to reflect the three-part (SAT) voicing of the singers. Ninth-, eleventh-, and thirteenth-chords may also be distributed among the voices and instruments to produce a jazz sound.

Falsetto is used extensively in African American gospel-jazz music, especially by the lead male singer with groaning, humming, moaning, sliding, and gliding (*portamento*), swoops, slurs, and smears. Occasionally, a rough, foggy, raucous style of singing is performed for musical effect and to reflect the text (Brooks, 1984). In Africa, the music is influenced by the rise and fall of spoken text (Nketia, 1974, p. 186). Francis Bebey stated, "If you can speak, you can sing" (Adzinyah, 1986, p. 2).

Unlike the spirituals that grew out of work performed on the plantations and cotton fields in the rural South (e.g., "Sit down servant, sit down, know you mighty tired so sit down," [Work, 1940, p. 65]), gospel-jazz music was a direct result of urban hardships. The text focuses on "(a) staying alive: 'It's another day's journey,' (b) health: 'I woke up this morning in sound mind . . . blood running warm in my veins,' (c) finances: 'I've been down and out, you know I didn't have a dime,' (d) conversion: 'But the Lord came in right on time,' and (e) assurance of salvation: 'Be sure your name been written down'" (Anderson & Moore, 1998, p. 4). Eileen Southern (1971) described the necessity for a different text and music in the gospel-jazz style: "When the Black people (African Americans) began pouring into the nation's cities during the second decade of the twentieth century, they took their joyful spirituals (of music and text) with them, but found the rural music to be unsatisfactory in urban settings and unresponsive to their needs" (p. 402). In both instances the text was religious (Christian) in nature to reflect the singers' reliance and dependence on God and hope for deliverance.

In West African and African American music, singing, dancing, and playing instruments are inseparable. Those who sing and play instruments also dance. The music and dance are primarily improvised; however, many songs may have a recurring refrain with an improvised verse or line. Improvisation and extended melismas occur as the moment dictates, that is, as emotions heighten. An African testament to the wedding of a song, dance, and instruments occurs in the writing of Equiano, who was the first to write about music of the region in English: "We are almost a nation of dancers, musicians and poets. Thus every great event . . . is celebrated in public dances which are accompanied by song and music (instruments) suited to the occasion" (Southern, 1971, p. 5). In both cultures, hand-clapping and foot-stomping constitute an important contribution to the music-making while others sing, dance, and play instruments. The instrumental ensemble in African American gospel-jazz typically consists of keyboard, bass guitars, and drums. Advanced ensembles include a wind section: saxophone, trumpet, and trombone.

According to Nketia (1974) several standard song forms from African music have been retained in African American music. The first is the simplest and most common call-and-response in which the second singer or chorus may echo the phrase of the leader exactly, or they may choose to extend the response. In the second form, the leader sings a few notes and the second singer joins immediately, and then they sing together to the end. Other forms found in gospel-jazz music are verse-refrain, an influence from hymns heard by the slaves on plantations in the South. Frequently, rondo is heard with the A sections (the repeated sections) performed by the ensemble and the contrasting sections sung by a leader or soloist.

In West Africa, music permeates every facet of daily life and is engaged in by all people in a community, village, or area. Performing music provides an opportunity to share in creative experiences, participate in music as a community, and communicate sentiments (Nketia, 1974). Adzinyah et al. (1986) confirmed this use of music by noting that "the African community is held together with a musical bond" (p. 2). Music is performed at every ceremony, rite, and festival, including religious ceremonies and rites. As observed by Thomas Bowdich, one of four delegates sent to Africa to bring back information about the Ashanti tribe: "The Ashanti thought it absurd to worship God in any way other than chanting and singing" (Southern, 1971, p. 5). The concert arena for African music activities can be any public or private place where individuals gather to participate in music (e.g., a regular place of worship, a grove, courtyard of a house, a street corner, a market place, or a dance plaza) (Nketia, 1974). Regardless of the arena, it is not easy to distinguish between the performers and the audience, except when instruments are used. Nketia (1974) describes this unique relationship in his writings on African music: "There is not a wide gulf or a clear boundary between them and the performers" (p. 33). Southern (1971), an African American ethnomusicologist, further described not only the physical involvement of the audience, but also their active verbal participation: "Onlookers also shouted words of encouragement to the performers (or disapproval, if they wished). Essentially then, there was no audience; all persons were actively involved in the music-dance performance in one way or another" (p. 12).

The performance or ministry of gospel-jazz music is a community event as well. The ensemble or choir provides the stimulus, and the audience responds by singing with the group, shouting affirmations to the performers and to God, and clapping and dancing in front of their seats and in the aisles. On occasion, the audience members leave their seats and gather around the stage to be closer to the performers. All participate in the performance and respond differently as inspired by the Holy Spirit. Students in the music classroom may behave this way when performing religious music from the African American culture. Therefore, it would be advantageous for the teacher to be knowledgeable about the performance practices that accompany the music.

HEARING THE SINGERS' VOICES

The personal stories in this section document the progression of four singers in Shades of Gospel. The four members are the first singer to join the group, the two singers who joined later, and the most recent member. My talks with these singers were based primarily on responses to a structured interview comprised of open-ended questions that facilitated the telling of their stories of personal involvement in the music ensemble. I met twice with each member of the group. Session one lasted thirty minutes, and session two was one hour in length. Members were encouraged to share information about themselves and their experience in the music ministry. Interestingly enough, many of the music traditions of Africa, as previously discussed, were referenced in the narratives, an indication that the African influence on African American music and culture continues.

In addition to being the interviewer, I participated in the telling of the singers' stories by encouraging unedited and flowing conversation, by giving the participants frequent affirmations of their accounts, and by interspersing my perspective on the part of the story being related. The content of the narratives was audiotaped and documented in my personal notes. However, I relied heavily on the audiotapes in recalling their stories and seeking emerging themes from the data. (The statements or questions I posed are labeled as "S" or "Q," respectively, and "R" indicates interviewees' responses in the transcribed, unedited dialogue that follows.)

Teresa

Teresa, soprano, is a fifty-four-year-old, single mother of two adult children and four grandchildren. She is an executive secretary at a manufacturing company in a small town fifty miles from Knoxville, Tennessee, the city where the gospel-jazz ensemble rehearses. For each rehearsal Teresa drives a total of 100 miles in order to follow what she believes to be her calling, ministry through Shades of Gospel. She has sung in choirs since high school and in her present church for fourteen years. She is punctual, frequently arriving at rehearsals before other ensemble members, highly organized, and takes on the responsibility of preparing song texts for rehearsals. She listens to each song that we will perform on a CD, transcribes the words phrase by phrase, duplicates copies for the choir members, and places the song sheets in their folders. There is no music in the folders, just words. All music is learned and sung by rote.

I first saw Teresa in the gospel choir when I visited her church. She immediately stood out because of the way she sang—with a smile on her face and hands raised. Later, when I was hired as the minister of music at that church, she agreed to assist me with clerical work pertaining to the music department. As a result of working together, we became friends. After I left the church, I had a call from God to do ministry outside of the church in a small ensemble. I immediately thought of Teresa and how an audience would relate to her, as I had when I observed her sing. I did not know the quality of her voice (a light, pleasing, pretty sound) or her ability to sing by ear—her pitch accuracy and gift to retain the soprano line after hearing it only one time. Instead, I was struck by her manner of communication with the congregation while singing. I asked her to sing for me and, as a result, we formed a duo that was the beginning of Shades of Gospel. Teresa chose my house for our interview conversations, because she had rehearsed there since the group began.

S: State your name and tell me about yourself (for example, where you grew up, et cetera).

R: My name is Teresa Hodges. I am 54 years young. I was born in Bronx, New York, but I only lived there a year. We moved to Queens, New York, where I was raised. I was married in 1974 and had two children. I was divorced in 1980, and I lived in New York until I left in 1987 with my future second husband. I moved to Albuquerque, New Mexico, in 1987 with my children and lived there, until I remarried and moved to Texas. We lived in seven different states, until we ended up in Athens, Tennessee, in 1993. I divorced my second husband; he left, and the children and I stayed in Tennessee. We've lived here for fourteen years now.

Q: Why did you decide to join Shades of Gospel?

R: How much tape do we have? Well, I would have to start with how I met you. That came about because at the church I was going to they were looking for someone to be over the music department. They invited you to come and that's how we met, because I was a member of the choir. . . . For some reason we just became instant friends. Since then I've gone through a lot of things at the church, not only being a member of the choir, but also part of the praise and worship team for over ten years. During that time, even though I knew the Lord had called me to be a part of the praise and worship ministry, it got to where it wasn't joyful anymore to do it. . . . I knew that the Lord had something more for me to do, but I felt that I had to be faithful in that position and do it. Then at one point, I felt at peace that He had released me, and I didn't have to be a part of that anymore. And when I did that, that's how the door opened, and it just seemed like once I was finished doing that ministry, the Lord had another one for me which I had no idea was in the making or even in my future, and that was Shades of Gospel. That's when you asked me if I wanted to become part of the ministry, and that's how I became part of the group. Because I felt that was the door the Lord had opened for me after closing the other one.

Q: How would you describe the mission of the group?

R: Well, even at the beginning, I saw us as being ministers not just to the African American culture but to those who have not even experienced what we know. It's like we are at the forefront to bring people to God, to the Lord, with this type of music that they've never experienced before. You know, something that's going to get them off their feet and be able to praise and worship the Lord like they've never done before and maybe they didn't even know they could do, because they have never been in that kind of atmosphere. I think that . . . that it is our mission to spread the gospel in places that maybe certain people may feel that they can't minister to them, because they don't know where they're coming from, but that's why we're going there so that they can know where we are coming from and where they're going in the Lord.

S: Describe your experience with the group. Tell me your story of the group as it involves you and your participation.

At this point Teresa, who was sitting at my kitchen table, sat straight up with her hands clasped as though ready, willing, and serious about telling her story. Her countenance, which is generally very pleasant, changed to an even more pleasant expression as if to remember happy times when just the two of us constituted the group.

R: At the very beginning, the Shades of Gospel was . . . the two of us, singing all the songs. We did have a piano player, Jan. Then the two of us went to Pat's church, who is a friend of yours. She graciously invited us to her church to do our first ministry outside of your home, and we went there, and God just anointed us, and the two of us just did our thing. The instrumentalists at the time were Jan, piano; Terry, bass guitar; Dennis, electric guitar, and Yashan on the drums. That's how the group started . . . that was the beginning of the group—two singers and four instrumentalists. We did our ministry. It was exciting because we just didn't think we were good enough, or that people would respond to us, or that we weren't ready. But it was just like, you know, once we got out there and started singing, it went from us singing to the Lord just ministering through us to the people because it was awesome.

After that, you brought on Francis as the tenor and Susan as the alto because you were doing all the alto (and lead) parts. Then Jan, Yashan, and Dennis left us; Sam, Twain, and Catrell (all from Chattanooga) came on board. Our group started to grow and expand, and so as the group expanded and grew, we had to find other places to minister so that the ministry could grow. We ended up getting an engagement from your friend, Tanya in Dayton, Ohio. . . . When we came out and opened our mouths the Holy Ghost just did His thing. I mean it was awesome. We had people standing up and clapping their hands, singing and dancing, who had never in their lives done those things before. When we went out to talk with the people at the reception after we sang, we got their feedback. They were saying, "We've never experienced anything like this before!" That's when I knew that is what we're supposed to do. Not just going places where people say, "Okay, we've got this black group coming in singing gospel jazz," and they know where we are coming from but we're going places where people have never heard, you know, they're like, "*Wow*, where has this been all my life?"

The main thing is experience. There are things that African Americans have been through and have experienced that no other culture has, and so our music projects that, and you feel that when you sing or when you hear gospel or jazz because it's all about experience. You can have a white (Caucasian) family living on one side of you and an Asian family living on the other side and you can all get along, but yet within the home you are experiencing different things. So I can hear Andre Crouch in my home and just relate to everything he is saying and worship God with it. But these other two families on the side are saying, "I don't know what she's talking about." So they are not feeling what I'm feeling, and so to me that's the difference with the African American culture. Even though they have their own experiences, they still can't relate to what we've gone through [historically, culturally, and in times of hardship]. I'm not saying that their worship is not right, but they don't worship the same as we do . . . it's different.

Because of the ensemble, I think I look more to what I can do as far as ministering to the Lord in the future. Before it was like, you know, I didn't know what the Lord had for me outside of church. I didn't know . . . I knew that all this could not be for nothing, just end. There had to be something more. So it's made me look forward to the future as far as ministering in a group to people that also makes me feel good. It's wonderful to be in a group with people who love the Lord the same as I do, who you can be friends with in a long-term relationship, not just well, okay we're going to sing and then we go off and do our own thing. So, it's more of a family. I have two grown children and when they're gone, well my son still lives with me, but when he leaves it will just be me but it won't be Teresa all alone, because I'll have outside things that will not only help me in my older years, but I can still do something that is going to minister God's word.

Francis

Francis, tenor, is a fifty-five-year-old, married male with three adult children and five grandchildren. He is a property clerk for the Department of Energy in Oak Ridge, Tennessee, but he lives in Knoxville. Francis is a trained classical singer who has held roles in various operas and is considered one of the leading local soloists for community events and at churches. He was also a member of a doo-wop group like The Temptations in his early career. He prepares the sound system set-up for rehearsals and performances. Francis chose to meet me at my office for our interview conversations, because it was closer to his home and after work hours when the music building would be quiet.

I met Francis in 1978 through his wife, Gwen, who became my hairdresser immediately after I moved to Knoxville. She told me about her singing husband and invited me to meet him. At the time, I was minister of music at the Methodist church and asked Francis to drop by at the end of his church service to sing for me. He did, and after that, every time I was asked to prepare the Christmas and Easter pageants, I hired Francis as a soloist. Francis has one of the most outstanding natural operatic tenor voices that I have heard in many years. After Teresa and I presented our first ministry concert, I thought of Francis, so I asked him to join us, and we formed a fine trio.

S: State your name and tell me about yourself (for example, where you grew up, et cetera).

R: My name is Francis Harshaw, fifty-five years old. I grew up in Knoxville, Tennessee, in a family of ten siblings, five girls and five boys.

Q: Why did you decide to join Shades of Gospel?

R: Well, let me say that I've sang [sic] with several groups in my life, and next thing you know they'd sing a little while and then fade away. I'm looking for something that's going to last at least until I stop my singing. . . . I can take my retirement and go sing and be perfectly happy the rest of my life. . . . That's why I decided; I kept saying, "Ms. Moore doesn't play. She means what she says, and she says what she means." It's gonna happen . . . it's gonna happen, and that was one of the biggies.

Q: How would you describe the mission of the group?

R: I think we're trying to reach people, number one. That's been my particular goal whenever I'm in front of anyone or with a choir. . . . When people come to me and [say], "There's something that pierced my heart," I'm like, "That makes me joyful too." I hope that's our goal—to minister.

S: Describe your experience with the group. Tell me your story of the group as it involves you and your participation.

As I asked this question, Francis, who was sitting forward in a comfortable red office chair with a high back, sat back, breathed a sigh, and began to relate his story by telling how important his role was to the group.

R: I'm the tenor in the group, and they [the members] kind of depend on me to do my tenor part. I joined the group four years ago and, of course, I'm anxious to see what we're going to do. . . . But I hope I'm going to be a steady person in the group and give what I can give. Everybody's going to give something, and I'm going to try to give until I'm full. What was our first performance? Claxton? Goodness, how did I forget that? We had some different musicians then, too. Ohio? Dayton, wow! We've done some things. It [the audience] gets kind of personal. Some of them shout, some of them stand up, hand-clap, say "Amen," and some of them sing along with us, too. Our music is a "feely" music too. You feel what you sing. You have to perform with feeling.

Our practices are always great, too. Of course, the people in the group [are great, too], and we have changed personnel several times, haven't we? But we always seem to bounce back. Pretty good, pretty good. When I came to the group, it was one male for a long time. That was me. The spirit of the group is good, too. If we keep that spirit going, it will take us a long, long way.

Quinton

Quinton, baritone/tenor, is a twenty-six-year-old, single male who lives in Knoxville, Tennessee. He has an undergraduate degree from the University of Memphis and a graduate degree from the University of Tennessee. He currently teaches music at a local elementary school and serves as an assistant pastor at his church. He completed a CD of his original compositions, recorded with a band and one backup singer who sang several vocal parts. Quinton recently performed some of his songs in concert. He assists with the sound system set-up for rehearsals and performances. Quinton also met me at the office for our interview conversations, because it was closer to his house, and he relates well in a more formal setting.

Quinton was a graduate student in music education at the University of Tennessee when I met him. He was one of my advisee students in my graduate classes and asked me to serve as chair of his master's committee. After observing his calm yet serious spirit in class and after his graduation from the university, I asked him to join Shades of Gospel. He did, and we formed a strong quartet. Quinton has a fine baritone voice that is capable of reaching many tenor notes. Therefore, he sings with Francis most of the time, because there are very few gospel-jazz songs performed in SATB.

S: State your name and tell me about yourself (for example, where you grew up, et cetera).

R: Well, my name is Quinton Rayford. I grew up in Memphis, Tennessee. I was actually born in 1980 to William and Ruby Rayford. And growing up in Memphis where the city was just surrounded by music, I had the opportunity to attend a performing arts school there in Memphis, majoring in music. I participated in the choir when I went to Colonial Junior High School. I left there and went to Overton High School, a performing arts school, and I had the opportunity to participate in a lot of different vocal ensembles, from show choir to concert and chamber [choirs] and all the other different activities. That was basically my upbringing in music. I also sang in the church choir.

Q: Why did you decide to join Shades of Gospel?

R: I put a lot of thought in it. I said, "I really don't want to be a part of a lot of groups." I have never joined an organization or group that I did not feel I could give my all to. And when you introduced me to Shades of Gospel, I was like, "Wow, Shades of Gospel." You were telling me that it was a gospel-jazz ensemble, and I became excited because I love to sing jazz. I love to sing gospel. And then as far as being a part of a group of people to come together that would sing gospel, it just blew my mind. I was excited about traveling. I was excited about ministering to a multitude of people of every ethnicity, and I was excited to be able to spread God's Word through song to others. This is so important, and one thing I've noticed is that Shades of Gospel is a wonderful, wonderful group name, because there are many different shades of not only gospel music but different shades of people, and I don't believe that God has called us just to minister to one group of people. So the thing about Shades that I love is that there are many different shades of people, and God has called us to share this love and share our gifts with the world.

Q: How would you describe the mission of the group?

R: We are about singing God's Word, singing God's praises, giving God the glory. Just being examples, not only for each other, but for the world through song. He has given us a gift, and we're gonna use it to give Him the glory, no matter what color. Like I said earlier, we're not here for fashion; we're not here for fame or fortune, but we're here to be a blessing because God has blessed us. It's all about giving, and believe it or not we will be blessed even more through our giving because that's what the Word says—give and it shall be given unto you.

S: Describe your experience with the group. Tell me your story of the group as it involves you and your participation.

Quinton sat back in his chair, crossed his legs and reminded me of the time he attended the first rehearsal at my house. As he continued, he began to talk as a pastor in relating the mission of the group and how being African American contributed to the sound of the music, yet reminding me that the Word of God is for all.

R: Well, I remember when I just came to the group. I can't remember the date, but it's been a while ago. I was very nervous when I first came to the group. I came in and saw everyone sitting around. It was you, Francis, and Teresa, and you were sitting around getting ready to start. I was actually nervous, because I was the youngest person in the group. . . . Actually, I was nervous the first two times I came, because everyone knew the songs except for me. I'm getting to learn the music and to learn the people, and it's a wonderful group of people that I'm working with and singing with. Everyone is just so loving, and hearts are just huge and kind, and I think that plays a big part in being able to get along with others, and being able to work together with others has a big role in any ensemble, whether it's African American or Caucasian. Can you work with the person you're called to work with? Can you follow the one who's in charge and leading? So, I think that plays a huge role in it.

Well, my role, more so, is to sing. I know that's my role, and I just go in and do the best I can. . . . I feel the nerves went away quickly, as I began to become more engaged in what I was doing, as I began to learn the music, as I began to sing out more, and as I began to just develop relationships. It was easier, and I feel that that's what makes a good ensemble easier, once you begin to develop these relationships. Once they see that there is a gift there and understand that you are talented, and once you see that for yourself, then it's very easy for you to go forth.

Being African American and growing up in an African American culture/community influences the performance of gospel music and the way one ministers to others. It has a lot to do with soul. I feel that we are a group of soulful—our culture is just based in soul. From back singing way before I was born over 400 years ago when we were still in slavery, our songs were birthed out of hardships. Our songs were birthed out of pain. Our songs were birthed out of agony. Our songs were birthed just out of hope for a better future and all of that being passed down it still inspires us today. Our songs are still birthed out of pain. Our songs are still birthed out for a better future and when singing gospel, our songs are birthed out for being with Christ one day, being able to see His face one day. You know our songs are inspiring to us even though we're in this world, we don't have to be of this world, and we have already received the victory over the enemy. I mean there are so many things that our songs do for us when we sing it, when we perform it, well not necessarily when we perform it, but more so when we're singing and ministering. We feel all of these emotions, all of these feelings are part of us, and they begin to become manifested through tears, lifting up of hands and just our style of worship, which is not just our style, but should be everyone's style according to the Word, because God does tell us how to worship. He does say, "Clap your hands all ye people." He does say, "Lift up your hands and lift up your eyes to the hills which cometh your help." All of these things play a part in it. We just experience all of these things and all of this because of who we are and the struggle of our lives. . . . We've seen so much through daily or weekly settings and outings, so it has just become a part of who we are.

Shades of Gospel has offered me an opportunity (currently I'm a music teacher and what I do currently is sing all day long with kids). It offers me the opportunity to go outside the school and sing with individuals who love music. It offers me the opportunity to learn new songs, to develop relationships, like I said earlier and just use the gift that I have and expound even more [upon] gospel jazz. It offers me joy. There's a joy about being a part of this group. There's a peace that comes with being a part of this group. I truly believe that peace is there because of the prayer warriors that we have in the group. It's just a joy to be a part of it. It's a very important part of our lives.

Erica

Erica, soprano, is a thirty-six-year-old, single mother of one son, who lives in Knoxville. She is a pre-certification and referral coordinator for internal medicine at the University of Tennessee Medical Center. She is the newest member of the group and relates well to the existing members, having sung with the ensemble for approximately one year. I met Erica after work at my house for our interview conversations, because it was en route to her home.

A current member of the group, Francis, brought Erica to my attention. He sang with her at a Martin Luther King concert celebration and discussed joining the group. I contacted her by phone to discuss the possibility of auditioning for the group. Somehow during our conversation, I knew she would work well in the group because of her frequent reference to God and how important He is in her life. I decided that if she could sing in tune and had a decent voice, not necessarily outstanding, I would ask her to join the group. Her audition far exceeded my expectation. She has a dramatic soprano voice that complements Teresa's sound.

> S: State your name and tell me about yourself (for example, where you grew up, et cetera).
>
> R: My name is Erica Wilkerson, thirty-six years old, native Knoxvillian. I'm a single mother. I've got one of each, a brother and a sister. My folks are still alive, and they're still very active in my life, and I'm still very active in their lives. I'm a church-going woman, working a full-time job. Pretty much that's all you're going to find me doing—working, church, or home. We grew up on about an acre in the city right up the street from my elementary school [with] my mother, her mother, my daddy, my brother, and my sister. But we always had God, always, for as long as I can remember. My daddy played piano— gospel. My mother played classical. Just one of those families.
>
> Q: Why did you decide to join Shades of Gospel?
>
> R: I don't think it was my decision, to be honest with you, because people will ask you, "Why don't you sing for me here; I got a program here." But I try my best, pretty much. "Lord, you tell me what to do"—because I don't want to go somewhere that God doesn't want me to be, getting myself in trouble. And I have been saying, "Lord, I'm truly giving everything I have to you to use how you see fit." Yeah, I got my own ideas about how I would like to go out and witness and testify, but okay, God just said, "Um, um, go ahead and sit down somewhere, and I'll let you know when I'm ready for you." And you said the other day that we can pray for stuff and ask for stuff, and we might not see anything, but when it comes it just . . . dah, dah, dah, dah, dah. So I feel like I was led by God, because it could have been somebody else asking me to sing, and I'd say I'll call you. . . . So, just the fact that he [Francis] was inviting me to do something with Shades of Gospel just impressed me so much that he would

even think of me. It just tickled me, because I'm just a little country pick. You're some praying people. Everybody seems to be diverse.

Q: How would you describe the mission of the group?

R: Well, I believe it was back in the New Testament that Jesus said, "Take this gospel and go and spread it." You're saying [that Shades of Gospel is] going to Australia. . . . We're not just going to sing down at the church. It's nothing wrong with singing in the church, but who are you singing to? You're singing to the saved folks that know the Lord. You don't know those people on the airplane that you're going to sit next to, and you don't know nobody [sic] in Australia. That's stepping out on faith. That's saying, "Okay, Lord, I'll do whatever you say, however you say." I do see you all as being that wildfire that's gonna spread. I believe that we need it not just here in the States, not just in our home, but we need that rebirth, that revival. I believe Christianity is just going to catch on fire.

S: Describe your experience with the group. Tell me your story of the group as it involves you and your participation.

Erica paused, thinking about how to tell her story, since she had only been with the group for a brief time. Once Erica began talking, however, she did not hesitate describing her time with the group and her feelings as a result of participating.

R: Personally, I did not know Francis well enough to say [that] at least when I get there [the rehearsals], I'll have a buddy. Although I had met you, everybody's face was still very new. But you guys were so very comfortable, easygoing, and the rehearsals themselves have been pretty much unlike any that I ever had, because you're going to teach us diction, too. You're going to teach us posture, too. And I love it, because I'm one of those people that I don't know. I'm country and a lot of the things that come out of my mouth are very country. The pronunciation . . . the older I get the worse it gets. I don't like that about myself, but I've never had anybody teach me. You guys are very much punctual. You have business set aside. You have prayer. You have rehearsals. You know, not having words or music is wearing my comfort zone. I'm forgetful. But what did I wake up to this morning in my head? I couldn't get that song out of my head. It's driving me crazy. It was the last song we rehearsed, "In All the Earth."

When I get off work, I may have had a trying day, but when I get here it's like a reprieve. I know there's not going to be any drama. There's not going to be any turmoil. There's not going to be any strife. I just love it. I can say I've never had another rehearsal like it. It's Jesus. Because we are African American, our music is not just a performance. Those words we're singing, we've lived them. We've had some hard times, but we've also had some really good times, too. We've come a long way. We've been delivered. We've been set free, and yet some of us are still enslaved. But they'll be delivered, and they'll get to witness and testify and shout and sing. I think back in my grandmother's time. She wasn't allowed to do the things I do. And I think back to my mother's time, she wasn't allowed to do those things either. But I know that my son will never see the things that my folks went through . . . being a little black girl being afraid to be on the street. Mother said she couldn't be on the street past six p.m., because the police would be the ones to pull you over and rape you, and little black boys would disappear and never be seen again, but in our performances, those that I have been a part of, they've been very professional, very respectful, very soulful.

Most people who call themselves a group do not know how to blend. But Shades of Gospel wants to pull together and blend. There should be no part higher or louder than the other when doing a choral arrangement unless it's a crescendo, unless it does call for that. Here, it's not that everybody wants to be heard. Everybody wants to complement one another, which is the way it should be. Everyone is so gentle towards one another. I think everybody's willing to help one another and to listen to one another. I have to listen to you to know where I need to be. It gives me peace, because I know that it's ordained. It's His blessing and His desire. It's not two ladies just wanting to get together and sing, because I sound good and you look good and we're going to make some money. I want to belong to something that He desires, not just doing my thing.

This is the first thing that I've done in a long time as a single mom for me. Everything is always revolved around my son. It's actually given me a little growing-up time. It's an education for me, but I love it. I just believe that God has something wonderful in store not just for those who are being obedient and singing His songs, singing praise to Him, and leading others to Christ, but I believe He has a wonderful blessing in store for those that will bear witness to Him and those that help along the way to get us where we need to be so that we can get out and minister to people. I believe that lives will be spared through this ministry. I believe this is just the Lord's blessing in store. I've already been blessed just meeting you all and singing with you. My mother and father asked what's going on at rehearsal, and my son even said, "Don't you have rehearsal?" He is interested in something I'm doing, for a change.

POSTSCRIPT

Thus, the chronology of my experience with four of the seven members of Shades of Gospel. Interviewing the singers was a labor of love. The more I listened to their stories, the deeper my understanding of their participation, especially as African Americans, became. Belonging to Shades of Gospel influenced their lives, directing their ministry and affecting their lifelong teaching and learning. As one singer described, "Those words we're singing, we've lived them." Another singer expressed, "The main thing is experience. There are things that African Americans have been through that no other culture has and so our music projects that." Experience also determined musical functions within the culture and the manner in which they were transmitted, acquired, and engaged, whether formally or informally. Further, these interviews confirmed the necessity of experience in the process of teaching and learning. Finally, my conversations with members of Shades of Gospel brought me closer to the singers and gave me insight into their lives.

The results of this project have implications for music teachers by pointing to how their instruction may become more effective. First, students are a product of the experiences they bring from their culture and community. Therefore, teachers should acknowledge and incorporate information that students take from these experiences into the teaching and learning process. In other words, it should be acknowledged that students bring valuable musical information, transmitted to them according to their cultural values and traditions, to be shared with others in the music classroom. Second, teachers being knowledgeable of and sensitive to students' learning styles can enhance students' learning. For example, if students are accustomed to learning music aurally and through physical involvement, then the implementation of these approaches into the music classroom would be beneficial to students who learn in these ways.

The singers' narratives depicted how everyday life experiences of the culture created a reliance and dependence on God. The singers regarded their experiences as the ingredients that made their music unique. The relationship they developed with God through their struggles and triumphs created a strong desire to transmit and convey the message of hope, love, and deliverance to others through their music. Religion for them was the foundation of their existence and their messages that they referenced consistently when referring to their music as being something they have lived.

REFERENCES

Adzinyah, A. K., Maraire, D., & Cook Tucker, J. (1987). *Let your voice be heard*. Danbury, CT: World Music Press.

Anderson W., & Moore, M. (1998). *Making connections: Multicultural music and the national standards*. Reston, VA: MENC.

Bebey, F. (1975). *African music: A people's art*. Brooklyn, NY: Lawrence Hill Books.

Bowdich, T. E. (1873). *Mission from Cape Coast Castle to Ashantee with a descriptive account of that journey*. London, U.K.: Giffith & Farran.

Brooks, T. (1984). *America's black musical heritage*. Englewood Cliffs, NJ: Prentice-Hall.

Campbell, P. S. (1998). *Songs in their heads*. New York: Oxford University Press.

Dewey, J. (1938). *Experience and education*. New York: Macmillan.

Equiano, O. (2003). *The new interesting narrative of the life of Olaudah Equiana*. London: Dover Thrift Publishers. Revised Edition, Penguin Classics. (Original work published in 1789).

Gioia, T. (2006). *Healing songs*. Durham, NC: Duke University Press.

Nketia, J. H. K. (1974). *The music of Africa*. New York: Norton.

Sloboda, J. (2005). *Exploring the musical mind*. Oxford: Oxford University Press.

Small, C. (1998). *Musicking: The meanings of performance and listening*. Hanover, NH: University Press of New England / Wesleyan University Press.

Southern, E. (1971). *The music of black Americans: A history*. New York: Norton.

Thompson, F. C. (Ed.). (1964). *The Thompson chain-reference Bible*. Indianapolis, IN: B. B. Kirkbridge Bible Company.

Work, J. W. (1940). *American Negro songs and spirituals*. New York: Bonanza.

16

Both Sides of the Coin: Experienced Musicians Tell of Lives Lived and Shared

Katherine Strand

This chapter is about three musical artists who devoted their lives to music-making and teaching. Their stories illustrate their backgrounds, opportunities, obstacles, and viewpoints on the lives they have lived and shared. Each has been recognized for her or his unique contributions to music and to pedagogy, and together they have enriched the lives of thousands of people. Their stories converge at the Jacobs School of Music at Indiana University (IU).

As a young faculty member, composer, teacher, and colleague, my interest in collecting and understanding the artist-teachers' personal histories came from a desire to learn how they managed their achievements. I was amazed to learn that, for them, creating and teaching were inseparable, two sides of the same coin. Their teaching practices informed their artistic creations and vice versa. I wondered how these examples might inform the readers' and my own creative artistry and pedagogy.

The purpose of this study was to examine the ways these artists reflected upon the interactions between their creative and teaching lives and beliefs. This chapter includes information about their lives and pedagogies, evaluations of their experiences and learning, and understandings of their life journeys. In addition to the artists' narratives, biographies serve as introductions to the narrators. Discussion of my findings follows each narrative.

I collected and analyzed three artists' personal narratives (Peacock & Holland, 1993; Riessman, 1993), created from their responses to open-ended questions, which served to initiate dialogue and encourage the participants to speak about their lives (Holstein & Gubrium, 1995). Following the interviews, I analyzed the narratives, after which I took my findings to the participants for member checks (Crabtree & Miller, 1999) in order to learn if the artists agreed with my analyses and approved of their reformed narratives.

Narrators use their stories to reflect upon events as they perceive and remember them. They also use stories to create meaning of life events. In this way, narrators both reflect and construct reality. For my analysis, I focused upon psychocultural and psychosocial techniques described by Peacock & Holland (1993) to learn how the participants viewed themselves as creative artists and teachers and how they understood the events of their lives in connection to their beliefs about creating and teaching. Psychocultural approaches examine self-identities that narrators assume and how culturally available plots, symbols, and metaphors influence them. According to Polkinghorne (1988), a narrator assumes one of four roles in a personal narrative—the romantic, the tragic hero, the survivor, or the victim. Psychosocial approaches focus on cultural markers that narrators use to define themselves and their relationships with their audiences. As an additional interpretive step, I sought to find common threads in the transcripts (Josselson, 2006) and themes to guide my own and the readers' creative and pedagogical growth.

JAN HARRINGTON

Jan attended Southern Methodist University, where he studied with choral conductor and composer Lloyd Pfautsch. He earned master of music and doctoral degrees at IU, studying choral conducting with Julius Herford and Fiora Contino. Before returning to teach at IU, he taught at State University of New York at Fredonia and at Oklahoma University. Harrington served as head of the IU choral faculty for thirty-two years before his retirement in 2007. During his collegiate teaching, he also served on the faculty of the Aspen Choral Institute and conducted at the Aspen Music Festival. He was cofounder and music director for the Music Festival at Grey Towers in Milford, Pennsylvania, and served on the faculty of the Dartmouth Conducting Institute. In 2005, he was awarded the Indiana University Chancellor's Professorship of Music in recognition of excellence in scholarship and university teaching.

Jan cast himself in the role of romantic as creator and teacher (Polkinghorne, 1988). His self-identity was established as an "everyman" character, developing special relationships with teachers and students with whom he felt a special resonance. Relationships emerged as a central plotline and a causal agent in his life, musical choices, and beliefs about teaching. Patterns and structures were common metaphors throughout the story. One can almost imagine him poring over his life in ways similar to his studying a musical score to find every nuance in its design.

Jan's Story

I probably decided to go into music when I was in high school. But I think there were lots of influences before. I have a very important memory from when I was two or three, maybe four. There was this recording, *"Variations on Under the Spreading Chestnut Tree,"* by a composer named Weinberger. I remember my dad sitting there, telling me stories about it. There was "This is the Lady in Red" and all these little stories about each variation. And since I remember that, it must have really formed the way of approaching and thinking about music later, when I knew about music.

I played tuba. My band director didn't think I should continue on tuba because she knew that I aspired to be a band director. She switched me to trombone and gave me one of her own. But when I moved to high school, she also moved to the high school and became the choral director, so I joined choir. She was my mentor for my musical growth. She was a thirty-year-old spinster—austere, tough, and very intense—and she gathered her students around her. We had a gang, a clique, of about five kids that she took everywhere, even to the symphony every week. She made me the student conductor and all those things kids do when they're in high school.

I ended up going to Southern Methodist University because I was a Methodist and got a scholarship. I went as a music education major with a concentration in piano, but then there was one day when my voice teacher found my vibrato, and she went screaming out in the hallway and had everybody come listen to me sing, because they were so relieved that I didn't have to be a piano major. My voice teacher took me seriously. She treated me like I was going to be an artist, and that was very important for me. She would say, "You know, Jan, you must never think you are going to be a performer, because your voice is too small." But, nonetheless, she treated me very seriously, and I think she thought I was artistic, and so I was very grateful for that.

By that time, I was going to be a choir director, and Dr. Pfautsch was a great teacher. He was developing his system, articulated in such texts as *Choral Therapy: Techniques and Exercises for the Church Choir* (Pfautsch, 1994). I was in the select choir from the time I arrived. I remember my audition. Dr. Pfautsch made me feel accepted and happy at my audition which, in retrospect, was very important. Dr. Pfautsch was very kind and he gave me an understanding of how you could be [as a teacher].

And, for the first time, in college, I had a theory class. Before, I couldn't memorize anything, because it didn't make any sense. Suddenly, studying theory, everything became systematic. I remember learning about the Neapolitan chord in second-semester theory and going to choir; a chord came around, and it had a name. All those things that I knew aurally [were] getting names. Things that I intuited were being given structure.

But my voice teacher was my strongest influence during college. She sent me to Indiana for graduate school to work with a conductor with whom she had sung and saw to it that I got an assistantship singing in opera chorus. Then I came into contact with Julius Herford and Fiora Contino. My first year, Dr. Herford gave a Schütz festival with lectures and performances. I went to the very first lecture, and I knew that this was what I needed—to learn his way of viewing music. I thought that what he had resonated with me. I always understood what he was talking about. I didn't always see what he was going to say, but once he said it I knew what it meant. But I also knew what it meant in sound. I don't know what that is. Maybe my dad telling me, "Here comes the lady in red." But I knew, if he said, "There's this chord, and isn't it wonderful?"— I knew that it was wonderful, and I knew how it should work. [Herford] was about timing and spacing of the form and how the form informed the progress of the music. Fiora had a great love of text. I felt a resonance with her and vice versa. Whatever it was that she saw in my music-making, which she said had to do with the relationship to text, was something she admired. Even though I felt that I was not the most skilled or had the best ears or could do the best things, both of them, these two opposite poles [Herford and Contino], something in me resonated with them or they with me.

One of the things Dr. Herford imposed on me was a structure of music study—that you have to have a framework to put the art into. From Dr. Herford we got a pattern of living. The idea is that you look at the whole and then you look at the small things that make the whole add up. And this is the way you approach a big piece and how you approach many problems in life. All the details add up into the big picture rather than starting from the small picture and hope that you can express the big picture.

As I was finishing my degree, the dean at Fredonia was on campus to interview someone else, and he wasn't happy. He asked our dean if there wasn't anyone else, so he told him to go over and watch me. And he watched and went home and called me and asked me if I would come for an interview. And I did, and that's how I started teaching [at] college. At Fredonia I had a two-hundred-voice choir, and I taught voice. Teaching voice was pretty funny. I would get bored, and I would just think of things to do. I said to a student one day, "Let's see if we can fix that high note, free it up. Get up on that desk, and when you get to the high note I want you to leap off the desk." I just wanted to see if she would do it. And she said, "Okay, Dr. Harrington. AAHHHHH." So, my life as a voice teacher was short but eventful. But I had a real studio. And maybe that particular experience influenced the way I relate to students in choral ensembles, because teaching voice is a very personal thing. I cared about them all very much, and they responded in kind.

There was a tenor who was very talented. I was investing a lot of my concentration in his personal development and how it related to his singing. He didn't come back after the first semester. And he didn't tell me. That was very revealing to me, because of the way I felt betrayed that he didn't tell me he wasn't coming back. I thought, at that point, that one of the problems that studio teachers have is that they give out, but they expect a lot back personally. They think the student owes them something for what they've taught. I decided that if you are going to teach, you give out this way because that's what I like to do. But you don't have to expect something back.

At Oklahoma, I was director of choral activities, and I directed a select choir, an oratorio choir, and the women's choirs, so I had a lot of programming to do. Programming is one of the things most creative about being a choral conductor—how you plan your program and your time. Thematic programming that has some sort of structure to it and that has a thread of thought about it, is something that I just love to do. I start with one piece, some piece that wants to be done, and I work out from that. For example, I wanted to record Libby Larsen's "Billy the Kid," so I thought, "What are we going to do with this?" Libby Larsen said the piece is about violence and the foundation of the whole American culture based on violence. For the rest of that concert, we did the James Macmillan piece about the violence against missing sons in Argentina and "Friede Auf Erde" (Schönberg). The concert was called "A World of Violence" and ended with "Friede Auf Erde," which was about someday something better coming along where power will not be achieved through violence. It has to do with a respect for structure and for thematic continuity, an extrapolation from Dr. Herford's sense of structure and Fiora Contino's great love of language, my own interest in literature, and maybe my dad saying, "Here comes the lady in red."

Here at Indiana, we have such great students, and there's so much to learn from them. The choir gives me many, many ideas. When they produce something from a line of music, you say, "Oh, here's something we can run with." I think what I try to encourage is a sense of musical responsibility and creativity. I notice that my singers, the ones that have been with me a little while, bring an awful lot to the way that they think about music. They can handle text better. What you try to instill in the choir is to find any sound that's beautiful, and that's the one you work from. If they're feeding me and something sounds beautiful, then I say, "That's beautiful," and work from there, and "Let's make sure we don't make any sounds that are worse than that, ever." And the next will be better, but none worse than that. I think it was the way I was treated by my teachers. They certainly didn't treat everybody that way. Whatever was in me resonated with them. So my life has been blessed.

Reflections

Jan's story reminded me that it is important to be open to the relationships and structures that exist in our environments. Jan viewed himself as the beneficiary of all that his teachers, colleagues, and students offered. He allowed himself to follow where teachers sent him. I also learned to value my connections with students and with an audience by engaging them in learning processes and creative musical expression.

MARY GOETZE

Mary earned a performance degree in voice from the Oberlin Conservatory of Music. She taught second grade in the public schools, married, and moved to Bloomington to complete a music teaching certification and a master's degree. After completing a Ph.D. at the University of Colorado, Mary taught at IU for more than twenty-five years. During her tenure there, she founded the IU Children's Choir, the Mountain Lake Colloquium for teachers of general music methods, and the International Vocal Ensemble (IVE). She also gained international recognition as choral conductor, composer, and educational innovator for her use of technology in teaching multicultural music. Additionally, Mary contributed to and served on the editorial boards of *Share the Music* (1998, 2003) and *Spotlight on Music* (2006), K–8 textbook series. She earned numerous awards for her industry, artistry, and ingenuity.

Mary established the identity of a pragmatic hero (Polkinghorne, 1988) in her narrative. Her journey began as a child having musical talent, recognized by a teacher in college who propelled her into a career of challenges. Mary responded to perceived community needs by teaching and creating. She made a career of finding wrongs and creating ways to make them right.

The prevalent metaphor in Mary's narrative was one of traveling. Several of her references to traveling, paths, directionality, lines, taking steps, and shoes added to the hero's journey plotline (Campbell, 1949). Her language throughout her narrative reflected her assumed role as mentor, to countless music teachers and to me.

Mary's Story

I was a musical child, and I grew up in a musical environment at a time when you sang instead of turning on an iPod or a radio. I was part of a small family church that involved a lot of singing. I was in 4-H with a song leader who led songs at meetings and camp. At the movie theater, everyone would sing following a ball bouncing over the words. It was not surprising that I fell into music-making. I was the fourth child and, odd as it seems to me now, I always thought of myself as the black sheep of the family. I couldn't do what my siblings could do, not understanding that they were older and that is why they were so skilled. So music was my default interest. Both in school and home, I was the youngest and felt as if I wasn't as able as those around me. So I opted into music because I thought, "Oh, I can do that."

We grew up on a farm, and farmers have to know how to do everything. We lived miles from town, and if something went wrong you had to fix it yourself. My father was a farmer, which means he was also a mechanic and a veterinarian. He knew the latest things about agriculture, and he had great intuition for raising crops. He could butcher, he could fix the water pump, and he could repair the car or any kind of machinery. And all of us grew up thinking, "I have to do this myself." I think that transferred to music. I taught myself to play by ear, thinking that if other people can do it, I can do it, so I just figured it out.

[In grade school] I attended a laboratory school. There were thirty people in my class, most of them the same group all the way from first grade through high school. Throughout high school, I was in band, orchestra, choir, and in small ensembles, all within the school day. In addition, I took piano as well as flute and voice lessons outside of school. So it was natural to major in music when I went to college. If my brother had chosen that, it would have been a problem. But I was a girl, and it was fine.

When I attended a little college in Kansas, I had a piano teacher who became my hero. He was rather amazed that I had no technique but, oh, did I have passion. He recognized that my ear and my passion took precedence over technique. My fingers responded to my love for the music. He was demanding, and I wanted to work hard for him. This college piano teacher started testing me on my pitch, and he'd say, "Did I play it in this key or this?" I always knew. He was the first person to tell me I was exceptional and that I should have a better background than what I was getting at that school. He had gone to Oberlin, and he had accompanied in the vocal studio of Robert Fountain, who was also the choral director, so he paved the way for me to enter his studio. I transferred in as a voice major.

Singing in the Oberlin College Choir under Robert Fountain was perhaps the most profound musical experience I had. I really credit him with the aesthetic I bring to choral music. Everything was about line. He'd say, "Music is up there [pointing overhead]. It goes along infinitely, and we're just going to pull it down and go with it for a little while, and then we let it go." I loved that idea. We were shaping the musical lines with forward motion and the beautiful sculpting of lines and shape toward climax and resolution. Robert Fountain also believed in memorization. He never gave us a pitch, and he never rehearsed with the piano. I would read, and because I knew I had to memorize, I could read it once and then sing it from short-term memory. The next day we would read it once more and after that, it was mine. It was a tremendous model. But it was more than that. We sang with amazing depth, and we truly communed with that music. To me, if you don't take a piece of music into your soul, it never really touches you and you're not going to have a chance of touching somebody else with it. That experience made me realize how little we ask of singers.

Well, I finished at Oberlin, got married, and moved to Indiana. It happened that this was a time when the profession desperately needed teachers. There were actually want ads in the newspapers for teachers. So I answered one, and I became a second-grade teacher and taught on a provisional certificate for three years. My sister was a primary-school teacher, and my aunt was a primary-school principal, so it was a respectable thing to do with a college degree. In truth, I had no idea what I was doing. However, it was a wonderful fit, and I was hooked. I remember coming home from teaching on the first day, and I said, "I've had the first truly happy day of my life." I had around twenty-two kids, with some kids with IQs of fifty-eight and sixty. I was like a hen with her little chicks, and we just fell in love with one another. I think I discovered that nothing matters in the classroom except the love you have for the kids. And you have to do right by them, and you have to protect their self-esteem.

My joy in teaching was a major turning point, because I said, "Okay, I'll get certified to teach. I'll either teach elementary classroom or elementary music." I sent my credentials to the state department to decide which. It was a shorter route to do music certification. I came to IU, because my husband had the GI bill. Someone had dropped out of a program in the schools that she [music education faculty member Miriam Gelvin] had developed called multiple arts. So in my second semester I was student teaching. Ready or not, she put me in that position, because she needed somebody to fill this slot in music in her school program. I had no background in art and dance. Again, I felt over my head, out of my territory, but Dr. Gelvin said, "You can do this," so I said, "Okay, if you think so." And I did it. Other people also identified my capabilities and put me in situations for which I was unprepared. People seemed to give me shoes that were too big, and I grew to fill them. I assume they recognized my potential. Sometimes that's a gift, and sometimes you feel very overwhelmed!

Around 1977, a music education faculty member at IU resigned in August. They asked Jean Sinor [music education faculty member] to take it, but she said she wanted to share it with another person. Since I had been working part-time because I had a preschooler, I accepted and shared the position with Jean. I taught and supervised courses for non-majors. Again, all new territory for me. In 1980, Jean and I started the children's choir because there were no children prepared to take part in IU choral and opera productions. I didn't like what they were doing with the voices when they had children in the operas. The proposal was also beneficial to music education students because it provided an on-site laboratory experience. I benefited by training kids to sing and applying Robert Fountain's approach. The only way I had of carrying forth that legacy was through the children's choir, and I felt I must do it.

I wrote music for the children's choir, and Doreen Rao took my arrangements [to Boosey & Hawkes]. They were taking the lead in providing good literature specifically for kids. My works sold well, so they offered to form a series in my name. For the next fifteen years, I was turning out one or two arrangements or compositions per year. When you're writing for children's voices, you are creating within tight limitations, given their vocal and musical ability and undeveloped part-singing skills. I find it satisfying to figure out how I can say something musical within the limitations that children's voices and skills provide me. It is like maneuvering inside a little box. I find inventive, sometimes funny, ways that will work pedagogically, while being satisfying to me musically and intellectually. I would say that I am a musical problem-solver. Limitations are the problems you have to deal with creatively.

My last professional chapter has been the most exciting and most important—my work with the International Vocal Ensemble (IVE)—for it brought a lot of my life together. I woke up with the notion that I could have this ensemble that could provide at least some music students the opportunity to make music from other traditions and to work with people of other cultures and colors. I was raised in a peace church, and then I went to Oberlin with all its social activism. I have always been keenly aware of racism in this country, but then I came to recognize it in the IU School of Music. There is no level playing field when it comes to academic and school music. That realization is what propels me to do what I can in the time I have left—to build some bridges to some of these musical traditions that aren't embraced by the academy and to find ways to bring them into school classrooms that honor non-European ways of making music.

The whole journey has been amazing. I feel as though everything came together in my work with the IVE—my choral and musical passions and the social agendas that are rooted in Oberlin, the peace church, and my family values. And I loved the pedagogical challenges—teaching in ways that are totally new, venturing into uncharted territory. So the fun of it for me was and will continue to be learning, making contacts, and making music in new ways.

Reflections

Mary viewed her journey as one of challenges and opportunities. From her narrative, I learned the importance of never allowing complacency or contentment to blind my eye to the needs of students and community. A hero's journey requires us to recognize the gifts we bring to the world of music, keeping an eye on making that world a better place.

DAVID BAKER

David Baker was born in Indianapolis in 1931. He attended Crispus Attucks High School, a segregated school in Indianapolis, and played trombone with the Hampton family band. He attended IU as a trombone performance major during a time when the university was segregated. After graduation from IU with a master's degree in 1954, he moved to New York to establish his career. David received the *Down Beat Magazine*'s New Star Award in 1962, but a car accident resulting in a jaw injury ended his career as a jazz trombonist. David reinvented himself as a teacher, conductor, jazz cellist, and composer. He has composed more than two thousand jazz, symphonic, and chamber works, has written seventy books and some four hundred articles, and he has been honored with numerous national awards. David is currently a Distinguished Professor of Music and Chair of the Jazz Studies program at the IU Jacobs School of Music and conductor and artistic director of the Smithsonian Jazz Masterworks Orchestra.

From my analysis of his narrative, David cast himself in the role of survivor (Polkinghorne, 1988), whose identity emerged in part because of racism. Community and high school were life rafts that kept him safe, and his love of music saved him from other futures. He acknowledged the experiences and people who aided him throughout his life. Doors and walls are metaphors that suffused in his narrative. David spoke of challenges and opportunities in terms of spaces that allowed passage and protection or those that formed barriers. He reported that he pushed through boundaries formed by his own limitations and those imposed on him by society.

David's Story

I wanted to start music in the seventh grade. There was a teacher who brought instruments. The teacher sent the instruments around the classroom, and the only instrument that was left when they got to me was the trombone, so I played the trombone. And at the end of a week, my teacher sent the fifty cents back to my stepmother and said that I had no talent. So I didn't get to start music then. But just before ninth grade, I sang in the choir at my junior high and in church, and my teacher noticed that I was really trying to learn. I had even taken a cigar box and put springs on it so that I could learn to play the fingerings on the tuba, because Mr. Brown [the high school band director] told me they needed people who played tuba. Mr. Brown gave me a tuba, so for the first two or three years I played tuba. And it was during that time that I began to get the notion that music was something I loved so very, very much. I had other ambitions that were not open to us [African Americans] at that time—to be a test pilot, a politician—but the first time that connection became real was when I wanted to become a music teacher and that was because of my music teachers.

Russell Brown remained my friend to the end of his life. He started me on tuba. He started me on cello when I had to quit playing trombone. He went to a pawn shop, bought a cello, glued it together, and gave it to me. Mr. Brown was passionate about music, passionate about kids, and intellectually curious. He was also a good disciplinarian. I remember we were playing the Martin Gould "Pavane," and that's the part that goes [singing straight quarter notes]. The girl I was dating played flute, and I had been listening to boogie woogie, so I was playing [singing swing-beat], and Mr. Brown said, "David, that's not the way it goes." And we started again, and I played [singing same], and by this time when he chastised me, my girlfriend was looking at me, so I'm being petulant. And he says, "Boy, I don't understand you. You run into a wall, and your solution when the wall doesn't move is to get back further and run faster into the wall. From now on, when I tell you 'Sit down, you're rockin' the boat,' just sit down."

The schools were segregated. The Klan had taken over politics in Indiana at that time, so we had the best teachers [in Indianapolis] because anyone who wanted to teach who was black had to teach there. So we had Ph.D.s! We had a band teacher, orchestra teacher, theory teacher, choral teacher, and it was because it was the only place where black folks could go. These teachers cared about us black kids, and they gave us a sense of self-worth. There was a saying when I went to high school that said, "Good, better, best, never let it rest until your good is better and your better is best." And my teachers really meant for you to learn that. Mr. Brown said that you could be anything you wanted. You can't be everything, but you can be anything. Mr. Brown acted as though symphony orchestras were going to be open to us, which was at the time certainly not true. These were times that shaped my life. I think all these things propelled me.

I grew up in Indianapolis, which was the center of jazz at the time. This was the only thing open to us. As a black person, you either went into rhythm and blues, rock and roll, or jazz music. I grew up around the Hampton family; Slide Hampton was my closest friend. They included me in their family band. I learned much from them, because if we played a song from a record, we each had to take our part off of the record. So we learned to transcribe and that was my street learning. It was as idyllic a situation as I could have had growing up, surrounded by people who loved me and [where] my skin color didn't matter. Maybe I lived in musical Valhalla or something like that.

I came to IU and played in the orchestra here. At the same time, I remember auditioning for another orchestra where there was an opening for bass trombone. And I remember him [the director] saying, "You're probably the best we've heard, but you know this is an exercise in futility. The board of directors is not going to hire a black player." So that was a learning experience for me. But I didn't take it that hard because I already understood that that was not open to me. By now, I had things to do. I played in the orchestra here [at IU]. I went from playing for fun to playing for the orchestra, to going out in the summers with professional bands like Lionel Hampton or Stan Kenton. I would go to play with people who were highly professional people, and they would help you.

If I hadn't had the car accident, I'd have probably stayed in New York. I'd have been a first-call bass trombone player, but God put it in a different way. You know, we think that when a door gets closed another door is opened. I remember I sat around the hospital every week thinking "Why me?" after the accident. One day it occurred to me that while there were also good things happening to me, I never asked, "Why me?" So, I just shut up with the whining and went about doing whatever was necessary to survive. I had some good luck because I went to Lennox Institute. The models for all the jazz programs across the country are based on that. That's the first time I had direction about how to go about teaching jazz. That's the thing that gave me the impetus that showed me that it is possible to teach this music and how to organize it. It was the model for what a jazz school could be like.

When I came back to Indianapolis, I began to teach privately. I started by having the students imitate the things I did. But then I started, more and more, to have them find an individual voice they had in order to have a foundation. I was able to put together a lot of things that I was working on. I've written probably seventy books, and many of them are the result of practical experience. I found out that the scale goes like this, this piece goes like that, or here's an easier way to do that. And every year I find myself revamping and reconsidering, finding different ways to teach.

There was no reason to assume there would be any career for me as a composer. There was William Grant Still and Ulysses Kay [African American composers], but you didn't write classical music. Forget that. I just stumbled into it. It was at IU when Joseph Gingold [violinist on faculty at IU] first asked me to write a piece for him. And when I wrote a concerto for Joe, the door sprung open. Basically, if he accepted a work, then it was Starker [Janos Starker, cellist on faculty at IU], then it was Beaversdorf [Tom Beaversdorf, composer on faculty at IU], then it was Phillips [Harvey Phillips, tuba player on faculty at IU]. And once I was really serious about it, then it was just a question of studying with people. I studied with anybody who would show me anything. At the same time I'm writing, I'm actually asking questions and studying. I study before I write, and then I study how they play so that I can write a piece reflective of who they are. And it's easy for me to write because I ask them to set all the parameters. I say, "How long is the piece going to be?" and "How many movements do you want?" and "What sound?" "What should the character of the piece be?" "What would you like?" and they tell me. And every time they tell me another obstacle, then it makes that piece much easier to write. I've learned so much from having to overcome obstacles, you know, because the obstacle is sometimes the *raison d'être* for the piece. Without any obstacles, there would be no piece.

Wilfred Bain [former dean of School of Music at IU] brought me back to IU. My charge was to build a jazz program. A thing intervened that made it possible for it to be an explosion—the civil rights movement. And it came along at a time when America was sensitized to black folks. And for the first time, everybody was trying to take at least one course that had something to do with the black aesthetic. There is something very satisfying about being on the ground floor of something new because then you can build it into anything you want it to be. I've got it to the point where I know what a class needs. Mostly students, those who are inquisitive, have shaped my teaching. I tell my students, "Look, if I tell you something, and I can't tell you how I know that, then you have no reason to respect me and do those things. If I can't convince you how I know, either experientially or through a source, then why should you accept *a priori* that I know those things?"

I really consider myself a Renaissance person. The only thing that's indispensable in my life is teaching, because that's the inspiration for everything else I do. It is a question of becoming acclimated to whatever the obstacles are, finding a way to go around the obstacle, go over the obstacle, or crush it. I find that I'm not willing to accept the words "can't be done." That's nonsense. I tell you, it's been a wonderful life.

Reflections

One of the most inspiring aspects of David's life is that he was born and raised during a time when race, by virtue of segregation, directed his musical experiences. His references in his narrative were, for me, poignant reminders that David has never stopped thinking about the influence that racial segregation had on his life and our American culture. From David's story, I learned the importance of accepting challenge and of continuous and tireless learning, and using colleagues, mentors, texts, and students as sources of knowledge.

CONNECTIONS

The artists' narratives exhibited four commonalities. The most striking similarity was the central role of a teacher (or teachers) who took interest in the narrators' personal and musical growth. Their teachers provided direction, guidance, and challenge, while also creating opportunities the narrators might not have otherwise experienced. The teachers' influence is evident throughout the narrators' lives. Each narrator also recognized the importance of university life in shaping his or her opportunities and beliefs about teaching and creating. For Jan, colleagues and students informed his musical practice. For Mary, the influence was the challenge to discover and solve problems in her situations. David attributed his growth as a composer to opportunities afforded him by his university colleagues.

Each narrator could have chosen to be a victim—Jan referred to himself as "nothing special," Mary felt that she had been thrown into challenging situations for which she was unprepared, and David experienced racism. Had they viewed themselves as victims, they might never have had the success or fulfillment they ultimately enjoyed. Rather, three narrators conveyed that their creativity was enhanced by the limitations and boundaries they experienced.

SUMMARY

The three narrators can prove music educators wisdom about the relationships between teaching and creating in music, collaborating with other teachers, and learning from our own students. They show that collaboration can lead to new possibilities and that artistry is served and challenged by music classrooms and rehearsal halls. The narrators also suggest that creating music and teaching music are integrally related. The impulses that lead to becoming a good teacher can also direct and inspire creative musical expression. According to the narrators, creating music meets a need to develop oneself, to organize the world around us, and to address the needs of our students.

The three artists' teachers exposed them to high-quality and powerful musical experiences. They recognized their students' talent, propelled them forward when they might not have had knowledge or connections to do so themselves, and remained important in their lives. Teachers have the power to form future generations of great artists and teachers. I challenge myself and other music educators to strive to live up to the models provided by these three artist-teachers.

REFERENCES

Campbell, J. (1949). *The hero with a thousand faces.* Princeton, NJ: Princeton University Press.

Crabtree, B. F., & Miller, W. L. (Eds.). (1999). *Doing qualitative research.* Thousand Oaks, CA: Sage.

Holstein, J. A., & Gubrium, J. F. (1995). *The active interview.* Thousand Oaks, CA: Sage.

Josselson, R. (2006). Narrative research and the challenge of accumulating knowledge. *Narrative Inquiry, 16*(1), 3–10.

Peacock, J. L., & Holland, D. C. (1993). The narrated self: Life stories in process. *Ethos, 21*(4), 367–383.

Pfautsch, L. (1994). *Choral therapy: Techniques and exercises forw the church choir.* Nashville, TN: Abington.

Polkinghorne, D. (1988). *Narrative knowing and the human sciences.* Albany: SUNY Press.

Riessman, C. K. (1993). *Narrative analysis.* Newbury Park, CA: Sage.

17

Dancing Inside: Dalcroze Eurhythmics in a Therapeutic Setting

R. J. David Frego

It often happens that when my body and mind are in tune with the movement of the music, I experience the feeling of stepping away from myself. I look down from above and see myself dancing in harmony with the music. In these moments I learn how to feel music and to grow stronger by synchronizing my mind and body.

—Luke

Luke is a middle-aged man infected with Human Immunodeficiency Virus (HIV)—a retrovirus that causes Acquired Immunodeficiency Syndrome (AIDS). This condition causes the immune system to fail, often leading to fatal opportunistic infections. Searching for ways to heal himself, Luke used music and movement as both a physical and emotional aid to rebuild his damaged immune system. It also provided a space for centering himself and for creative expression and exploration. In the reconstruction of Luke's story, we come to see the connections he has made between music and movement; how the use of these expressive art forms helped him learn to feel trust, resiliency, and spirituality in his life; and how music and movement could offer guided learning initiatives and palliative alternatives to learning to lower stress.

Over a period of ten years, Luke has experienced connections with music and movement through Dalcroze Eurhythmics, an active-based approach to teaching music through movement. Luke's experiences occurred mostly, but not exclusively, during healing weekends, which were clinical and instructional weekends designed for people infected and affected by HIV and AIDS, and in hospital settings for medical doctors, nurses, case workers, and psychological professionals.

313

Luke's story of learning and healing reflects his need for music and movement in his life and his experiences with Dalcroze Eurhythmics. Sources used to gather information on Luke's learning through music and movement included interviews, field notes, and his writings. These sources are compiled into an amalgam to create a cohesive story that spans Luke's journey from youth to illness to emotional and physical healing.

A case study method was employed based on Creswell's multiple sources of evidence. This approach uses multiple sources to provide a detailed in-depth picture of the phenomenon being studied (Creswell, 1998, p. 37). Six modes of collecting information for this project include documents, archival records, interviews, direct observation, participant-observation, and physical artifacts (Yin, 2003). Informational data for this case study were gathered through my formal and informal interactions with Luke, my observations of him during movement classes, field notes, Luke's own writing, interviews with other professionals familiar with him, and my lesson plans. I served as researcher and participant in this study, teaching the Dalcroze Eurhythmics lessons, keeping field notes, and conducting interviews following movement classes. Trustworthiness of the findings was obtained through close collaboration with Luke during the data collection, writing, and editing processes.

A full description of Dalcroze Eurhythmics can be found in music education (Bachmann, 1991; Mead, 1994; Spector, 1990) and therapy resources (Dutoit, 1971; Frego, 1995; Frego, Gillmeister, Hama, & Liston, 2004). Originally conceived as an educational tool to internalize and physically demonstrate all aspects of music, Dalcroze Eurhythmics has expanded to include treatment for physical and emotional trauma. While Luke's treatment regime is the focus of this chapter, it is worth noting that my previous applications of Dalcroze Eurhythmics in therapeutic settings included people with autism, cancer survivors, people with post-traumatic stress disorders, land-mine survivors, and adult survivors of childhood abuse. Each therapy group experiences music and movement activities unique to the members' needs by employing a treatment that promotes physical and emotional well-being (Dutoit, 1971). Throughout the process, participants address inner discoveries and outward social growth. The educational goals of using music and movement to connect the brain and the body are primary in a therapy session. Secondary goals involve helping the individual to connect feelings and cognition and to connect to other people (Nunes, Kappes, & Carr, 2007; Ochsner, 2007).

In these therapy settings, I taught Dalcroze Eurhythmics lessons in which individuals helped learners discover personal rhythm through walking and quick reaction games, partner activities used creative movement and singing in reaction to improvised music, and large group activities used *plastique animée*, often described as a loosely structured choreography that reflects the music in motion (Frego, 2007). Participants used discussions and journal writings to reflect on their experiences.

Music is thought to stimulate the brain and force the body to react (Frego, 2003). My goal in eurhythmics sessions with participants affected by post-traumatic stress disorders or emotional trauma is to create experiences where the participants may open up and address issues within themselves that have been masked due to trauma (Frego, 1995). Using Dalcroze Eurhythmics in therapy sessions shares some commonalities with dance therapy. According to the American Dance Therapy Association, "Dance/Movement Therapy is the psychotherapeutic use of movement as a process which furthers the emotional, social, cognitive, and physical integration of the individual" (ADTA, 2007). The Dalcroze Eurhythmic sessions I constructed incorporated music education concepts into the integrated whole of the individual's body and mind. After twenty years of implementing Dalcroze Eurhythmics in therapeutic settings and by observing hundreds of clients in movement therapy, it is apparent to me that rhythmic movement may stimulate feelings that can be translated to named emotions. I work with participants to help them learn to connect their brains and bodies through experiences that challenge the brain to focus on the music and to express that music in physical and musical acts.

The purpose of this chapter is to examine how Luke describes his connectedness to music and movement and how his experiences with eurhythmics helped him learn. The first part of Luke's story sets the stage and leads us to understand how music and movement play a role in his life. The second part addresses the Dalcroze Eurhythmics experience from Luke's perspective. The third and fourth parts address how music and movement contributed to Luke's physical and emotional growth. The text for "Luke's Story" is derived from two lengthy interviews, excerpts of notes from Luke's writing, and eurhythmics class field notes taken when Luke was a participant. This process allowed for a cogent, chronological narrative. Follow-up reviews and editing occurred through several e-mail communications. After numerous exchanges, we felt that the collaborative writing had evolved into a unified structure with a seamless first-person writing style. Luke chose not to be formally noted as coauthor of this chapter.

LUKE'S STORY I

"You can dance inside." That's what I thought as I lay in my hospital bed, motionless with fatigue and the toll that AIDS was taking on my body. While listening to music from earphones, I felt the beats and the rhythms that always motivated me to get up and dance and to feel music as it should be felt—physically.

I don't know if a lack of motion in your body can depress you, or if depression causes a lack of motion. But through these last months, this disease had taken motion out of my life. Music could motivate me to move inside, but even raising my arm was now a struggle.

I faced a serious AIDS illness and a prognosis of three months to live. It was a dark time for me. And while I struggled to move beyond the statement that "you have three months to live," a voice inside told me I had to get up and start moving again. I had to reconnect my body to the rhythm that has guided me all my life. In my mind, moving was living.

Thinking back, music and movement were always central in my life. In high school I played trumpet in marching band and I sang and danced in musicals. In college I took modern dance classes. During these moments I knew that music and dance transported me. In the euphoria of feeling the music, I could look down from somewhere above and see myself moving. I stopped dance training at the end of the first year of college, and truly regret it. I look back now and wish I could have been stronger inside and bold enough to follow my passion for music and movement instead of succumbing to outside peer pressures.

In graduate school, I majored in health and fitness. Thinking about it now, I see that aerobics allowed me to find success in music and movement without being labeled as different. After college I moved to a larger city and took a job as a bartender and waiter. This life also allowed me to dance and perform, but in a social setting. Behind the bar I could move, dance, and entertain customers until the bar closed at midnight, then go out and party until well into the morning.

This lifestyle takes its toll, even when you're young. We think that we're invincible. Sadly, that's not the case. I found out that I was HIV-positive two days before Christmas in 1985. That's when my world came crashing down. At that time, there were no medicines or any thoughts of a cure. The prognosis was six months to two years to live. So live I did! My destructive behavior of recreational drugs, alcohol, unprotected sex, and sleep deprivation accelerated with no thought of the future, since there was no future. It was the *now* that counted.

It wasn't until I passed that two-year mark and a family intervention that I began to look at my life and realize that I might live beyond the point that was given to me. I had to get my life and my health back. For the first time in five years, I began to rebound and focus on the future. I realized that the lifestyle in which I had participated was not what I wanted for myself. No one ever plans to destroy his own life —it is usually a series of events that lead us there. I needed to feel a connection to the world again, not just hide from it, which I now realize was what I was doing. I knew that there was a better life for me, and for the first time I was determined to try to make that happen.

I left the restaurant industry in 1990 and began work as a fitness and aerobics instructor. This was a new and healthier way to express movement through music. It was music that had always motivated me to move and express myself. I was now choosing music that encouraged and inspired movement in my clients. The music had a strong beat and a vitality that would often allow my aerobics clients to get caught up in the feelings that I always had—feelings of youthfulness, vigor, and drive. During aerobics classes, the flow of time ceased to exist, and the energy kept everyone in deep focus—almost like a trance. When we all emerged at the end of the class, the euphoric effect was almost like a runner's high.

I loved what I was creating in my life. I was happy to be a full participant again. I think because I was so happy, my desire and passion for my work made me work far too much, and I began to take my health for granted. With increased hours, I began to experience weight loss, fatigue, and shortness of breath. I cut back on my working hours, but my decline in health continued. Then in 1993 came the diagnosis of disseminated histoplasmosis, a condition that affects the lungs by causing a short-term, treatable lung infection. My T-cell count had dropped to zero. I was hospitalized and placed on permanent disability. Now I was struggling to breathe and any movement exhausted me. I was missing the movement and fell into a depression.

Reflecting on this, the combination of depression and the lack of movement really had a crippling effect on me. I still played recorded music, but I could no longer feel it. The feeling of how music made me want to get up and move was gone. After weeks of depression, I realized that I had to get that feeling back inside of me, if I were going to get better. Coupled with a new drug combination and a determination to get moving again, I began to bounce back. This happened in stages. While lying still and listening to music, I forced myself to dance inside—to visualize myself dancing, to breathe with the music, and to imagine my health returning.

It was around this time that I began to discover complementary therapies. This included massage, acupuncture, and guided imagery and movement therapy. Consequently, throughout the next ten years I continued to heal physically and emotionally. Physical healing came with massage and reflexology, but also with weight-training and cardiovascular activities. Emotional wellness was experienced with individual and group therapy and with movement therapy. The emotional therapies helped me to cope and to keep bouncing back when physical dips would occur along the road. During this time, developments occurred in pharmacological care that helped my immune system. I am now on the same drug regimen that I began eleven years ago. Ten years of being on disability insurance was enough. I was offered a job at a local hospital and haven't looked back.

Reflection I

Luke's story is similar to that of many people affected with AIDS during the 1980s and 1990s. A sense of hopelessness and shock is often followed by an increase in destructive behavior (Kylma, 2005; Rosenfeld, Gibson, Kramer, & Breitbart, 2004). For some people, slides into self-destructive behavior may lead to more opportunistic infections and, ultimately, death (Hendershot & George, 2007; Irwin, Morgenstern, Parsons, Wainberg, & Labouvie, 2006). Luke was fortunate that he had a family that cared for him and intervened in his life. By enrolling in a research clinical trial, Luke was able to get the assisted medical and pharmacological help he needed. He chose to take charge of his health, using movement to propel him out of depression and into better physical and emotional health.

Luke often referred to music and movement as a single thought. This concept is similar to other cultures whose perception of music and movement is of one entity (Merriam, 1985). To Luke, movement requires music, and music compels him to move. The concept of dancing inside is one that can transfer to music education. As educators, we want our students to feel music within themselves and to express the music in some way. Music, consequently, becomes more than a cognitive function; it is something that is also felt viscerally within us. There are many studies that refer to music and emotion. The most common among them are the studies that measure the degree of perceived emotion with the aid of the Continuous Response Digital Interface (CRDI) (Coggiola, and Madsen, 2001; Madsen, 1998). A related CRDI study that examined perceived artistic tension in music and dance showed that observers can perceive emotional tension without having to name it (Frego, 1999). However, all of these studies involve the participant measuring emotions while in a seated position. To date, no studies report real-time response to music while engaged in locomotor movement.

The terms *emotion* and *feeling* are synonymous, according to the Merriam-Webster dictionary. Yet throughout Luke's narrative, he refers to feelings more than emotions. In a later conversation with Luke, I questioned him about his choice of words. Luke perceives *feeling* as unnamed emotion—something that is more viscerally experienced. Emotions, on the other hand, are more cognitive and are identified as joyous, sad, tense, and frightening, to mention only a few. Music inspires feelings in Luke that makes him want to move. He did not feel the need to consciously identify them.

In a subsequent meeting, Luke discussed his initial reaction to Dalcroze Eurhythmics in a therapeutic session—thus, the second of Luke's stories.

LUKE'S STORY II

Dalcroze Eurhythmics was a unique experience for me, because its goal was to integrate the brain and the body through rhythm, to empower people to feel music and in turn, to feel within themselves. This was different than the dance therapy sessions I had done, because rhythm in movement, rather than self-expression alone, played a larger role in these experiences. The other unique challenge was the need to focus attention on the music and on the immediate moment. We didn't have time to dwell on any problems that we brought into the room. We had to deal with the *now*.

My first Dalcroze Eurhythmics class was in 1998 at an AIDS healing weekend. There were about twenty-five people in the room; all of us were either infected or affected by AIDS. The room had plenty of floor space and was furnished with chairs around the edges and a piano at one end. We started by just walking around the space—trying to orient ourselves and to find our comfortable pace. For some of us, that pace was as fast as a walker could accommodate. For others it was as fast as a stroll through the park. We would stop from time to time to see if we could feel that walking pace while standing in silence. Then we'd walk some more, but purposefully change our walking speed. This forced me to listen to myself and to feel the natural rhythms inside of me. All of us could feel our rhythm, and it was surprising to learn that we were all different. While we walked, the leader went to the piano and began improvising at the speed that one of us was walking. Our job was to figure out whose walk was being played on the piano. This allowed us to think beyond ourselves and to really look at others—to connect what we saw or felt with what we heard. Over time we became more synchronized in our pace and the subtlety of the music began to have an effect on *how* we walked. A heavy sound played on the lower keys of the piano allowed us to tramp through the space, while a light touch on the piano keys compelled us to walk more buoyantly. What struck me as odd was that walking buoyantly made us all smile and, for a time, even forget our condition.

Another activity in this session involved bouncing rubber balls—first on our own, then with a partner, then in a star-shape within a group of five—to various rhythms played on a drum or a piano. Working with a small group of people forced us to think cooperatively and to get into a combined focus where we operated as a unit. The activities weren't strenuous, but involved tremendous concentration.

There was a partner activity that combined the need for trust with the goal of feeling what someone else felt while listening to the music. With our partner, we sat on the floor beside each other. One person in the pair was selected as leader; he placed his palm under the partner's palm. We got into a position where we could move the other person's arm freely. Once the music started, the leader guided the partner's arm around the space, changing direction when the music changed. The follower was then asked to be guided (with eyes closed) and to trust that the leader would feel where the arm needed to move to be connected to the music. We changed leaders and tried it again. Each time we changed, we felt more connected to the other person and we sensed how that person felt the music.

We ended with a relaxation and guided imagery activity while lying on the floor, and then sat up to talk about what we had all experienced. While everyone experienced eurhythmics differently, the common theme among us seemed to be a heightened sense of awareness and an ability to feel more connected within our bodies and with those around us. And with all of these feelings was a sense of rhythm in our bodies.

This first experience of Dalcroze Eurhythmics really changed me. It validated my belief that music and movement are vital to my physical and emotional healing and growth. I found it empowering because of what it made me do. I really heard music in that session and felt rhythm as a moving force within me. I connected myself more deeply to music and found a sense of joy and calm at the end. Music was different after this; not just as something to cheer me, but as a force that could change me and help me cope with my illness.

As a new advocate for this type of movement, I encouraged the planning committees at subsequent healing weekends to include Dalcroze Eurhythmics as part of the movement sessions. These sessions were complements to the expressive movement classes held during those weekends. As participants got out of their chairs, they began to realize connections between physical health and mental health. The number of participants in a eurhythmics session ranged from twelve to twenty-five people who were infected or affected by HIV/AIDS. In each session, people left with movement ideas to try with music of their choice, and they were encouraged to keep a journal of what they did and what it meant to them.

Reflection II

Prior to any therapeutic Dalcroze Eurhythmics experience, the goals of the session are articulated verbally and in writing so that the participants can feel that they *own* the experience. Based on my field notes, Luke described the class accurately but presented little information about his personal feelings. He was also accurate in relating goals of the experience.

During editing sessions for this chapter, Luke mentioned that he had been challenged to think of music and movement in a different way—not just as an experience to be lived for in the moment, but one upon which to reflect. While reflection is part of the way he thinks, he had not yet reflected upon his physical reactions to music. "This has been good for me," he recently said. "I'm learning how I learn to heal myself through the editing process."

Prior to our final meeting, I gave Luke a list of unfinished phrases to consider. The following phrases were springboards for him, since he felt that he needed parameters to consider how music and movement affect him on visceral and emotional levels:

To me, music and movement mean . . .
Dancing makes me feel like . . .
Being connected means . . .
To move from risk to trust involves . . .
To be honest with my feelings means . . .
Resiliency involves . . .
Spirituality means . . .

We met in a coffee shop with notes and previous drafts of this chapter. Although this was our final meeting, we continued our telephone calls and e-mails as later drafts of this chapter emerged. Conversations did not center on completing the unfinished phrases, but the phrases did appear in Luke's later comments.

LUKE'S STORY III

I have always felt that music and movement are powerful tools. During these past weeks, I have begun to ask myself how it works for me. First, I have to say that it is always situational. By that I mean that it's not only the music and the movement that lifts me up, but it's also the environment, which includes the space and the people who share that space with me. Music, movement, and space all combine to make the experience more real and perhaps more meaningful for me.

Music can't be just background sound. When I hear music, I can't tune it out, nor can I multi-task with reading or casual conversation. Even this coffee shop has music playing that makes me struggle with my focus. It takes over my brain functions. Also, I feel lost without my iPod. It's a comfort tool for me at the gym or while I am jogging. It's interesting that what I just described also involves movement. I don't just sit and listen to music. I run to it; I lift weights to it; I drive to it. It's a way to know that I'm doing something. Music inspires me to move, and movement creates these emotions within me. This probably explains why dance and rhythmic movement are such a meaningful part of my relationship to music. Dance makes me feel more alive, energetic, joyful—even tingly. I feel my body more. Dance is not associated with negative emotions. I rarely feel like dancing when I'm down. Perhaps I'll sway to a ballad, but that's rare. I have often asked my-self if dance was what I was supposed to be doing with my life. I do regret not doing more with dance.

Music and dance can also be tools to help me get past my insecurities. I often remember the rubber ball activity in eurhythmics, and think that the "rebound" metaphor works for me. Music and movement help me to re-bound and deal with my health issues and my own insecurities.

Being HIV-positive tends to bring out insecurities in all of us. You can see others having similar experiences when they avoid eye contact or con-sciously put themselves down. There is this underlying societal feeling among us that you have participated in a behavior that you shouldn't have. The fear of disclosure of your disease to others is so high among HIV-posi-tive people, because there is fear of judgment and rejection. With structured movement, such as a eurhythmics class, some of these insecurities come forward. How am I being perceived? What are people thinking of my movement—meaning me? These insecure feelings will pop up at the begin-ning of a eurhythmics class. *Is this risk worth the effort? Will I drop the ball?* I remember all my childhood experiences with baseball. I cringed at the thought of having to catch a ball. I had that same reaction in eurhythmics class, but gained more confidence in this trusting environment. That is why I think that a eurhythmics class is a microcosm experience of moving from risk into trust.

Even though we know that we are in a eurhythmics session in order to move for physical health and to feel more connected to ourselves and oth-ers, we all begin with the awkward sense of not knowing the people in our space or the tasks at hand. There is uncertainty in the room, which can bring up uncertainty in our own disease. I'm always asking questions, such as: How will my health hold up? When will be the next bout of illnesses? How can I keep myself from catching an opportunistic virus? We always start a session doing something that we all do every day—we walk. That al-lows me to connect with the space, to look at other people and to just work out some nerves. Sudden changes in the music make me react in different ways, which in turn makes me more alert. In a sense, the beginning of these games starts to give me a little more trust in the experience and with the other people who share this space.

When we move from an individual experience to a partner experience, the sense of risk and insecurity returns, but perhaps less intensely. You're given a task to express a musical phrase or nuance with a partner, and now I have to look at my own control issues. If my partner has an idea, I need to acknowledge and honor it. In an example that comes to mind, my partner and I had to express antecedent and consequent phrases. If my partner ex-presses the antecedent phrase one way, I need to respond similarly, but change the end of the movement to express a closing phrase. This requires a quick reaction and trust that the person would honor my interpretation of the music. Soon I am attracted to another person's energy. I look into their eyes for meaning, and I try to see their soul in the experience. When connecting musically with that person, I start to forget about my own insecurities, and begin to trust myself to be in the moment while trusting others not to be judgmental. This trust experience was truly the first time that I moved when I didn't care what other people were thinking. The sense of letting go of vulnerability and opening up to the experience was one of the most liberating moments of my life. Trust changed inside the room as we made connections with others on an aesthetic level. I recall leaving the space in the room feeling that it is okay to trust again. People *looked* different after that class.

One particular experience near the end of a session still haunts me. There were a dozen of us in the room. Half of us were holding votive candles, and the lights were turned down. The goal of one movement activity was to pass the candle gently to someone who didn't have one at the change of a musical phrase. The music was a gentle rocking triple meter and made me feel like swaying in my movements. Dynamics would ebb and flow, which made us increase and then decrease our energy. There was also a big sense of anticipation when the music would slow down and speed up. That made us work to pass the candle with precision because of the pulling and pushing of the tempo. We all were doing our own movements with a similar outside purpose. Everyone was experiencing personal emotions inside. I saw it from the outside, watching others, but also felt it within me. It felt like a gift to receive a candle, which meant that people accepted me with all of my personal faults. I also felt my own emotions of joy and sadness. It was interesting to hear other participants reveal their inner stories when it all ended. Heidi, a caregiver, told us that she was thinking of her grandmother who had recently died. As the last of the music faded, Heidi's candle went out. Through her tears, she said that she felt that her grandmother was comforting her and that she was giving Heidi permission to let go. The music was perfect for the activity, because we had to share our candles with others when the phrases began again. The sharing of the candles carried over to the stories that we all shared with each other at the end of the session. Heidi's story changed me. I realize that we are affected by movement and music, but all affected in unique ways.

Reflection III

Luke remained concerned about how he might be perceived by others during a movement activity. He mentioned that he wished he could have been an anonymous participant, where no one would know him or about his disease. Research shows a distinct connection between HIV/AIDS and guilt and shame that accompany the disease (Duffy, 2005; Lee, Scragg, & Turner, 2001). The underlying societal feeling is that the person with HIV/AIDS has participated in a behavior that is considered taboo; thus, the person suffering often feels isolated and internalizes shame. When Luke revealed his vulnerability, he expressed the general insecurities of people with HIV and AIDS. During the eurhythmics activity, music, along with a movement response, provided the catalyst for all of the participants to confront their isolation and feelings of guilt or shame. When passing a candle at the change of a phrase, the participants appeared to share a gift. Later, his narratives reflecting on the experience revealed the uniqueness and depth of each person's response to the music and to the disease.

Luke is unique, and as such, his story can only be viewed in the context of his experiences. Luke's lifetime of dance differs greatly from someone who has had very little experience in rhythmic movement, or where music has been perceived only as background fill. Luke acknowledged music and dance as his saving graces. He readily adapted eurhythmics concepts and made them his own. He saw non-verbal communication and rhythmic movement as a means of enhancing his physical and mental health. Luke was physically active, thus boosting his immune system. He communicated music concepts and the aesthetic feelings he derived from music through movement to himself and others. He felt less isolated and more part of a group effort.

Throughout the eurhythmics sessions, I made informal assessments of participants' progress and their interactions with each other. I noted them in a journal in order to assess progress over a period of time. Five qualities can be measured or assessed during a movement therapy session using Dalcroze Eurhythmics: length of focus, stamina, locomotor control, connection with the music, and interaction ability (Frego, 1995). Length of focus and stamina can be measured as temporal events. During an activity, the participant is required to be engaged in tasks that reflect music through movement. Breaking concentration can be indicated by stopping motion, dropping arms, or losing synchronization with the music. Stamina is connected to strength and agility, but also endurance. Locomotor control is assessed through observations of how the individual moves through and within the physical space. While coordination of the body to the music is part of any assessment, a movement specialist may also assess the quality of the movement as it reflects the nuances of the music. Flowing movement to *legato* music indicates an attentiveness to nuance. More vertical gestures and short connections with the floor by the foot may reflect a *marcato* style in music.

At the beginning of the class, Luke exhibited behaviors that would be labeled as *bound*. His hands were clenched and his jaw appeared to be tense. Luke later described this initial contact as "working hard to get it right." It was not until the first half of the session that Luke began to relax his upper body and to move about the space with a lighter gait. Luke showed an extraordinary ability to concentrate. He appeared not to drop focus throughout each ten-minute activity and responded joyfully to each new challenge. By the end of the first session, Luke's movements were fluid and synchronized to the music. What was more interesting was Luke's ability to predict the changes in the music and demonstrate it in his body in real time. Luke explained later that while he did not know the music, he felt that the music was going in a certain direction and that he was able to make his body go along with the changes.

Engagement in an activity is not measured in time, but with observable indicators. I have found that participants in my eurhythmics sessions often indicated an engagement in the experience and a connectedness with the music in the moment through gestures I observe. These gestures included alert postures, eyes wide open, an ability to react quickly to changes, and joyous faces. These are also indications that people experience a euphoria following an experience that is challenging and rewarding. Csikszentmihalyi (1990) described the experience as a mental state of operation where the individual or group is fully immersed in a challenging and goal-reaching activity, which is characterized by a feeling of energized focus and where success is both in the process and the product. This state, referred to as "flow," occurs in many applications, including education, sports, and spirituality. Movement and dance are among those possible flow experiences cited by Csikszentmihalyi (p. 99). Activities that connect the brain and the body in focus-based games, such as those of Dalcroze Eurhythmics, are conducive to entering this state.

The ability to interact with others during a Dalcroze Eurhythmics class is crucial to music education and therapeutic situations. Music is experienced in social contexts. The creative activities in these Dalcroze Eurhythmics sessions fostered sharing in pairs, small groups, and with the entire class. These interactions were often non-verbal in nature and required that participants work with others to reflect the music in new and subtle ways. Observers in this study noted participants' spontaneity, problem-solving behaviors, and creativity in their responses. Luke commented that he discovered more expression in people's faces and an increased desire to look into people's eyes for meaning and communication.

A study that engaged participants with AIDS in weekly eurhythmics sessions over a six-week period showed that people were able to increase stamina and agility over time, increase coordination in locomotor and non-locomotor activities, reduce personal stress, and increase social interaction (Frego, 1995). While stamina and coordination were observable events, participants kept journals and reported through interviews about their stress levels and social interactions. A similar study measured the effect of aerobic exercise on people who are HIV-positive and found that stamina increased over time with timed exercise to music and reduced depressive symptoms (Neidig, 1998). Relating these studies to Luke's story provides us with an insight on how aerobics and eurhythmics may assist in people's mental and physical well-being.

Luke's compelling story is grounded within another story of resiliency. Resiliency, or coping, is a relatively new area of health research. Mosack (2001) conducted a study on the resiliency of people with AIDS and found that resiliency correlated to self-esteem, depression health, locus of control, and social support from friends. People who tend to be more resilient to adversity or stress may live healthier and more meaningful lives. These individuals may also seek out other treatments that are helpful in their own healing and growth. Characteristics of these individuals, cited by Valentine and Feinaurer (1993), reflect strong reasoning abilities, internal locus of control, advocacy, positive outlook, and a spiritual orientation. Luke demonstrated many of these characteristics when interacting with others in our sessions, but particularly in his capacity as patient intake coordinator at the infectious disease clinic in a major research hospital. His positive outlook and modeling of locus of control created a benchmark for people new to AIDS. Music and purposeful movement to music may be a resiliency tool that Luke learned to use to "bounce back" from a stressful day. I spoke with Luke once more in order to probe the role of music and movement as a coping mechanism—his resiliency.

LUKE'S STORY IV

There are days when I don't feel particularly resilient. There are times at work when I feel like I am the low man on the totem pole, a feeling of being beaten down. I also replay old stories in my head. I was on disability for ten years. Who would want to take me back as an employee after ten years of not contributing to society? That makes me put up even more barriers.

The bounce back may come from the way my parents raised me. They always instilled the need to set and achieve goals. That may be part of being resilient. I also work to surround myself with a support group so I can retreat to a safe place when needed. I make a point to verbalize my strengths, even on days when I don't feel them. Advocacy also plays a big part in my life. I had to learn how to advocate for myself, particularly when government case workers would treat me unkindly. Advocacy made me be the one that other people looked up to. When I speak at AIDS conferences, I tell people to advocate for yourself first, then *pay it forward* and advocate for others.

In order to bounce back from bad news, bad health, or just a dark period, I need to have music and I need to move. In order to rebound, I think that I choose the music carefully. Something that is fast and has a heavy rhythm is too far away from where I might feel emotionally and that music just won't resonate with me. Classical music is a good friend in this situation, and I may gravitate towards that. I'll put on headphones and walk to the music, change my pace, and start swinging my arms to the rhythmic patterns. The effect starts to happen soon, and my focus becomes the music and my connection with it. In the same sense, Dalcroze Eurhythmics has helped me bounce back more quickly. It has provided me with the tools to be resilient. I can call up some of the activities that we did and turn my attention to becoming the music.

Spirituality has also added to my resiliency. I had long ago rejected my structural upbringing in the church. Over time I have discovered that my spirituality has necessitated that I focus on the inside and not on the structure—on the journey and not on the prize. In turn, this has helped me move through changes. Change is difficult, but after moving through all of the changes, you get stronger. The more times I have to pick myself up and change, the more I feel successful and that I can go on. At one point during my years on disability I said to myself, "I just can't live in this *what if* life any more." We can't be fearful of change.

CONCLUSION

While Luke's narrative is unique and can only reflect outcomes based on his behavior, it does speak to the transfer of teaching and assessment techniques used in music education to therapy applications for adults with terminal illnesses and for people at the end of their life.

Adults with life-threatening illnesses can approach their remaining quality of life with aesthetic understanding through a combination of music and movement therapy experiences. In hospice settings, I have met people left motionless from fatigue induced by a disease. They allowed me to help them feel the tension and relaxation of musical lines and phrases by letting me connect our hands together with elastics. Medical research on exercise to counterbalance muscle wasting in HIV/AIDS cases supports this approach (Dudgeon, Phillips, Carson, Brewer, Durstine, & Hand, 2006; Lynch, Schertzer, & Ryall, 2007). This physical connection has a secondary effect of lowering stress in the individual, of increasing the feeling of connectedness within themselves, and in developing a sense of inner calm (Galantino, Shepard, Krafft, & Laperriere, 2005; Kemppainen, Eller, Bunch, & Hamilton, 2006).

Luke used music and movement to make connections with his feelings and cognition. Specifically, Luke learned how to use music to help him become resilient to the physical and emotional challenges that he faced. Resiliency is a personal attribute that is relevant to all education and therapy situations. It helps learners cope with change and trauma in their lives. Through the experience of moving purposefully to music, people might be led to find the resiliency within them.

Luke appeared to be even more unique than I originally thought, since he regularly connected music to movement and, consequently, approached music as an active experience that was felt deeply within himself. Movement allowed Luke to be in the moment with the music. Even "dancing inside," as Luke said, allows him to imagine the movement in music.

REFERENCES

American Dance Therapy Association (ADTA). (2007). Fact sheet. Retrieved May 31, 2007, from www.adta.org/about/who.cfm/

Bachmann, M. L. (1991). *Dalcroze today: An education through and into music*. Oxford: Clarendon.

Coggiola, J., & Madsen, C. K. (2001). Pioneering inquiry in the new century: Exemplars of music research, part II: The effect of manipulating a CRDI dial on the focus of attention of musicians/nonmusicians and perceived aesthetic response. *Bulletin of the Council for Research in Music Education, 149*, 13–22.

Creswell, J. (1998). *Qualitative inquiry and research design: Choosing among five traditions*. Thousand Oaks, CA: Sage.

Csikszentmihalyi, M. (1990). *Flow: The psychology of optimal experience*. New York: Harper & Row.

Dudgeon, W. D., Phillips, K. D., Carson, J. A., Brewer, R. B., Durstine, J. L., and Hand, G. A. (2006). Counteracting muscle wasting in HIV-infected individuals. *HIV Medicine, 7*(5), 299–310.

Duffy, L. (2005). Suffering, shame, and silence: The stigma of HIV/AIDS. *Journal of the Association of Nurses in AIDS Care (JANAC), 16*(1), 13–20.

Dutoit, C.-L. (1971). *Music, movement, therapy*. London: Dalcroze Society.

Frego, R. J. D. (1995). Music movement therapy for people with AIDS: The use of music movement therapy as a form of palliative care for people with AIDS. *International Journal of Arts Medicine, 4*(2), 21–25.

Frego, R. J. D. (1999). Effects of aural and visual conditions on response to perceived artistic tension in music and dance. *Journal of Research in Music Education, 47*(1), 31–43.

Frego, R. J. D. (2003). Psychic energy, psychic entropy, psychic ecstasy. *Orff Echo, 35*(3), 47–51.

Frego, R. J. D. (2007). Dalcroze eurhythmics as a therapeutic tool. *Canadian Dalcroze Society Journal/Bulletin de la Société Dalcroze du Canada, 1*(2), 3–4.

Frego, R. J. D., Gillmeister, G., Hama, M., & Liston, R. (2004). The Dalcroze approach to music therapy. In A. A. Darrow (Ed.), *Introduction to approaches in music therapy* (pp. 15–24). Silver Springs, MD: American Music Therapy Association.

Galantino, M., Shepard, K., Krafft, L., and Laperriere, A. (2005). The effect of group aerobic exercise and t'ai chi on functional outcomes and quality of life for persons living with acquired immunodeficiency syndrome. *Journal of Alternative and Complementary Medicine, 11*(6),1085–1092.

Hendershot, C., and George, W. (2007). Alcohol and sexuality research in the AIDS era: Trends in publication activity, target populations and research design. *AIDS and Behavior, 11*(2), 217–226.

Irwin, T., Morgenstern, J., Parsons, J., Wainberg, M., and Labouvie, E. (2006). Alcohol and sexual HIV risk behavior among problem drinking men who have sex with men: An event level analysis of timeline followback data. *AIDS and Behavior, 10*(3), 299–307.

Kemppainen, J. K., Eller, L. S., Bunch, E., and Hamilton, M. J. (2006). Strategies for self-management of HIV-related anxiety. *AIDS Care, 18*(6), 597–607.

Kylma, J. (2005). Dynamics of hope in adults living with HIV/AIDS: A substantive theory. *Journal of Advanced Nursing, 52*(6), 620–630.

Lee, D. A., Scragg, P., and Turner, S. (2001). The role of shame and guilt in traumatic events: A clinical model of shame-based and guilt-based PTSD. *British Journal of Medical Psychology, 74*(4), 451–466.

Lynch, G., Schertzer, J., and Ryall, J. G. (2007). Therapeutic approaches for muscle wasting disorders. *Pharmacology & Therapeutics, 113*(3), 461–487.

Madsen, C. K. (1998). Emotion versus tension in Haydn's 'Symphony No. 104' as measured by the two-dimensional Continuous Response Digital Interface. *Journal of Research in Music Education, 46*, 546–554.

Mead, V. H. (1994). *Dalcroze eurhythmics in today's music classroom.* New York: Schott.

Merriam, A. (1985). African music in perspective. *Ethnomusicology, Journal of the Society for Ethnomusicology, 29*(2), 374–377.

Mosack, K. E. (2001). *Development and validation of the R-PLA: A resiliency measure for people living with HIV/AIDS.* Unpublished doctoral dissertation, The Ohio State University.

Neidig, J. L. (1998). *Aerobic exercise training: effects on depressive symptoms in HIV infected adults.* Unpublished doctoral dissertation, The Ohio State University.

Nunes, J., Kappes, B., & Carr, J. (2007). Cognition and emotion. In O. Sahler & J. Carr (Eds.), *The behavioral sciences and health care* (2nd ed.) (pp. 73–78). Ashland, OH: Hogrefe & Huber.

Ochsner, K. N. (2007). How thinking controls feeling: A social cognitive neuroscience approach. In E. Harmon-Jones & P. Winkielman (Eds.), *Social neuroscience: Integrating biological and psychological explanations of social behavior* (pp. 106–133). New York: Guilford.

Rosenfeld, B., Gibson, C., Kramer, M., and Breitbart, W. (2004). Hopelessness and terminal illness: The construct of hopelessness in patients with advanced AIDS. *Palliative & Supportive Care, 2*(1), 43–53.

Spector, I. (1990). *Rhythm and life: The work of Emile Jaques-Dalcroze.* Dance and music series, no. 3. Stuyvesant, NY: Pendragon.

Valentine, L., & Feinaurer, L. (1993). Resilience factors associated with female survivors of childhood sexual abuse. *American Journal of Family Therapy, 21*(3),
216–224.

Yin, R. K. (2003). *Case study research: Design and methods.* Thousand Oaks, CA: Sage.

18

Voices of Experience: Lessons from Older Adult Amateur Musicians

Don D. Coffman

Truly, it was a magical moment. The outpouring of genuine appreciation for the band's performance was something the director had rarely, if ever, experienced to that degree. Each piece had its share of small flaws, yet the concert had received a standing ovation that lasted long enough for a couple of curtain calls. Afterwards, one player asked, with an expression of utter amazement, "Did they like us because we're good, or because we're *old*?" It was a joy to be able to reply that the applause had been heart-felt, not merely courteous, certainly not out of sympathy or pity, because this band of senior adults had played so musically.

—Coffman & Levy, 1997, p. 17

I have recounted this brief episode on many occasions, because it captures the feelings of surprise and delight that I witness repeatedly in people who observe or participate in my band. Since January 1995 I have been involved with a project that is a joyful blending of the teaching, research, and service components of my work as a university professor. I am founder and director of the Iowa City/Johnson County Senior Center New Horizons Band (NHB). This concert band is designed to provide retired seniors with instruction in music. No prior musical expertise is required of participants, and the band attracts both novice and veteran players.

The leading edge of the baby boomers, the generation born between 1946 and 1964, began turning sixty in 2006. Much has been written in the popular press about how this generation is redefining the concepts of retirement and old age (Cohen, 2000, 2005; Sadler, 2000; Valiant, 2002). Boomers are more active than their predecessors, and there is considerable interest in what is sometimes called "successful aging" (Rowe & Kahn,

1998). Thirty years ago, our society essentially dismissed senior citizens because they were in the twilight of their lives. Now, society finally embraces the notion that older adults have much to contribute. Over the past thirty years, researchers of adult development have demonstrated several factors, ranging from genes to environment, that contribute to successful aging (Warshofsky, 1999).

One shift in beliefs about aging centers on socialization. Formerly, researchers held to a theory of disengagement; elderly people were viewed as being in decline and therefore more likely to withdraw from society. Starting in the 1970s researchers began to demonstrate links between social engagement and a variety of positive outcomes, including effects on cognitive ability (Barnes, Mendes de Leon, Wilson, Bienias, & Evans, 2004; Fratiglioni, Wang, Ericsson, Maytan, & Winblad, 2000), mental health (Dean, Kolody, & Wood, 1990; Dean, Kolody, Wood, & Matt, 1992), and mortality (Glass, de Leon, Marottoli, & Berkman, 1999; Lennartsson & Silverstein, 2001).

Making music with others is a social activity, and there is a small body of research that documents the social and psychological benefits of playing a musical instrument for older adults in amateur music organizations (Coffman, 2002, 2006; Rohwer, 2005). A few researchers have demonstrated links between music-making and physical health. A recently completed longitudinal study (Cohen, 2007) showed that older adults participating in professionally conducted arts programs displayed fewer declines in emotional health and functional health, and in some cases, improvement in their health, compared to a control group.

New Horizons Band participants reported that music making and socialization was either "very important" or "essential" to their quality of life, rating them as high as family relationships and good health (Coffman & Adamek, 1999). Yet, ratings of importance do not reveal specifics about tangible benefits. What specific benefits do NHB members perceive?

Data for this chapter come from observations, conversations, letters, and e-mails that I have collected for nearly thirteen years and, more recently, from a survey of band members who wrote short essays in response to a simple question: "What does making music mean to you?" This question has also been the basis of my past research with older adults.

The chapter has four sections. The "Program" section briefly describes the history of the band and how it operates. The "Director" section explains what motivated me to begin a New Horizons Band and how it has influenced me personally and professionally. The "Players" section offers the views of these adult amateur musicians, arranged thematically. The "Bottom Line" section relies on the eloquent writings of some players that I believe capture the essence of the experience. I encourage readers to ponder the following questions as they read the chapter: Why is performing music so meaningful, even for members who do not play particularly well? Does playing an instrument as older adults mean something different from when they were youngsters? Does their involvement in music making cause them to view themselves in new ways? What role does creative activity have in successful aging?

THE PROGRAM

The Iowa City band is part of a growing association of musical organizations that began in 1991 with a vision of providing instruction and performance opportunities for older adults. The first New Horizons Band began in Rochester, New York, in 1991, under the leadership of Roy Ernst, professor of music at the Eastman School of Music (Ernst & Emmons, 1992). My band was one of the first of what has become an international movement of over 120 bands, choirs, and orchestras across the United States and Canada called the New Horizons International Music Association (NHIMA). NHIMA is an affiliation of musical organizations that share a newsletter on an Internet website (www.newhorizonsmusic.org), and national institutes (i.e., gatherings of players for a few days of intensive music making). Most groups rehearse once or twice a week in music stores, schools, or churches. Each NHIMA group usually works with a local music merchant who offers support that could include rehearsal space, administrative oversight, discounts on purchases, underwriting, and so forth. Each ensemble is autonomous.

Groups are usually led by one to three retired high school or college ensemble directors or by college professors with flexible schedules. My program is not typical, because I rely on a teaching staff of six to eight assistant instructors who are either undergraduate music education students or graduate students with teaching experience. As a teacher of future teachers, I am pleased to note that over one hundred undergraduate music students have gained practical experiences in real-life New Horizons Band situations prior to obtaining their degrees. Teaching adult beginners is a supportive, low-stress field experience for my students. I am delighted that three of my former doctoral students have started their own New Horizons Bands. The insights I have gained from teaching and researching in this area have revolutionized how I teach.

My band and most other New Horizons groups differ from other amateur community performing groups because we do not simply rehearse music for an imminent performance. I am dedicated to teaching participants how to play better. For many players, the band is an opportunity to improve skills they acquired years ago in school. For some players, this program fulfills desires for making music that they have dreamed of for decades. For others, this program is an invitation to an experience that they thought was not possible for them.

Twice per week we congregate at the local Senior Center for forty-five minutes of small group instruction or chamber ensemble coaching, followed by a sixty-minute band rehearsal. The center is a multi-floor former post office from the early 1900s with ornate woodwork and a sweeping staircase. The building has been renovated to house a modern ceramics room, exercise room, assembly room/cafeteria, computer lab, television production studio, library, and consignment shop. On New Horizons mornings, music emanates from rooms on all three levels of the building. From 8:30–9:15 a.m., the brass all meet in one large room on the top floor to rehearse brass choir and expanded brass quintet music under the guidance of a music education student who has complete responsibility for running all rehearsals. Across the hall, another student coaches the saxophones in mixed trios and quartets. Down the hall some less advanced clarinets do the same kind of rehearsing with a student instructor. Moving down one level to the mezzanine, which is the library room, a fourth student leads a mixture of flutes, oboes, and bassoons. On the main floor in the assembly room, which is also the lunchroom, a fifth student instructs percussion players. A sixth student works with the more advanced clarinetists in the visiting nurse's office in the basement. These groups spend the semester preparing for a chamber concert.

I have seen tremendous growth in musicianship and confidence over the years. At first, only the brass choir was interested in performing publicly. However, over time, all the groups now eagerly anticipate these chamber concerts, so much so that I had to create two days for the hour-long concerts (one for woodwinds, one for brass and percussion), which occur every December and May. During coaching sessions, student instructors also teach technical aspects of playing the instruments. I am amused when players ask students for additional opportunities to practice technical skills (e.g., scale and arpeggios) and thrilled that this chamber program has spawned other self-directed groups of musicians who rehearse weekly on their own. We concur that the concert band's technique, tone, and intonation are much better because of the instruction that occurs in these smaller groups.

The concert band has nearly tripled in size, from twenty-six players in 1995 to seventy-seven at present, and the program has expanded from one band to many ensembles. Some groups were formed and named through members' initiatives, such as the Polka Dots, Dixie Kids, Tempered Brass (a low brass quartet), Second Wind (a woodwind quintet), and the Old Post Office Brass (quintet). In 1998, I added the Silver Swing, which plays big band swing music from the 1930s and 1940s and has been led by a series of student instructors. As the concert band matured in musicianship I recognized the need for a new entry-level band, so in 2004 I added a Monday evening band for novice players (they call themselves the Linn Street Band), led by a doctoral student in music education who is assisted by undergraduates from my Band Methods class. Because this band meets after the typical workday, adults who have not yet retired from work can participate. Some members of the Linn Street Band have matriculated to the more advanced Tuesday-Thursday morning band.

We rehearse year-round, pausing for four weeks over the winter holidays and during August. Nominal member fees and donations sustain the program expenses for student instructor stipends, music, and equipment. The concert band averages eleven concerts annually, most typically in local venues such as the Senior Center, concert halls on the university campus, the historic Englert Theatre in downtown Iowa City, pedestrian malls, shopping centers, parks, churches, schools, and area adult care centers, but we also have traveled a couple of dozen times to other Iowa towns. Our most prestigious appearances have been for two state conventions of music teachers and the Governor's Conference on Aging. The small groups play over ninety performances annually.

My interest in lifelong involvement in music making has led to promoting local intergenerational band concerts with players of different ages, from elementary bands through university bands. A highlight of these concerts has been combining the bands for massed band performances, allowing players of varying ages to literally rub shoulders musically and socially. It takes some planning, but I design seating arrangements that intersperse my players in the sections of the school bands. Then we briefly rehearse some music and allow time for players to visit within the sections. When we rehearse with youngsters, the adults take the lead in talking to the children. Glenn, a retired high school choir director and French hornist, once remarked, "Music is timeless. We don't think about age, we just make good music together." However, when we rehearse with college students, the adults often follow the lead of these advanced musicians. Bill, retired architectural consultant and sousaphone player, was in awe of his younger counterparts' talent. The respect extends in both directions, because the youth are often surprised at the abilities of the older musicians, remarking that music is something they can participate in throughout their lives.

THE DIRECTOR

Before becoming a professor, I was a school band director. I enjoyed my students, yet I frequently wished that I could reach more students. As is unfortunately the case in many U.S. high schools, 90 percent of the student body was not involved in the school's music program. In addition, I recognized with sadness that most of my students would stop playing after high school graduation. I wanted ways to increase music-making opportunities for amateur adult players, especially for those who had missed the opportunity in their youth.

When I decided to pursue a career in higher education, I knew its path would lead me away from the rehearsal hall and into the classroom. Further, my university duties would center on lecturing, directing graduate research, and on my own scholarship. Leading a band was not something I could foresee.

Fortunately in 1995, I was able to establish the New Horizons Band and return to making music. After meeting with Roy Ernst in the spring of 1994, I worked with our Senior Center to prepare video promotions and press releases. We held one organizational meeting for interested players in December 1994 and started rehearsals on January 17, 1995. For the first six weeks, the players met in small groups having similar instrumentation to learn or re-learn how to play their instruments. By mid-March we added meeting times during which the entire band rehearsed together. Our first concert was to a standing-room-only crowd at the Senior Center in early May 1995.

Over thirteen years, 125 performances, and 450 tunes later, I can attest that teaching adults is much like teaching elementary school children and high school adolescents, but with three differences. First, older adults *want* to be there, and their parents are not forcing them to practice. They are attentive, generous, and responsible. While it is also true that young persons can be attentive, generous, and responsible, my rehearsals never approach the contest of wills I sometimes witnessed in school bands. People actually *thank* me for the band program.

Second, New Horizons Band members have taught me that having fun and never losing sight of fostering social relationships are as important as making music. I had viewed directing my high school band students as having a job to do together, and I worked to make sure we did it well. Now my goals also include laughter at every rehearsal and enjoying each other. No matter how well or poorly we play, I want members to look forward to the next rehearsal. I now exhort music education students about the importance of having fun while teaching, telling them that if they finish a rehearsal without everyone having experienced some moment of enjoyment, musically and socially, they should consider the possibility that they have failed their players to some degree.

Third, New Horizons players have shown me how everyone can be a teacher and learner, a giver and receiver. These older learners mentor my university student instructors, and they have also inspired and guided me. Many times I have ended a rehearsal feeling better than when I arrived.

THE PLAYERS

The best way to describe the New Horizons experience is through the play-ers' words and stories. Every member has a unique story. This section re-ports the actions and thoughts of some, but not all, of the band members. What follows represents the most prevalent themes that arose from my ob-servations and their comments. I developed these themes after a content analysis of texts that included field notes, e-mails, letters, and survey responses.

Dedication

Band can become the center of life for some players. For example, Joan C., a retired professor of psychology, learned to play percussion in the New Horizons Band. Not a musical novice, she had developed an early interest in music and in psychology after taking a music aptitude test, Carl Seashore's *Measures of Musical Talent*, as a child. She studied piano privately and almost became a piano major in college, but she chose psychology be-cause of performance anxiety concerns. She eventually came to the Univer-sity of Iowa's Department of Psychology as a professor, the alma mater of Jacob Kwalwasser, who had administered the music aptitude test to Joan af-ter completing his doctoral training with Seashore. Joan became interested in percussion while observing all the fun her son had playing drums in the high school band.

Joan is very dedicated, having become a self-acknowledged "percussion junkie." After a couple of years of playing, she acquired a mini-van to haul percussion equipment, as well as the array of instruments that filled the lower level of her home, including timpani, keyboard percussion, two drum sets, and suitcases filled with sticks, mallets, and small hand-percussion in-struments. She attends on average six band camps across the U.S. each year, is on the NHIMA board, and has been featured as a percussion soloist on many occasions. She believes that by learning to be more comfortable with herself, she has also learned to manage her performance anxiety.

Other band members display comparable dedication. For instance, Del-mar makes a two-hour-round-trip drive twice a week to attend rehearsals. He and his wife drive to several adult music camps all across the country with his tuba in the back seat. Another player, Judy, who played bassoon in high school, learned to play the oboe in the band because the oboe is a less expensive instrument. However, after a couple of years, she acquired a bas-soon and now plays both in several groups. Nancy, a trumpet player, books performances for the four groups in which she plays. She also secures the funding and handles the logistics for our annual band festival, which gathers other Iowa New Horizons Bands. Glo plays clarinet, French horn, trumpet, and euphonium in more groups than I can keep track of.

Humor

It takes a sense of humor to put oneself in situations where there is a risk of making audible mistakes. Everyone does their best, so I sometimes tease them gently about playing problems. The band members love to tease, too. Recently, Brett, an undergraduate assistant conductor, remarked to the percussion section, "You're short today." What he meant to convey was that he could see that they were short-handed, because only three of seven players were present. One player, Sheila, replied with a smile, "I beg your pardon, I've always been considered rather tall" (she is probably 5'-11"). Of course, teasing is part of the overall emotional tone. These remarks could have been delivered sarcastically, but that would never occur in this band.

Our goal is to balance playing our best with not taking ourselves too seriously. Without our capacity to laugh, this group would not have progressed to its current state of excellence. If someone plays at the wrong place, misses a pitch or rhythm, there is never any embarrassing awkwardness—someone is bound to come up with a gentle witty remark about it. For instance, Janice wryly remarked during one rehearsal, "At our age, every day is sight-reading!" While the novice players often fret about holding back the more advanced players, everyone is eager to make allowances for others' mistakes. Two members' comments echo my observation: "Making music is a *joyful* activity. I don't ever see people being cranky when they are making music." "The more I get to know the other band members, the more I enjoy my participation in the band. All are so encouraging to a beginning player like me."

Socialization

The band functions very much like an extended family. Band participants go to lunch together, rehearse at members' homes, and attend concerts together. Some single women travel together on vacations abroad. Two marriages have resulted from friendships formed in the band.

From Martha: The band has been the main influence in finding my way into the community. Band activities give me a natural way to get to know men—something not easy for a widow new in the community.

From Duane: I enjoy "making music" and being part of a band. . . . I was able to join the high school band at eighth grade. . . . It was fun then to be part of the groups making music, the friendships, trips, the feeling that we were having worthwhile experiences. It never seemed hard. It was always enjoyable. When we were about juniors, nine of us started a dance band. It was the "big band" era, playing good music for fraternity and sorority parties and various other occasions. These engagements were fun—and we made a little money at it! . . . In 1995 . . . I joined the NHB and have had a ball ever since! It was quite easy to pick up the drum sticks, etc., again and [it] was great to be back making music. At one time, six of us who had played together in high school in the 1930s were back playing together in the New Horizons Band. Older people can make music together and with the wonderful leadership we have had, older people can make good music. We continue to do it because it is so enjoyable and brings us together with many folks who have a similar interest.

The small chamber groups have become quite important to members. A clear example is the Polka Dots, who have met weekly and performed approximately twice a month for the past eleven years. Wally, a founding member, explained it this way:

> I consider all of the band members to be very good acquaintances. And given an out-of-band situation, each would come to another's aid. Given the age we all are, it is less likely that a goodly number would become close chums, because we all have too many other personal, health, housing, and financial concerns. Yet there is a togetherness as we come together in band and sectional practices. . . . Maybe it is because we are more dependent on each other's presence at each gig for our success. We compliment each other a lot and do cause each to put in extra effort because we want our group to do well. The NHB and its many subgroups are the catalysts for a group of people to do many activities together, who otherwise would probably have few if any associations with each other.

Mentoring

My university students and I are the teachers in the program, yet we learn a great deal from our elders. Most student instructors come to the program with understandable nervousness about how to present themselves. They also lack experience in detecting performance errors, expressing how they want the players to sound, how to pace the rehearsal, what music is suitable, and so forth. The older learners guide the student instructors, suggesting gently and with the utmost deference how these preservice music educators might approach pedagogical difficulties. Sometimes they simply tell the instructors what they are having trouble playing or understanding. Sometimes they ask for a clearer conducting pattern from the instructors. On rare occasions, they have private conversations with me to let me know about an instructor who seems disorganized or unsure.

Band members also reward their instructors generously with wonderfully creative expressions of gratitude. Student instructors have fond memories of cash gifts, personalized poems, baked goods, and my favorite—a tuba duet of "I Love You Truly" composed for a female instructor and performed for a rehearsal on Valentine's Day. The fledgling instructors, struggling to display competence and confidence, sometimes seem remote and reluctant to reveal their inner selves. The band members' good-natured camaraderie helps them to relax as teachers, because the students sense acceptance.

There are instances of peer teaching among the adults in the small chamber groups that rehearse on their own. A few of the adults are former music teachers, and the other players rely on their judgments of what to play and how to play it. Within sections of the band the typical hierarchy of a section leader is not evident. Because players are not seated by audition, but through a combination of self-assignment or my suggestions, sections handle decisions by consensus. Stronger players usually offer suggestions, but the spirit of accommodation and deference prevails.

I have learned from New Horizons that people are more important than music. This is something I thought I already knew, but my awareness has increased. Early on, I decided not to single out players for mistakes. For example, band directors often single out players in front of the ensemble, calling attention to performance errors. I address problems by identifying group problems (e.g., tubas, or woodwinds, or melody line), or by teasing them gently so that we can laugh at ourselves. I might say, "We all have the right idea about that rhythm, but we're not quite agreeing on when to play it." My conviction is that everyone is trying to do his/her best, so I wish to protect them from unnecessary embarrassment. They are all wonderful people with interesting and successful lives who have taken a risk to perform music in a culture that expects perfection. I do my best to honor the trust they bring to the experience.

Creativity

Cohen (2000) modifies Einstein's famous formula to explain the importance of human creativity in his book *The Creative Age: Awakening Human Potential in the Second Half of Life.* In his $C = me^2$ formula, "Creativity" requires a "mass" of accumulated knowledge multiplied by "experiences" (internal and external) that interact to produce new insights.

Cohen proposes four phases of adult human potential: (a) Midlife Reevaluation (ages forty to sixty), motivated by a crisis or quest to create meaning in life; (b) Liberation (late fifties to early seventies), characterized by the question "If not now, when?" and signifying the freedom and desire to try new things, often after retirement; (c) Summing-Up (seventies), a desire to pass on one's life and wisdom; and (d) Encore (eighties), a desire to affirm life and make lasting contributions. Members of the New Horizons Band range in age from the mid-fifties to early nineties, so I am able to observe all of these phases.

Most players join the band after retiring, but this life change can leave them searching for a way to structure their time (Midlife Re-evaluation). Others joined after the death of a spouse, which is perhaps a quest to create meaning in life. Some remarked that they always wanted to learn an instrument and dreamed of doing so during retirement. This thinking corresponds to the "If not now, when?" perspective (Liberation). The later phases (Summing-Up, Encore) may be seen in band members' mentoring of student instructors. Several of the players are former teachers and have often offered advice about the practice of teaching or their subject matter expertise (e.g., statistical consulting for my doctoral students). One member established a School of Music endowment to fund student travel for making presentations at music education conferences.

Cohen asserts that one of the keys to living life well is to make use of our creative potential, even in small ways. I have seen this exemplified in band members in small things, both practical and musical. For example, early on some players decided that the traditional music folders were a problem because the music scattered if the folder fell to the floor, so they began putting their music in three-ring binders. One woman who had difficulty remembering clarinet fingerings made multiple copies of the fingering chart, clipped copies of difficult fingerings and pasted the diagrams in her music near the problem notes. Players often comment that they learned to play more expressively than they did when they were younger. Alice put it this way, "Now I can focus more on telling a story using the alphabet (which instrument keys produce certain pitches) and grammar (counting, rests, sound levels, and speed of playing) . . . contributing to the whole of the group, creating something together that cannot be achieved individually."

There have been other examples of creativity, too. Dick and Gene are clarinet players, one with training in music composition and the other who is self-trained. Both regularly compose and arrange music for their clarinet quintet. Chuck, a former music teacher, uncovered a previously unknown talent for composing and arranging and has created thirteen compositions for the concert band. Wally, a retired dental professor and tubist, invented, patented, and markets a "tubasisst" tuba holder (www.tubassist.com/). Jean, a former state senator, became a self-taught video production expert to develop a ten-year documentary DVD of the band's history.

Sense of Mastery

Wayne C. Booth, retired English professor and amateur cellist, wrote an autobiographical book on amateur music making, *For the Love of It: Amateuring and Its Rivals* (1999). He posed a fundamental question: Why pursue an endeavor when some version of failure is certain? Booth argues, and I agree, that amateur musicians enjoy the pursuit of mastery far more than needing to attain perfection. Abilities vary dramatically within the band, yet even the best players apologize about playing imperfectly. What continuously emerges from members' comments is the value they place in contributing to the total sound of the band. Here are comments from two members who responded anonymously to my recent survey:

> I had continued to sing in church choirs, so never left "making music" behind entirely. However, I had forgotten the very real pleasure that comes from being part of an ensemble where the total is greater than the sum of the parts. There is great satisfaction, to say nothing of the fun involved, in making music with a group. Even when it doesn't go well, it's fun to play—and in those occasions when it's better than we thought possible, it becomes a spiritual adventure. There is a physical and emotional high that comes from being a part of the band that I don't find in anything else that I do.
>
> I think making music does more for me spiritually and emotionally than anything else. What makes it fun is that it is challenging and even if I am not great, I can get better than I am now. Piano and voice have hit their peak for me and it's all downhill. But with a new instrument I can progress. With music, the whole is great than the sum of its parts. I do not enjoy being a soloist and I play (and sing) much better in a group. I can't make myself practice for myself (piano) but I work hard to bolster my section in the band. And every now and then this band of blue hairs and aches and pains, people who forget their short comings and concentrate on their parts, this band makes glorious music and I'm proud to be a small part of it.

I often receive e-mails from band members after concerts, but the following messages from two members after one particular concert are especially revealing about how mastery is important, but not the ultimate goal. On the program were two lyrical selections, "While I Watched the Yellow Wheat" and "the echo never fades," written in memory of a high school saxophonist who had died.

> *From Dinny*: My son said he could see the yellow wheat swaying in the breeze. His wife was touched by "the echo never fades" and had tears in her eyes during the sax solo. And seven-year-old Shannon liked everything—and was really grooving to the last two numbers. I thought we managed to pull it together pretty well.

> *From Bev*: To the members of the New Horizons Band: I do not know whether I played well or not but I do know that I made an impression on one young man. He thought I played well and that was a giant compliment to me. A mother, son, and daughter were waiting for me in the lobby at Clapp Hall. The young man around twelve, with his program in hand, approached me and asked if I was the Beverly Mueller listed in the program. I told him I was, and he asked to shake my hand. His mother also shook my hand and said her son loved the sax. I asked him if he played and he said he was playing the Eupho-

nium but wanted to play the sax as he really loved it. The realism of playing in the New Horizons Band really hit home. We are actually making an impression on the younger generation. I thank each and every one of you for the opportunity of playing with you all.

Health

Members' health is an issue. While generally their health is good, it is not unusual for members or their spouses to suffer sudden setbacks (heart attacks, strokes, broken bones, cardiac bypass surgery) or long-term ailments (Alzheimer's, Parkinson's, cancer). Many times ailing members make remarkable recoveries so that they can return to the band. The importance of the band as a genuine community is evident during these tough times. When one person copes with illness, other members help with visits, meals, and transportation. And while many recover, this past year alone four members had to stop participating because their deteriorating health would not let them continue. Several years ago, George wrote this response on a survey I had distributed: "Members of the NHB are friends who share a common love for making music, and in some cases are companions, role models, and mentors as I engage my own aging process." Last year he was diagnosed with cancer. I have learned much from him and other members about illness, chemotherapy, and coping with optimism and grace.

We have experienced loss through death as well, and band members have taught me and each other much about facing mortality with courage and composure. In cases of bereavement, members provide what comfort they can. According to Joan B.:

> The NHB has become my main group. I love the men in the clarinet group—they are concerned about me and for each other, like when someone doesn't make it to rehearsal. One member even came to the visitation when my husband passed away, and I had just met her! That's the kind of loyalty the band has for each other.

THE BOTTOM LINE

Several members wrote eloquently about the multiple benefits they derive from making music:

> *From Ann*: The New Horizons Band fits my needs perfectly to: (1) stretch my musicality, (2) work on a new challenge with discipline and direction, (3) feel that I am accomplishing something, (4) be with fellow music lovers and enjoy their company.

From Helen: Making music is a positive experience that contributes to the health of body, mind, emotions, and spirit. It helps the brain grow through concentration and coordination. It boosts the immune system by creating positive energy. It creates companionships through sharing in the activity. It brings joy through the happy awareness of creating beauty.

From Sally: The most astounding aspect of my involvement in band, chorus, and orchestra is the extreme enhancement of my joy in listening to music. The education of my ears and that part of my brain adds immensely to the intellectual, emotional, and kinesthetic pleasure of listening: deepens and expands it. And, therefore, my life. Where else are people crazy enough to haul a bass drum, timpani, and a xylophone across rough terrain to play music with the wind ruffling the pages and overturning music stands and call it FUN? It's satisfying at this age to be part of an educational experience that demonstrates that performance really improves with practice. One may not get "good," but one gets better! An atmosphere which encourages all learners is a very good place for a retired person.

From Margaret: It's a relief to find like-minded souls. Musical amateurs seem to have many common political, social, recreational views. In addition, they have similar family backgrounds to mine. Music was the *leitmotif* in my family life—all kinds, not any one type. I see and hear about it in other band members. . . . Making music has been the fourth meal of my day ever since the neighbor who dressed me at birth became my piano teacher. Singing in the family and especially together in the car was a given. Words and rhythms were put to music like other families work puzzles together. Music means memories. Music brings joy.

From Catherine: Returning to band and playing clarinet once again after years away from it felt like a wave had washed over me and I'd woken up to discover life.

From Keith: New Horizons is a shot of cortisone for your retirement.

From Bob: Part of my "need" to be an amateur or recreational musician is that I just love music, but I have wondered if part of it is also that I once planned on going into music education and when I chose a different profession I may have felt that I let some folks down—maybe even myself. Let me explain. . . . I decided about my freshman year in high school that I wanted to be a music teacher like my favorite teacher, David Boyd, who came to our school when I was in the 8th grade. Mr. Boyd was a magnificent teacher. . . . Mr. Boyd invested a lot of time in me, accompanying me in solo work on the tuba and encouraging me to enter the student conducting competition at state music contest. . . . The point of all this, I guess, is that when I decided to enter the ministry and later higher education, along with marriage and raising a family of four boys, and earning three higher ed degrees, I really gave up music except as a listener. I did continue to play the piano at home a little, and Beth and I enjoyed music by dancing (which I love), but no performing. I missed it for forty-two years. There simply was no time as a minister, then a university administrator and professor, etc. AND I also thought Mr. Boyd may have been disappointed that I didn't follow through with music education after he invested so much time and effort in my musical and personal development. Of course, he never said anything to that effect. And I thought my mother was a bit disappointed too, but she never expressed it. I was no doubt projecting those feelings. In any case, I have found an opportunity in retirement to "play out" some of my musical aspirations, not in the way I once thought but in a wonderful way nevertheless. *This would have been very difficult to do to this degree if you had not started the New Horizons Band and made it possible for me to reclaim a lifelong ambition— something I just had to do!*

What does making music mean to these older adults? The seven themes briefly described in this chapter reveal many of the reasons. They have multiple links between them, such that discussing one factor inevitably brings in other factors. If one views the first four themes (dedication, humor, socialization, mentoring) as aspects of music-making pursuits and the final three themes as aspects of music-making outcomes, then it is possible to fashion a structure to the nature of the players' experiences in New Horizons. These amateur musicians work hard at what Robert Stebbins calls "serious leisure" (1992), and with doses of humor they are able to enjoy the process. They have reciprocal relationships with people (peers, student instructors, and a director) who encourage them, support them, and teach them. They acknowledge that they "may not get good, but [they] get better," yet they find pleasure in their creative accomplishments and experiences that benefit the body, mind, emotions, and spirit.

Music educators generally assert that music is a lifelong activity, yet teaching focuses on youth. Opportunities for adults to make music are limited in comparison. New Horizons adults are excellent examples of what is possible, and I find their love of music making inspirational. I hope to inspire other music educators as well by sharing the experiences of these amateur musicians.

These voices of experience provide remarkable insight into the music-making process. They are not just people whom I teach; they are my friends. It is impossible for me to separate the music of New Horizons Band from the people who make that music. Knowing the players of the instruments is what makes the experience so rewarding.

REFERENCES

Barnes, L. L., Mendes de Leon, C. F., Wilson, R. S., Bienias, J. L., & Evans, D. A. (2004). Social resources and cognitive decline in a population of older African Americans and whites. *Neurology, 63*(12), 2322–2326.

Booth, W. C. (1999). *For the love of it: Amateuring and its rivals.* Chicago: University of Chicago Press.

Coffman, D. D. (2002). Adult education. In R. Colwell & C. Richardson (Eds.), *The new handbook of research on music teaching and learning* (pp. 199–209). New York: Oxford University Press.

Coffman, D. D. (2006). Voices of experience: Interviews of adult community band members in Launceston, Tasmania, Australia [Electronic Version]. *International Journal of Community Music, 6.* Retrieved April 16, 2006, from www.intljcm.com/articles/Volume%204/Coffman/Coffman.pdf

Coffman, D. D., & Adamek, M. (1999). The contributions of wind band participation to quality of life of senior adults. *Music Therapy Perspectives, 17*(1), 27–31.

Coffman, D. D., & Levy, K. (1997). Senior adult bands: Music's new horizon. *Music Educators Journal, 84*(3), 17–22.

Cohen, G. D. (2000). *The creative age: Awakening human potential in the second half of life.* New York: HarperCollins.

Cohen, G. D. (2005). *The mature mind: The positive power of the aging brain.* New York: Basic.

Cohen, G.D. (2007). The impact of professionally conducted cultural programs on the physical health, mental health, and social functioning of older adults. *The Gerontologist, 46,* 726–734.

Dean, A., Kolody, B., & Wood, P. (1990). Effects of social support from various sources on depression in elderly persons. *Journal of Health and Social Behavior, 31*(2), 148–161.

Dean, A., Kolody, B., Wood, P., & Matt, G. E. (1992). The influence of living alone on depression in elderly persons. *Journal of Aging and Health, 4*(1), 3–18.

Ernst, R., & Emmons, S. (1992). New Horizons for senior adults. *Music Educators Journal, 79*(4), 30–34.

Fratiglioni, L., Wang, H. X., Ericsson, K., Maytan, M., & Winblad, B. (2000). Influence of social network on occurrence of dementia: A community-based longitudinal study. *Lancet, 355*(9212), 1315–1319.

Glass, T. A., de Leon, C. M., Marottoli, R. A., & Berkman, L. F. (1999). Population based study of social and productive activities as predictors of survival among elderly Americans. *British Medical Journal, 319*(7208), 478–483.

Lennartsson, C., & Silverstein, M. (2001). Does engagement with life enhance survival of elderly people in Sweden? The role of social and leisure activities. *The Journals of Gerontology. Series B, Psychological Sciences and Social Sciences, 56*(6), 335–342.

Rohwer, D. (2005). Teaching the adult beginning instrumentalist: Ideas from practitioners. *International Journal of Music Education, 23*(1), 37–47.

Rowe, J. W., & Kahn, R. L. (1998). *Successful aging.* New York: Dell.

Sadler, W. A. (2000). *The third age: Six principles for growth and renewal after forty.* New York: Perseus.

Stebbins R. (1992). *Amateurs, professionals, and serious leisure.* Montreal, Quebec, Canada: McGill-Queens University Press.

Valiant, G. E. (2002). *Aging well.* Boston: Little, Brown.

Warshofsky, F. (1999). *Stealing time: The new science of aging.* New York: TV Books.

About the Contributors

Carlos Abril is assistant professor of music education at Northwestern University, where he teaches courses in general music, multicultural music education, and philosophy. His research focuses on the sociocultural dimensions of the music teaching and learning process, policy, and music perception.

Cecil Adderley is chair of Berklee's Music Education Department and an accomplished educator and performer. He has also written a number of published articles on topics that range from teacher preparation and strategies for teaching with technology, to the climate of the high-school music classroom.

Margaret Berg is associate professor of music education at the University of Colorado, where she teaches undergraduates and graduates in string music education and qualitative research. She has used qualitative methods to investigate sociocultural and sociological influences on student chamber ensemble participation.

Patricia Shehan Campbell is Donald E. Peterson Professor of Music at the University of Washington, where she teaches courses at the interface of education and ethnomusicology. She is the author of numerous books and articles on content and method of world music cultures.

Don Coffman is professor and head of music education at the University of Iowa. He teaches courses in conducting, instrumental methods, introduction to teaching music, psychology of music, and techniques for researching and measuring musical behaviors.

Lori Custodero is associate professor of music and music education at Teachers College, Columbia University. Her research focuses on the musical lives of children from infancy through preadolescence and on adults as musicians, teachers, and parents.

Patrick K. Freer is head of the music education division at Georgia State University. He is the author of *Getting Started with Middle-Level Choir* and the DVD series, *Success for Adolescent Singers: Unlocking the Potential in Middle School Choirs.*

R. J. David Frego is professor of music education at the University of Texas, San Antonio. He is a licensed instructor in Dalcroze Eurhythmics and has been using Dalcroze Eurhythmics in palliative therapy by combining music improvisation and purposeful movement.

Maud Hickey is associate professor and coordinator of music education at Northwestern University. Her research is focused on the areas of creative thinking in music, technology in music education, and the connection of these two areas.

Marcia Earl Humpal is music instructor/therapist for the Cuyahoga County Board of Mental Retardation and Developmental Disabilities in Cleveland, Ohio. She also taught general music and served as a music therapy consultant for public schools and private therapy groups.

Beatriz Ilari is associate professor of music education at the Federal University of Paraná in Curitiba, Brazil, where she runs a music program for babies, toddlers, and children. She has been conducting research on infants' and children's music perception and cognition, as well as on musical parenting in early life.

Jody L. Kerchner is associate professor and director of music education at the Oberlin Conservatory of Music, where she is the secondary school music and choral music education specialist. Her research interests include children's responses during music listening, choral music education, empathetic leadership, assessment, reflective thinking, and music teacher identity.

Chee Hoo Lum is assistant professor in the Visual and Performing Academic Group at the National Institute of Education / Nanyang Technological University, Singapore, where he teaches courses in elementary music methods, and foundations and research in music education.

Kimberly McCord is associate professor and coordinator of undergraduate music education at Illinois State University, where she teaches courses in elementary and general music, graduate integrated arts, and curriculum and courses in Black Music and Music for the Exceptional Child. Her research includes collaborative research in the area of assistive technology for children with disabilities in music.

Marvelene C. Moore is professor of music education at the University of Tennessee where she specializes in choral and classroom music for students grades K–8. An author and singer, she is also certified in Dalcroze, Kodaly, and Orff methodologies.

Katherine Strand is assistant professor in music education in the Jacobs Schools of Music, Indiana University, Bloomington. Her research interests include qualitative research methodology, teaching creativity, and classroom composition.

Matthew D. Thibeault is assistant professor of music education at the University of Illinois, Urbana-Champaign. His recent research has focused on qualitative, narrative, and action research approaches to understanding and improving teaching and learning in music and science education.

Wendy Valerio is associate professor of music and director of the Children's Music Development Center at The University of South Carolina, where she teaches graduate and undergraduate music methods courses, teaches early childhood and elementary music, and guides and conducts research. She is a member of the Gordon Institute for Music Learning Mastership Certification Faculty.

Betty Anne Younker is associate professor of music education and associate dean for academic affairs at The University of Michigan. Her research areas include philosophy and pedagogy of music education, and critical and creative thinking in composition.

Breinigsville, PA USA
29 April 2010
237021BV00003B/2/P